THE DANCER'S IMAGE

points & counterpoints

WALTER SORELL

On the title page: Don Redlich's design for *Reacher*.
Photograph Barbara Benzinger, Wisconsin.
Courtesy Don Redlich.

On the facing page: Helen Tamiris in *Negro
Spirituals*. Photograph Marcus Blechman.

Copyright © 1971 Columbia University Press
Library of Congress Catalog Card Number: 75-170923
International Standard Book Number: 0-231-03249-8
Printed in the United States of America

TO THE MEMORY OF

Helen Tamiris

. . . it was March 1968. I remember a blonde nurse demeroling me slowly into a state of unconsciousness while preparing my body to be operated on. Feeling how I was losing my grip on things, I quickly forced myself to think of what I could think about.

As I was trying to hold on to my wife's image, a few dancing figures whisked along the empty white wall in front of me, followed by a scenic image which could have been a stage design to the second act of *Swan Lake* in the twilight of my mind because I remember having heard a few bars of Tchaikowsky and then through it came a familiar voice: "Another season . . . that I have always to start from scratch each year, fighting, struggling for a new life—just like spring!"

I am no longer sure the voice said "just like spring" or that I now think she could have said it to make it more meaningful. But her words fell like drops into me, slowly, dragged out like drowning drawls. When for one last moment I tried to concentrate on the face of that voice, it was suddenly Helen Tamiris who looked at me. I knew how serious she could be, even when she smiled. How she could smile while being serious! And then I thought I heard the surgeon say in passing while putting on his gloves: "Our last will. . . ." I knew, while looking at Helen's questioning face, I should have made my last will. I stretched out my right hand as if I could have written down quickly what I wanted to say. . . . It can't be too late yet . . . my last will to the dancer . . . but I no longer felt my arm move, I no longer felt being.

When I came to, the blonde Irish nurse held my hand. She reminded me of someone. Only when I called her Helen, which was not her name, I knew who she was not. A few hours later she remarked: "You know what you said when they gave you the anesthesia?" "Tell me . . ." "It's so easy to dance into nowhere."

It was then and there that I decided to write my last will for the dancer, my testament to the dance—whatever it may be worth to whomever may read it.

ACKNOWLEDGMENT

I wish to thank my fate for having had the opportunity of viewing and reviewing dance and drama on two continents for several decades. I wish to include in my thanks the many dancers and choreographers, actors and stage directors, painters and composers as well as editors and press agents who have made it possible for me to gain insight in a world of make-believe whose reality, beauty, and excitement added joy and meaning to my life.

My thanks go to the many friends I have found and lost over the time past and who have enriched my knowledge in heated and casual debates; to my students who have challenged me and kept me on my toes and youthful in spirit; and to my wife who gave me courage to endure.

I would like to thank those magazines in which some of the material appeared, even though in different form: *Ballet Today, Dance Magazine, Dance Observer, Dance Scope, Focus on Dance, Impulse, National Sculpture Review, Shakespeare Quarterly,* and *University of Kansas City Review.*

Last, I wish to express my gratitude to the Rockefeller Foundation for a travel grant which enabled me to see more of dance and drama here and abroad than I would otherwise have been able to and made it possible for me to write some of the essays collected in this book.

CONTENTS

Part one

DANCE
& DANCERS

THE AGE IS
OURS

The lifelong search

THE MOST IMPORTANT search in life is the search for
one's own identity. Who am I? and Why am I the way I am? We
look into the mirror. A face looks back at us, vaguely familiar. Features of our parents stare at us. The past, in other words.
We look into our most private mirror, the mirror within ourselves. What we see there we think to know, but the image is
blurred in its complexity. Are we really what we are, what we
feel we are? And then the last mirror we cannot escape: the mirror in which we are only an infinitesimal spot on a huge canvas;
our little self in that giant reflection that daily shouts at us: I
am your fleeting time, I was your yesterday, I will be your tomorrow, I am your world, the world in which you live.

Those three mirrors exist. They are imaginary mirrors at moments only when you try to see yourself detached from reality.
But reality has a way of forcing you to recognize her immediacy,
her inescapable power. Only a few men are endowed with will,
endurance, and vision to break through the boundaries of reality,
to live on its fringe, to widen its horizon. These men are able to
ignore the pressures from without and try to find the real meaning of their being in the world of their time. They ignore all dan-

3

ger signs: Beware of going too far! Are you not afraid of so much loneliness? Are you not frightened of being misunderstood? Do you have the courage to shout at the crowd that the emperor has no clothes on?

The stronger the inner pressures, the more tumultuous the inner chaos, the stronger is our drive to discover the world beyond reality. And what seems to be a journey into nowhere is actually a short flight into the Self. It is a search for this torturing and perplexing, this wonderful and enjoyable thing that lives in the shell of our body.

No doubt, I have tried to allude to the compulsion that makes an artist an artist. But, in fact, we all search for our identity, for the key to ourselves, for some kind of recognition—however obvious or crude—for the unriddling of that strange puzzle that is: Man. We all hope to find it, whatever it may be, in the oddest way and in the strangest places—in companionship or politics, in business or pleasure.

The artist is subjected to the very same feelings and drives, but he has a particular gift and an often undefinable urge to express himself through an art form. He can channel the search for his identity through his artistic talent. This may lead to some degree of fulfillment, but does not make his search nor his life any easier. On the contrary. I am reminded of the scene designer Robert Edmund Jones looking over a class of eager students, who all thought they had their passports to fame in their pockets, and saying: "I can see that some of you are doomed." And then, after a moment of silence cut short by a deep sigh, he added: "Doomed to be artists."

The artist creates out of the world that has made him in order to remake it according to the image of his inner world. His struggle to give this image meaning and form is basically a struggle with himself. It goes without saying that he is tortured by a compulsive feeling to express himself through his artistic medium. He is cursed with a heightened sensitivity and awareness to do so. He feels hurled into a lifelong struggle, using and discarding the heritage of yesterday, finding the true expression of today which, at the same time, envisions the face and shape of another tomorrow. In other words, no artist can deny his past, and even in rebelling against it he pays his negating respects to it. He must realize that yesterday was a living today as much as he must be aware of the fact that there will be no artistic tomorrow if his today is not burningly alive.

The artist's struggle on so many levels and the awesome reality of his loneliness, the loneliness with his work, done or not yet begun, have become cliché by now. We know of that frightening feeling of the writer or composer to face the empty white sheet of paper, or we can visualize that forbidding moment when the dancer-choreographer steps into the staring emptiness of a studio, and even more forbidding if it should be peopled with dancers, waiting like a mass of clay to be shaped, to be made to live.

We know all that, but we rarely picture the creative artist coming from outside into the studio, the outside which is a world full of screaming headlines, a few blossoming or fading flowers, of turbulent events and a faint smile here and there; and the artist leaving the studio to face the same world again, full of different opinions and opinionated differences, a factual and factitious world to which he presents the realization of his dreams.

His artistic responsibility is threefold: toward his art, toward the world, and toward himself. Has he come close enough to the fulfillment of his artistic dream? Has he grown in and through his work? Did he remain true to himself without remaining a slave to his own achievements? A cynic once said—I believe it was Picasso—that you may copy everyone except yourself. And the world which never stands still will ask the artist: Man of today, what have you done for tomorrow? Have you caught the spirit that is now and have you pointed the way for those who follow you and for those who must follow you in order to break away from you one day to find their own road, their own identity?

Also, his art will take him to account for the same reasons: Have you learned from the past to be able to express your experiences in the spirit of your world? Have you extended the symbol, or the thought, that was revolutionary yesterday into a new reality of artistic expression? Don't forget that while you grow in your craft, the world also grows and changes; and your growth has to keep step with the world—no, it had better show it the way.

We call our artists modern because their mode of expression is of now. Or, is it rather our attitude toward life that is modern dictated by the changes within the cultural climate? Alwin Nikolais once said that being of our time is a state of mind rather than a means of expression. Is not every innovator a modern artist in the eyes of the majority of the people who always take their time to find out what was modern yesterday? Did not Jean Georges Noverre appear extremely modern to the theater-goers in the eighteenth century?

Must it not have appeared as a modern device or technique, when the ballerinas began to stand on their toes? This happened at the dawn of the industrial revolution, when gaslight was introduced, when the first machines began to roll and the railways began to move man at the unheard-of speed of twenty miles an hour. It was then that the artist escaped into a romantic mood, and the ballerina began to rise on her toes to demonstrate—or did she protest?—that she is not of this mad world of steam and iron, that there is more reality in the unreal, in the wings of grace, in the lightness of flight. What she did was modern because it was an attitude of her time, it grew out of its historic-sociological events. It turned into the triumph of the classic-romantic ballet as an expression of its time, the nineteenth century.

At the turn of the century ballet was a Sleeping Beauty, but the Prince who kissed her was not a prince and much too preoccupied with the state of the world and his own inner turmoil to be charming. Come to think of it, he did not kiss her, he rudely roused her from her sleep. When she awoke she realized that the world had changed. She gradually adjusted to the new sights and sounds, even though she often tried to turn around to fall asleep again.

It was no longer a beauty sleep for this Sleeping Beauty. The unsettled, revolutionary, searching spirit of the new century soon showed its effect on her. The illusion of utter grace and the pretense of having conquered gravity were gone. The drama of conflicts expressed through angularity came with the motivations of Freudian complexities. At a time when man began to circle Earth into the stars, the romantic image of the conquest of gravity was lost to the artificial stars, and the ballerinas did not mind rolling on the floor. If the coming of the modern barefoot and soul-searching dance would have had no other purpose than to remind the ballet of the facts and realities of twentieth-century life, it would have fulfilled its mission after mid-century. And, it certainly has from the viewpoint of the ballet.

Some thoughts on the total man as an artist

The natural talents of children are amazing. It is just as amazing how quickly they can be destroyed by life—by the confines of our environment, by the gradual narrowing-in of natural impulses, by the crippling adjustment of our demands and desires to the realities of society, by the yielding to a lifelong bargaining position with principles and values, by our attempt to find some other outlets for our rising frustrations, by the crude necessity to make a living in order to betray life for the sake of mere survival. But there is no way of saying how and when the need to create would crack and break through the veneer of all the superficialities of our existence. The very same stifling process may actually help accumulate dramatic and traumatic strength in us which, one day, could be channeled into creative expression, however gradual or volcanic its manifestations may then be.

Since our school systems omit the teaching of two of the most vital subjects, namely, "A philosophy of Living" and "The Appreciation of the Real Life Values," we are left without spiritual guidance and a nonmaterial goal when thrown into the jungle of existence. Of what avail is the knowledge of higher mathematics if we do not master the simple algebra of living, if we fumble because we lack a viewpoint, if we stumble because we have no vision?

I strongly believe that mankind can be divided in creative and uncreative beings whereby creativity is not limited to the arts alone. A teacher who, beyond the conveyance of his subject matter, opens up the avenue of new understanding in a child is creative. So is a physician who, beyond his reliance on laboratory tests, can see through symptoms and recognize their cause and possible future effect. A cook whose senses are seasoned and whose palate is inventive can be creative.

There are no limitations set for the creative urge and need of man as long as they are channeled into some activity outside the realm of artistry. Our competitive society—the society of modern man since the Renaissance—has brought about more and more the desperate longing of the individual to prove his mettle in public, to yield to the performance principle in an industrialized and compartmentalized society. In this age of technology and the leveling process of democracy, the will of the many has come to triumph over the dictate of an aristocratic elite of the spirit. (The days are over when a culture was made by twelve people, as Ezra Pound once claimed.) In this age of the masses and their electronic media, it is the individual who cries out in anguish and anxiety, he wants to be heard, to be seen, to be recognized. The key sentence in Samuel Beckett's *Waiting For Godot* is the desperately imploring reply of the tramp Vladimir to the messenger's question: "What am I to tell Mr. Godot, Sir?" "Tell him . . . tell him you saw me and that . . . that you saw me. . . . You're sure you saw me, you won't come and tell me to-morrow that you never saw me!" Not to drown in the masses, to be recognized is the neurosis of our time.

There are many ways of using one's sense experience, of giving one's artistic imagination an opportunity to unfold, if you are not hungry for applause. I strongly believe that in everyone's life things are growing toward you if you have the patience to let them grow. It is a half-truth that we are the masters of our fate; you certainly cannot force your creative ability to use its full potential at any given moment. This is the result of many imponderabilities and the one fact that you have worked incessantly with your tools and on yourself. In all the arts there is an uplifting and, at the same time, terrifying interrelation between the artist's growth as a man and as an artist.

Certain truisms have intrinsic value and should not be treated with the contempt we have reserved for them. For instance, outside recognition is not what matters. The easy little victories are deceptive and futile. When you are honest with yourself, they will leave a very unpleasant taste in your mouth and soul. It is there that the West can learn a great deal from the East.

It seems necessary to find a center of our personal identity.

So much of what we are and what we are doing is little more than trying to get through the Scylla of meaninglessness and the Charybdis of hostilities. More often than not, we live and act against something instead of for something. Our entire existence suffers from the dichotomy of reason and unreason, intellect and senses, morality and nature. We are cheating ourselves by reading the Sunday book reviews instead of the books themselves. Nowadays the stress lies more on information than real knowledge through enlightenment. We have not yet learned that we may be happier with less when it is meaningful. We are always taking short cuts to be somewhere fast for no purpose. We may thus miss the experience of an irretrievable hour of beauty, the image of a landscape that may have had meaning for our mind, that may have been the very thing to replenish our soul. In this age of the jet, everyone should—the artist must—find time to stop and turn, to look inward a little.

Experience constitutes a great part of man's full awareness, and so does knowledge. I doubt that we can produce masterpieces if we have not learned to feel life, to walk with all our senses fully awake through existence. "Works of art are projections of life," Henry James said. The intensity of felt life helps to heighten our artistic capacities and to transcend our own limited reality. I also doubt that we can produce masterpieces if we do not take the trouble to widen and deepen our grasp on the past. It is not enough to be introduced to life by the *Reader's Digest* and to Dostoevski through the film of one of his novels. A student at Columbia University once said in class that Goethe's *Faust* is trash, and two years later he was hailed by the press as the youngest and most hopeful producer on Broadway. I do not suggest that the artist carry along insignificant cargo of the mind. The deepening of knowledge ought to be an adventure that creates a wide enough frame of reference, the images of which are well-organized, visible in all their contrasting colors, in their cyclic movement through the centuries. But knowledge without experience may be little more than a bloodless charade, and experience without knowledge may remind us of a rising edifice whose architects forgot to lay the proper foundation.

Man's limitations are set off by man's dreams, and art is the result of his desire and endeavor to reach beyond himself, to give *Gestalt* to the conflicts arising from his limitations pitted against his dreams. The first drawings of the cave man were the expression of a need, perhaps to beautify the cave, perhaps to glorify a feat, a triumph over beast and nature, but in essence to hold on to an image primitive man must have had. Undoubtedly, the drawing gave to him a feeling of gratification. But the very moment he may have had qualms about his drawings, about the full expression of a line here and there when gaining perspective to what he had done, then the artist in him was born. And when he called in the man from the neighboring cave to show the drawings to him, the second act of the birth of art began: the realization that a work of art only lives when the experience from which it emerged can be shared.

Movement is the essence of life, dance its ultimate expression. Also, life only lasts the very moment of our awareness of it, and all that remains is, as in the dance, the memory we can retain of it. As time is the most fragile fabric of which our life is made, so is the moment it takes the dancer to move. This moment is an ecstatic state of being; it is telescoped timelessness. Because of it, the urgency, the power of immediacy, is stronger in the dance than in any other art form. But permanence in general, and particularly in the arts, is fictitious. Beethoven felt that "every true creation of art is independent, mightier than the artist himself." Each creation, if true and of momentous importance, lives on because no great achievement ever dies, however fleeting it may appear at the moment. It continues to live its own existence, and if only through its influence and inspiration.

Is art a subliminal manifestation? Who tells us how much our unconscious processes have helped it to come into being? All we know is that we master our craft. Beyond this, we may realize that suddenly we had an idea without quite knowing how it propelled itself into the foreground and took on form and substance in our mind. Craft, discipline, and self-criticism are the pillars on which our work rests. The point of view that is, more often than not, the reason for working on something is our guiding light. It is always the idea which looks for its only fitting form, and the organic structure depends on how thoroughly we have thought through that which we try to give artistic realization. The compelling urgency and the power of imagination are the wings of our creative effort. The poetry, the mystery, however, is locked as secret in all of this. If it is there, it is there because the artist could not help putting it there.

The artist who does not deprive himself of the great adventure to search for the indefinable truth, the perhaps nonexistent beauty of life transformed into a work of art, will triumph. His triumph is the satisfaction of the total man.

From meaning to mystery

What should we expect from a dance created as a theatrical experience, no matter how experimental it may be, or how much it may rely on and move within the traditionally known and familiar? We can only judge the truth of any work of art by its intentions to express an idea, to find the suitable form for its content and the physical manifestation of its soul, or as Stark Young expressed it: "Behind any work of art is this living idea, this soul that moves toward its right body, this content that must achieve the form that will be inseparable from it."

It would be deceptive to view the dance as human bodies moving in space and time without considering motivation and meaning. Dancing is no longer unrelated to life when performed on a stage and, therefore, must have meaning. Even the most non-objective, impersonalized, nonliteral work of art is an abstraction of some realized experience, because all art, if not cliché-ridden photography (which is no longer art), is an abstraction or extraction of life and transcends the actuality of happenings or the happening of the artist's visualization of a reality.

We see not only movement per se on stage, but a human being, costumed or in practice clothes before a black curtain or an elaborate set, moving in light, alone or in relation to other people. We have been invited to share an experience which may range from a mere kinesthetic response to emotional and intellectual gratification. Unconsciously, we are bringing with us our own little world. Assuming we never became aware of motivation and meaning of the dancer's movement and would only absorb the image of a human body within space and time, we could do so only with the help of our visual experience which, at that moment, is neither completely detached nor isolated from past experiences. We are carried away by dancing because it does and means something to us, to our senses, to the sum total of our being. In other words, stage dance will always be communication through visual stimulation.

Whatever the dancer does on stage gives him or his choreographer away. Every creative artist presents us with a world in his own image, with a segment of his thinking and feeling. And the artist's personality also speaks to us through dances which have no apparent message, in which the familiar concepts of the dramatic or emotional gesture and the unfolding of a story line are eradicated.

The great artists of all times are able to reach us across many centuries only because—whatever their theme has been—they created it out of the spirit of their own time. There is no such thing as an "ivory-tower" artist in the theater, because the stage is a platform connecting man's imagination with the world of his day. We, the contemporaries, who are called upon to witness the artist's translation of the image of his era may react to his work as differently as we are attuned to or out of tune with our time. Particularly in transition periods as ours, we may easily harbor hostilities and even reject ourselves as a symbol of the time, an unconscious process which, of necessity, must prejudice our judgment of the artist.

As we, the audience, enter the theater from the street with the nakedness of everyday thoughts and feelings, so does the artist. He may help us forget them or he may use them as a point of departure. In whatever he intends to do he will best succeed when giving us an abstraction of his own world and re-creating for us the epitome of order and chaos, of beauty and ugliness in the life he lives. But he can only do so when he has a point of view, a philosophy, a conception of life.

If he has something to say, he will say it most forcefully if he feels an urgency about it. There must be a passion in him—not only for his own art, but also to communicate and express himself. If we are absorbed and impressed by a work of art, then this intangible urgency has helped to establish an atmosphere of oneness between the dancer and his audience. On its most convincing level this urgency conveys the inevitability of a work of art.

In reshaping a new world consisting of movement, sound, and color, he may not necessarily be able to open the doors and

windows for which we look in our own search for truth and a new
experience in life nor give us the answers to the eternal questions
of what, who, where, and why we are. Should he achieve any of
these, he has created one of those rare moments of ecstatic existence, moments born of passion and wonder, which have made
the theater live through thousands of years. What we may expect
him to do is to take us away from ourselves by making us share
with him his experience, to help us find some justification for our
being, or by giving us a heightened sense of living.

He may wish to puzzle or shock us, to create a feeling of
unease. But whatever he does, he must bear in mind that the original sin of art is boredom. However, of late some artists have
made of boredom a cult in order to demystify art. They may want
to present us with a put-on, with art as non-art which is happening in front of us in the context of everyday living in a constantly
and unpredictably changing world. Art holding up the mirror to
nature and life cannot be static—as little as nature and life themselves. This explains the eternal flow of styles and formulae in art
and their timebound existence. When Nietzsche saw in the philosopher a man not so much in search of truth as of the metamorphosis of the world in man, the same can be said of the artist.

"The whole visible universe is nothing but a storehouse of
images and signs," Baudelaire said, and it depends on the power
of the artist's imagination how he can absorb the ideas and images
of his time, how he can fuse them with his inner world to transform them into artistic expression. There is never one way only
to find this goal, but there is only one way at any given moment
for any artist.

We expect from him at that moment that he pours the "images and signs" of the outer world and his inner world into his
creation in such a fashion as to catch our own imagination una-

wares and escape with it into new experiences. Because—and this only sounds contradictory—dancing is of such physical immediacy, it can best realize the imaginary and is the most perfect stage translation of the intangible and the transcendental. The task of the choreographer and dancer is to evoke a poetic feeling of reality in us, to open up the vast field of dreamlike existence that we know lives within us.

It does not matter what the dance is about as long as it creates a high form of empathy.* The action may belong to the past, present, or future, or the dance may express a mood, the mere joy of moving. But whatever its motivation or purpose, the dance ought to convey the impression of complete abandonment which alone makes dancing on stage kinesthetically contagious. Neither artistic sophistication, nor the most stupendous technical and acrobatic abilities can be substitutes for the realization of that inner ecstatic blending of the dancer with his material which gives the impression of his total surrender to movement itself.

Finally, any great dance—as any great work of art for that matter—has the most indefinable of all attributes, most hidden and most obvious at the same time, which may best be described as mystery. No dance work can fully exist at the very moment of its being nor survive this moment in our memory, if it does not have some mystery which lives in the secret of its elusiveness, in the magic of what we see, or think we see, in the surprise of visual

---

* There is, of course, also the compulsive ideologist, the depersonalized anti-art-artist, who will try to evoke the realization of an off-stage world on stage, or of life reduced to the banality of its being, to rehabilitate the commonplace, to use a Cocteau phrase. To this "instantaneous" artist the act of creation is more important than the result. He entertains with the nonentertainment of what is happening "now," and the artist often solicits your active participation. The empathy he is out to create may have negative connotations, it may range from numbing our senses to an artificially whipped-up and orgiastic ecstasy.

excitement, profound and inexplicable, evocative and provocative. Paradoxically, the revelation of most works of art come to us
through their mystery.

The poetic image

Art is the most personal language in a most universal idiom.
It can only grow out of an experience and can only live when this
experience is shared. It is the visualization or re-creation of that
indefinable truth which the artist finds at one of the many crossroads between reality and his inner life. It must become the expression of a relived vital reality, conveying its complete significance in a newly discovered meaning for our life. The artist may
find it an almost Don Quixotic adventure in which the windmills
turn out to be real giants. In his quest for and search of the ultimate, he may stumble upon a tiny segment of it or only upon a
new question leading to more adventures; his critical mind riding
the flames of his feelings may find a beautiful image at the preci-
pice between the definite and the indefinite.

Man suspects that there must be harmony in all chaotic complexity, there must be some reason for his own existence and
some final answer to all questions. In his search for the secret he
has found the key in art. It may not fit the last lock or open the
ultimate gate, but it makes him walk through a thousand little
doors and, with each door he leaves behind, he feels as if he had
come one step closer to finding the secret.

There is hardly a great artist who does not seek the poetic
expression of the world around him and of his own self. Even if
he depicts nothing but the filth on earth, he looks for the flower
of poetry within the flower of evil. Behind the incessant urge of
man to create and re-create lies the desire to deliver himself from

the bondage of being merely human, to rediscover his intrinsic values, to catch the music of the spheres or simply a spark from his Maker's glory.

It is not necessarily poetry itself which shows the most poetic feeling, the poetic image at its best. It is everywhere in life; in a human gesture of kindness and in the sparkling dust of stars; in the questioning eyes of a child as much as in the petal of a rose. If it is wherever we can see it, then it is we who are charged with the tremendous task of discovering it.

The poetic sense is one of the most essential elements of all art. Leonardo da Vinci must have felt the same when he wrote in his *Notebooks:* "Painting is a form of poetry made to be seen." It seems that the sociological development has a great deal to do with how and where the poetic image is strongest in certain eras, and it may very well be that future generations will say about our time that there was poetry in the formulas of an Einstein, or in the little artificial worlds circling the globe; or that the poetic image found its most contemporary expression in architecture. Some people in the year 2000 might even say that it was also found in the dance.

Plato defined poetry by saying, "It causes a thing to emerge from non-existence into existence." Poetry is a tiny fragment of eternity caught as a reflection in the mirror of the poet's soul. Poetry is deep insight into reality from the flight of someone riding a cloud to catch the next rainbow. And from up there he can often grasp more of the inexplicable and the essence of life than he would were he too close to it.

As soon as the inexplicable is found, or almost found, it can be put on paper, on canvas, or into stone. It is then there to endure, to be enjoyed and shared. Not so the dance. Wedded to the moment, it is as fleeting as the time it takes to move, and all that remains is the memory we retain of it. Since the dance is so much tied to time, it has something of time's preciousness, its urgency, and timelessness and has that dreamlike quality which we associate with the irretrievability of a moment passed.

The dance is the purest art. It uses no artifice, no instrument for its communication but the dancer's body. It has therefore an immediacy no other art has. The body would remain a mere silhouette moving from now into then if it were not animated by something described by many poets as the flickering flame of its soul, the ultimate compressed into a moment's ecstasy. In this state of rapture the dancer would extend his leap into the infinite if he would not have to become himself the very instant he is lost to it.

Through the ages and beyond all barriers of cultures and nationalities, man saw in the dance a primary force. This is explicit in the Chinese proverb "One may judge a king by the state of dancing during his reign," as much as in Balzac's cryptic, but all-embracing, statement that "The dance is a way of being." When Ralph Waldo Emerson and Margaret Fuller saw Fanny Elssler perform in Boston during her tour of America, the poet-philosopher whispered into his neighbor's ear: "Margaret, this is poetry!" "Waldo," she corrected him, "this is religion!" This anecdotal story is as revealing as the reports about the impact Isadora Duncan had on her audiences when we read that upon seeing her perform, old men wept into their beards.

If only minds of minor caliber had fallen prey to the charms of Terpsichore, we could easily overlook her inducement to enthusiasm and ecstasy, and write it off to frivolous lightheartedness, erotic titillation, or any other stimulation through our senses. But some of the greatest poets, thinkers, and artists championed the dance wholeheartedly and, let us admit, often with naïve exaggeration, as did Pushkin or Stendhal.

All arts are interrelated in one way or another. Works of the plastic art would obviously be closest to the dance since we can easily visualize a sculpture as the one arrested movement out of a succession of many movements leading to the climactic point the sculptor chose. In its total linear effect, the dance is certainly close to painting and in its spatial use as much as in the geometry of its pattern it is a first cousin of architecture. Jean-Louis Barrault is undoubtedly not the only one who termed the dance a child of music; we know only too well the deep interrelation of these two art forms. And the dance accepts a great deal from literature in general which receives, in turn, its share from the dance. Somewhere in time, space and form all the arts meet, cross, trespass, overlap, lean on, liberate, give, borrow, and take from one another. But when we think of the poetic image and the dance we visualize something that is no longer peripheral, but inherent in dancing. It is a vital part of it.

The Greek essayist Plutarch called dancing silent poetry and added that "Dancing and poetry have all things in common." This statement goes beyond the Aristotelian definition of dancing as the representation of passions, actions, and manners or the realization of the instinct for imitation, harmony, and rhythm which he saw in poetry. In the course of its development theater dance has vacillated between the concept of the *ballet d'action* which displays actions, passions, and manners and dancing for the sake of dancing which embraces poetic imitation, harmony, and rhythm. Diderot went one step further when he wrote in 1757: "A dance is a poem. This poem should have its independent representation. It is an 'imitation' by virtue of the movements, an imitation which presupposes the collaboration of poet, painter, musician and pantomime-dancer." Diderot anticipated by one hundred fifty years what Diaghilev fully realized in his Ballets Russes.

When in the beginning of the nineteenth century Viganó wanted to speak to the heart of the spectator and create "a movement of the soul," he knew that, though the dance is expressed through the body, the soul is as much involved in the artistic idiom of dancing. Since the word *soul* is used here for heightened sensibility and receptivity acutely attuned to all those impressions and vibrations which escape the ordinary perception, it is part of the very poetry which is found at the core of this art.

Of all theatrical arts the dance asks either the most of the spectator, or the least. It will not fail to unfold its magic whether you approach it with complete unpreparedness and the pure joy of the innocent, or with the most intimate knowledge of its technique. It fills one's eyes. But of all worlds of make-believe dance is the one to most enrich those spectators who have learned to give themselves wholeheartedly to unreality, to a dream, to a thing between the things which hold a miracle out to those who can see it. Ibsen said, "To be a poet is chiefly to see." Those who can see, the dance turns into poets.

The first feeling or taste we develop for any art is purely unconscious and sensual. Only gradually do we become absorbed while absorbing it. This feeling or attitude is important for the dance. From the pleasure of seeing animal grace of movement to the intellectualization of what the choreographer may have meant is a long way filled with a thousand and one variations of pleasure. The effect may be different, but the source is the same. You may start with the impression of the little boy who, upon seeing a ballet for the first time, only saw people jumping through the air, whirling and flying around, and wanted to know how it was done. Or you may finally say ecstatically with Baudelaire that dancing is poetry composed with arms and legs or agree with his compatriot, Stéphane Mallarmé, who felt that ballet is "preeminently the theatrical form of poetry," a paradise of all spirituality. Dreams, poetry, and dancing live in the same sphere of the inexpressible or absolute. It is the thing that is and is no longer if you cannot

catch and hold it in the arms of your memory. Word and movement are freed from their utility through poetry and dance alone.

Dancing like poetry is a symbolic art, reduced to the most essential, to the allusion rather than to the direct statement. Mainly
in its suggestiveness dance is poetic and transforms reality into a
matter of remoteness which, in its effect, is stronger than the most
beautiful of concrete realities. It is stronger because its suggestiveness opens up a wider field and penetrates the mysterious world
of our emotions more easily by working with the essential only.
Its ethereal quality, its elusiveness is strongly mingled with reality, with a world of make-believe all its own and can evoke sensations in us which otherwise might remain unexperienced. It
makes us fully realize that we all share as a common dream the
ability to give our daily life meaning beyond the obvious, to escape the averageness of our existence—not for the sake of escape,
but to create a stronger affirmation of our being, to reach into a
sphere of nonreality in order to give us greater understanding of
our reality.

The age of surprise

"Étonne-moi!"—the now legendary words hurled by Serge
Diaghilev at Jean Cocteau as a personal challenge have assumed
universal importance. Their symbolic significance is inescapable
when one looks back at what has happened in the arts and in the
smaller world of the dance during the last five or six decades.

Nijinsky's introduction of archaic forms in his choreography
for *L'Après-midi d'un Faune* and even more so for *Le Sacre du
Printemps* preceded Cocteau's concepts and undoubtedly inspired
them. But with *Parade* in 1917 Cocteau opened the curtain to a
new beginning. His was a decisive first break with all clichés in

the world of dance, a poetic montage of everyday banalities, the triumph of irrelevance. He could not have had help better than that from Satie, Picasso, and Massine in wrecking the past and in giving the future the artistic license for experiments for the sake of experimenting.

In his enthusiasm Cocteau foresaw an immediate continuation of all forms of experiments which, however, did not materialize, at least not with the same intensity and logical absurdity as they were taken up in the Fifties and Sixties—and even then not in the all-embracing manner he had visualized. He desired total theater on an experimental basis "in which the fantastic, the dance, acrobatics, mime, drama, satire, music, and the spoken word combine to produce a new form; they will present with very small means, plays which the official artists will take for studio farces, and which nonetheless are the plastic expression and embodiment of poetry itself." What he called "poetry *of* the theater" in contrast to "poetry *in* the theater" was the fulfillment of a theatrical magic in which the Greek chorus was fused with a music-hall atmosphere in a final triumph of surprise and shock.

What was still a playfully creative concept with Jean Cocteau was attacked by Oskar Schlemmer and the *Bauhaus* in Weimar—which, in the words of Walter Gropius, "sought a new synthesis of art and modern technology"—in a far more scientific manner and with methodical exactness, during the Twenties.

Schlemmer complained that "this materialistic and practical age has in fact lost the genuine feeling for play and for the miraculous." In order not to remain the victim of the traditional rules for staging a theatrical event, he sought stage realization under conditions of the greatest possible freedom, independent of writer and actor, in an area of "the anonymous or mechanically controlled play of forms, colors and figures." He built a spiritual and factual bridge from the naked man to the abstract figure. His ideal goal aimed at having the stage designer develop optical phenomena for which a poet could then find the appropriate language. In the course of his experiments to fit man into space he transformed the *Tänzermensch,* the Man as Dancer, into the mechanical human figure, the *Kunstfigur.*

A dehumanized pathos was achieved, a grand gesture of the nonreal, of an artifice to which perfectly free-ranging fantasy can give poetic illusion and meaning in terms of visual beauty. Oskar Schlemmer's ballets remained, even in their final stage version, the paragon of experiment; their full artistic realization was a question of "time, material, and technology," as he himself admitted.

His *Triadic Ballet,* the best known of his theatrical adventures, shows the concentrated effort to eliminate all literary or logic-intellectual aspects and to rely on geometric patterns in space, on plastic images, eccentric or beautiful shapes in motion. Oskar Schlemmer began as a painter and sculptor, and what he created on stage was a dancer's theater seen with the eyes of a painter and sculptor who became fascinated by the architectural possibilities in moving apparently living shapes in space. Inspired by the then new technological facilities, by the geometric logic of cubism, by the Dadaist's flagrant denial of any traditional aesthetic feeling, and, as the child of the *Neue Sachlichkeit,* by the new functionalism of the mid-Twenties, this dance theater was the outgrowth of a nondancer's fantastic dreams.

Rolf de Maré's Ballets Suédois also flirted with experiments —Cocteau collaborated with him—which moved in the same direction, but it was not until the early Fifties that Alwin Nikolais gave this idea the exciting effect of a very personalized total theater. One of Schlemmer's coworkers, the architect L. Moholy-Nagy, answered the question How shall the theater of totality be realized? with a statement which anticipated Nikolais' basic concepts: "Theatre is the concentrated activation [*Aktionskon-zentration*] of sound, light (color), space, form, and motion. Here man as co-actor is not necessary, since in our day equipment can be constructed which is far more capable of executing the *purely mechanical* role of man than man himself."

The ideas of Cocteau and the *Bauhaus* were a breakthrough into a new world, but they were stopped dead by adverse political circumstances, by Fascism and its philosophy which did not tolerate any experimenting spirit, and by the advent and advances of the modern dance.

The movement of Symbolism at the end of last century and its attempt to free the poetic from the obvious and concrete, from syntactic arrangement at the risk of avoiding intelligibility, had great influence on Cocteau almost twenty years later. There are only vague spiritual links between Symbolism and Isadora Duncan's rebellion against the sterile and stereotype of ballet as the heir to romantic classicism. Her discovery of the "soul" as the propelling force of her artistic expression remained, together with the very individualistic presentations of her "felt" dance visualizations, in the realm of the romantic. The gradually progressing mechanization of the world at the end of last century cried out for symbolistic and neoromantic trends as antidotes to reality. Just as neoromantic in spirit was the eclectic program of the Denishawn group from which the second rebellion emerged in America.

Martha Graham and Doris Humphrey entered a wilderness of unknown possibilities in order to find themselves, the artistic realization of the time that was theirs and of the folkloric background of the country in which they functioned as human beings. But what they danced was not so much a rebellion against the past and its tradition as it was for the shifting of its symbols onto another emotional plane. Aztec princesses and Oriental goddesses were replaced by primitive mysteries, by images from an era in which the frontiers were moved westward, by the memory of the Shakers, and later by Biblical and mythological figures. Freudian symbolism, the division of the portrayed personalities into psychic components, became a predominant theme.

In spite of the vast range in the freedom of artistic expression, in spite of its return to ritualistic forms and myth, in spite of daring angularity and dissonance, the art of modern dance as it developed in the early Twenties in Germany and somewhat later in that decade in America did not reach beyond its expressionistic concepts and remained essentially romantic in its self-reflective manner. It ignored the *Neue Sachlichkeit* of the *Bauhaus* and Cocteau's experiments with the creation of surprise.

The modern dancer was so surprised to have discovered his own existence and the tremendous scope in which to explore his inmost conflicts with his fellowmen that in the wilderness which he ventured to conquer he lost himself in the process of finding himself and his freedom of expression. Like Isadora, only with a great deal of technique added, he represented the process of his psyche in a most literal and narrative style.

Beyond his sociohistoric role in making Isadora Duncan's dream come true and in giving basic dance its most sophisticated representational form, the modern dance also played a major part in reshaping the aesthetic values of the *danse d'école*. Contemporary ballet no longer believes exclusively in extolling the airborn dancer and in proving his disdain for gravity. The floor as a fourth dimension, a new expressive plane, was established, the elements of distortion, some discontinuity and surprise were introduced by George Balanchine and others.

The so-called modern dance solidified its own image at the end of the Forties. It had experienced growth, recognition, and the self-complacency of maturity. It did not escape the Hegelian law of creating the antithesis to its own thesis, and thus gave birth to a third rebellion, this time against the sterile and stereotype of the representational modern dance. The fight against the obvious and easily legible of the expressionistic form of dancing started in the early Fifties, and, fighting the establishment, the *modern* modern dance began to establish its own image. The new revolution very logically continued where the modern dance as the apparently rebellious movement had intercepted the first great adventure started by an intellectual elite for which Cocteau and Schlemmer were prototypes.

Corresponding to the theater of the absurd, the dance eschewed all literal connotations, divorced itself from meaning, and wanted to be little more than *to be* and to be accepted for what it is, the moment it is, to whoever watches, with whatever emotional reactions. The ideas Cocteau had presented and written about three decades previously were broadened and vulgarized. The need was no longer to express oneself but to let *it* express itself. The threshold of tolerating the slightest dependence on or encroachment of past traditions became constantly lower. Compromises were anathema. The negation of the so-called laws of so-called beauty, that is, of any aesthetic notions, became more hardened because a feeling of futility in the Fifties and Sixties had been added to the despair of the Twenties. Tristan Tzara's "optimistic" statement in his manifesto of Dadaism "Measured by the scale of eternity any activity is futile" was toned down to: Measured by any scale man's activity is futile. The realization that it is impossible for man to resolve the paradoxes of existence gave him a feeling of aloneness. He saw everything out of harmony with reason, purposeless, cut off from all roots. Life became the triumph of incongruity and, in this sense, absurd.

From the vantage point of the beginning Seventies, the rebellion of the early Fifties was tame because one could recognize what it was all about. Even though John Cage shouted "we must start from scratch!" he actually continued where the intellectual progressives had stopped after having won the first two rounds. One recognized the dadaistic and surrealistic influences and, in a fundamental way, existential philosophy. Some of the principles of Zen Buddhism—even though misunderstood in their applications—and *I Ching,* the book of changes, played their part. In its mystifying way, the Oriental influence was obvious in such dancers as Merce Cunningham, Merle Marsicano, and Erick Hawkins. It led to the acceptance of stillness in movement and movement in stillness, of chance and whim to express the apparently inexpressible or indefinable, letting, for instance, the dancer's body discover its own direction in "automatic movement."

The shock value of surprise was there, the anticliché had become the cliché of the time. The discontinuous and incongruous were there. But all this and more had reached a climactic turning point in the Sixties. Jean Cocteau had opened the door for a free-for-all movement, a revolving door which began to turn so fast in both directions that one no longer knew what was real or irony, what was serious in intent, in negating the world and debunking life or what was put-on, deflating its own surprises and hoaxes. In *Parade* Cocteau still wedded the banal of reality to the imaginative innocence of the poetic that lives in the wonder of childhood. But all poetry is lost when an artist hangs a toilet seat (with or without flushing implements) on your wall as an *objet d'art.*

This is like pulling the last aesthetic tenets from under our understanding of what art is and is not. When John Cage has the pianist sit four minutes and thirty-three seconds at the piano without touching the instrument's keys once or banging its strings at least and calls this piece *4'33",* I know there must be some purpose behind it. Does he protest loudly against composing for and playing the piano or tradition per se, or against our absurd traditional notion which still makes us clandestinely hope that someone sitting at the piano in public would do something to the instrument and us? By protesting so loudly through silence or by kidding us while saying, "Stop thinking a piano is a piano is a piano! Those Gertrude-Stein-days of the twenties are over!" he demolishes the last hope that the public may find some sense in what he is doing. He does not mind inviting such protest against his manner of protesting or rather experimenting with the music of silence. I know he is serious about it but does not realize that the music of silence he wants us to hear becomes lost in the cacophony of our confusion.

Cocteau and the Twenties did not foresee such finality of nothingness. They only made its emergence possible. They also prepared the aesthetic passport to the *happenings,* which, at their best artistic behavior, are well-rehearsed improvisations. The absence of scripts or clearly premeditated choreographic concepts, with the dancers giving expression to their momentary mood within the framework of a general idea—which characterizes, for instance, some of Ann Halprin's work—somehow closes the circle and, with the experience of many cataclysmic events, returns to the individual improvisational approach of Isadora Duncan without, of course, the flamboyance of soul acrobatics.

It is remarkable how much of the artistic activities in the Sixties had the stamp of a neoromantic trend, even though fraught with electronic vibrations. The earlier realization that our age has lost the breath and taste for continuous narrative, for any traditional rules and that it can only be coaxed along a staccato existence by quick turns of surprises, became refined into a sophisticated version of the vulgar. Hoaxes, self-delusions, and contradictions climaxed the struggle of being different at all costs and mainly at the expense of the poetic in each creation. Most artists who wanted to be *in,* understood that you were only *in* when you were *way out*. It also demanded less artistic discipline and almost wiped out the border lines between art that is art and a free-for-all art.

"Why must it be art?" I hear the youngest generation say. "It's life."

But then what is art to you? Define!

"Why try to define art, define life," is the reply.

James Waring, however, once defined art by saying that dance is any aimless movement motivated by no motivation or motive, guided by no aesthetic principles, propelled by no passion or compassion nor intent on arousing any emotion or stimulating any thought. A program note of Merce Cunningham declares:

Dancing has a continuity of its own that need not be dependent upon either rise and fall of sound (music) or the pitch and cry of words (literary ideas). Its force of feeling lies in the physical image fleeting or static. It can and does evoke all sorts of individual responses in the single spectator. These dances may be seen in this light.

John Cage: "Theatre is seeing and hearing. I go to happenings. That strikes me as the only theatre worth its salt. We aren't having art just to enjoy it. We are having art in order to use it."

Time moves a bit hastily these days. Perhaps it has already passed them by, and Waring, Cunningham, and Cage have not yet noticed it. Taking their accomplishment, art or non-art, as a point of departure where will the new generation go? Will the young follow the proverbial pendulum by going back? Or will they move forward into a new bewildering wilderness and leave their footprints there while denying they had any thought of immortality? Or will they go forward without noticing that they returned to the past with a new look and wonder in their eyes?

In a critical and facetious mood George Bernard Shaw once

said forty million Frenchmen cannot be right. It has happened before in history that an entire generation was wrong.

The age of surprise for the sake of art or for the sake of surprise has not yet ended. And yet something happened to the old war cry: Étonne-moi! It was no longer the great challenge in the late Sixties. If said at all it was said with a grin of despair in a kidding mood.

No doubt, the artist will continue to search for his identity. He will remain as restless as his time. One day—to his own and everyone's surprise—he may find out that he has found himself.

TRENDS, TRAPS, & TRAUMAS

Titles and program notes

TITLES ARE A MEANS of identification. A rose is a rose, even if we call it by another name. But speaking of a rose evokes images in us of a certain color, form, and fragrance. These images may vary, but they channel our instinctive reaction, they orientate our thinking. Moreover, the naming of a thing is in the last analysis a mere necessity to facilitate communication.

A work of art is no exception in this respect. However, as a product of our imagination, of our artistic will, it is a new manifestation of man's creative ability. Although this manifestation exists within a generic category, it lives its own existence without awakening in us any associations, any images of a familiar certainty.

Giving a work of art a name, that is, a title, is a creative act in itself, because beyond identification a title must have meaning. It must have deep roots in the creation, it must relate to it as if it were blood of its blood, flesh of its flesh. If the notion of a "rose" channels our reaction, orientates our thinking in a direction shaped by experience, the title of a new work is supposed to be the point of departure toward a new experience to be added to those we carry with us as the light burden of knowing and the heavy baggage of accumulated knowledge.

Theoretically, there is merely one title that is not only the best but the only right one. The finding of it puzzles the artist more often than not. It would not puzzle him were he aware that he cannot really search for it, that a title comes "towards" him. We often hear artists say that they are bad at finding a title, whereas in reality they do not sense that it has already suggested itself while they worked on their idea. Also, it could have occurred to them simultaneously with the conception of the idea itself. There could be easily something wrong with the idea of the work if hitting upon a right title is wearisome, if something that is so much part of the entire creative process should be unyielding.

A title does many things to many people. Above all, it impresses us as does a person who introduces himself. At that very moment we do not yet know anything about the person, though we instinctively react to him by forming a subliminal image of him which may be of quite some significance when we are afforded deeper insight into his personality. Somehow we constantly try to correct, or to complete, as it were, the image caused by our first impression without being really conscious of how strongly this first impression is guiding us in our reactions to and feelings for the bearer of his name.

The same holds true for titles. When we say that a good title can "sell a piece" (the thought of having to market our artistic endeavors is a nauseating, but undeniable, fact), we admit how very important this first encounter with our public is. In his understandable eagerness to succeed the artist may be inclined to look for a "catchy" title, thus engendering greater expectation than his creation warrants. What I would call a catchy title need not necessarily be as long as the marathon *Oh Dad, Poor Dad, Mamma's*

Hung You in the Closet and I'm Feelin' so Sad (with which the playwright Arthur Kopit at least prepares us for a wacky session of loose-joint and gimmicky ideas). Erick Hawkins who has a fine ear for linguistic tricks has come upon a catchy and all-embracing title with *Here and Now With Watchers* which is as intriguing as it is suggestive. It rings as true as the piece itself and therefore is of one piece with his piece.

Knowing you must be more daring to risk less, Hawkins called another dance *Sudden Snake-Bird* or *Earth-Sky* or *She-He* or *Soft-Loud*. This is very close to the *Oh Dad* type of title. It proclaims the ambiguity of all oneness, putting suchness into the center of a circling entity. This is how it struck me. But I felt it aimed too far, sounded too proclamatory. To paraphrase Hamlet, I would say, "the title doth protest too much, methinks." If your aim is to strike at your audience with sound and mood in contrast, then Martha Graham's *Acrobats of God* is a classic example.

Most of her titles have a monolithic feeling about them. Either they are direct in their appeal and then almost prosaic as in those cases in which she uses the names of the heroines she creates (*Phaedra, Clytemnestra,* for example), or she evokes a poetic image with a precision whose secret lies in its brevity, with a seeming simplicity in the choice of her words. Iceberg-like, the bulk and weight lie submerged and an image expressed through and compressed into two or three words are visible in their powerful suggestiveness. Already the titles for her first dance creations from *Dance* or *Fragments: Tragedy, Comedy* to *Frontier* and *Primitive Mysteries* show a percussiveness and tautness which betray the form and feeling of her creations. As little as anything decorative ever creeps into her dancing, so has a title never been chosen by her for the purpose of embellishing the viewer's expectations. She puts her cards on the table (read: program bill). The cards do not lie. On the other hand, they reveal little more than the direction in which we will find the heart of the matter.

Among her longer titles are *Canticle For Innocent Comedians* and *Every Soul Is a Circus* which still have the calm ring of a statement despite their length. Both have a universality about them. In the latter, the meaning is all-embracing, moves on the thin edge between the tragic and comic foreshadowing both. In the former, the innocent comedians equal every soul, but what "circus" does for the one title, "canticle" does for the other. Each sets a mood, each holds out a promise for us which the dances fulfill. Particularly the dancing in *Canticle For Innocent Comedians,* its heightened lyricism, the intenseness of the intangible in it would have misled many other choreographers to a far more lyric-sounding title (perhaps something in the order of Lucas Hoving's title *Strange, to Wish Wishes No Longer* which seems to be too poetical for the dance's good).

The poetic in a title ought to be far more hidden and evocative than spelling it out in its verbal image. *Do Not Go Gentle Into That Good Night* (which belongs to my favorite lines and poems of Dylan Thomas) would nevertheless be a bad choice for the title of a dance, if for no other reason than its directness, but *Deaths and Entrances,* as revealing it may be, does not disclose more than we need to know. It may turn out to be a blind battle of sisters, or the Brontë sisters in particular. However, the juxtaposition of death and entrance is laden with a hidden drama of tremendous tension, and the plural of both images gives them the rhythm of eternal change as much as of universal stability. In other words, the broadness of the title's meaning is at the same time confining our mind to the specific dance creation. Thornton Wilder's *Our Town* refers only seemingly to Grover's Corner while, in fact, it embraces all the towns everywhere.

Consider Martha Graham's *Dark Meadow,* a title of stark simplicity though vibrant with poetic mystery. As the reader of a program bill, I cannot help thinking of something enigmatic, of something unreal-real like a huge carpetlike meadow in full bloom but shrouded in darkness as if sun and moon conspired to hide something beautiful from me. These two words have the same intensity in their suggestiveness as does Pearl Lang's *Windsung,* which evokes a sweeping, swishing image that cries out in movement. This image is light and floating, while *Dark Meadow* reveals a frightful fascination with earth, past, and depth. I expect from it either a medieval or archaic presentation bordering on the ritual.

Alwin Nikolais has a way with words which fits his kind of creative imagination. In the totality of mechanization in which inanimate things are blessed with the power of life, in which life and sound move as much as the human shape, in his theatrical realization of a marionette-like complete unawareness of movement, his titles show a playful intellectualization or an intellectualized playfulness. *Nascent Psalm, Reliquary,* or *Rite of the Caped Man,* sections of his *Totem* have a potent quality which, if nothing else, arouses a curiosity in those who are unfamiliar with his work and creates a clear conception—in broad outlines, of course—of what we have to expect if we know his work.

Some titles evoke the feeling of non-titles. The most obvious would be: *Dance.* But even a title such as Merce Cunningham's *Sixteen Dances for Soloist and Company of Three,* despite its factual length and clarity, says little more than *Dance.* Wassily Kandinsky also had great title problems because of the sparse abstractions of his imageless imagery which, in their pure lines, have musical rather than literary or architectural affinities. He wrote in a letter to his biographer, Will Grohmann, in 1928:

My titles are said to make my paintings uninteresting, boring. But I have an aversion for pompous titles. No title is anything but an unavoidable evil, for it always has a limiting rather than a broadening effect—just like "the object."

A non-title is far less objectionable than an inexpressive title, a choice of no-choice. The choreographer may wish to be noncommittal using titles such as *Variations* or *Story*. The only case of alienation through non-titling a dance occurred, as far as I can recall, in the Fifties when James Waring—then on a "way-out excursion into nowhere" from where he fortunately returned—simply gave his dances Roman numbers.

It is a kind of apology for not having found a suitable title when a choreographer chooses the title of the score he uses. George Balanchine's self-indulgence in not bothering to find the right, or any, title for so many of his masterly works borders on disdain for his audience. (One does not present a dirty or torn visiting-card when introducing oneself.) The range of Balanchine's titles leaning on the score is overwhelming; it runs from *Ivesiana* to *Glinkaiana*, from *Brahms-Schoenberg Quartet* to *Metastaseis & Pithoprakta*, from *Symphony in C* to *Liebeslieder Walzer*. These title choices are more *Capriccio* than *Brillant*.

Michel Fokine choreographed a work in 1908 which was shown in St. Petersburg under the title of *Chopiniana*. Taglioni's famous ballet *La Sylphide* was suggested by the costuming of the second version which Fokine staged for Diaghilev's Ballets Russes a year later. It was Diaghilev's genius to have changed the title to *Les Sylphides*. Even though the Russians still adhere to *Chopiniana* whenever they perform Fokine's work, the title reduces this by now classic work to the image of a musical potpourri and lacks the evocative spirit of airiness and the dreamlike atmosphere of *Les Sylphides*.

Fiction and nonbelletristic prose works often have subtitles which more precisely define what a general title withholds and which point out the direction the reader's imagination should take. Subtitles are rarely used for plays and hardly ever for ballets. Cunningham's *Summerspace* is an apt title which helps to attune our mind to the ballet. Its subtitle, *A Lyric Dance,* seems unnecessary and in no way extends the suggestiveness of the *Summerspace* image. Agnes de Mille's *Rodeo* was premiered by the Ballet Russe de Monte Carlo in 1942 with the title *Rodeo or The Courting at Burnt Ranch.* Fortunately, the "or" description was dropped and is hardly remembered any longer. A similar case is August Bournonville's *Napoli or The Fisherman and His Fiancée.* One cannot imagine a more fatally prosaic subtitle. It seems that no one has yet tried to put a poetic image into the subtitle which could easily eliminate the need for a program note.

When in 1957 Pearl Lang choreographed her Persephone she called this dance *Falls the Shadow Between.* It then struck me as a good title, but there was something that bothered me about it, something that seemed to be of a cumbersome and a-bit-too-much nature. When, a year later, the title was changed to *Falls the Shadow* I realized how heavy and clumsy the word *between* was and how much it took away from the clear-cut suggestiveness of its shorter version. In the 1957 production the title was further burdened with six lines of an e.e. cummings poem:

> what if a dawn of doom of a dream
> bites this universe in two . . .
> Blow soon to never and never to twice
> (blow life to isn't: blow death to was)
> —all nothing's only our hugest home;
> the most we die, the more we live

The 1958 program only gave us its first two lines:

what if a dawn of doom of a dream
bites this universe in two . . .

While the six lines took the mind away from the expected dance
—our thoughts unwillingly lost themselves in the weird, contrasting beauty of cummings's imagery—the two lines took on the role
of a mental guide, of implied meaningfulness. In expectation of
the reality of a make-believe world, title and program note (if
needed) must prompt our present state to open up our memory,
to let the *was* and *will-be* fuse into *is* (to borrow from e.e. cummings), to help draw the curtain from the unfolding mystery of
the ideas-and-act turned revelation-in-movement.

The artist is aware of the hidden potencies that lie in the
title. He often superimposes the title on his work instead of listening to the work's own heartbeat which longs to let him in on
the secret of its name. To be able to be suggestive to us, the title
must have been suggested by the core of the creation. Then, and
only then, no shadow will fall between here and now with watchers and leave us unprepared for that inevitable look at lightning
when, in an imaginary dialogue of seraphic remoteness, those lovable and sometimes exasperating acrobats of God try to divert and
bewitch, to enchant and amuse us.

what if a dawn of a dream of a title
embraces the many and one . . .

Although the problems of whether to add a program note to
the title—and if so, what it should be and do for us, the viewers
—are different from the problems of choosing the right title, the
conclusions will point to similar pitfalls and the same potentialities.

In some cases program notes are chosen because the artist
gropes for a crutch, because he does not quite trust his own work

to be valid and viable enough to speak for itself. Does the artist mistrust his public to be able to grasp his visual imagery, to penetrate the depths of his thoughts? And does the dancer-choreographer therefore wish to make quite sure that our expectations are channeled in the right direction, that neither our mind nor heart could leave the track he traced for us and on which he wants to lure us into the mysterious world of his imagination?

No doubt, there may be a touch of uncertainty in this need for emphasis, in the artist's desire to explain something of which no one can know in advance whether it needs an explanation. On the other hand, the idea of the motto is an old and justified one. The greatest writers have used it by heading their books—and even each chapter—with quotes from other writers or philosophers in order to create a mood in the reader suggestive of the content to follow. Such a motto should not be a direct statement spelling out and embracing message and meaning of the content. The subtler its suggestiveness, the more effective will a motto be. In essence, its words try to give hidden wings to those who are about to enter a yet undisclosed realm of creation. In its relative brevity, a motto is like a magic chord whose sound is supposed to swing open invisible gates and carry us on the back of its echo right into the subject matter.

Thus, a motto seemingly performs a feat which is the exact opposite to its etymological meaning, for its source, in Latin, is the word *muttum* which stands for a mutter. Although the purpose of a motto reaches from helping a lame dog over a stile to quickening the visual emergence of a poetic image, there is a great deal of a mutter about it if we go back to the dictionary and its definition of being a "repressed or obscure utterance." For all a motto should be is a whish of an illusion to the heart of the matter: the adumbration of a feeling, the implication of a thought. Its actual concern ought to be with something that has no direct bearing on the essay, book, chapter, or dance in question. Yet it must have the power of intense poetic suggestiveness broad enough in its meaning to reach from the particular into the universal and narrow enough to build a straight line, a bridge, as it were, from the universal to the particular of the created work.

If a poem or poetic line inspired the dancer to choreograph a work, then its inclusion as a program note is not only justified, it also has a special meaning pointing from the genesis of the work to its fulfilled identity. In such a case, the artist must only concern himself with the right and balanced choice of lines and words. More often than not, one or two lines will be stronger, may have a more propelling power than a whole stanza or longer quote. If the dance has several sections that lend themselves to be titled, then very short phrases from the poem used for subtitles would easily create a feeling of intimate intensity. I could imagine that these subtitle lines could be very effective in taking the place of the motto. Erick Hawkins presented *8 Clear Places* without a motto, but being as poetically articulate as he is, he called the fifth and sixth section of the dance *sheen on water* and *inner feel of the summer fly,* images which have as potent an allusiveness about them as some of the best lines written by e. e. cummings.

Sometimes a seemingly prosaic wording of a title can have a dormant poetic potency as Katherine Litz's *The Fall of the Leaf* or her *Twilight of a Flower.* There is something absolutely tragic in the juxtaposition of twilight and flower. This image creates the feeling of something beautiful fading away. Or, it would have been utterly redundant, had she added only the shortest motto to her title *The Story of Love from Fear to Flight.*

It is quite obvious that the nonliteral dance creations, those which avoid the narrative and revelation of the self through any form of dramatization, do not need any verbal lead or descriptive avant propos. Their kinetic appeal is purely sensuous, their intent does not transcend the articulation of body images. They are self-sufficient in their visualization. Nor does a clearly representational dance demand much in the way of a suggestive poem. The legibility of its story, the demonstrative display of its feelings in their stark staring unmistakability quickly reach the observer. To use a program note in these cases could only be thinkable if its choice could, to some extent, obfuscate and mystify the obvious.

Of course, there are a great many dance creations that fall between these two extremes of the representational and nonliteral. Sometimes the choreographer may deem it wise to protect himself by way of explanation, as Jerome Robbins did with *The Cage*. Consciously, or less so, he must have sensed the danger of being misunderstood or misinterpreted, although he could always have pointed to the classical source of his inspiration, the second act of *Giselle* in which Heine-Gautier's Wilis take revenge on the males by dancing them to death. But, as writers who realize the similarity of their figures to living persons deny it in a prefatory note, Jerome Robbins must have felt the need to direct the thought of even the most enlightened public to his real intent while clearing himself from all suspicion by inserting the following program note:

There occurs in certain forms of insect and animal life, and even in our own mythology, the phenomenon of the female of the species considering the male as prey. This ballet concerns such a race or cult.

There is nothing new about the use of longer program notes. Every Roman pantomime was introduced by a herald who recited the content of the story to be enacted by the mime. This was done to refresh the audience's memory as much as to create a mood of receptivity. The Romans probably did not mind being told by innuendo that the artist was not sure whether they knew their mythology which, after all, was part of their cultural-religious existence.

It is far more justified to assume in our days that not everyone in the audience is familiar with Greek and Roman mythology. At the risk of insulting the intelligence of some, the majority of the audience needs to be instructed. Moreover, the Freudian overtones usually added to the mythological events, the changed emphases, in other words, the twentieth-century reinterpretations of an old legend justify some information. It will have to be longer than a motto. But it serves no other purpose than to annoy the audience by making it read one long paragraph after another to be prepared for the intricacies to unfold. This leaves a bitter taste in one's mind, as if being scolded for not having done one's homework properly before going to the theater.

As everything she does, Martha Graham's approach to program notes is of an almost ecstatic intensity. Sometimes it is also puzzling. There seems to be a heightened sense in her that the dancer should speak to his audience, or rather speak as though a third person—an imaginary teacher for the serious creations, an imaginary master of ceremonies for the light and lyric pieces—would step before the curtain. In her program notes she speaks of herself in the third person.

In the creation of her famous classic impersonations, the feeling that enlightenment comes before entertainment becomes obvious through the detailed retelling of the mythological or Biblical story in her program notes. After the teacher has given his basic information which varies in length—*Clytemnestra*'s program note runs more than one full page in the smallest print—he then tells his listeners how they should follow Martha Graham's conception of and approach to this basic story. Also, after telling of Oedipus, the note says: "In *Night Journey,* Martha Graham's dramatization of this great myth, it is not Oedipus but the Queen

Jocasta. . . ." After the detailed background story of Troy, Agamemnon, and Clytemnestra, we are told: "Martha Graham's Clytemnestra begins in the underworld. . . ." After the introduction to the tragic tale of Phaedra: "Martha Graham's *Phaedra* is focused upon that time outside of time when at the pitch of her lust. . . ."

It is notable that the language she uses goes beyond the mere telling of facts, but has a lyric touch and dramatic terseness which is very expressive. This verbal intensification is even more manifest when the teacher dons the cloak of the master of ceremonies in her lighter fares. He cannot always forget his original vocation, as, for instance, in *Acrobats of God* when he says:

To their contemporary biographers, the early Church Fathers who subjected themselves to the discipline of the Desert, were athletae Dei, the athletes of God. This is Martha Graham's fanfare for dance as an act . . . a celebration in honor of the trials and tribulations, the disciplines, denials, stringencies, glories and delights of a dancer's world . . . and of the world of the Artist.

The master of ceremonies also tells us exactly what we have to expect in viewing *Diversion of Angels,* namely "a lyric ballet about the loveliness of youth, the pleasure and playfulness, quick joy and quick sadness of being in love for the first time." In *Embattled Garden* he tells us, with tongue in cheek, that

Love, it has been said, does not obey the rules of love but yields to some more ancient and ruder law. The Garden of Love seems always to be threatened by the Stranger's knowledge of the world outside and by the knowledge of those like Lilith (according to legend, Adam's wife before Eve) who lived there first.

A Look at Lightning is introduced in a highly suggestive way of how Hesiod eavesdropped on the Muses' chatter about the difference between true and false things and about the artist who, encountering his Muse, looks at lightning. Lately, only *Secular Games* condenses the program note in the three subtitles of this dance.

It seems that whenever Martha Graham has encountered her Muse and perceived the difference between true and false, more often than not, she cannot help telling her audience all about this encounter before giving us the movement visualization of her inner experience and ecstasy.

Doris Humphrey, who was very much dependent on inspiration that came from lyric passages, has used mottoes rather sparingly, but with great effectiveness. For her, verbal imagery was often a point of departure, to free her own fantasy, and little else. She may have needed a spark to ignite her imagination, but then she usually was on her own. Only in her *Lament for Ignacio Sanchez Mejias* did she make Lorca's words "At five o'clock in the afternoon" move with the dancers in an almost percussive mood like verbal drum beats. It was in her *Dawn in New York* that she used more profusely the motto quoting ten lines from Garcia Lorca's poem and, though they were very illustrative of her choreographic concept or rather because of it, this program note seems to be, particularly in retrospect, a bit overdone.

In general, the British do not indulge in overstatements nor do they show too much inclination for verbosity. Balanchine's English counterpart, Sir Frederick Ashton, hardly ever fell back on the title of the score as title of his ballets. In the one case in which he did, it is fully justified. Edward Elgar's *Enigma Variations* not only serves as musical accompaniment, it is the very theme of the ballet's story.

Even Elgar's subtitle, "My Friends Pictured Within," makes sense as a subtitle for Ashton's work since he peoples his ballet with them in their specific Victorian atmosphere. Each character with all his idiosyncracies is very much alive. But do we need a verbal snapshot under each figure, such as "Richard Baxter Town-shend, An amiable reedy-voiced eccentric who rode about on a tricycle," particularly when we see this eccentric ride about on a tricycle? You cannot miss that on stage. In describing the character Dora Penny, Ashton adds to her name: " 'The movement suggests a dance-like lightness.' An intimate portrait of a gay but pensive girl with an endearing hesitation in her speech." All these descriptions have a narrative feeling as if taken out of a novel and most of them allude, strangely enough, to vocal peculiarities.

Here Ashton erred. Even if every description were taken from Elgar's score—and they were taken from a variety of Elgar sources—dance characters need more evocative epithets than "Charming and romantic" or "Her gracious personality is sedately shown." Such descriptions are pedantic and pedestrian, and, as a matter of fact, they are superfluous. I could imagine that a few short and whimsical words with an inherently poetic feeling may, in this case, add spice to the visual stage image of the character, but then the word must not be identical with what we see on stage.

Frederick Ashton painted an almost Chekhovian picture in this ballet which demands from the spectator to listen between the lines or, to be more explicit, to see what remains uncreated between the movements. He not only paints such a picture, he also ends the ballet with a cliché-dénouement characteristic of the nineteenth century. A telegram is delivered which foreshadows Elgar's breakthrough as a composer. Using a real incident as a basis, Mr. Ashton felt the obvious need to let us in on Elgar's story and on how the *Enigma Variations* brought "international fame to Elgar and immortality to the 'Friends Pictured Within.' "

The ballet succeeds to the very moment when reality, the banal arrival of a telegram, breaks into a picturesque sequence of poetic vignettes. I go so far as to say that the final program note pinpointing historically the incident of Elgar's triumph proves the ending of the ballet to be as prosaic and programmatic as the program note itself. In his *Les Illuminations* Frederick Ashton demonstrates so well that he knows how to transcend reality and how to transfigure a life experience into the rapture of a poetic reality.

It seems that program notes can be used as artistic barometers. Rising atmospheric pressure caused by program notes should make us weatherwise.

To workshop or not to workshop

Ours is the age of haste. Fruits are expected to ripen during their transport to the market, not on the trees.

Any work of art needs time to grow and mature to full ripeness. The artisans in pre-Renaissance days worked with devotion and love for the work itself and its purpose; they did not feel the need to see in it the reflection of their Self. Gratification lay in the process of giving shape to something where there was nothing before. These master craftsmen—who often took ten years to create one altar, as Pacher did in St. Wolfgang near Salzburg or Grünewald with his Isenheimer altar—may also have done their work to satisfy their egos. But they were mainly driven to serve their community and honor God. They may even have felt they were competing with other craftsmen. But no one hastened to present the final product so as not to be forgotten or to feed his vanity with reviews and sandwiched trivia at cocktail parties.

The haste with which we have learned to live today has deprived us of a focal point within ourselves. It took Leonardo four years to paint his Mona Lisa. But we know that he experimented incessantly with colors and the fresco medium, in particular, and was less interested in the enigmatic smile of that lady than in the solution of another enigma—the work itself.

Everyone wants and needs recognition, but, in the long run, hunger for applause and the easy little victories spell self-defeat for the artist. The French mystic Simone Weil pointed out that it is immoral to reach a destination without having made a journey. It is against the fundamental laws of all arts to rape one's respective Muse when she is not willing to yield to the artist's courtship. In his intercourse with her, it is not finality that counts, but the playful and creative process leading to it.

The need for the "workshop" is an initial step in the course of creativity. It cannot be described nor prescribed in general terms since background and temperament of the individual artist remain the only determining factors in this process. It is not a new idea in the arts, and certainly not in the dance field. The creative dancer and choreographer may at times underrate its importance, but he will, in the long run, pay for it.

There are different notions of what a dance workshop is and of how and on which level it should function. This is determined by the circumstances under which the artist works, alone or with a group. But in all cases the workshop activity is, or should be, a preparatory phase, a steppingstone leading to the final result of his work as it will be presented to the public. Essentially, it serves as a clearinghouse for a work to be tried out and prejudged. The workshop's trade mark is the work-in-progress. It is difficult to say at which point a creative work is in its final stage (if ever at all!). Criteria and standards exist for it, but they vary with our demands on life and on the arts. Many publicly performed ballets and modern dance works are often artistically unjustifiable and at best workshop material which should have been discarded. On the other hand, some of the greatest works of the dance repertory have emerged from workshop productions.

Only a very few choreographers, such as Balanchine and Nikolais—to mention two extremes—have enjoyed the opportunity of a company and a home which have enabled them to show their experiments to the public. The American Ballet Theatre instituted a workshop which has functioned intermittently without having a base from which to work. The company has tried to give some of its younger or less experienced choreographers a chance to try out certain ballets, unconventional or daring in their conceptions. In the late Fifties and early Sixties, its workshop presented a few stunning works, such as Herbert Ross's *The Maids*, based on Genet's play, and Donald Saddler's *This Property is Condemned* in which some of Tennessee Williams's lines were integrated in the movement patterns. These works were truly experimental and keyed to a limited audience—an initiate or balle-to-manic public. Both were fascinating and exciting works; the former was almost a *scandale célèbre* when first produced as a workshop creation but aroused no puritanic reaction when taken into the repertory of the American Ballet Company during the rather permissive era of the late Sixties.

The growing pressure in dance for more and more conformity (the inevitable dilemma of democratization) makes the dance workshop almost obligatory. First, it offers the choreographer a framework for challenging himself, his time, and contemporaries; and in getting rid of excess "genius," he will more readily create in terms of the generally acceptable. Second, it tests the theatrical effectiveness of a semiexperimental work, such as Kenneth Mac-Millan's *Journey*, which found its way into the repertory of the American Ballet Theatre.

Sometimes the aura of a workshop—perhaps in a heightened sense of the word—is an inherent part of an entire company. One of these rare cases is the Ballet Rambert. Dame Rambert has always put emphasis on working on an experimental basis, free from outside pressures, removed from the atmosphere of the commercial theater. Ballet Rambert does not have the apparatus, equipment, and technical facility of any of the leading companies, nor does it wish to compete with them. Being a tremendous spiritual force within the British dance world, it appears next to the Royal Ballet, or even the Western Ballet, as a workshop of serious intent with the implicit desire to further the creative talent of the choreographers and the understanding of the dancer's stylistic needs.

Besides Antony Tudor, Dame Rambert nurtured such artists as Frederick Ashton, Andrée Howard, Walter Gore, Kenneth MacMillan, and, the youngest of them, Norman Morrice. The famous ballerina Tamara Karsavina ended her spectacular career with Ballet Rambert, and such a star as Alicia Markova was a mere beginner when she joined Rambert's company. Dame Rambert has an uncanny feeling for talent and, when she has found it, is able to awaken in the artist the spirit that creates, the mind that understands, the strength that endures. I give Dame Rambert much emphasis because, coming from Dalcroze and via Nijinsky to ballet, she is a unique example of an individual best equipped to give the concept of a dance workshop the strongest profile and constant sustenance.

In spite of the fact that Ballet Rambert is inherently experimental, it has always desired to retain the outer appearance of a regular company. As a result, a near relative of it came into being in the early Fifties, simply calling itself Ballet Workshop. It was founded and directed by Marie Rambert's daughter and son-in-law, Angela and David Ellis. Its workshop character was far more outspoken than that of the Ballet Rambert, its program a bit more experimental, and, as often happens in workshop enterprises, students from the Rambert School were used for small parts.

One of the dangers of workshop activity is the intrusion of or deterioration towards amateurism. This danger is more serious in the field of the modern dance than in ballet, because it is more accessible to the amateur in basic movement and self-expression than in the stylized balletic form; because the need of the dancer-choreographer to experiment in terms of the world in which he lives and the one he visualizes is far more intense; and finally because the creative ability is a great deal richer among modern dancers than among their counterparts in ballet. Of course, there is no way of stopping dilettantism in any artistic activity. But it very quickly eliminates itself by virtue of its being what it is. The border cases, however, the talented dilettantes, will always use the workshops as justification for their existence.

The young artist has a responsibility towards his art, himself, and his future, as well as his potential audience. He must have humility. He must learn to have it. He must learn to be simple and to the point. He must realize that quantity is no substitute for quality and that at times it may be more important to sharpen one's self-criticism than one's wits; that it is more important to be able to wait until one knows—and not only thinks—one is ready.

The artist expects a sympathetic approach from his audience and his critics when he presents his works in a studio. The stage with its distance and better lighting equipment, with all the accouterments of stage illusion gives any choreographic work a fullness and theatricality which no studio production can have. One can easily make mistakes in judgment and see more in a work viewed so closely in a surrounding of informality or, on the other hand, slight its potentialities because the work is deprived of its theatrical make-up that is a part of the stage secret. A studio production is cruel to the dancer and hard on the choreographer. If one cannot help feeling the artistic inevitability of a work under these circumstances, then it cannot lose anything of its inherent theatrical image in its more appropriate environment, the stage.

Soon after World War II the Choreographers Workshop in New York offered many young dancers an opportunity to prove their creative abilities. Valerie Bettis and Lucas Hoving turned out to be the strongest talents, and Herbert Ross gave initial shape to his ballet *Caprichos,* a work which is now constantly in the repertory of the American Ballet Theatre.

The Choreographers Workshop soon disintegrated as did most of the other workshops that followed it in quick succession: in the early Fifties the Stage for Dancers and the Theatre Dance Workshop whose roster of performers shows a few star names— Tony Charmoli, Pauline Koner, Ruth Harris, Nelle Fisher, Merle Marsicano, Glen Tetley and many others. Contemporary Dance Productions, starting its activity in the late Fifties, could count on Lucas Hoving, Marion Scott, Jack Moore, Don Redlich, and Doris Rudko. This group brought Gus Solomons, Jr. to the fore and made it possible for Jeff Duncan to prove himself as a choreographer. Duncan, more recently, has become the driving force behind the studio programs of his Dance Theater Workshop which feature seasoned choreographers next to the very youngest, which show most serious attempts at expressing the beauty and horror of living beside spectacular dances of the unspectacular absurd. For a short season Jeff Duncan's Dance Theater Workshop took some of the more successful works from the studio atmosphere into an off-Broadway house.

Were they no longer workshop pieces then? It will always be the most awesome moment in the life of any creative artist when he feels convinced that, in the process of growth in the studio atmosphere, the work matured as best as could be expected. Whenever the artist contemplates moving his work from the studio (from where printed criticism should be excluded) to the stage, he must face the fact that certain works will never quite make it and will persist in remaining workshop pieces. Theater presentations expose a work to a more severe standard of criticism. The glamorous reality of stage illusion can create new unexpected traps for a dance work.

That there have been so many attempts at studio productions and workshop-theater presentations lately speaks loudest for the workshop as institution and for the vital strength of the theater dance. But workshops need artistic leadership, as does any company, and probably an even stronger personality to guide them on adventurous journeys through the artistic Scylla and organizational Charybdis. The emergence of so many dance workshops can only have one motive: the creative urge of the young dancer-choreographers and the lack of sufficient opportunities to test their abilities as choreographers through possible errors but few trials. That so many of the workshops also vanish so quickly has probably to do with a lack of genial leadership and the precariousness of human relationships.

Experiment we must. All the workshop activities remind us —whether we make use of those existing or try to call new ones into being keyed to our personal artistic aims—to move on, not to stop in self-complacency. They admonish us that art and the growth of the artist is a never-ending process. It demands work and work and work: to compose and shape, to weed out and eliminate. And there is no better place for it than a "workshop."

Swan Lake in our age of anxiety

We live in a curious world of half-truths and sham wisdom. Since the 1920s the creative artist has more or less consciously lived off the work of one pioneer who dared to plunge into the labyrinth of that elusive something that makes man tick. Our age —the Age of Anxiety, as it was so aptly called by W. H. Auden— will, in all its shades and variations, go into history as a "psychological" epoch. Today nobody can keep away from the clichés and jargons of psychoanalysis. Giving our life a second look, we cannot help realizing that we have surrendered our entire existence to the semiknowledge of our soul submerged in its subconscious. Whether the Id or the Superego remains triumphant, from early morning when the first sounds of the radio begin to hammer psychologically prepared advertisements into our subliminal existence to the very moment when we finally succumb psychosomatically to the hollow din and the grim horrors of our time, we are surrounded by the consequences of Freud's discoveries.

Of course, man had a subconscious—often very loosely referred to as his soul—in pre-Freudian days, and, along with many others interested in the conflict of reason and feeling, action and motive, Dostoevski, for instance, most successfully penetrated its depths; even more than two thousand years ago Euripides treated man's traumatic experiences dramatically; and most artists have "unconsciously" probed man's psyche in their endeavor to give *Gestalt* to the image of their world.

But too often modern psychoanalytic knowledge has become a toy rather than a tool in the hands of creative man, and it has prepared more traps for him than it has helped to tighten and solve his artistic problems. Time and again it has been proved that the poet's vision is stronger if it is not supported by crutches of psychoanalytic textbooks. It is unthinkable what might have become of the scene between Hamlet and his mother had Shakespeare not been the great poet he was and had he been burdened with the psychological "insight" of our era. This statement has been proved by the many interpretative aberrations on stage and screen of this very scene in the last few decades.

Although we can heighten the awareness of man, we can never quite penetrate his subliminal state scientifically in the way a surgeon can cut into our mortal being with his scalpel. The dramatist has to create the reality of the hidden being in man. Living suspended between knowing more but not knowing enough of what makes man "tick," he is weakened by having gradually learned to rely on semiknowledge instead of relying on the ecstasy of his insight, the unerring power of his vision.

The God-given spark of creative intuition channeled by experience and checked by reason is more reliable and productive than is knowledge and reason combined, however well supported by a flair for this and a knack for that. If only the dramatist could let his own conflicts fight it out on the keys of his typewriter with clarity of purpose and unmistakable vitality! If he could only let loose the fairies and furies of his subliminal self to render himself a service as a stand-in for his characters and their universal meaning! Being a product of his environment, the contemporary dramatist cannot help bringing with him a certain amount of psychological knowledge. No doubt it is his greatest problem to make it work for him without eclipsing his intuitive gift.

The choreographer faces the same, or very similar, problems, even though his tools and working methods differ from those of the dramatist. He also cannot exclude himself from the effects of his environment, since no artist can claim to be not of his time. And, since the 1920s the choreographer has been indoctrinated by Freudian concepts.

A strong link ties the theater dance to Freudianism. There is in Freud a deep current of romanticism just as it is inherent in the dance. A sense of the power of symbolism permeates both and so does a poetic rather than rational spirit. Psychotherapy has recognized the interrelation between man's make-up and movement expression and has successfully employed movement experience as release and relief of psychic disturbances. However valuable this may be in its therapeutic area, it must not penetrate the realm of artistic creation.

The body, being the shell of man's soul, being most intimately related to the complexities of our emotional mechanism, is an ideal instrument for self-expression. There is nothing closer to us than our own self, and the creative spark is, more often than not, ignited by unresolved conflicts within ourselves.

Martha Graham compartmentalized her leading characters and created major facets, either two or three of one and the same personality in order to penetrate the psychic depth of a human being. She gave *Gestalt* to more than one phase of existence, whether it be the duality of Emily Dickinson in *Letter to the World* or the threefold facets of Saint Joan in *Seraphic Dialogue* with their varied psychological motivations. In *Herodiad* a servant is used as her mirror reflection, or alter ego; the wild beast in *Errand into the Maze* is the destructive power within the human being. In her dramatic works she proved a growing ability to penetrate analytically the psyche of her many mythological, historical, and Biblical heroines, the complexity of motive and deed.

The dancer-choreographer of the representational modern dance was, at times, unable to reach from the personal towards the universal. Essentially being self-expressive, this form of the modern dance too often lost itself in the re-creation of psychodramatic experiences, and the inner torment of the dancer was inflicted on his audience. Merce Cunningham, uncrowned rebel king of the nonliteral dance movement, could state with dignified disdain in the early Fifties: "If it is self-expression you are after, then the proper place is the psychoanalyst's couch."

Cunningham's credo is the negation of the literal statement and the obvious involvement of the choreographer's personal feelings. He believes in detachment that has a non-Brechtian quality. He has no message and shuns the concept of "meaning." If his dance impresses the spectator as communication of noncommunicativeness, this impression is gained at his personal risk. And if Cunningham, in the finale of one of his works, slips with desperate, jerky movements into a plastic bag and rolls himself into nonexistence, any interpretation is, according to Cunningham, done in the willful association of our mind trained to perceive dance in literal terms.

However far removed his dances are from any psychological motivations and implications, they are just as remote from dances for the sake of mere dancing. Cunningham and his followers introduced the concept of the meaningfulness of meaninglessness, or the meaninglessness of the meaningful, depending on the mood of chance or the chance of mood. Such Dances of the Absurd should not be viewed with eyes whose visual nerves are traditionally oriented. It poses new problems of which the intrusion of the nonartistic into the realm of artistry is the most crucial and vexing one. It represents nothing except a vital part of our *Zeitgeist*. By blurring the demarcation line between the symbolically heightened reality and the most ordinary banalities, these dances demand a new critical approach the criteria of which are not yet established.

The revolt against the classic modern dance, known as the representational aspect of it, has led to the extremes of non-dance and those absurdities which consist of negation for negation's sake and deny all aesthetic rules. A witty "put on" can be enjoyed for the sake of its wit. It no longer is dance per se, and many of the innovators of the new style of nonstyle have recognized and admitted that their freedom, their total break with the past, and the last bit of ornament have led them into a new field of stage presentation which has nothing in common with theater dance in the customary sense. They are of course unaware that most of their non-dance creations are psychologically motivated. Any analysis of their theatrical doodling would bring forth the calamity of our *Zeitgeist* more clearly than their attempt to express it on stage while consciously staying away from any psychological involvement.

The only dancing free of any psychological aspects is the dance for the mere sake of dancing. The archaic word *tripudiate* means to dance as well as to rejoice. Even then the joy of moving expresses the liberation of feelings and opens blocked channels through the jubilation of the body. It seems there is no escape from psychological implications whatever we do, or rather not do, or pretend not to do.

Dance per se of which there is so much in all classical ballets attacks all my senses which are ready to surrender while absorbing the beauty of the visual images, fleeting as the minute to which they belong. This is a very feminine act: to surrender while absorbing. This is conceiving and being fructified. On this emotional level I can accept *Swan Lake* in our age of anxiety, even though the intellect is not overly engaged.

Dancing for the sake of dancing in the classic-romantic ballet either has a trace of formality—as proved by the *pas de deux* in which Marius Petipa gave expression to the bourgeois dream of courtliness—or tries to overwhelm our senses with sheer abandonment bordering on acrobatic virtuosity with jetés, pirouettes, or fouettés. When all this titillating excitement passes by, I ask for a touch of poetic mystery in the total context of the production to offset the impression of little more than a clinically clean production with perfect mastery of mere technique.

When seeing a classic ballet, romantic or modern, we must

realize that ballet appeals essentially to the unconscious. A world
of unreality and dreams is brought close to the threshold of our
rationalizing mind, but not so close as to make it reject the naïveté of make-believe which is the ballet's prerogative. The greatest literary minds have often used allegory, fables, and fairy tales
in order to hide their messages within gentle stories. With a
silken touch they have tried to illuminate human foibles and fail-
ings, actions and reactions, desires and dreams. The choreographers of *Swan Lake, Giselle,* or *Coppélia* were not prompted to
teach mankind a lesson as was Voltaire when he wrote *Candide,*
but many of the modern ballets carry within them meaningful
implications. Also, the nineteenth-century ballets reach back into
our subconscious to recreate the joys and anxieties of our childhood experiences.

These ballets are far less an escape from reality—as it may
seem—than a penetration of our unconscious and a visualization
of the kind of imaginary life which somehow reconciles our waking mind with reality. For the same reasons we find many ballets
concerned with inanimate objects with which we liked to play as
children: *The Nutcracker, Coppélia, Petrouchka, La Boutique
Fantasque, Iron Foundry* (Adolf Bolm's Ballet Mecanique).
Today we can see many psychological quirks and implications in
these ballets, a realization which corresponds with our desire as
children to take apart our toys and to investigate them.

Surrealism with all its Freudian aspects of uncontrolled, automatic reaction and the blending of weird dream images can also
be found in the ballet, although the dance "sugar-coats" the more
fantastic and frightening symbols. It is no mere coincidence that
the advent of the film in the Twenties and surrealism (André
Breton's Manifeste du surréalism: 1924) had great influence on all
the arts and, in the final analysis, influenced one another. They
were both historically conditioned by their era, and their overt

and covert impact on the development of the theatrical dance has been striking. The ballet renaissance, beginning with Diaghilev and growing steadily ever since, parallels the rising importance of the film as a new art form. Ours is an age of inherent movement and everything visual. Marshall McLuhan defined film as a "jerky mechanical ballet of flicks that yields a sheer dreamworld of romantic illusions." The classical ballet has always had favorite subjects, namely the elusive expression of dreamlike myths, legends, and fairy tales. The Freudian awakening of mankind after World War I only helped deepen their symbolistic significance and universal meaning.

A realistic ballet—in the sense in which we find realism in dramatic literature—is self-contradictory. Topical ballets with a realistic background such as Kurt Jooss's *The Green Table* or Jerome Robbins's *Age of Anxiety* succeeded because their realism was heightened to symbolism. When Antony Tudor turned from poetic symbolism to a very realistic theme as in *Echoes of the Trumpet,* a ballet dealing with the brutal conquest of a town, he failed. He has never failed when his point of departure was a realistic situation or story which remained a silhouette, remote and yet real, against which the danced events flowered into poetic symbolism.

Fokine, still following the footsteps of Noverre, wanted to make the ballet an imitation of life, whereas Antony Tudor deepened it to an interpretation of life. While still using the vocabulary of the classical ballet, he infused the *danse d'école* with the expressiveness and the essential purpose of the modern dance. Tudor's work shows a refined understanding for motivations and the ability to clarify feelings through movement. The essence of movement and gesture emerges from the figures he shapes. His themes are rather ordinary. A young woman has a sexual experience before she finds fulfillment with the man she loves, as in *Pil-*

lar of Fire. Jardin aux Lilas is the lyric expression of a moving drama of lost hope and love between two couples whose passion yields to reason and convention. Tudor can create an atmosphere of explosive tension as poetically as he can reveal the secret of beauty. It is not easy to dance Tudor "tudoresquely." Every gesture, every step is fraught with emotional meaning. If the dancer cannot materialize the lightness that lies on the threshold of the soul's depth, he fails Antony Tudor.

"For all alike, in differing degrees, the *real* is mere appearance and something else exists, that is not appearance—and does not always bear the name of God," André Malraux once wrote. We are much closer to the unreal, whatever it may be, than we are willing to admit. Perhaps it has something to do with the undeniable dualism in man which Goethe expressed so well with the phrase about two souls dwelling in our breast. Living with reality as we do, we must undoubtedly learn to accept it. If we must reassure ourselves about learning to accept it—as we daily say and hear it said—then the implication is that basically we are not so easily inclined to do so. It also seems that man can only endure reality by holding out to himself the possibility of escaping the very thing he knows he must accept.

Man invented many devious means to make the real acceptable. One of them is the fairy tale. Fairy tales are written not only for children but for the child in man. They can only survive if the adult mind sees something in them that goes beyond the surface acceptance by the child, that touches, in its allegory, our life's experiences. This is why ballet is so close to us and will never die.

Ballet is often identified with romantic escapism. I am convinced that just our era needs romanticism as a means of escape and actually creates its own scientifically oriented romanticism by making all the things possible which were still in the realm of man's dreams a few decades ago. It may be another brand of romanticism, strangely blended with reality. But many scientists believe, as do I, that man's ability to bring the heavens down and to come close to re-creating the mystery of God belongs to a new sphere of romanticism. It is escape, man's escape from the reality he knows into another reality, full of more secrets of the eternally unknown. All that man has achieved is to bring fulfillment closer to certain dreams, while opening new channels for his fear of reality which drives him to more and more escapes.

We may be frightened by our own abilities and cleverness. Horizons may have shifted, concepts and values changed, but deep "within" man remained man. I do not think that we have outgrown the child-in-man stage because we have reached the moon. Because we have reached the moon we will need the fairy tale more than ever. Only our mind which now knows so much more will have to adjust itself to the story or the story to our more sophisticated mind.

Edwin Denby once tried to explain *The Nutcracker* in psychological terms:

Thinking of Christmas, I remembered the Christmas tree conspicuously on stage and the Christmas party in the first scene of *The Nutcracker,* the venerable fairy tale ballet that Petipa's collaborator Ivanov set long ago to Tchaikovsky's lovely score. Has the action anything to do with Christmas? What is its nonsense plot really about and how does the Nutcracker create its mild and beneficent spell? This serene old vehicle complete with all the 1890 ballet conventions—pantomime scene, ballroom dance, grand pas de deux, divertissement —all of them strung in a row on a story nobody pays attention to—still works as a theatre piece. . . .

The Nutcracker is not foolish in form, nor is it foolish either in its literal content. It is a fairy-tale ballet and certainly looks like nonsense. But nowadays with psychoanalysis practically a household remedy, grown-ups take the nonsense of fairy tales more seriously than children. We call them narratives in free association and solve them like cross-word puzzles. *The Nutcracker* is an easy one—the title gives it away. The story begins at Christmas eve in an upper-class home, the locus classicus of ambivalent anxiety. An elderly bachelor with one eye gives a pre-adolescent girl a male nutcracker (the symbols and inversion could not be more harrowing). Her young brother tears it away from her by force and breaks it. But she takes it up from the floor and nurses it; she loves it. She dreams that *The Nutcracker* turns almost into a boy. Then she dreams of a deep forest in winter with restless girl-snowflakes and a handsome young man who keeps lifting up a young lady (and who is this lady but the little heroine's own dream image?). And after that she dreams she is watching a lot of dancing Chinamen and oddly dressed people—all of them somehow 'sweet'; and at last the previous young man and the previous young lady turn up again, too. They furnish a brilliant climax, and that leads to a happy dazzle for everything and everybody everywhere at once.

The Nutcracker has gone through many versions and one of the more daring ones was Rudolf Nureyev's restaging of this familiar E. T. A. Hoffmann story (*The Nutcracker* and *The King of Mice*) for the Royal Ballet. His version met with resistance from most balletomanes, but I found his attempt at modernization refreshing and intriguing.

This ballet always suffered from its dusty, all-too-naïve story which Nureyev streamlined by including a great many Freudian touches. Clara's dream adventures are still in the foreground, but she herself is the fairy princess, attacked by nasty rats which symbolically tear off her skirt; she finds herself in the mysterious grotto persecuted by strange shapes which finally turn out to be her parents, relatives, and friends. All this is Freudian-new and so is Nureyev's innovation of having the sinister Herr Drosselmeyer turn into the handsome prince.

The contemporary choreographer may take liberties with the classical ballets and make them more acceptable to our taste. (John Cranko: "I try to preserve the nucleus, to dust it off and in this way to turn the old into something vivid and alive.") The basic vocabulary is still the same as it was at the time when Marius Petipa reigned supreme at the Imperial Russian Theatre. But our aesthetic tenets, approach and emphases have changed; classical dancing is far more intricate and demanding today. There are several courses open to the choreographer to restage a classical ballet. George Balanchine took one of Petipa's works and made it into a contemporary tribute to the master by streamlining and modernizing it to such an extent that we can speak of a complete paraphrasing of the old idea. He called it *Ballet Imperial*. All he kept of Ivanov's original in his Act Two version of *Swan Lake* was the central adagio and the pas de quatre of the cygnets. The rest of the choreography was undiluted Balanchine.

The contemporary choreographer can take the basic idea of a story and completely modernize it as Jerome Robbins did with *The Afternoon of a Faun*. The hills on which we once found the faun, the faun himself, and the nymphs are no longer valid. We see the hazy outlines of a modern dance studio. One of the dancers lies on the floor, dreaming, languorous as the faun on the hill. A ballerina enters as if carried by a breeze. She seems to be more interested in her mirror reflection than in him. Then they dance together, somehow aloof, hardly being aware of each other. The boy brushes a gentle kiss on the girl's cheek. She is surprised, not frightened like the nymph. She puts her hand on the cheek where he has kissed her as if reassuring herself that the kiss was real. But the entire experience can only be a dream. She leaves as she entered, carried by a breeze. The boy lies down again and continues to dream.

This is the most perfect translation of a semiclassic ballet and romantic theme into contemporary terms. It is Nijinsky, vintage 1953. I consider it a classic of its kind, as an outstanding example of how older ballets could be treated if the choreographer is daring enough. But probably we cannot do the same so easily with classic fairy tales on which romantic ballets are based. Again, Jerome Robbins was daring when he boldly borrowed the second act of *Giselle* and turned the Wilis into fictional animals in *The Cage*—and, in more than one way, he "got away with murder." He triumphed with a dramatically beautiful and choreographically exciting ballet in which, allegorically, the rapaciousness of the woman is damned and the male, in a world of unsatisfied women, is doomed. When it was first shown in Europe, it was booed in many cities, perhaps because of its forthright homosexual implications or the allusion to the struggle of the sexes. Nobody would have booed the romantically sugar-coated revenge of the Wilis on the male for being deprived of the enjoyment of sex and the bliss of matrimony. Of course, the "sexplosion" of the late mid-century makes *The Cage* appear as a gentle homily.

Tinkering with the traditional versions of the nineteenth-century ballets occurs all the time everywhere. Choreographers are naturally tempted to alter a bit here and there, but usually the changes are not too drastic and rarely remarkable enough to survive. There are exceptions: the Bolshoi's new *Swan Lake,* which I saw in 1959. It had very little to do with the familiar choreography that has come down to us from Ivanov and Petipa with the help of Sergeyev. This version was originally made by Alexander Gorsky and remade by Asaf Messerer and Alexander Radunsky, with a fourth act and a happy ending by Messerer which I found disturbing and embarrassingly naïve. All the mimed scenes were omitted (which I did not mind missing), but a new character was introduced in the person of a jester, who, like the devil always having the best lines in a morality play, had wonderful things to do in the first and third act. But taken all in all it was not an improvement over the older versions.

This happens only too often, and the reasons for it differ from one attempt to the other. Some ballets, like *Giselle,* seem to defy major choreographic changes, probably because the dramatic story is tightly structured, while other ballets tempt the choreographer. *The Sleeping Beauty* belongs with the latter. As it was originally conceived and as we know it through Sergeyev, it centered on the ballerina and neglected the male dancers. Several of the new adaptations, particularly the Frederick Ashton–Marius Petipa version staged by Peter Wright, tried to remedy this injustice. Ashton added quite a few dances and new nuances which have made this fairy-tale ballet more colorful. Among the many additions was a new adagio solo for the Prince in the hunting scene, a pas de trois at the wedding, and a very impressive pas de deux for Aurora and the Prince. The poor décors of the Royal Ballet version evoked the memory of the sumptuous Bakst designs which gave Diaghilev's *Sleeping Beauty* the stamp of a remarkable visual spectacle.

To call *Giselle* the *Hamlet* of the ballets is, if nothing else, a misleading comparison. Kenneth Tynan, one of the most astute drama critics, felt prompted by this comparison to see *Giselle* and came away from it with the observation of having seen a most stupid concoction.* A comparison between the two may lie mainly in the difficulty, the challenge, and the great possibilities that both title roles offer actor and ballerina. There is hardly an actor who does not dream of playing Hamlet one day as there is no ballerina who does not wish to prove herself as Giselle.

* *"Giselle* itself is something of a hoax: where else but in the ballet world would you find a grown-up audience ready to believe that the betrayal of a village maid by a nobleman in mufti . . . was an emotional experience comparable in intensity to *Hamlet?"*

This ballet works theatrically, although it defies all basic dramaturgic rules. The second act of the supernatural Wilis story came first. Gautier realized it would not suffice as a one-act ballet —which, moreover, was not in vogue at that time—and needed some "logical" and dramatically satisfying justification. He thought of a princely hall with a great many divertissements before he and his collaborators hit upon a more realistic solution. Giselle—before becoming a professional Wilis charged with the destruction of deceiving males—was to be a simple country girl. To make the betrayal scene work, this rustic girl had to suffer from a heart condition, the heart being associated with love. But to let her recognize the betrayal and drop dead, seemed to the scenarists plausible, yet too abrupt and undramatic. Giselle had to earn her well-deserved death. Being frantically in love, the sudden disappointment ought to be killing. She could have killed Prince Albrecht—Did she not manage to get hold of his sword? —or Helion for that matter. Then Giselle would have been a Greek tragedy or a Renaissance revenge play, not the romantic ballet it is. Giselle's character had to be noble, full of selfless love, and, at the very end, she must save her betrayer's life. Woman, the unattainable ideal, had to be noble. Nobility does not exclude a fragile mind, and, obviously inspired by Hamlet, feigning madness, and Ophelia, going mad, the solution was found (and there is the only other parallel with Shakespeare).

Giselle is a serious case of a manic-depressive, leaping out of Freud's books. She was only given a few minutes—and what dramatic minutes!—between the gradual exultation of madness and the excitement affecting her heart. This short-paced metamorphosis is the ballet's climactic moment, challenging the dramatic skill of the ballerina. Many a ballerina has lived for that one moment, that is, to be able to die as Giselle.

The male betrayer had to be a prince. This is in keeping with the fairy-tale atmosphere. Although about that time Karl

Marx began his studies which led to his *Das Kapital,* Gautier did not think of exploiting any class difference. Princely blood was a conventional and convenient counterpoint to peasant simplicity (peasantry was idealized during the romantic era as was the child and the noble savage).

By being robust and realistically tragic (I almost said class-conscious), Galina Ulanova gently hinted at the contrast between rustic simplicity and playful aristocracy. On the other hand, Alicia Markova, just as famous for her Giselle, created a fragile little thing, doomed to die because of her frailty and the wayward touch of a neurosis which permitted her to be all tenderness, a gossamerlike dream in the second act. Between these two lies a variety of interpretations. Because of these possibilities, Giselles will come and go, be madly in love and die in madness, and the audience will behold this frail flower of ballet and take it apart: "I love you, I love you not, I love you. . . ."

Swan Lake is another case in point. To have two different ballerinas take the roles of Odette and Odile, as is often done, is to deprive this fairy tale of one of its essential points. When Odile betrays Odette, is not a very complex human mechanism at work, the positive and negative in us, the split personality, symbolized by the white and black swan? How often we betray ourselves, not knowing what we want and so often not knowing who we are!

Seeing the Swan from Prince Siegfried's viewpoint, we find expressed in it the eternally unfulfilled dream image of the woman we crave for. It is the craving for things or for a human being that makes us lose our perspective and better judgment. Of course, there is also the fickleness of the male, whatever excuse he may find. The white Swan, on the other hand, triumphs in romantic fashion as the incarnation of dignity and courage of the woman in love.

She is beauty made noble and teaches us the most obvious

lesson which life must apparently teach time and again: that there is only an ephemeral certainty to whatever we hold in our arms. In reality so much is unreal.

The sacred dance

Art is the highest form of love—total absorption and timid re-creation of our existence—and the highest form of love is closeness to God. There has never been any doubt in my mind that the great and almost great artist creates from that deep withinness where also lies his awareness of divine power. The greater he is, the closer he will come to master the eternal themes in all their variations. In that sense, the artistic and the religious are brethren in spirit.

The aloneness of man was evidently as frightening to the caveman who cut the first picture into the stone of his wall as it is to us today. Out of desire and need to reach beyond this aloneness we begin to express ourselves. And in our silent discovery that we can give form to feeling, expression to thought—and beauty to both—we praise Him who has made us in His image and was willing to share with us the spark of creativity, however minute and microcosmic it may be in our hands. But man is not alone in his aloneness, in fact, it seems to be his curse to have to share it with others without being able to free himself from it. Only by communicating his experience through symbols that have meaning to his fellowmen, through something bigger than life and his mere existence, he triumphs over his human confines.

Thus in its deeper sense, art is the communication of spiritual truths and its highest task is to ennoble man's concept of himself. The dance as the most immediate form of self-expression can most easily bring about the highest point of self-realization, a feeling of rhythmic wholeness.

We know that man's need of ritual existence is today as

strong as ever, and so is his drive towards common movement which is as old as man himself. We do not like to admit that what separates us from primitive man is a rather thin veneer of culture which can so easily crack and a skin-deep civilization which, at the slightest provocation, can be lacerated. Our tribal instincts still run amuck and, speaking figuratively, we continue to dance wildly to evoke the spirit of victory as well as fertility. Why, then, should we not join the all-embracing rhythm, the mystery of the divine cosmic dance in our worship and glorification of God as primitive man has done? Or does, after all, this skin-deep veneer create invisible barriers when we want to manifest our feelings of awe, of pure love and frightful fear through movement? We have built cathedrals to create outside stimulation and to help us visually in our meditation, prayer, and ritual, in our attempt to come closer to the unification of our true, naked self with God. We use images and music as wings to carry us more quickly out of our everyday existence. Why not the dance which, in an abortive way, is even embodied in the Holy Mass?

With a mystic consciousness prevailing in primitive societies, all goal-directed life activity was sacred because it was religious. All dances of primitive man were sacred since early man saw in bodily activity the fullest realization of being and an identification with the power of creation. He danced, and danced ecstatically. In the ecstasy of the dance man felt he could shed his earthbound being and reach beyond himself, thus dividing the sacred from profane existence.

No doubt, there is nothing more basic than movement, and dance is measured rhythmic movement, the perpetual part of a living totality, or, as Havelock Ellis expressed it, "the diversity of the Many balanced by the stability of the One." Dance as symbolic movement is the eternal connection between now and then, birth and death, the corporeal and spiritual. Our body as the shell of our soul is a preserver and instrument. Only with its help can we exist and free ourselves from mere existence.

Through the centuries many factors have combined against the notion of the dance as something pure. The repercussions of the romantic glorification of dancing in balletic form and, by the same token, the bourgeois' conception of its flippant nature and sheer entertainment value during the last hundred years can still be felt to this very day. Historic misunderstandings easily slip into our consciousness as dogmatic facts. Ruth St. Denis, this valiant fighter for the realization of a rhythmic choir, has pointed to the dichotomy of body and soul as caused by the teaching of Saint Paul. Since then we have learned to mistrust our body, we have become too much aware of it as the devil's disguise of our human weaknesses. But seeing evil in the body does not keep one from sinning any more than going to church necessarily makes one religious.

In our attempt at approximating the sacred dance we must separate self-expression as a personal experience in worship from the creation of an artistically valid experience that is supposed to communicate. As long as we stay within the limitations that exclude audience reaction and participation we are on safe ground. Out of silence and stillness will emerge the movement of the moment which, in its spontaneity, in its unrelated self-evidence, will then be pure and justified because it needs no other justification than your personal feeling of satisfaction in having found the expression of inner freedom. It matters little whether you do it at home alone or in the basement of your church with a group of people who seek with you to become part of the universal ritual in celebration of the Creator's creation.

However spontaneous your movement may be, it will be less genuine and less intensely felt than any movement by primitive man for whom movement was, and still is, a way of thinking and feeling, a way of living with himself and God. You may be closer to the dancing of the prophets who, more advanced in their culture, danced in the context of divine purpose and gave meaning to their ecstasy. In the shedding of our humanness we may feel the awakening of a power which is the embodiment of the spirit in us. You and only you alone can feel the "reality" of this experience. You can share it, to some extent, in rhythmic harmony with others as the Shakers did.

It becomes a different matter when a professional dancer or choreographer is called in to "stage" the sacred dance. Although I feel there should be room made for, and use of, the dance by and in the church; the difficulty, as I see it, lies in the realm of artistry. It is not so much a question of whether it should be done, but how it could be done if it can be done at all.

To interpret a Biblical theme, scene, or figure in form of a dance is not yet sacred dancing (though we must not exclude its motivating and inspiring content). But there is no great artist who has not drawn from the Bible. Then, of course, the best "sacred dancing" would have been done in concert halls and theaters, because there can be nothing more sacred than great art from wherever it emerges.

There are dance works by inspired men, inspired by voices speaking within the artist which carry the clear connotation of something holy. José Limón's *Missa Brevis* is one that comes to mind or, in textural contrast to that, Leonide Massine's *Laudes Evangelii;* both have the suffering of man and his resurgent spirit as their basic themes. I cannot imagine a more cleansing and uplifting feeling which the spectator can derive from such ballets. Movement moves us, brushes our skin, penetrates to our nervous system, infects our muscles and mind. But to achieve a heightened sense of oneness or wholeness that borders on the holy, a ballet does not necessarily have to display allusions to a "religious" theme. Any great work of art deals with the ultimate, or at least vital, questions of life, however disguised, and conveys artistically a sense of spiritual liberation. The Reverend William Glenesk said,

A creative work of dance opens up its audience to the fresh air of freedom simply through the use of space. If we be carried away, as it were, there seems to be a supernatural element involved. The dancers, like angels, take to flight as athletes of God, possessed of forces beyond the ordinary mortal.

We have advanced far in the development of the expressive dance in all its artistic manifestations. It now has such a highly sophisticated form and face that it must be difficult for the dancer of our time to return to a grand simplicity so basic for the creation of the sacred dance; to an understanding, rather than the feeling, that everyone of us carries within him a secret temple and it is from there, and there alone, that he must find an artistic form and perfect expression of the holy purpose of the moment. It is like finding inner truth in its purest artistic expression that has always stirred man most.

Above all, the dancer would have to leave his false ambitions, his egocentric mania outside the church door in order to find the road to this new simplicity and, through it, to a new exaltation. "Instead of taking from without, he would have to learn to give from within," to paraphrase one of Ruth St. Denis's sayings. I only wonder how the modern dancer, who is so strongly attuned to an overcivilized civilization and to his own sophisticated needs, can do it.

Perhaps, and I say only perhaps, the secret to, and the fulfillment of, a sacred dance may be found in the words of the dancer and dance teacher Diane Davis, who once wrote to me of an experience that helps explain the pitch of concentration that is essential for true communication of a spiritual message:

To me, all *real* dancing is a highly religious experience—an experience in which all conflict is erased, all black and white; and all one's energies and concentration focus into a kind of unity that makes one untouchable and peaceful.

One does not experience an ecstatic state often, and most people never. It symbolizes a complete oneness of being. It has happened to me twice. I remember vividly the second time it occurred. It arose out of my previous weeks and weeks of practice of dance, a limited food and sleep supply. I danced a series of dances with a kind of inner concentration I have not had before. I felt the dances executed with fantastic vitality. When the performance was over, my whole being was in a complete state of peace that lasted for two days. I can only express it by saying that I was untouchable for that period—as one who floats in air without effort. These experiences changed my whole life. Dancing is to me the most complete expression of God manifest—only most people do not see dancing, or feel it. The majority of our dance on stage is only an expression of incomplete artists still caught up in the turmoil of their own frailties. . . . We neither understand nor accept what fantastic stories and images the human form tells as it moves. We live on the periphery of movement. To become aware of the real language of movement is terrifying—it gives a kind of God-like power which can be used constructively or destructively.

An experience I personally had while participating in one of the annual meetings of the Sacred Dance Guild may shed some more light on the limitations and potentialities of the sacred dance in action. It was at Drew University, Madison, New Jersey. Early one morning there was an outdoor worship service. For some time the dancers stood around in an almost helpless manner trying to move in a unified and coordinated way. But seemingly paralyzed by the overwhelming presence of nature, none of the many attempts crystallized.

Then Vija Vetra, a Latvian-born dancer, who had introduced the sacred dance in Australia and had come to the New World from a sojourn in India, mingled with the group. Suddenly she led the dancers in ever-widening and closing circles, at moments with all arms united and reaching toward heaven as if with spires of many cathedrals, then she led the group in serpentines and achieved what, at that moment of experience, seemed to me to be the key to sacred dance in our time: with artistic intuition, but with spontaneity, these bodies moved, and there was a wholeness about them, they were bathed in the coolness of the morning, they became integrated in the image of awakening nature. In fact, these circles and serpentines against the background of bushes and trees had something almost pagan about them, uniting mother earth with the spirit above. Each of the participants was overwhelmed by the dance of which he or she was a part; and, as an observer, I could not help applauding God.

I suppose such moments are rare. As in this case, such experience may have come about by an artist's instinctive feeling of how to project across the footlights of nature, as it were. I doubt that what I have seen can be rehearsed and repeated for an audience. It just happened.

This brings us back to the question of artistry and the sacred dance. In every other area the artist has as much the right to fail as he has the duty to experiment. In front of the altar, a failure not only strikes a strident note or insults your aesthetic and artistic feeling but could throw you back into cold reality and might even carry a blasphemous connotation. A failure would have to be felt and experienced by the dancer-choreographer so deeply and so genuinely in order not to be profane in its cheapness; but then it would no longer be a failure.

To the great artist the religious problems are the living, as well as the moral, issues of his time. As long as he is concerned with them on an emotional and sentimental level only, he will fail. This, in particular, is the major trap for the creator of the sacred dance. When the religious problem becomes mainly an intellectual one, the artist will be able to let his emotions flow freely. The great danger is that, more often than not, something phony may be used to heighten something holy.

Through the centuries we have witnessed the growing process of secularization of the dance as an art form, a process that paralleled all other human activities. The dance, too, went the way of all civilization. After World War II, when all old values collapsed with the dropping of the bomb, religious drama was seen on stages everywhere, and the churches opened their doors and the space around the altar for the dramatist's words. The churches also invited the dancer, and during the last few decades many attempts have been made to bring the dancer back to the Church. Were they justified?

During the Middle Ages when almost all art had sworn allegiance to the Church and not yet to the princes, the creation of sacred music had its place and fulfilled its function. Later, however, when Bach wrote his music, his genius created the need for his work.

Some people may feel today, when technology is rampant and ready for an all-embracing dance of destruction, when the hands of the scientists try to lift veil after veil from the hidden secret of the Creator, that man should revert in more than one way to himself as he was, to past simplicity. This feeling shows man unconsciously counteracting the arrogance of his waking self. Through movement he may again seek the shortest distance from his soul to his Redeemer. These people feel that the free and co-ordinated rhythmic movement has spiritual reality and may help draw humanity together in a mystic union. It can happen here and there, as I have tried to demonstrate.

But can it be realized on an artistic level? Even if the choreographic equivalent of Bach's genius were among us today, it is more than doubtful that he could overcome century-old barriers and unfold the blessings of divine power through his creativity.

Written on the margin of time

I have always wondered why so much trash is produced when it is just as difficult to create something worthwhile.

*

When an artist does not bother to find the heart of the matter, he may easily miss the matter of the heart.

*

Whenever I am exposed to something in the theater staged for the relaxation of the patrons, I get very nervous.

*

Strange, that sometimes an infinitesimal spark of creativity can ignite so much fire that leaves one cold.

*

Each intermission was twenty minutes long. The first one was promising, the second showed signs of exhaustion which caused a long queue at the fountain, the last one was inexcusable. At the end friends stayed to cheer and to give the artistic funeral of the evening a festive appearance.

*

Most modern ballet groups which officially represent their country and the country's history in a folkloristic manner face the difficult task of being modern enough without belying the past, of fusing technical proficiency with the characteristics of spontaneous dancing as done in the past or present by their people. There is a big enough margin for both these elements to become an artistic oneness. But the danger is just as great that either the folk quality overshadows the necessary theatrical effectiveness or the theatricality of the dance makes us forget its folklore background.

*

Most artists would be better off not finding out in which direction the last bandwagon moved so that they are not tempted to jump on it.

*

It is not enough to create newness for the sake of newness. There ought to be something new about a work of art.

*

I found out that you can lead by standing still and by giving time a chance to catch up with you. I also found out that you are not necessarily a square if you don't stand in that circle which moves around you like a merry-go-round.

*

Each dance work consists of the very same few steps: to stand still, walk, run, jump, hop, skip, slide, gallop, and turn. How very little goes into a dance and what a world of difference makes the whole of so little.

*

Some contemporary artists stretch other artists' imagination too far.

*

One cannot help noticing that we live in a fast-paced world. Terpsichore is no longer desired and courted, she is immediately fingered. That reminds me of the saying, "Mademoiselle, I don't make love. I'm used to getting it ready-made."

*

An impresario is an entrepreneur with his heart in the arts and his eyes on his bank account. When his eyes get too big, his heart begins to murmur and, finally, to fail; when his heart beats too loud, the scales fall from his eyes in the form of dried-out zeroes. An impresario must be a psychologist who has the right answers and pills in the right doses for all the idiosyncracies and whims of his female and male prima donnas; he must be an organizer who brings an artist to the public and a public to the artist; he must have imagination and foresee the change in temper and taste of the audience; he must have instinct for who and what is right at the right moment; and he must be daring enough to challenge the public in the name of art to ensure the survival of both public and art.

*

Improvisations can become a tricky business. Some artists like their improvisations so much they copy them night after night.

*

Whenever we create a work of art, we should do it in the spirit that tells us this is the very last thing we would ever be able to do.

*

Some artists never outgrow their childhood reactions: In order to spite their elders, they spit into their own faces.

*

We pride ourselves on having a sense of humor. Nobody stresses the point that he has a sense of the tragic—which only goes to show that humor is not easily come by. Comedy in dance is not quite as rare as the comic in music, but rare enough. Verbal wit is mostly based on associations rapidly working in our mind on two different levels. Kinetic humor depends on similar reactions, but since our eyes seem to be quicker than our ears, our visual associations are more demanding.

Everyone has a threshold of humor as he has a threshold of pain. They cannot be too far removed from one another since humor which escapes us can hurt. The most inescapable humor lies in clowning as much as in the subtle fun inherent in a ballet idea. One of the best examples of the latter is Jerome Robbins's *Fancy Free* or the kinetic wit in some of George Balanchine's twentieth-century ballets and in the first movement of his *Bourrée Fantasque*.

The clown and his more intellectualized brother, the fool, are basic to any comic effect. They personify laughing misery, they are the clumsiest acrobats, and they only get up in order to fall down and overcome obstacles they prepare for themselves in the hardest way. The best dance humorists have used absurdity as an extension of logic, man's limitations and life's incongruities; they let the cliché explode in their hands and play on kinetic *non sequiturs* as their most popular instruments. As an example, Paul Taylor plays it expertly most of the time.

Parody is a favorite form of dance humor. It presupposes total familiarity with another choreographer's idiosyncracies and is at its best when the parodist feels compelled to liberate himself from too great a love for another choreographer's work. Frederick Ashton's parody of a Petipa pas de deux in *A Wedding Bouquet* is a striking case in point. On a far broader basis Antony Tudor parodied in *Gala Performance* the French, Italian, and Russian schools of nineteenth-century ballet as well as the eccentricities of ballerinas in general. But, more often than not, parodistic finesse gives way to burlesque and caricature in this ballet.

James Waring has a special flair for humor which employs all tricks of the skilled entertainer. Discontinuity, the most illogical *non sequiturs,* burlesque and parodistic elements are among his kinetic surprises. Most of the time they are used to reveal the zany-ism of the questionable sanity of our world. *A Poet's Vaudeville* and *Spookride* are good examples of Waring's sophisticated humor which often hides behind obvious and crude ideas saved by his uncanny sense of timing.

This sense of timing reminds me of Charles Weidman who, admittedly, began employing the most obvious humor, the sadistic type of humor, the effect of which is almost guaranteed with every audience. It has been a long and arduous way for him to develop via *Kinetic Pantomime* to the visualization of Thurber's *Fables for Our Time.* By adjusting to Thurber's gentle irony Weidman gave his predilection for the grotesque gesture of the clown a polished facade. Weidman is far more literal and literary than Waring, and watching both of them in their funniest antics one cannot help feeling that, at any moment, their material and ideas would explode in their hands into pyrotechnics of brilliant fun and biting satire. That it so rarely does has less to do with the skill of these two artists and more with the difficulty of creating humor at its kinetically best.

Iva Kitchell's weakness and forte was in leaning towards the theatrically stronger caricature at the expense of parody. Her unforgettable caricature of Martha Graham earned her, most deservedly, Graham's hatred. Kitchell's chiaroscuro method differed greatly from Martha Graham's self-parody in *Acrobats of God,* one of the finest examples of humor with tongue-in-both-cheeks.

Another form of the parody, most often used, is the one on a period's predominant style of life. Bronislava Nijinska's *Les Biches* pokes fun at the *dolce vita* atmosphere of the Twenties with more sophistication than Ashton's *Façade* which deals with the music hall and social dances of the same period. If a work such as Trudi Schoop's *Blond Marie* exposes the inanities of our social life and the ridiculous customs of so-called civilized man, then the satiric overtones become unmistakable.

However, in the name of satire too much in the dance world goes the way of all "art." There has been a variety of comic dances with no invective and specific target in mind, lampooning institutions, habits, and human situations in a good-natured manner and with the personal skill of the dance comedian. The only great satire, the *Lysistrata* of the dance, is Kurt Jooss's *The Green Table*. There is little comedy in it which only proves that satire is a brother to tragedy.

In our sophisticated age the sly, on-second-thought humor, the cleverly stated ironic aside is the most effective. The surprise of the unexpected will rarely fail. But the danger of the visually obvious is momentous. A dance humorist is only good if there is more to him than meets the eye.

*

Everyone can look and does so, but only a chosen few can see.

*

Every human being has his own rhythm, and so has each dance work.

Dance can create its own music. I have never been more aware of rhythm, melody, and pulse than when I saw Jerome Robbins's unaccompanied *Moves*. He accepted silence as a challenge and proved that it is not something that can be overcome but something that can liberate the music locked in the dancer's body.

The melody should give the choreographer the feeling for the over-all design, but the division of time—which is all that music really is—should be responsible for the dance figures.

There are dance works which happen *to* the music, *against* the music, and *within* the music. The movement realization of a score experienced within the music seems the happiest to me.

The ideal dance music will make you hear the dance and see the sound. On the other hand, no one can claim that for some of the modern dancers—Merce Cunningham and Erick Hawkins, to give two examples—music has not worked as an aural décor. John Cage's or Lucia Dlugoszewski's musical accompaniment lives a life all by itself. With the artistic umbilical cord of mutual inspiration and mushy emotionalism cut, both dance and music enjoy their freedom and independence. Instead of having a marriage of convenience or a union in which the partners tolerate each other, they go steady, each doing his own thing in harmonious togetherness.

It is a cliché and a false one that someone is a born dancer because he is rhythmically perfect. No one can maintain that Vaslav Nijinsky—known for his bad rhythm—was not a born dancer.

There is music that calls out for choreography. It may call out so loudly, as Igor Stravinsky's score *The Rite of Spring,* that it dominates the stage however impressive the dance may be. There is music that will not yield to the dancer. Used, nevertheless, it will not let you doubt for the duration of a bar and step that this is a rape. There is also music that wants nothing else but surrender to the dancer's body.

Great music never immortalized a bad ballet. But great ballets were choreographed to bad music. Moral: A good ballet can easily become better if accompanied by a good score. Postscriptum: We can but look with wonder and incredulity at the long stretch of balletic accomplishment in the nineteenth century which triumphed with only one Tchaikovsky while overcoming the mediocre creations of a Schneitzhoeffer, Pugni, Adam, and Minkus. Nineteenth-century music was most often the obedient servant of ballet whose femininity whipped music into servitude. Twentieth-century music became the dancer's inspiring partner.

The score for a dance work should always be unexpected but predictable. It should merely support the action while calling for each movement to follow the next, and it should paint the emotional climate readying the dramatic accents. Briefly, it should be distinct in an undistinguished manner and be distinguished in its indistinctness.

*

It is not enough to have talent. You must also know how to make your critics forgive you for having it.

*

When Théophile Gautier put on a red waistcoat or a pink doublet in the 1830s and 1840s, he wanted to spite the bourgeois.* The artists of the 1960s intended to do the same by taking off their clothes. This proves two points: the endurance of the object of spite and the change of fashion.

*

A dancer cultivates the awareness of his artistry in a world of mirrors. In facing himself, he discovers his self. He may have been a narcissist before becoming a dancer, but he must cer-

---

* According to the Brothers Goncourt, Gautier declared that "it was not a red waistcoat he had worn at the opening night of *Hernani* but a pink doublet." On another occasion he said, "The costume was fairly well calculated to irritate and scandalize the Philistines."

tainly become one as a dancer. In this reflective world his body speaks to him day in, day out, telling him who and what he is and creating a new sense in him of highly objectivized egocentricity.

The writer's profession is one of torturing lonesomeness in which he faces a blank paper and the awesome uncertainty of his inner self. There is no province in the arts in which the creative or recreative mind would not have to struggle in an atmosphere of aloneness. But the dancer's aloneness is doubled by the constant presence of his mirror image. It is his real shadow, his best friend, and hardest taskmaster. It is his inspirational alter ego and prompter when his movement loses sight of itself.

The ballet dancer embraces the very idea of himself in the reflected image as fulfilled movement in its moments of elegance and ecstasy, grace and ease. The modern barefoot dancer, torn between searching and protesting, dissecting and creating, asks more from the mirror than the mere image of his self. He asks for its fulfillment.

*

Man is a born ritualist. His mind, in its lucidity and aberrations, cannot divorce itself from all kinds of rituals. If not conceived as mere entertainment, dancing is an invocation, a summoning of all life forces in response to life itself. It summons in order to exorcise, it creates to free itself as one gains by losing.

The mirror reflection is part of the dancer's ritual that crystallizes into artistic form. The photograph of a dancer in movement is one such reflected moment preserved for the future. The shot should never be a pose. Any artistic photograph must have the sculptural quality of an arrested movement that retains the flow of what preceded it and foreshadows the moments to come. Despite its disadvantage of not being three-dimensional it must contain the inner drama, the motif of its motive power, cadence and pace of the movement phrase. Of course, at its best a photograph can only give us a vicarious feeling, for no part can be as weighty as the whole. But every shot should convey a clue to the essence of the dance as a few bars of music can intimate its leitmotif, as the telling line of a poem bares the flight of thought, the depth of its imagery.

*

Our time has become suspicious of beauty after having deflorated, violated, and raped her.

*

Each age has the art it deserves.

*

A critic must take his task, but not himself, seriously. He ought to be passionate in his charity and charitable in his passion. A critic must be aware of publishing his opinions at his own risk. As any artist he has the right to fail, to be obstinate in his passions, and, pleading guilty, to hope for the charity of his critics.

To be a critic

For it is much more easie to find Faults
than it is to discern Beauties. To do
the first requires but Common Sense,
but to do the last a Man must have Genius.
        DENNIS (*The Impartial Critick*)

First was the creation in its explosive abundance, its burst of beauty and waste of wisdom. Then, and much later, the critic came down from Mount Olympus with his commandments, codes, and credos. Only in a moment of creative despair, of doubt in himself as an artist, could the artist in man have provoked the appearance of a policeman, prosecutor, and judge in one personification who called himself critic. He cleverly chose this epithet from the Greek *kritikos* whose meaning is "able to discuss."

In the beginning he must have been a teacher who had the ability to discern and verbalize his impressions and thoughts. In our age art has lost its hallowed purpose as an act of gratitude towards God for our heightened awareness of being. It has become a commercial commodity between a producing craftsman and a consuming humanity, and the critic turned into a middleman who lives on supply and demand which he helps stimulate. He may put on the hood of the historian to explore the present through the eyes of the past; he may rush from a performance to his newspaper to get his copy ready by midnight; or he may talk shop in a trade paper. Essentially, he is a one-way interpreter who tries to explain the language of the artist to the understanding of the reader.

The function of criticism is to judge a work of art. But the critic, as we know him today, is a relatively recent phenomenon. In ancient Greece the critics were ten judges chosen by lot in the theater on the first morning of the competitive productions. The ten judges were taken from a large list of candidates nominated by the Council. Criticism was then in form of prizes, and the selections for first, second, and third prizes were written on tablets of which five were chosen by an archon at random. These judgments were accepted as the final response to the plays, the acting, and the dancing.

In contrast to our own time in which the potential audience depends on the critics for guidance, the Greek judges, as Plato complained, too often decided according to the applause in fear of the crowd and thus debased the theater art through, what he called, this "theatrocracy."

Written criticism came into being only after the Renaissance, notwithstanding the ground rules for tragedy and comedy laid down by Aristotle. The first influential critic of the theater was Nicolas Boileau-Despréaux (1636–1711), a zealous polemicist with a satiric bent, who, as a spokesman of classicism, was considered a literary lawgiver in the eighteenth century. With newspapers and periodicals in circulation—the first issues of the *Mercure de France* appeared in 1672, the first newspaper in England in 1702—critical reviews had a chance to be aired. But the importance of the newspapers and magazines as organs of criticism begins with the nineteenth century, preceded by Jean-Georges Noverre's *Lettres sur la Danse et sur les Ballets* (1760) in a letter-writing epoch, and by Gotthold Ephraim Lessing's *Hamburgische Dramaturgie* (1769) in form of essayistic reviews which were originally published by the Hamburg National Theater over a period of two years in the first house organ of any theater in the world.

Criticism is considered a secondary art because its existence depends on the existence of a creative act preceding it. One cannot exclude the possibility, however, that it may be superior as a piece of craftsmanship to the creation it criticizes. As no artist can function if his critical faculties do not play their proper part in his creative process, no critic can put to paper his viewpoints successfully if not endowed with the sensitivity and sensibility of an artist.

This is said in full awareness of the ailing condition of most professional criticism which often lacks the necessary understanding of one or the other disciplines which are part of the critic's requisites. Moreover, those familiar with the tricky task of translating one language into another will realize the difficulties in communicating the dance through words of many-faced values.

Thus, dance criticism suffers from its own complexity, which keeps it from being well written, convincing, and brilliant.

Should we not ask ourselves what validity any criticism has and to what end the writing of reviews is pursued if not for the mere purpose of recording events for a posterity whose interest in all of them is rather questionable? I have heard it said more than once by established artists that they could no longer take critics seriously; but when unanimous raves haloed their endeavors they collected all the reviews to set them off in the nicest offset re-print. Also, I have always wondered whether it is really true—as I was made to believe—that dancers are only reading the bad notices of their colleagues.

It is an awesome feeling to realize that a person is supposed to judge a work of art at one sitting and within a very limited time at his disposal, to put down his reaction to a work that may have taken many months of thinking and feeling before it ripened to the point of being put into its final, or near-final, shape. A creative process takes many weeks and hours of struggle which the artist has to fight within himself and with many external forces unknown to the critic. On the occasion of receiving the Capezio Award in 1969 John Martin, then no longer dance critic of the New York *Times,* virtually apologized to all dancers and choreographers for whatever he may have written about them.

He may have thought of the many unavoidable hurts he had to cause, of the many judgments that had to be revised over the years, of the many disappointments some artists afflicted on him by belying his hopes in their future work. The critic's pitfalls are as treacherous and unpredictable as anything in life. We must never forget that, in the last analysis, a critic is little more than another member of the audience. I have often found it deeply disturbing how cruelly, flippantly, and insensitively most members of an audience usually react to what happens on stage. They of course have the right to say whatever they wish since they have paid for their admission, while the critic is paid for his judgment for which he is often taken to task.

Sometimes a critic may be deadly opposed to an artist. Such adversity is mainly of interest when the critic is nearly as important as the artist. The feud between critic and artist may take three different courses. The critic may turn against the artist on all possible occasions. What I would call criticism with a vengeance—however sincere the critic's revulsive motivations may be—takes place when, even if not reviewing the artist, the critic strikes out against his pet hate to hit him, so to speak, in parenthesis.

John Martin did not review nor mention Merce Cunningham for many years and at a time when Cunningham had started on his revolutionary path. Martin, champion of the modern dance in the late Twenties, in the Thirties and Forties, may have realized that Cunningham was about to unleash a movement to administer the deathblow to the representational, literal modern dance. Martin may have recognized this revolutionary trend as a sign or stigma of the times, inevitable as much as intolerable. His silence was a vociferous disapproval. During those years John Martin embraced ballet, in particular George Balanchine's company, and helped Alwin Nikolais to his deserved reputation with the aid of several Sunday features. I do not take this as mere coincidence. At the crossroads of history critics play a major role. Sometimes they even create crossroads.

The critic can try to kill with silence, he can also shout his diapproval for years and become embroiled in a personal feud with an artist such as Eduard Hanslick did with Richard Wagner. In this feud, now legendary, the artist was as powerful and articulate as his critic, and, ultimately, invective replaced all reason. Undoubtedly Hanslick was a great music critic, but his rather conservative attitude made him oppose Richard Wagner's "music of the future" in a lifelong struggle. Towards the end of his career Hanslick admitted—without thinking he was wrong in his main objective—that he may have become hardened through bitterness, attrition, and frustration in a fight which he knew he could not win. He did not deny Wagner's genius. "I know very well that he is the greatest living opera composer and in a historical sense the only one worth talking about. . . . But . . . Wagner's operatic style recognizes only superlatives, and a superlative has no future." On another occasion Hanslick said:

I and some others who share my views probably should have written more dispassionately about Wagner had not our pulses been agitated by the immoderate, often ludicrous, exaggerations of our opponents. The consciousness of being in the minority embitters the most honest soul and sharpens the vocabulary.

It makes no difference which art form is criticized. Everything depends on the critic's choice of words (and I will have to come back to this crucial point). An adjective can make an artist appear ridiculous, a verb can stab him in the back. The satiric approach is the easiest to show the critic's brilliance at the expense of the artist. For instance, Claude Debussy, who composed exquisitely senstive music, was insensitive as a music critic and often indulged in cheap attacks. In reviewing a Grieg concert it was a blow below the lowest level of journalistic decency to write:

At last I saw Grieg. From in front he looks like a genial photographer; from behind his way of doing his hair makes him look like the plants called sunflowers, dear to parrots and the gardens that decorate small country stations.

Admittedly, there is hardly a critic who has not succumbed to the temptation of a witty remark. I remember—mea culpa—to have been disturbed, in fact, annoyed by the ear-puncturing noise effects with which John Cage accompanied Merce Cunningham's dances. Cunningham's *Night Wandering*, which I have always considered his most lyrical and human creation, has music by Bo Nilsson. In praising *Night Wandering* I could not help saying that whenever Merce Cunningham is unCaged he feels free to be his better self.

To write for a daily paper such as *La Presse* in Paris, as Théophile Gautier did during the greater part of last century, puts a tremendous, awe-inspiring power into the hands of the critic. He cannot help being aware of his power, and yet he must pretend even when alone with himself and his deadline that no such power exists. Edmond and Jules de Goncourt tell in their *Journals* (January 2, 1867) that they dined at the princess's with Gautier and others. Gautier must have spoken harshly about the dramatist François Ponsard, a blown-up zero who managed skillfully to be a fashionable success.

When we had finished, someone asked Gautier why he did not write the things he had just said. "Let me tell you a little story," Gautier replied with perfect self-possession. "One day, Monsieur Walewski [minister for foreign affairs of Napoleon III] told me that I was to stop being indulgent to writers, I had his authority to write exactly what I thought of all the plays produced. 'But,' said I, 'it is So-and-so's play that is opening this week.' 'Indeed?' said he. 'In that case, suppose you begin the week following.' Well, I am still waiting for the week following."

Or, as a postscriptum, let us turn back in the de Goncourt *Journals* to August 23, 1862:

Gautier began once more to express his judgment of *Le Misanthrope* —a Jesuit-school comedy written to be performed at the beginning of the new term. "Oh! the swine. What language! What foul writing! But of course I couldn't say so in print. After all, I have to go on earning my living. I am still getting letters abusing me for having dared compare *Timon of Athens* with *Le Misanthrope*."

I doubt that critics have the power to break or make an artist, even those critics who, due to their alignment with all-powerful papers, hold a trumpet-tongued position. True, they can sometimes slow down an artist's career, or they can become his unsalaried press agents and secure bookings and jobs. But I agree with Carlyle that if any artist can be killed by one or many critiques, the sooner he is so dispatched the better.

Every artist looks for recognition, and rightly so. If he is clever he will try to find out the predilections of the critic and then match the critic's response to what he intended to create in the light of these two different worlds that face each other. He should take neither praise nor fault-finding literally. Both should caution him, make him think, and compare the mental notes of the critical reaction with the original visualization of his work—because both always fall short of their goal. For any criticism to be constructive, the artist must be willing to give the critic his due.

How very personal—and of the one-man's-poison-another's-meat category—criticism is, is proved by the fact that not all critics have the same to say, not even if they basically are of one opinion in their praise or disapproval. Furthermore, it is at least as confusing and irritating for the critic as it must be for the artist if the critical reactions to one and the same piece are completely contradictory as to the whole work, or to any of its details. But as the critic must not then despair in his integrity and judgment, neither should the artist despair in criticism as such nor in his own artistry. It only demonstrates that art is the intangible of something very tangible.

A work of art may seem enigmatic and cause divergent interpretations. This is not the artist's fault, who, in the process of creation, must draw the widest possible circle of implications and must abstract from life and his own experiences the essence of a thought, feeling, and vision. When Gerhart Hauptmann was questioned about which of his critics' interpretation of his play *And Pipa Dances* was, in his opinion, the correct one, his only possible answer was: "They all are right." The wonder of creation is that a created work may have a different meaning for each of its beholders.

Since we live in a world in which art has become a property, a commodity and even an investment, a world in which the artist has to sell himself, the critic's role as the one who does the inadvertent selling was imposed on him by the artist and the public alike. The public which relies on the critic for guidance in its judgment is eavesdropping on another person's heartbeat to gauge its own pulse. Both should memorize Lord Byron's lines:

Seek roses in December, ice in June;
Hope constancy in wind, or corn in chaff;
Believe in women or an epitaph,
Or any other thing that's false, before
You trust in critics.

It has been said Raphael would have been the great painter he was even though he were to be born without hands. I expect the critic to be such an artist, born as a sage and seer who develops all his perceptive and creative faculties without using them in that one particular field in which he functions as a critic. The dance critic will come closest to this far-set goal if he shows an unusual literary gift—as a matter of fact, if he himself is a poet, because only the immediacy and remoteness of the poetic image can picture the visual image of the rhythmic sweep of human bodies in space and time, can make us relive and remember the elusive quality of the dance.

The great writers on the dance were literary men who, if not practicing poets, were endowed with the power of poetic vision. From Stendhal and Gautier, from Baudelaire and Mallarmé to Cocteau and Marianne Moore, they all have caught the essence and the spirit of the dance with that intense subtlety of the word which gives lasting existence to the illuminated illusion of a moving reality. The Russian-French critic André Levinson is probably the most outstanding example of a nonpoetic critic who had the ability to present the dance with absorbing intensity and to develop, as no one else before him, a philosophy of the dance. Even though his approach to the art was uncomfortably conservative, his writings are important. There are of course many more who have contributed to the understanding of the dance through their critiques and enlightened essays, carried either by the impetus of their passion for the art or by being dancer-choreographers who have had something to say about their own work or the dance itself—and said it rather well. (There is a surprisingly great number of dancers, who are not only articulate but articulate with a touch of the poet.) However, it is the professional critic who interests us here, and the name of Edwin Denby is most often mentioned among the contemporary writers as particularly knowledgeable and gifted in catching the dance and dancer in the mirror of his word. He not only views the dance with the distant look of the philosopher, he is also a minor poet of major sensitivity.

Baudelaire spoke of the art critic, but he could have referred to the music or dance critic as well when he wrote, in *Salon de 1846:*

I sincerely believe that the best criticism is that which is amusing and poetic; not that cold and algebraic kind which, under the pretext of explaining everything, displays neither love nor hate, and voluntarily strips itself of every shred of temperament . . . Thus the best account of a painting can well be a sonnet or an elegy.

Amusing, I hope, was meant in the archaic sense of bemusing, to cause to muse, or in the obsolete sense of absorbing, of occupying our attention. I see some danger in the critic's intent to entertain in a light, playful, or pleasant manner or to try to appeal to our sense of humor. He then invites a bantering tone and could easily slip into wit for wit's sake. There is no good writing that would not entertain, and need not be vitriolic, as Shaw sometimes was, or Kenneth Tynan in our time.

Oscar Wilde, who had a knack for the formulation of epigrammatic thoughts, liked to sprinkle his reviews with little poisonous asides. In *The Critic as Artist* we are told that "There is no sin except stupidity" and that "The difference between journalism and literature is that journalism is unreadable and literature is not read." Exercise in sophisticated wit, that is, the desire to entertain, can easily lead to pronouncements which, on the surface, have a brilliant sheen, but do not stand the test of a second thought. Although Oscar Wilde felt that art was "deeply incriminated" with life and that the artist lives on life as much as the critic lives on art, he nevertheless could not help writing that "All art is entirely useless"—a statement which can be only accepted if one believes that life is entirely useless.

Baudelaire juxtaposed *amusement* to "a cold, mathematical criticism" and had not in mind the paradoxes of polished witticism, but amusement as the result of temperament that knows how to present its likes and dislikes in a nonprofessorial manner. Baudelaire pleaded for "partial, passionate and political" criticism which should be "written from an exclusive point of view, but a point of view that opens up the widest horizons." Herbert Read, in his essay *Farewell to Formalism,* referred to Baudelaire as a symbolic critic, saying that "all criticism that was ever worth anything and that has survived its brief day of topical relevance, was symbolic in this sense, taking the work of art as a symbol to be interpreted, rather than as an object to be dissected."

The critic as poet remained at the core of Baudelaire's approach to criticism, he came back to this idea time and again. When he wrote his defense of Wagner he made his viewpoint unmistakably clear:

All great poets naturally and fatally become critics. I pity those poets who are guided by instinct alone: I regard them as incomplete. But in the spiritual life of the great poets a crisis inevitably occurs when they feel the need to reason about their art, to discover the obscure laws in virtue of which they have created, and to extract from this study a set of precepts whose divine aim is infallibility in poetic creation. It would be unthinkable for a critic to become a poet; and it is impossible for a poet not to contain within him a critic. Therefore the reader will not be surprised at my regarding the poet as the best of all critics.

When we speak of the obvious requirements of a critic as those of an intimate familiarity with the art he deals with and the craft enabling him to utter his criticism, we usually forget another feature which, in its self-evidence, is basic to both these aspects: namely, that the critic is only human. Therefore, he must have the right to be wrong and, what is even worse in the eyes of some people, to change his mind. His critical faculty grows—at least, we must hope so—and growth means change.

A crucial point is his integrity. As a critic he cannot afford to indulge in partisanship, but as a human being he cannot help having preferences. As we all do, he cannot avoid living in the narrow world of those whose interests he shares, and the dance world is particularly small. Will knowing the dancer and choreographer not warp his viewpoint, influence his judgment? It certainly will, if he is not strong enough to withstand the inner pressure of his infatuations or animosities. But then he runs the risk of giving himself away. His approach will be feeble or too forceful, his adjectives too glaring or underplaying the facts. If we know how to read, style unmasks the writer.

The critic's prejudices may be annoying. But are not all our preferences dictated by the secret of affinity, by those attracting and repelling forces embedded in our animalistic instincts over which we have no control? To demand that a critic be objective is to ask him to deny that he is human. On the contrary, I expect him to be very much involved, emotionally and intellectually, in what he is criticizing. (Oscar Wilde: "A critic cannot be fair in the ordinary sense of the word. It is only about things that do not interest one that one can give a really unbiased opinion, which is no doubt the reason why an unbiased opinion is always absolutely valueless.") If the critic is also deeply and honestly concerned with the art as such, then his devotion will keep him from failing his public as well as the artists.

In self-defense Bernard Shaw wrote in 1890:

People have pointed out evidences of personal feeling in my notices as if they were accusing me of a misdemeanor, not knowing that a criticism written without personal feeling is not worth reading. . . . The artist who accounts for my disparagement by alleging personal animosity on my part is quite right: when people do less than their best, and do that less at once badly and self-complacently, I hate them, loathe them, detest them, long to tear them limb from limb and strew them in gobbets about the stage and platform. . . . When my critical mood is at its height, personal feeling is not the word: it is passion: the passion for artistic perfection—for the noblest beauty of sound, sight, and action—that rages in me.

On the other hand, the best critic is shortsighted when too partisan. André Levinson, for instance, strongly believed in the need to uphold the *danse d'école* and to defend it against any violation of its dogmatic rules with all verbal pirouettes and entrechats at his disposal. In turning against Diaghilev and his Ballets Russes, Levinson did not realize the historic role that Diaghilev was destined to play in the development of the theater dance. In spite of his love for and understanding of the dance, Levinson was out of tune with his time. As an adherent of the old classic dance and art for art's sake, he condemned Diaghilev's company for giving each step a dramatic emotion as its *raison d'être,* for seeking inspiration outside dance itself. But time sided with Diaghilev against his critic. Even though Kenneth Tynan described a critic as a man who knows the way but can't drive the car, we cannot always be certain that the way known to the critic moves in the right direction, that is, at least forward, not backward.

I expect the critic to enter the theater with a feeling of awe and the awareness that something of God lives in every creative attempt. There should be a sense of humility in him that something emerged into existence from nonexistence (to paraphrase Plato). He must realize that the purpose of art is to be, its only function to give itself to whomever can see in it whatever this particular expression means to him.

The critic must try to feel his way into each work, to sense the artist's intention. With every curtain going up he will have to adjust himself to the object he criticizes. He should be guided by neither his emotions nor his intellect but by all his faculties at the same time. It may, however, depend on the work of art whether the stronger demands are made on his emotions or his intellect. A great deal of his judgment will depend on his ability to recognize this at once.

Ideally, the critic should have left the imprint of the day with his coat in the cloakroom, or shove both under the seat—more so than any other spectator. He should not sit there with his arms and mind crossed, but with eyes and ears open, with the attentive curiosity of a child and with the wisdom of the aged and experienced amateur (*amateur* in the original sense of the word denoting 'someone who loves the art'). He should want to embrace his object with absolute freedom and be completely free from any absolutes. He is out to explore what feeling qualities are embodied in form and content, what the work means to him, and what it may mean to the man next to him. In trying to find this out, he should be guided by principles, but not by theories.

When the curtain falls his total involvement ends, his first step into an undefinable state of detachment begins. He now faces the stupendous task of holding on to the last impression with which he was left and to think backwards in order to catch some vanishing images and to look down on the remaining design and movement sequences from those towering moments that seemed memorable.

The artist creates in response to an inner need and to outside stimuli. The framework within which he creates is his personality, circumscribed by its limitations, no matter how prolific and many-sided he may be. It is an infinitesimal segment in comparison to what the critic must respond to who is exposed to the expected and unexpected, to the possible and impossible. An artist mostly creates out of a certain experience. How wide has the range of the critic's experience to be to match those of each artist! Fortunately, man feeds his awareness with many vicarious experiences. Moreover, there may be as many different expressions as there are original artists, but all these expressions can be reduced to a few basic conscious events.

T. S. Eliot pointed out that the most important qualification of any critic is a "very highly developed sense of fact" and his task is to put "the reader in possession of facts which he would otherwise have missed." Eliot spoke of a literary critic, but the same—and in a far more drastic manner—holds true for any critic of the theater, particularly of the dance. Theater as the performing branch of dramatic literature and even opera as a part of the world of music have always evoked criticism of a proved method with a sound tradition, with a technique and terminology. These two performing art forms demand an intellectual approach and permit an emotional identification. This is true of the dance in a far lesser degree. But the fact that the kinesthetic response is an added factor of great significance in the dance not only points to the strongly physical and elusive quality of the art, it also widens the scope of dance critique and, at the same time, narrows the critic's chance of grasping the intangible literally and literarily.

His knowledge must encompass all the theater arts, since ballet as much as modern dance can only be viewed in conjunction with their close relation to music, within the frame of the stage décors and the costumes. Lighting, the use of projections, all this can easily change the quality of the moving body. Usually, the critic has to form his judgment after one seeing, and very few critics have the ability to hear the music with the same intensity with which their eyes absorb the visual image. Costume and stage architecture are constant in contrast to the flight of movement which, born of time and lost to space, ceases to be while it is.

The critic's mental burden while watching a dance performance makes comparison and analysis, the keystone of all criticism, difficult. His awareness of the theater arts—as badly needed as it may be—is of little avail if not complemented by a broad knowledge of literature and a sense of history because the dancer-choreographer heavily leans on mythological, Biblical, and literary material.

It seems to be a moot question—though often raised—whether the critic should have had some dance training or will fare better if he once was a dancer or choreographer. It is obvious that the experience of how the body moves and how it feels to move is of great help in sensing a movement quality. (Goethe made the apodictic statement that "He who does not know the mechanical side of a craft cannot judge it.") But was Nijinsky justified in saying angrily when, no doubt, his vanity was hurt, that "Svetlov had never danced in any of the ballets he wrote about and did not know what dancing means"? If Svetlov had danced in them and then became a critic rather than remained a dancer, should we not be more suspicious of a failure in his craft sitting in judgment on his peers? Does not frustration distort our responses? As an artist I would prefer a critic who approaches my efforts with innocence, an aesthetic and ecstatic feeling for what I am doing rather than with a detailed technical knowledge out of his own experience and a hidden grudge against his fate. Since a vicarious knowledge of technique can be acquired, the non-dancing critic is in no way inferior to the dancer-turned-critic. However, the critic should have a clear concept of dance composition, of the ethnic roots of all rhythmic movement as well as of ballet tradition. Only then can he grasp and quickly coordinate the spiritual values and technical coherence the very moment movement unfolds.

Let us assume that the critic's mind plodded through comparison and analysis, that his visual memory successfully retained most of the highlights of what he saw and that he is now ready to translate his visual impressions into verbal imagery. It is only then that his greatest difficulty begins, his bout with semantics.

His troubles start with the adjective whose easy descriptive power of common provenience is most treacherous. He relies on it because it is pliant and pleasing and, above all, the next best to the only and ultimate word which often is trapped on the tip of his tongue. He then realizes that it is no longer a matter of his right judgment alone. A single word, a certain idiom, or an uncertain phrase can give his pronunciation a different slant, a distorted meaning.

If we were to collect a critic's descriptive terms such as the more popular *radiant, brilliant, superb,* or *breathtaking* and make the critic face the dancers whom he adjectivized as radiant, brilliant, superb, and breathtaking, he would believe neither his own eyes nor his words. Can we maintain that Anna Pavlova as well as Margot Fonteyn can fit with equal justification these four descriptive words? And does not our own mental image of these two ballerinas give these words another quality?

Her technique is of a sort to dazzle the eye. The most difficult tricks of the art of the dancer she executed with supreme ease. . . . Grace, a certain sensuous charm, and a decided sense of humor are other qualities that she possesses. In fact, it would be difficult to conceive a dancer who so nearly realizes the ideal of this sort of dancing.

This is a fair sample of better dance criticism. The description may easily fit a dozen ballerinas—although, in fact, Carl Van Vechten wrote these lines about Pavlova in the New York *Times* in 1910.

The critics' choice of words is indicative of their personalities as well as their points of view. Therefore, the editorial *we* is either a megalomaniac attitude assuming that everyone working for the magazine or newspaper would not shrink from sharing the same opinion or it is a cowardly flight into a half-hearted anonymity. What their eyes see, only their *I*s can express. In one of his letters to his editor, Kenningale Cook, Oscar Wilde wrote in 1877:

I always say I and not "we." We belongs to the days of anonymous articles, not to signed articles like mine. To say "we have seen Argos" either implies that I am a Royal Personage, or that the whole staff of the . . . visited Argos. And I always say clearly what I know to be true, such as that the revival of culture is due to Mr. Ruskin, or that Mr. Richmond has not read Aeschylus' Choephoroe. To say "perhaps" sports the remark.

George Bernard Shaw wrote little about the dance, but while engaged in reviewing the theater for the *Saturday Review,* he encountered the problems of dance criticism. He, who had a scant knowledge of the purely technical aspects of the dance, recognized, nevertheless, that it is not enough to parade the most beautiful French terms in one's critiques and, on the contrary, it is easy to hide one's insensitivity to the inherent beauty of the dance behind a splash of enticing-sounding words which pretend the connoisseur. He must have been aware of how beneficent it is to see that a dancer terminated a phrase, let us say, repeating the fourth position from which it began—but will it give the critic the final revelation or the aesthetic realization of what he saw?

On August 27, 1890, Shaw wrote:

The worst is that the only journalistic scrutiny as yet brought to bear on dancing is of a sort now all but obsolete in every other art. The very vilest phase of criticism is that in which it emerges from blank inanity into an acquaintance with the terms, rules and superstitions which belong to the technical process of the art treated of. . . . unfortunately . . . a critic with no artistic sense of dancing may cover up his incapacity by talking about rondes de jambe, arabesques, elevations, entrechats, balonnés and the like, threatens to start a technico-jargonautic fashion in ballet criticism.

As a music critic George Bernard Shaw said that he could reduce any able editor and the public to a condition in which they cannot help but accept any "pompous platitude" when he uses a technical jargon by writing that "the second subject, a graceful and flowing theme contrasting happily with the rugged vigor of its predecessor, appears unexpectedly in the key of the dominant." And Shaw, reacting to a critique of Musical Criticism that had appeared in a magazine article, suggested to form a "Vigilance Committee of musicians for the exposure of incompetent critics."

John Martin once advocated the erasure of the word *grace* from the dance critic's dictionary. By the same token, one could plead for keeping many a threadbare word out of the critic's vocabulary. Words such as *ease* and *grace* certainly have a timeworn, tired look vying in triteness with many adjectives. Yet, they are indispensable. I feel they can be used with grace and ease when placed within a cliché-free image, or even in conjunction with an adjective of contrapuntal quality. No critic can completely escape the curse of the adjective. As a matter of fact, I find that *superb* can have a *radiant* power when superbly used, and *breathtaking* can be made to fit brilliantly a final descriptive exclamation that brooks no further superlative.

We must acknowledge a great deal of circumstantial evidence against the dance critic, an evidence accumulated through the decades. But we must also take his testimony into account that although the English language has 600,000 words of which a substantial part are adjectives, more often than not, the only right word and the exact phrasing eludes him in describing a dancer or dance movement because of the inherent elusiveness of the art itself.

The least successful is the "schoolteacher" in the critic who grades a work instead of putting it into its right place by evoking images suggestive of the work itself. This is why only the "poet" in the critic can really do full justice to a dance piece. He works with tools similar to those of the dancer and choreographer, tools that create an illusion, the magic of illumination, the realization of something unreal. He can communicate the core of his experience. Since he can see and has the vision to see into the inmost within and far beyond the narrow strip of the horizon, the poet-critic can make us see. He can awaken a feeling of expectation or heighten our sense of appreciation. He can quicken our sensual response to the sensuous brilliance of the dancers. His perception can conjure up and capsulize the dancers' movements—limb for limb, body in unison with or juxtaposition to body—in a sentence that has the verbal power, the rhythmic subtlety, depth, and lightness to make us feel the inexpressible, the movement-woven wonder of the dance.

When thinking of a critic at a time when I myself did not yet belong to this privileged circle, I imagined him to be a kind of Westernized Brahmin. Webster defines a *Brahmin* not only as 'a Hindu priest, a highly cultured person,' but also as 'a supercilious or exclusive intellectual.' The delightful novelist Aubrey Menen says of a Brahmin in his book *The Ramayana* that "Any man could become a Brahmin provided he set himself up to know better than his fellowmen, and was sharp enough to get away with it." That the Brahmin are priests of a faith that extols anticipation of blessedness through extinction of desire and pleasure seems unfortunately applicable in some cases of professional—I had almost said, sacerdotal—criticism.

In my weirdest dreams I have imagined that the critic was born when one artist, whose egomania overlooked the scathing consequences of his deed, wanted to destroy his rival; or that the first critic must have been an artist who failed in his creative efforts, but felt he was able to criticize what he was unable to do. Whatever his genesis, he has become an unnecessary necessity in our complex society, and sometimes his trade has luckily been joined by artists whose creative genius functioned properly in one or another field of artistic expression.

I cannot believe that anyone could feel the desperate urge at an early age to become a critic. In spite of the fact that criticism is an art for which one must be born, one only discovers it after having reached a more or less mature stage. Most often the critic slips into this profession by a thousand coincidences and the one ability: to be a critic.

Criticism and chaos

History has the curious habit of writing its own obituaries and postscripts. Our Age of Confusion distinguishes itself by obliterating totally any distinction between the arts and between art and life. Moreover, the traditional concept of art to create order out of chaos has come full circle: art is to create chaos out of an orderly functioning life, as Morse Peckham points out in *Man's Rage For Chaos*. Art is no longer one of the means "whereby man seems to redeem a life which is experienced as chaotic, senseless, and largely evil," to quote Aldous Huxley. Rather, we could equate man's rage for chaos with André Malraux's definition which states that "all art is a revolt against man's fate."

In the process of all revolts reason yields to disorder and confusion which, in turn and of necessity, lead to a state of chaos. We like to speak euphemistically of this condition as a transition period in which such notions as indeterminancy and relevance have magnetic power in their pertinence as much as in their vagueness. The apparent ease with which the artist "does his thing" stands in utter contrast to the mounting problems the critic faces. The idea of continuing a stage presentation with happenings in the theater's foyers during intermission or the daring attempt to wipe out any illusionary audience reaction by creating forcefully an audience-performer interaction in a seemingly nonchalant manner paralyzes any critical reaction based on the critic's traditional approaches—or call them crutches—of comparison and analysis.

At one of the Pop Art exhibits, where the boundaries between art and life were completely blurred, I stood in front of a refrigerator, the door of which was intriguingly kept ajar. When another visitor tried to close the door, I involuntarily blurted out: "Don't touch it! This is an object of art!" The man withdrew his hand with an apologetic nod, already half-convinced that my reaction was not born of mockery but the exalted belief in *la vie pour l'art.*

At that moment I asked myself: What, in reality, is my critical approach to an exhibited refrigerator as an *objet d'art?* I have always viewed refrigerators with cool indifference but emotional gratitude for their utilitarian purpose. However, the aesthetic beauty of the one exhibited with its door artistically kept ajar made me shiver because of its deplorable existence removed from its natural atmosphere and deprived of its obvious function. I felt certain that no other critic could have a better "refrigerhetoric" knowledge than I had, historically, sociologically, and economically. Even though I was unable to verbalize my aesthetic judgment, I knew that whatever I could have said about it would have been sound and enlightening.

I had far greater critical qualms when I had to react to fully dressed dancers who brought a tank filled with water on stage, stepped into it, and then, dripping wet, left the stage. Certain choreographers intend to denude their movements from any self-reflective feelings. The result is usually pure gymnastic non-dance, ordinary and repetitive movement. This eludes any critical evaluation in the traditional sense. If—as was the case several times—simultaneously a film is run with the stage action in order to prove that the naked body has no more artistic or aesthetic validity than a piece of furniture has, then a point is made which restates, in another medium, the ordinary walk or run of the non-dancing dancers on stage. If another film is added—as was the case—which made the detailed descriptions of the Kama Sutra seem like primers for second-graders, the critic has then at least enough material for comparison and analysis from personal experience. The critic's aesthetic and kinesthetic reactions to such visual images—however unnecessary and revolting they may appear—are less taxed than when he sees a group of people repeatedly entering the stage, forming lines, freezing in their positions, and disappearing, and all this done with the ideological compulsion of the anti-art artist.

In such cases the critic may at best describe what he has seen, but he will have to relearn to see with the eyes of a generation raging for chaos in order to know what he has seen. What a critic coming to the theater still equipped with his out-dated tools of comparison and analysis must do in viewing such spectacles is to hide his tools under his seat, his intellect in his pockets, while liberating himself of his emotions from yesterday's experiences.

In 1918 Hermann Hesse, who refused to join the avant-garde, the futurists, expressionists, and dadaists of his time, recognized the difficult and problematic position of the critic. Hesse thought that the critic should neither reject the old nor the new and if he wants to be fair to both he has "a bitterly hard time of it. But why shouldn't critics have a hard time?" Hesse asked and concluded: "That's what they are there for."

Of course, it would be easy for the critic to point out unequivocally that the Emperor *has* no clothes, were not the artists—or non-art artists—quick to retort: Any child can see that the Emperor is without his clothes and that that isn't the point at all which, by the way, no one can miss as long as the Emperor is without his clothes.

The critic needs more than experience and intelligence today, surrounded as he is by a stormy sea of newness for the sake of newness, by the barkers of tomorrow's fakes, by the genuine artist who dares look into the blushing face of his time and for a creative expression of his anguish and jubilation to be a part of it. The critic needs spiritual strength and physical skill not to be run over by the bandwagons filled with curators, impresarios, press agents, and critics howling in unison. He needs courage to put out the many "put ons" as if they were nasty brushfires and to say No to the nonsense sold as art at cut-rate prices even before it is stillborn. He needs the same courage of going it alone as once some of the great artists did before the invention of the computerized madness on steamrollers which makes mayhem of man's prerogative to be creative. The critic must also have a great measure of that sense of humor enabling him to laugh with the gods when he sees this desperate creature "man" trying to fool history while making fun of himself.

PROFILES
& MEMORY PIECES

Isadora Duncan: an American memento

SHE STILL HEARD the voices of her friends warning her not to drive out in that Bugatti racing car, but she turned around and said: "I'll do it, and even if it is the last thing in the world I should do." She stepped into the car and it was the last thing in the world she did.

That was the way she lived, danced, and died. She was the exaltation of life in movement. She was the torchbearer of a new idea, the rebel who laid the groundwork for the dance of the twentieth century. Isadora Duncan gave man back the awareness of his body. "To express what is most moral, healthful and beautiful in art—this is the mission of the dancer, and to this I dedicate my life," she said. And her entire life was a fight for her ideals, a fight which she so often thought she was losing.

To dance is to live, she felt, and it is the highest and oldest form of living when the body expresses one's thoughts and feelings, when the body must move because the spirit moves it. Isadora's dancing was of the imagination and spirit, not of the body which only obeyed the orders of her "soul." In her dance she

111

tried to find the way back to the beginning where man only danced when he felt he had to, when his dance was the expression of his self, his innermost self, when his dance movements built cathedrals for his soul communicating with God. But she also realized that the dance of the future would have nothing of the uncontrolled wildness of the primitive, that it would be imbued with the refinement of modern man, that it would reflect his cultural achievement. "The dance of the future," she said, "will be one whose body and soul have grown harmoniously together that the natural language of that soul will have become the movement of the body. The dance will not belong to a nation but to all humanity."

It was in 1927, on the Riviera where she stepped into that Bugatti racing car. A few days previously Isadora had yet promised herself and her friends to prepare new dances. She had said: "Adieu, all my old dances, I will create one that will replace them; through hell and its tortures I will pass, and to paradise I will dance." But she could no longer work on them, she could no longer go through hell and its tortures in order to achieve a new climax in her career. The only thing left for her was to dance to paradise.

Her step into the hereafter was a second or two of fright and pain when her scarf—caught in the rear wheel of the car—strangled her. That moment must have been too short to make her fully realize what had happened to her, let alone make her grasp the finality of it. She faded into the endlessness of space filled with music of which she had always been so fond. A warm voice which sounded like the luring language of bells approached her: "Isadora Duncan . . . Isadora . . . this way, please!"

She thought, she always believed her body moved with such

ease, but now she felt as if she hardly touched the ground. "You do not touch ground," the voice continued as if her thoughts were no longer her secret, "you are upward bound."

It was true, now she too was aware of it, though in a different way from how things often suddenly used to become clear to her before. She always taught her children to move up their arms, to keep up their heads; she always warned them that to become real dancers—not just good dancers—their souls must float and their bodies would then seem to leave the world.

"You have left the world, Isadora." The voice was back with her replying to her thoughts.

"I have left the world . . . left, you say?" She paused. It was a second of hesitation in which was crowded all the surprise and trepidation of the moment.

"Step nearer . . . Yes, that's right, to this desk, please."

Isadora turned around to see from where the voice came, but she saw no one anywhere. Her eyes could not penetrate the gray-blue of space. It makes no difference, she thought and then said aloud: "I know you must look like a young Greek god hewn in stone by Michelangelo!" She heard the voice laugh, and it was a warm laugh that seemed to envelop her. She became more uncertain and added: "Or perhaps like the archangel Gabriel."

"You will learn to see up here very soon. It takes only a short while until all the formalities are settled. Though you will have to dig into your memory, it is quite painless now. I shall ask the necessary questions as fast as I can. You were born in . . . ?"

"San Francisco."

"Your age?—There are certain questions which you do not have to answer."

"I don't mind. From here age seems without time. My heart feels like twenty, it beats the rhythm of impetuous drums, it hums the melody of tomorrow. My mind feels like fifty, it carries the cross of crushed hopes, it breathes the mellowness of resignation, or let me say: of beginning resignation."

"In other words, shall I write down fifty?"

"No. Forty-nine," she said quickly.

"Your profession? Or avocation?"

"I am a dancer, an international dancer; no, write down: An American dancer. As the poetry of Walt Whitman springs from the womb of America, so has my dance its origin in the very lifesource of my country."

"Your father's name?"

"Joseph Charles Duncan."

"And your mother?"

"I was named after her: Isadora . . . Isadora O'Gorman Duncan."

"Any sisters or brothers?"

"Yes, we were four: Elizabeth, Raymond, and Augustin . . ." And closer instead of fading out, she suddenly heard her mother's voice calling: "Children, where are you? Elizabeth, Raymond, Isadora, Augustin!" Then Isadora saw herself coming from the dingy yard and running up the dilapidated stairs to their apartment in San Francisco.

"Yes, mother? What is it?"

"I wish you would stop playing these stupid games! You must learn to think of more serious things. You are old enough now to show how talented you are! You must forget the world and serve the arts alone. The world is wicked: all art is sublime. We shall live for the arts, children! This morning I decided to rehearse plays with you. We'll invite our neighbors and they will have to pay if they want to see great art. Children, I said great art . . ."

This was the way her mother spoke and lived: she was impulsive, eccentric, erratic. Some people said Isadora resembled her. She loved music, oysters, and champagne; she divorced Mr. Duncan and was always in a fervor of enthusiasm. She gave piano lessons, knitted, and made embroidery which Isadora peddled from door to door as a little girl. At that time her older sister, Elizabeth, had learned to dance so that she could teach it. And all Isadora wanted was to prove that she could do better than her sister and she begged: "Mother, let me learn to dance!" She remembered it as if it had been yesterday.

Her mother looked at her and said: "Don't be preposterous! Elizabeth doesn't dance, she teaches a few nitwits how to move. That is nothing for you, my dear. Look into this mirror! And now dance, Isadora. If dance is in you, you can dance!"

And she danced. She danced before the mirror and discovered the beauty of the body and the magic that lies in movement. One evening her mother took her to the ballet. "Look at the prima ballerina!" her mother whispered. "How she glides through the air, how she floats and arrests her movement coming down on her toes as if she were a feather. That's art! The fruit of years of relentless labor."

"But why do they dance on their toes, mother?"

"That's the way one dances, stupid."

"Oh no, mother! This is unnatural! No body moves like this. . . ."

Music and image disappeared when the voice next to her asked: "When was your first dance recital?"

"At the turn of the century, in Chicago. I danced without corset, my garment was thin, my feet were bare, I danced with flowers in my hair."

She had to laugh when she remembered the manager, how he

pushed open the door to her dressing room, how he stood there on the threshold for a moment, frozen protest of a world hurt to its bones, and how he then paced the room: "What gave you the courage to do this to me? To appear half naked, and with no ballet shoes, and not on your toes. . . . Do you know what you have done? You shocked the first rows, you made the balcony boo! I think you won't be surprised when I tell you that we are through."

She smiled at his fury. "I discovered the dance. How dare you reproach me when I am dancing the soul of man. I give the dance what the dance gave me: the rhythmic movement of wind and wave and the winged flight of bird and bee. . . ."

He threw his arms up and yelled: "You ruined me, you made me ridiculous, you insult the eye! The public was shocked, the whole audience annoyed. You broke your contract, that is clear!"

"I don't quite see your point. The contract said I must dance, not how; it spoke of no entrechat, arabesque, of no pirouette."

"Our contract is null and void!"

At that moment a well-dressed, good-looking gentleman stood in the frame of the door: "I beg your pardon, I knocked at the door, but there was no reply and the door was not locked." The stranger visibly enjoyed the embarrassment of Isadora and her manager. Then he said matter-of-factly: "I overheard your conversation, I could not help it. . . . If you don't mind, sir, I offer her a new contract." Turning to her, he added: "Miss Duncan, do you accept?"

"I do . . . But who are you?"

"Uh, pardon me! My name is Augustin Daly."

He took her with him to New York where she danced in *A Midsummer Night's Dream* for the first time, on a real stage. Isadora discovered the dance. The rich ladies of society paid much money to see her in their clubs, to be shocked and annoyed. She was the vogue, but she wanted to be understood. Hardly an hour passed in which she was not pursued by men: "Miss Duncan, I expect you on my estate—Isadora, my carriage will wait in front of your door—this ring, Isadora!"

And, at that time, what was still her answer? "I'm sorry, gentlemen, but I'm already engaged. . . . ."

"Engaged . . . .? Did you say engaged . . . .?—Who is he . . . ?—Who conquered your heart?"

"It is the dance, gentlemen, I belong to my art!"

Then she heard the voice again: "Well, I'll put down: belongs to her art. And from here? What shall I say? These are formalities, but I must fill in your chart. . . ."

"Say: it was the beginning. I had to obey my inner voice, I had to trace the source of all art: simplicity, and I had to seek its soul in my soul. America remained too remote, too aloof. I fled to England on a cattle boat. As I said: it was the beginning. In the British Museum I studied the poses on Greek vases, the Tanagras, the secret of their ecstasy, the symbol of their gestures. From their mystery came my dance. Yes, I saw in ancient Greece all grace. I wedded my soul to the harmony of beauty. But I hit all convention in the face, my sandals left traces of scandals and triumphs. I was the rage. Oh, I dealt blow after blow to the Victorian age of corsets and curtains of Turkish beads!"

"Next station?"

". . . was Paris, 1900, the world exhibition. I danced: inhaling life and exhaling art."

Yet she knew she was still so far from reality at that time, far from herself, from the woman in her. One of her first admirers was Rodin.

"We have so much in common, Isadora," he said. "You transport the soul of man into movement and I chisel it into stone. Your rendition has the disadvantage of being created for a fleeting moment. . . . Let me cut it into stone."

"I could come to your studio for one hour tomorrow afternoon."

"One hour, Isadora, is not enough!"

"Then let me see—I stay in Paris several weeks."

"My memory of the dancer Isadora is so rich that it may take years. . . ."

"But years, Master, could mean a lifetime!"

"I would not tire of it."

She laughed, threw her head back, and moved her arms up. Rodin kept this moment on a piece of paper. For himself. For the years to come when he would want to look at it.

Isadora was restless. Time was too precious for her, was something she could not afford to lose. A theater agency in Budapest invited her to dance. It was a success. From there she took Germany by storm. Still many people were shocked and some booed from the galleries. Now she danced to the music of Gluck and Wagner, of Chopin and Beethoven. The dance was no longer cheap entertainment. Not Isadora's dance.

"My body sang, my body spoke. I created the reality of a dream. Those among the Germans who were dreamers saw in my dance the poetry of the moving body. Yet success and scandal became more and more the twin brothers of my days and nights. I had conquered Europe, Europe had conquered me: Berlin, Athens, Paris, St. Petersburg. I awoke to new life. I had grown mature. I frightened the philistines and stirred those who were enlightened. And then—then I met Gordon Craig."

They were sitting in her studio with the huge blue drapes and the many cushions on the floor and with the atmosphere of daring greatness.

"You cannot always be spray, Isadora, spray that dances on the crest of the waves and lives the miracle of an iridescent life. The surf carries the spray to the shore from where it must return to the endlessness of the sea."

"I think I know what you mean, Gordon."

"It is the great artist who decides what art is. You have so much to give to mankind, you simply can't afford to flash up like a flickering flame and then extinguish. You gave the world a new idea, a new art. Shall it die with you?"

"No, it shan't, it must live. I can see the letters: Isadora Duncan School. Schools are tools in the hands of creators. Isn't it so, Gordon? Tools of the future, tools of time. You are so right, Gordon, so right. Schools are what I need."

She paused and then turned around as if she knew where the desk stood from where the voice was questioning her, and said: "You may write down: I was no longer alone, I was going to live! And life was no longer vague, I could see the road with the many milestones. I had a child by Gordon Craig."

"What followed then?"

"Triumph and tragedy. Call it the beginning of the end. It was a tragicomic trend. There was my work. Victory step by step. And my private happiness. My two children: Patrick and Deidre. Oh, how I loved them . . . !"

"If I understood you correctly," the voice interrupted her, "then you said your career had reached its climax. Is that correct?"

"From the bleak wintry nights of Russia to the cold clarity of American mornings, I was the dance. I was supreme. And I lived the extreme. And then—while I was drunk with myself and men, suddenly—Oh, God! I shall never forget that shrill cry of the bell. I lifted the receiver. Hello . . . !"

"Madame Isadora Duncan?"

"Speaking."

"This is the Police Department, Madame. I am sorry to be the bearer of bad news."

"What happened? My children . . . ?"

"Yes, Madame. Your children . . . an accident on the Pont Neuf this afternoon . . . your car, Madame . . . ?"

"Are they badly hurt?"

"No, Madame. I regret to inform you that they are dead."

The voice was back with her again: "What followed next?"

She met a poet whose language she did not speak. He was a Russian, and she engaged a lady to teach her his tongue. After the first lesson she asked Isadora: "Aren't you proud of yourself? You have learned so much today!"

"Yes, so much. Now I can say in his language . . . : What is this?—This is a pencil— What kind of a pencil?— This is a blue pencil!— But when he comes to see me tonight I don't want to say that the pencil is blue! You must teach me other phrases, such as: Oh, my last love!"

"This is against the rules of the Berlitz System!"

"But I must be able to say: I worship the ground you walk on!"

"This is nowhere in my book."

"Then throw it away and teach me: I won't forget you, I will wait for you! And you?"

"And he?" asked the voice.

"Oh, I know he loved me too. But then—there was his temper and alcohol and the maddening labyrinth of his Russian soul. I cared for him as for a child—he was so young! But his genius eloped with him into the clouded land of insanity where he killed himself. Oh, this horrible moment when they told me! But after all—I still had my work—my school—to teach thousands of children how to move, how to let their souls fill their bodies with music and ecstasy . . . !"

"And your school?"

"It never grew, it never lasted. The only thing I really wanted so badly: rebirth through the new generation!"

"Then you would say your life . . . ?"

". . . was a triumph without success. Stories that had—out of shame—their text erased. Despair and distress and the overdue bills. And then the scream of headlines and everywhere the hissing of vicious tongues. I knew there was no fulfillment, only the groping dream for more in life. I wanted to drown myself, but a British Naval officer dragged me out of the Mediterranean and back to life. I no longer wanted to live!"

"Well," the voice said, "then we shall have to call the witnesses for you. Witness Auguste Rodin!"

"She danced life and lived the dance. From her emotions emerged movements which were flawless sculpture. Miss Duncan has borrowed from the Creator the breath of genius."

"Genius . . . ? Talent . . . ? Oh, God! I lied before when I said I did not want to live . . . but it was no lie, I really did not want to, and yet—I loved to live. I wanted to give, to give myself until it hurt; where the grief has outgrown its own pain. Oh, how brief was the freedom from knowing what we have known! I walked through a desert of words where the words were like sand and dirt. . . ."

"Next witness: Elie Faure!"

"Monsieur, I am speaking in the name of all artists who loved her. My profession was that of a critic, but—I confess, monsieur, I wept when I saw her. It was no longer to our eyes, nor to our ears; it was no longer to our nerves that she spoke. From deep within us, when she danced, there arose a flood that swept away from the corners of our soul all the filth which had been piled up there by those who for twenty centuries had bequeathed to us their critique, their ethics and their judgments. . . ."

"Oh, stop, please stop! I can't hear you say it. For me, there was no such feeling, there was no end to the madness that drove me and drove me—where to? I no longer knew since it was without aim, without direction. Was it to forget? Or that I was ashamed that I wanted to forget? Wherever I could I threw myself into naked embrace. I had but my body to feel, to be sure that I was, that I could endure the night and the dawn which was out to betray its own yesterday. And when I cried, I cried the tears of forgotten fears."

"Witness Sergei Alexandrovitch Essenin!" called out the voice.

"My name is Essenin. Am I still remembered? Only remembered because my star exploded in her fire? I thought the world would have died with my suicide. I could say so much and now I can no longer speak. My love has lost its tongue, the tongue which has once sung of her. What I have come to seek I found in ecstasy and death, and both lay hidden in her breath. I left you furtively, it's true left through a door which bore the sign: "No Exit." I did see it and walked through, ready to pay my fine. Goodbye, my friend; oh, don't be sad and do not cry. It is not new to die nor is it any newer to live on."

"I lived on, I tried to, at least. I drowned myself in the world again. But the world gave me up and I yielded, yard by yard, bit by bit. Life was so rich and life was so hard. It was always the same. The struggle for money. And everywhere the laughter of children; its sounds cracked like so many whips. I had left but the memory of a dream. I wrote my memoirs. I was going to create new dances. I saw myself riding a wayward gleam, but I could not call back the rider from there, nor could I wait, nor did I care. I knew my inner voice was on the verge of succumbing. Fulfilled and silent now. It had its share. And this was all I had to spend. If the end had not come, I would have come to the end. . . ."

She had come to an end which, in itself, was a beginning only. The doors of her memory closed and the uncertain space before her grew more and more into a definable shape. Now she smilingly recognized that the voice which had questioned her did not belong to a Greek god hewn by Michelangelo.

And while all this happened: this sweet dissolution of a tired life, this willing surrender to the greater unknown—the telegraph wires hummed from country to country: "Fatal accident of eminent dancer on Riviera!" The night editors changed the headlines of their morning issues and letters of bold-faced type drummed into the world: "Isadora Duncan dead!" And curious eyes everywhere scanned the story in small print: "The tragic end of the great dancer has come to all lovers of the arts as a shock— There is hardly anyone among us who does not realize what a great loss the dance world suffered—Yesterday the famous dancer met a young man who drove a Bugatti—She stepped in with a long scarf around her neck—She laughed and turned around to say goodbye in French with her heavy Californian accent: 'Adieu, mes amis, je vais à la gloire!'—The scarf caught in the wheel— The car stopped at once, but it was too late: Isadora Duncan was dead—Isadora, who—" today is more alive than she ever was.

She lives the life of her legend. She lives the legend of her life.

Mary Wigman*

Mary Wigman, what did she dance about when she and this century were younger? About man, his joys and tribulations,

* In 1966, on her eightieth birthday.

about man in relation to man and his environment. "Man needs man," she once said. "Art is communication spoken by man for humanity in a language raised above the everyday happening." She danced about the ultimate things in life: visions, fate, sacrifice, death. Yes, her preoccupation with death has so often been considered characteristic of her Germanic background. But, in fact, it was the artistic realization of those devastating war years, of the upheaval which caused inflation of all factual and spiritual values. Mary Wigman was then so deeply rooted in life, and so strong and positive a person, that she saw the vision of death only as a counterbalance to the dynamic energies of life.

I was reminded of her dances of death when I saw her in the summer of 1965, near Lugano, to discuss my translation of her book, *The Language of Dance*, with her. Then, her life was hanging on a thread, with a wicked bronchial cough relentlessly pounding at her weak heart. I still remember how she dragged herself from her bed into the living room to be bedded on the couch; how she strained to overcome her weakness—"one must not give in so easily, nicht wahr?"—but how an hour's talk showed her dwindling strength, her lake-blue eyes covered with a film of mist. The coughing spells, the tired gestures of the bony hands trying to frighten away an invisible shadow. "Our book," she had said, "we want to leave something that has meaning to those who come after us."

It was time to leave. I assured her that it will be a beautiful book, a book of lasting value. "Only try to get it into the hands of the right people, the young people, the dancers of tomorrow." She hid her head while embracing my wife. When I wanted to kiss her goodbye, she said, "No, no . . . I'm too sick . . . you never can tell" and pressed my hands against her cheeks. One does not forget such moments so easily. They carried with them the frightful knowing of being and not-being.

What a joyful Wiedersehen it was in the summer of 1966! Friends had rented a cottage in Ascona, glorious lake country in Southern Switzerland, for Mary so that she could spend a few restful weeks in the sunny Ticino on the Lago di Maggiore. Her faithful companion Hesschen was with her. As usual. Hesschen, a resolute, strong-willed woman with sparkling eyes and a devilish sense of humor had been with Mary for four decades. She speaks of Mary as "my baby," cares for her like a friend and nurse, like a cook and secretary, caring for Mary has become her *raison d'être,* and Mary could hardly exist without her.

Both expected us. On our arrival in Brissago, a few miles from where Mary lived, we found her letter: "Hope you arrived well. . . . Come and see us on Saturday. We want to celebrate 'our' book."

It has always been a great experience for me to be in the shadow of her sun. The grandeur of her simplicity is moving. To hold her hand, freckled and warm, with the pressure that speaks of the unspeakable: the love that communicates beyond mere words. We sit and sip tea which cannot be strong enough for her. And one cigarette after the other.

We speak of the events of the past year while her eyes follow two naked children running across the nearby lawn: "Isn't it wonderful to look at them!" she said as if wishing to absorb the never-vanishing tomorrow. "Watch the girl move! The perfection of innocence!" We speak of the seasons passing so fast. "It only seems to us like that." She pointed to the children. "For them time is timeless." Another cup of tea, another cigarette.

"No, I haven't seen too much lately, neither in Berlin nor in any other city. My school means a great deal to me. There is no lack of students who would like to study with me. They are coming from all over the world. However, I cannot help closing the doors to the many who feel the urge to dance but are not chosen.

And with being painfully strict in selecting the students, their number dwindles and always creates hazards for the continuation of the school."

Another cigarette. The apprehension with which I light it again, is answered with a smile. "The doctors wouldn't allow her to stop smoking at this point of the game," Hesschen explained.

"But whatever I have seen in the last few years, I have found such a repetition of sameness in the theater dance. Movement and the whole visual image is so often repeated, and there is always the same tempo whether the music is by Bach or a modern composer."

What are the possibilities of the modern dance in Germany today? "They are almost nil, hardly worthwhile speaking of them. Of the generation that followed me, the only strong personality in the modern dance was Dore Hoyer, and she devoted herself to solo dancing, has rarely worked with groups. Where are the days when Kreutzberg and I could tour Europe and appear in the smallest places in Germany? Even my most gifted pupils have no chance to develop. Once in a while they can be seen in Berlin. Perhaps they can give a recital in Hamburg. And there it rests. But only with opportunities for experience can one grow and unfold, find and reveal oneself. I remember how the doors of the world opened for me and how this helped me in my work. Now all this happens to your modern dancers in America, it no longer happens here. Well, what can a gifted dancer do here? He escapes into being avant-garde and remains the avant-guardian of a small new idea until his potentialities wither away."

Mary Wigman interrupted herself and pointed across the lake towards the mountains. "There is another lake beyond that hill, much smaller than Lake Maggiore. I wonder why the people call it the Eye of God." We both remained silent.

"I had quite a gifted student who gives the impression of

being a very manly, virile dancer. He works with four of my students. But he imprisoned himself by sticking to one clearly defined approach and style that permits no outburst of feelings, no dynamics. That's what I enjoyed so much when I saw the Alvin Ailey Company. Ailey made me believe in the future of the modern dance. Finally, I saw dancing again. People didn't just stand around on stage. They moved and moved me. They did something to me for which one must be very grateful, particularly in my years. When I left the theater I felt young again, the world went on dancing." She stopped for a moment. "But this seems to be the exception nowadays. There is so little rejoicing, nor any real suffering any more. If the time wills it so, then so shall it be. But it cannot stay that way."

We spoke of her travels and her recent trip to Greece. "There you have it," she said. "Delphi, the source of forgetting and remembering, of knowing unconsciously. In Greece I had to think of the new generation of dancers. If they only knew the secret—that you must possess the past in order to be able to be of your own time. Greece gave me a great deal, the experience that comes through the people and the landscape, with the landscape shaping the people, with the people forming the landscape. I have often brought with me unforgettable impressions from there, also of folk dances which, in spite or because of their untheatricality, are beautifully alive.

"Recently I lingered on a Greek Island. On Sunday a wedding was celebrated in a small village which seemed lost high in the rocky landscape, only accessible up a narrow path that had on it a few stone steps for mules and human beings. They brought me up, the mules and the people. They were all dressed in their most festive Sunday costumes. The bridegroom wore a dark suit which was much too big for him, the bride was in her native garment. I can never forget how radiant he looked and how he enjoyed being the center of this little world for a few hours. The musicians began to play at four o'clock, and the dance continued without interruption until one o'clock in the morning. The couple and the oldest people of the village danced best. Most often the dancers formed four circles. What impressed me so much was the mixture of utter joy and dead seriousness with which they all danced. Yes, and the expression on the bride's face: resigned, calm, almost unhappy as if she had already experienced and put behind her the joys of love and was now expecting what life has usually in store for these women, tasks and toils."

One facet of being with Mary Wigman is the pleasure of silence which cannot be put onto black and white, but which one can fully absorb and enjoy together with her. She radiates the feeling of accomplishment, of peace with herself, though not necessarily with the world. Still ready to come to grips with all problems she may face, ready to fight and overcome them, one can feel she has gained that final and enviable distance to herself and the events that shape her life: to know her purpose yet without taking herself too seriously.

"Everything will fall into its place," she wrote me after her return to Berlin where she found a few thorny issues to be settled. "In such a case one must not lose one's nerve."

The city of Berlin plans a special celebration of her eightieth birthday, friends, former students, coworkers and well-wishers will converge on her from every corner of the world. "Already now," she wrote on September 15, "my birthday casts its shadow! Radio and television interviewers storm my door. And I don't feel like doing it at all. These are the first cloudy and cold days since we met in Ascona. And immediately my body feels uncomfortable. I will have to make great efforts to be up to the impending strain."

More than ever before Mary Wigman loves the sunny south,

the calm of the day that replenishes her strength. I often observed that look of gratitude and wistfulness in her eyes when the sun disappeared behind the hills, and the expression of a defiant and sulking child when Hesschen put a shawl or a jacket around her shoulders. This was always a good time to make her speak about the dance.

"I feel that ballet lies outside of life, however beautiful it may be. Well, considering what is being done now I don't think one can speak of classical ballet any longer, but only of modern ballet. I have seen a few ballets which impressed me very much and which clearly showed the direct or indirect influence of the modern dance. Take for instance Balanchine's *Agon*. It engulfed and involved me, it made me open up and gave me something that became a radiant experience.

"I think the world has to acknowledge the achievement of American dance. My strongest impressions came from American companies. One of the great masterpieces of our time is José Limón's *Moor's Pavane,* it is absolute, incontestable, you cannot add to it nor take anything away from it. I'll never forget having seen Jerome Robbins's *Afternoon of a Faun,* danced by a Negro and a blonde girl. What contrasts between the dark faun full of chaste grace and the girl full of innocence! And the entire work had the making of a dream, was purity per se, fraught with eroticism."

How does she feel about the British influence on the German theater dance? "I do not mind whether an English, Russian, or American ballet master comes to Germany. Dance has never known borders. Noverre did wonders in Stuttgart. Why should not John Cranko repeat history? The Russian Tatjana Gsovsky withdraws from Berlin to let another Englishman take her place. Ballet masters come and go. Only the results count. I never read a program to find out who dances what. I always mix up names. A

name has never meant anything to me. I've never been interested
in being together with famous people. Whenever I meet someone,
it is the impression he makes on me that means something to me.
Some names I cannot forget because I cannot forget the man and
what he stands for. All I am still interested in is the work, the
dance."

She took my hand and smiled. "I am an old lady. Now I am
no longer interested in being tolerant about all kinds of dancing.
But I am still madly in love with dance. This love hasn't left me.
It will only disappear with me."

Anna Pavlova

So little is left: the faint and fading memory of the few who
have seen her and are still alive and can settle back with a sigh
and say: "Ah, Pavlova!"

Then, there are the written words of those who have tried to
verbalize the image of something seemingly so inexpressible that
such different minds as Serge Diaghilev and John van Druten escaped into the same poetic simile. Van Druten likened Pavlova to
"the wind passing like a shadow over a field of wheat," and Diaghilev thought "she could walk over a cornfield without breaking a stalk."

Diaghilev knew what he expected from a dancer: a fusion of
precision and lightness, of technique and expression. That he
could have let her walk over a cornfield and she would not have
bent an ear is the greatest compliment he could think of. He always, and unjustly so, suspected her of sheer virtuosity, and this
image would then be justified. But van Druten's is the poet's metaphor of floating like a mysterious shadow and whisking away,

windlike, as if it were a magic trick and helped by an incomprehensible furtiveness.

The poetess Harriet Monroe tried to answer the question of why Pavlova called forth such imagery when she wrote in her eulogistic poem:

Pavlova, your foot is lighter than the perfume
of lilies—Brighter than the sparkle of waves . . .

To say of Pavlova that her foot was "lighter than the perfume of lilies" still creates the sensation of floating, of air carrying something that is no longer indescribable; it is as airy and enchanting as a fragrance, fleetingly passing, but recognizable. The image of delicacy or frailty, of sweet swift tenderness embracing you, and, above all, of a sensuous delight is called to your mind; when the critic Carl van Vechten said of her, "the little dancer is lithe and exquisitely formed" or Arnold Haskell referred to "her ethereal qualities, in striking contrast to the more robust strength of her contemporaries," then they both claim the same in plain prose.

Only a dancer who can give her entire being the illusion of lightness is, in the spectator's eye, on her way to conquering gravity. It is not only the moment of jumping or sailing through the air which counts: strangely enough, it is the impression of how she comes back to the ground, that is, to our level, which conveys to us the feeling of her being "so" light or the impression of how light she must feel in her partner's arm who lifted her or into whose arms she jumped.

The secret does not seem to lie in technical skill, for many a dancer of our days is technically better equipped than Pavlova ever was. In fact, she rarely turned more than two or three pirouettes, but "she executed them with such a *brio* that they had the effect of half a dozen." Then it was far more the spirit in the body than the body itself which created the illusion of her being "lighter than the perfume of lilies." The decisive witness as to her lightness can only be a dancer with whom she performed, and we received such testimony from André Oliveroff who remembered:

I knew . . . she would be easy to lift—but I had not divined the uncanny lightness of her. When I caught and supported her in mid-air, I was scarcely conscious at all of her weight; her elevation seemed to continue after she had come into position, held up in the air by my hands. Some ballerinas, when you hold them like that, seem to be made of stone . . . but . . . she seemed always to be reaching up, giving you the illusion that she was very much lighter than she really was. . . . You almost felt she might fly away on the wind at any moment, like a piece of swan's-down.

The undulating movement, the rippling of water, the ever-recurring rolling of waves, full of sparkle, or light as foam are other comparisons often introduced to do verbal justice to the unfathomable impression this dancer made on her audience. Even a critic as sober and sound as Arnold Haskell wrote: "What struck me the most about Pavlova was not just the fact that her dancing seemed entirely spontaneous, but that it seemed a natural phenomenon, like the ripple of a pond, the opening of a flower, or the leaves being whisked and whirled by the wind." Such imaginative descriptions may seem extravagant, and they are used by a critic who usually mistrusts them profoundly, but they represent the only manner in which one can convey something of the impression created by Pavlova. Though it is understandable that Haskell felt puzzled at his own surge of emotions, it is one more proof of Pavlova's uncanny power of projection.

Two other images, well-established metaphors in describing a dancer, are the flight of birds and the flickering of flames. The flame has always been a favorite comparison with the dancing body, and such a brilliant poet and philosopher as Paul Valéry has seen in the "flame-body" meaning and explanation of the dance. In fact, for Valéry, the dancer seemed enwrapped in an atmosphere of fire and was like the flame itself. But fire and flame are not merely the image and beautiful spectacle of the final ecstasy of movement, they also carry the connotation of something so powerful and strong that it inevitably leads to destruction and death—but both fire and flame are strangely absent from all descriptive phrases which try to capture the impact of Pavlova's dancing. The nearest to it can be found in Cyril Beaumont's lines:

Pavlova dances with her whole body, from the crown of her head to the tip of her toe. She danced with such abounding vitality, with such ecstasy of the spirit; she surrendered herself so completely to the mood of the dance; that she became a being transformed. She glowed, became almost incandescent, as it were, from the lavish outpouring of her nervous energy and muscular force. Sometimes there was just a pale luminosity which filled the spectator with an exquisite sadness as in *Le Cygne,* sometimes the glow burst into flame as in *L'Automne Bacchanale.*

Though Pavlova danced "with such abounding vitality," we do not have the impression that the word *vitality* is used to express physical strength. It must have been a vitality born of "the ecstasy of the spirit." Her fragility, stressed time and again by all writers who tried to translate her graceful appearance into words, seems to have been far more akin to the ease and elegance of elevation and the felicity of flight, for most often we can find similes of the airborne lightness of birds.

Carl van Vechten reporting on his impression at the Metropolitan Opera House when Pavlova danced in New York for the second time, wrote:

Pavlova twirled on her toes. With her left toe pointed out behind her, maintaining her body poised to form a straight line with it, she leaped backward step by step on her right foot. She swooped into the air like a bird and floated down. She never dropped. At times she seemed to defy the laws of gravitation.

André Levinson, the famous Russian-French critic, said in painting the picture of her *Giselle* (as translated by Marianne Moore):

Arms folded, on tiptoe, she dreamily and slowly circles the stage. By even, gliding motions of the hands, returning to the background whence she emerged, she seems to strive toward the horizon, as though a moment more and she will fly—exploring the confines of space with her soul.

Anna Pavlova's name has become a symbol for absolute achievement, a trademark of ballet per se, and persistent dreamers of her greatness still see her dancing through heaven—without wings, of course, for her feet have always carried her as if they had been wings—"exploring the confines of space with her soul".

What was her "soul" like, what was the animating principle, what the actuating cause of her life, the essence of her drives which burgeoned into such breathtaking bravura that the memory of her has outlived all other dancers in awe, intensity and inspiration?

She was born in St. Petersburg on January 31, 1882, a frail and premature child. It was expected that she would not live, and she was sent to Ligova, a place outside the city, where the invigorating air seemed to have helped a great deal. Her early contact with nature had certainly had its effect on her entire outlook on life.

Of course, she could not recall these first few years when she sat down to write a short autobiography which she began with the words: "My earliest vivid recollections take me back to the time when I lived with my mother in a small apartment in St. Petersburg. I was the only child, and we two were alone in the world since my father had died when I was two."

This first paragraph states with simple finality her sense of isolation and insecurity. There she was, alone in the world with her mother, "poor—very poor." She could not forgive her father for deserting her and leaving her with her mother impoverished. "She used to reminisce sometimes about her childhood in Russia," André Oliveroff reported. "She spoke tenderly of her mother. . . . She hardly ever referred to her father, but when she did her face would harden and she would drop the subject quickly, as though it were a distasteful one." Later, Oliveroff also observed that, in her company, she would devote far greater attention to the girls than to the male dancers during rehearsals: "I have never known her to focus her criticism upon a man. . . . But of the girls she was unsparing."

She tells us little of her early youth. At the age of eight she was taken to the Maryinsky Theater where she saw a performance of the *Sleeping Beauty*. Her reaction differed little from the one of any other child. It was to be expected that she would want to become a dancer. But while other children would forget, or soon turn to new desires, Anna insisted on being taken to the director of the Ballet School. She had to wait for acceptance until she completed her tenth year. "And so I had to wait two years during which I remained sad and dreamy." But this sadness and dreaminess remained with her all her life, for it was said of the famous ballerina that there was a great tenderness about her, sadder than a child's. She looked for secluded spots in the woods when she was with her mother in the country during her summer vacations "and would sit under a shady tree to build in the air the fragile castles of my dreams."

The same girl, however, told her mother she would enter the

Ballet School, even if it meant leaving and hurting her mother (there were plenty of tears), and the same girl cried because at one of the czar's visits to the school he took her schoolmate Belinskaya in his arms and not her, and she cried until she was the center of attention.

At sixteen she was premiere danseuse, and, about that time, when she read Taglioni's life story she decided she would be seen as a dancer in the whole world. Taglioni was then the most popular name of all the ballerinas of the past. She had danced "at Paris, at London, and in Russia, where she is still remembered." Here her ambition recognized an unlimited incentive: to outdo Taglioni, to out-travel her. Theodore Stier, Pavlova's musical director for sixteen years, tells us that he traveled 300,000 miles, conducted 3,650 performances, and more than 2,000 rehearsals for Pavlova.

She became the traveling saleswoman par excellence. She sold ballet to the world and with it her name. She danced before audiences who had never seen dancing on toes, she appeared in regions where people had been inimical to ballet or without understanding of the art. In Java as well as in Mexico, in Japan as well as in India. Pavlova was the name, and ballet schools opened up wherever she went. Mothers permitted their daughters to become dancers because they had seen Pavlova dance. Little girls dreamed of becoming a "second Pavlova."

People—not connoisseurs—saw the beauty of her movements, the winged grace which enraptured them and they realized that the fleeting sensuous pleasure they derived from it all made them forget their drab existence and made them dream of something which they now knew existed behind the invisible curtain of their everyday. Pavlova had the justification for her mad race through the continents: the people needed her, "everywhere our dancing was hailed as the revelation of an undreamt-of art." She had become a pioneer, a propagandist.

At one of her tours through Europe she stood on the balcony of her hotel in Stockholm. A huge crowd which had followed her from the theater stood there cheering her.

I bowed from time to time. Finally, they sang the national anthem in my honour. I asked myself in vain how I could show my appreciation. Then I had an idea, I went to my room and returned with the baskets of flowers I had received in the theatre. But even after I had thrown my roses and lilies and violets and lilacs to them they did not want to withdraw. . . . I asked my femme de chambre, But what have I done to get them so enthusiastic? "Madam," she replied, "you've made them happy because you made them forget for an hour the sadness of life." I have never forgotten those words.

"She is, I think, the most sincere woman it ever has been my good fortune to meet," said Theodore Stier. One must assume she meant what she said when writing about this incident in Stockholm. A dancer "must sacrifice herself to her art. Her reward will be the power to help those who come to see her to forget for a short while the sadness and monotony of life." Only someone who had such great understanding for sadness, is, so to speak, on intimate terms with it, could stress this point as much as she did. It was the inner justification she needed for her ambition. It was not only the applause she craved for but the proof that she has done it and can do it again, the satisfaction of the conqueror whose own conquests do not let him stop and rest.

Success and happiness were major questions in her life. That they were, in their effect on her, far more complex than she thought, goes without saying. In her autobiographical pages she came to the conclusion that "the secret of success" is "to tend, unfailingly, unflinchingly, towards a goal." Pavlova was a strong disciplinarian and hard worker.

The dancer must practice her exercises every day . . . must feel so perfectly at ease so far as technique is concerned that when on stage she need devote to it not a single thought, and may concentrate on expression, upon the feelings which must give life to the dances she is performing.

All this is taken for granted. There is hardly any great achievement registered in the human annals that was not the fruit of hard labor and self-sacrifice. "But success, what exactly is success?" she asks. "For me," she answers, "it is to be found not in applause, but in the satisfaction of feeling that one is realizing one's ideal." Did she not forget that an interpretative artist, an actor or a dancer, cannot very well realize his ideal without outside success and thus needs applause as she needed it? For the artist, applause is the loud manifestation of being accepted and liked, and this warming feeling ought to have nicely compensated the poor little girl who had felt so utterly left alone in the world.

Pavlova comes closer to the core of the matter when she continues to say, "as a small child . . . I thought that success spelled happiness." In other words, neither the superficiality of applause nor the realization of one's ideal could make her happy. "I was wrong," she went on. "Happiness is like a butterfly which appears and delights us for one brief moment, but soon flits away." But when happiness is merely such a fleeting experience, did she not rather equate happiness and applause which certainly delighted her for many a brief moment, but, applause being what it is, faded away.

We are told by many observers that she could be a relentless taskmaster at rehearsals. Victor Dandré, her husband and manager, said, "she was firm because she knew she was right." For her, art and life were synonymous, and no one could have lived up to her maxim of "sacrificing herself to her art" more precisely than she did herself. She never stopped learning, not even in the days when the world celebrated her. There was always a teacher to whom she listened, to whom she looked up. She realized that when you cease to learn, you no longer grow, and not growing means for any artist fighting lost battles of retreat.

Pavlova was not beautiful in the ordinary sense, but everything about her was in full harmony. Harmony seemed to have been the keyword to her entire appearance. "Balanced harmony, in her thinking and in her motions, was her very self," said Marianne Moore, but harmony must have been absent from her emotional life. Otherwise, she could not have loved to dance the many tragic parts she chose, she could not have excelled just "in the portrayal of the pathetic, of some ephemeral being that came to life and then withered and died all on a summer's day," as Arnold Haskell wrote, who might have more appropriately changed the "summer's" to an autumn's day.

Harmony, though, was in her perfectly proportioned physique, in her arms and fingers, in her well-shaped legs, so rare with dancers. Her face was framed by long dark hair, and, if not conventionally attractive, it was like an instrument with a wide range of expression on which she played to perfection. Her head sat just right on the shoulders. Although she never really suffered from bad health after her early childhood days she made a delicate, almost fragile impression on the stage which accentuated the inimitable grace with which she moved. Only to see her walk on stage to take a bow was music of movement, people said; to watch her made Sunday out of every ordinary day.

"She is the greatest ballerina in the world," said Diaghilev, "excelling both in classicism and in character." He engaged her to open the unforgettable season of 1909 in Paris. The posters carried her name and portrait; her greatness was one of the inspirations that led to Diaghilev's now historic artistic venture with the Ballets Russes. But at the end of the first season she left and went to England to form her own company. What had happened? Nijinsky was, no doubt, favored by Diaghilev—male dancers of such stature are always rarities—and he also got better notices than she did. Even Ida Rubinstein had a somewhat better press. Moreover, Diaghilev was a despot and so was Anna Pavlova. They both believed in art as such, but both spelled it with different letters which read D-I-A-G-H-I-L-E-V and P-A-V-L-O-V-A, respectively.

Diaghilev saw in the total effect of dance, music, costume, and décor the realization of a theatrical miracle that would enchant the audience with his brand of magic whose trick remained his secret. Pavlova, one could simply say, had a rare stage personality. In fact, she personified her brand of theatrical magic, she not only rose above her material, she also took it along with her. She created out of the trite the tragedy of life, she lifted the language of movement onto a level of artistry which left the layman bewitched and the expert puzzled. But, as Haskell stated, the dancer is part of a complicated organism, and her personality and artistry must not be allowed to become the sole *raison d'être* of ballet.

Diaghilev, no doubt hurt that she had left him, thundered, "Pavlova was never really interested in art as such. The only thing that mattered to her was virtuosity," and he added, giving the devil his due, "and she is a virtuoso without equal." But Pavlova realized the unbridgable rift between them when she would ask the critics, "Are you on my side or Diaghilev's?" and she replied to his accusation in her autobiographical sketch by saying: "I was essentially a lyric dancer . . . never was interested in purposeless virtuosity."

It was not virtuosity which made her unique. The spectator could identify himself with her, could completely surrender, or was forced into it by a purely kinetic as well as emotional response. No artist can project so intensely if he is not intense and able to relive an experience which need not necessarily be the result of having actually gone through it. But mostly it is. Her great portrayals were symbols of grief, of renunciation, and of triumph only in a figurative way. She had died many deaths. When she died as a swan or a flower, the entire beauty of life seemed to die with her at that very moment. "One suspects," said Marianne Moore, "that she so intently thought the illusion she wished to create, that it made her illusive."

Her heart was always on fire. Victor Dandré told us how she would admonish the dancers in her company to express their own experience on the stage. "Why do you go about expressing nothing?" she used to say to them, "Cry when you want to cry and laugh when you want to laugh." But, of course, she knew it was not the actual crying or laughing that was needed. It was the recaptured and activated memory of it, the poetic allusion to the inner experience.

The question of what it was that made her so exceptionally wonderful has often been asked, and just as often have the experts tried to find an answer. Anatole Chujoy said succinctly, "she was great because she was Pavlova," and Cyril Beaumont thought that "it was not so much what she did, as how she did it." All of them, however, agreed that the painter-critic Alexandre Benois hit upon the happiest phrase when he wrote of Pavlova's dance, "la danse de toujours, dansée comme jamais." But when the ordinary dance was done as never before, what means were employed? If the "how-she-did-it" overshadowed whatever she did, no one could actually lift the veil from her secret. Even such an articulate critic as Carl van Vechten resigned himself to the statement (while reviewing her *Giselle* in the New York *Times*): "It is almost impossible to describe the poetry of her dancing."

But, at least, he seemed to have found the key word: *Poetry*.

It is the romantic at heart who loves Nature in a very subjective way. He is not willing to see Nature the way she really is, not only her relentless rhythm, her omnipresent and majestic beauty, but also her cruel nakedness in the fight of each against each to the finish, the rampant power of the elements, her careless attitude towards the individual flower. The romantic sees Nature through a poetic prism; he spells her in letters of a literary translation; and he buries his own dreams in her lap while reaching for a rainbow.

Pavlova was such a romantic. Already as a child she would weave herself "a wreath of wild flowers" and would imagine herself "to be the Beauty asleep in her enchanted castle." She went on writing about her relationship to nature as a young girl: "I often would explore the woods close by the cottage. I enjoyed the mysterious aspects of the cloister-like alleys under the fir trees, all peopled with dancing butterflies."

When she wrote these lines for a French magazine in 1913—unfortunately, it remained a half-hearted attempt at putting down her memoirs—she was thirty-one years old and at the peak of her career. She was a mature woman then and as such we must see her recapturing the memory of her youth. Characteristically, this article was called "Vers un Rêve d'Art," since her entire life was attuned to a dream of divine art with herself as the high priestess. True to the romantic, there is a guileless simplicity in the telling of her story or, as André Oliveroff said, " certain child-likeness that was very characteristic of her speech."

She wrote these pages of her life at her little dacha, the cottage in the country, "with the dimension of a doll's house . . . in the same setting which I love so dearly since it speaks to me of my childhood." She liked to dream herself back into childhood, the romantic's escape into the past. And only one in whom the sentiments play a major part would write, "The wind rustles through the branches of the fir trees in the forest which lies opposite my veranda—the forest through which, as a child, I loved to walk.

The stars shine through the gloom of the early evening." It was a loosely connected description before summing up her account, since the next sentence reads: "I have come to the end of these few recollections." This insert, an abrupt transition at that point, makes us actually see her putting down her pen and looking half-searchingly into the woods where once a child had dreamed of happiness and thought to find it in success.

At such moments, as at many others, nature was a décor—a stage set for her own hopes and disappointments. Nature lent herself so easily to the reflection of her ego, a fact that became particularly obvious when she, who was identified with *The Dying Swan,* kept swans in her pond at Ivy House in London which she made her home. Of course, her strongly literary approach to nature found its expression on the stage, too, where she could be seen dancing in such favorite parts as: The Snowflake, The Dragonfly, The Butterfly, or Fleur de Lys.

There must, however, have been more to her relationship with nature. Where her feelings were involved, she knew no half-heartedness. She was not only a romantic, she was—as we know from her stage presentations—able to relive the tragedy of reality as well as the reality of tragedy. She must have been in harmony with nature, must have found a sense of security in the rhythm of the seasons, in the feeling of nature's universality and timelessness. Eternity and herself—there was something, she must have felt, that was akin to her own aspirations of greatness, something with which she could identify herself. Art in the sublime, the creative pulse beat of Eternity, and there was she, Anna Pavlova, ever ready to sacrifice everything and everyone for the creation of sublime art.

On the other hand, she realized that her choreographic creativity was limited, and as every great artist she sensed her limitations. She did not feel the daring drive for the intellectual adventure, and if she did, she also knew only too well that creativity entailed failure and that was one word she had erased from her dictionary. All she wanted was to be the first in class, and no one will dispute that she was. She knew by heart what she was taught and could recite it with inimitable brilliance. She found it unnecessary to add to the dance vocabulary she knew.

With the exception of a few divertissements and one ballet (if we neglect her hesitant excursion into the literary field with a few pages of her life and into sculpture with a few statuettes of her dancing likeness), we have no proof of her creative ability, though a great many critics maintained that she was able to wipe out the difference between "creative" and "interpretative" art when she danced by making her interpretation as personal as if it had been her own creation.

There is one we know. It is a "choreographic poem" in one act called *Autumn Leaves,* which she created in 1918 and first produced in Rio de Janeiro. It calls that sentence to mind, standing so lonesome, without context, at the end of her memoirs, as lonesome as only a Russian can feel and as Pavlova must often have felt. "The stars shine through the gloom of the early evening." Dusk falling over the landscape of her life, the wind rustling through the autumn leaves, a sweet melancholy permeating her entire being. 'Happiness, where are you?' she must have heard that cry inside of her a hundred times. Out of it came this choreographic poem:

A beautiful chrysanthemum is seen in a park, when a wild autumn wind sweeps through it, whirling around the fallen leaves and uprooting the chrysanthemum;

A poet strolling around in the park picks the flower up and indubitably enjoys its looks and fragrance.

But the wicked wind returns and dashes the flower from his hand. More careful this time, he carries her (the flower) to a fountain, puts her on the soft cushion of moss and readies himself to read. But the wind had its eyes on the poor flower, grabs her again and whirls her about among a lot of leaves, until the flower is left lying in the last rays of the setting sun, out of breath which is about to escape for ever. The poet tries to revive her, but in vain. The poet's fiancée with whom he had a rendezvous in the park comes to meet him. He leaves the flower and, life being what it is, departs with her.

"Pavlova had a special affection for this ballet," wrote Cyril Beaumont, "and took particular pains to ensure that a high standard of performance was maintained. . . . The ballet was a charming conception in which Pavlova gave a fine performance as the Chrysanthemum."

She could best conceive herself in terms of nature and nature in poetic terms. The season most close to her heart was the fall. In this ballet she tried to create the inevitability of "Alles Vergaengliche," but also epitomized her resentment against always being rejected in the final analysis. For the poet's tenderness is only caused by a fleeting feeling for the flower's beauty, for its fading fragrance, perhaps by not more than pity for the doomed. The moment when reality's cue makes his betrothed appear, the flower is forgotten.

When André Oliveroff quoted her as saying, "You must dance your love, you must spiritualize it, you must turn it into grace and beauty of movement and line. . . . In the end, that is the only way for any artist to love, who would be great. And that is the only love that endures, the only love that never changes!" then we realize that she had expressed this same sentiment in her choreographic poem *Autumn Leaves.*

No one who knew her would contest that she radiated

warmth and kindness (she established a home for Russian refugee children in Paris, she herself would pay the salaries for her company whenever on one of her far-flung tours they were suddenly stranded); but she remained "curiously aloof" towards everyone, as only a person would who was afraid of being hurt again. Had she—who, as a little girl, felt the biting cold of isolation and shortly after came to fear poverty and insecurity—had she ever found love, was she ever able to share, to surrender her ego? "To be a great artist, you must have loved, you must know all about love . . . you must suffer with love. But—listen to me, *galupshik* —you must learn to do without it!" she said to Oliveroff.

Had she learned to do without it? Did she go through such experience, "suffer with love," and then decide to have none of it? Or was it only a secondhand experience, well intellectualized, to prove herself right for channeling all her feelings into her ambition which may have worked so comfortably as defense against any emotional involvement?

In 1913 she wrote: "People ask me why I do not marry. The answer is very simple. I believe that a true artist must sacrifice herself to her art—absolutely. . . . She has no right to demand of life the quiet joys of the fireside, which lie in store for other women." A year later she married Victor Dandré, her senior by 12 years. He was a shrewd businessman, a capable manager whom she needed on her side. He was a mining engineer when she met him in St. Petersburg. She had to have a reliable person to act as liaison with the impresarios, the press, the world at large, which she set out to conquer. There he was, unassuming, correct, and efficient. "He was first and last a good businessman," Oliveroff said, "and he had a consuming admiration for Madame, an unswerving faith in her career. . . . I do not know at precisely what point Dandré and she cast their lots together. . . . I believe their marriage was first announced in Boston—as a publicity stunt or, possibly, to reassure the Watch and Ward Society."

She felt that art was the only love that endures, that never changes; it would never be able to hurt her if she only worked relentlessly, unflinchingly and gave it all there was in her. No one could contest that art returned her love with growing passion and undying devotion, growing even beyond her grave.

By putting her fortune backed by her entire being on one card, consistently from her tenth year on, she had to win. The amount she won was, of course, due to her great gift and a few imponderabilities along her way which always throw their weight so decisively on the scale of those people whose character does not defeat their genius. When it can be said that every century has its Napoleon, but not every Napoleon his century, it has become obvious that Pavlova was ready for her time and the time ready for her.

Beside all this, however, she would have been a great ballerina at any time—though perhaps she might not have become the legendary dancer she now is—because she found the solution to the one decisive problem which every artist faces, a solution which varies with each but, basically, remains the same: It was said there was

something novel in my dancing. Yet what I had done was merely to subordinate its physical elements to a psychological concept: over the matter-of-fact aspects of dancing—that is, dancing *per se*—I have attempted to throw a spiritual veil of poetry.

Anna Pavlova will remain the shibboleth whispered from one generation of dancers to the next. If any young girl should dream of becoming a "second Pavlova," she should remember that Pavlova only became what she was because she did not want to be a second Taglioni; she should remember that, at best, she can only become herself, but her very best self, as Pavlova proved it. And, after all, nobody can beat a legend.

The magic of Ruth St. Denis

Her face crowned with white hair bore the immaculate imprint of its past beauty. She would immediately have interjected in self-irony that this was only made possible with the help of the scientific craft of modern beauticians. But, even then, the craftiest beautician's art, conniving with chemicals and nature, could not delete the story of eight decades and several years if it were not for that burning light in her eyes. These eyes seemed to command the attention of the angels; and, unwillingly called upon to witness this communication, the audience was fascinated by this woman who knew not of the triumph of defeat, who denied death his due, as she stood there on the platform delivering her message.

"Freedom, freedom! Everyone shouts it into his neighbor's face, and it has as many meanings as lips that say it, as many colors as eyes can see it." Ruth St. Denis had raised her arms, and the broad sleeves of her white gown which gave her the appearance of a priestess, opened up like wings. Now she lifted her head towards the heavens:

But who is aware of the core of its reality which is obedience to the only law, the law eternal, the law of life against death, of truth against lies, of order and harmony against disorder and disharmony, of beauty against ugliness? Where are the mighty prophets of our time to whip the double-dealers out of our temple, those fiends of mankind who pile up the dark heap of human mockeries, who try to sell your soul

and mine to the first best bigoted bidder, who, in turn, will re-sell
your soul and mine down the river?

Did Ruth St. Denis speak about the sacred dance? About a
new ballet pageant she was planning in the near future, massive
as the Rocky Mountains, gigantic as her belief in America? Or
was she campaigning for her pet idea of an art colony where the
artist can live, be himself, and sell what he creates to be independent from the competitive craziness of a money-mad world? (I
heard her mention that one day she'd go to the governor of New
Jersey and say to him: "Mr. Governor, I've grown up on a New
Jersey farm. I can still see myself as a little girl standing on a hill
behind our old farm house, lifting my arms in an unconscious gesture of oneness towards the magic glory of the moon. I was listening to the whisper of a faint breeze as it gently swayed the tips of
the tall pines. And so I began to move as a tiny part of the mighty
cosmic rhythm with a motion of complete joy, as a free being in a
world of infinite depth and beauty. I know, Mr. Governor, you
haven't got the time to be much concerned with beauty and the
artist who makes life beautiful. But once you must have stood on
a hill and looked up at the mystery of the moon and down at the
land you govern. You must have felt a tingling, titillating sensation, something giving you a feeling of wings. Governor, I want
to give you a feeling of wings forever. Keeping the crooks in jail
and the politicians out of it, building roads and schools is not
enough to make you immortal. All the governors have done so
from California and Nebraska to Maine and Florida for many a
decade. But a New Jersey farm girl gives you the chance of your
life. Be big enough to give her a few thousand acres of land for
people like her who need the beauty of freedom to give freedom
its beauty!')
Ruth St. Denis was a traveling saleswoman of beauty all her

life. With the Bible in her head and a philosophy in her heart, she roamed the country in one-night stands and beleaguered the world in a one-life fight to see holiness in the wholeness of body and soul. The long-fostered ecclesiastic idea of the eternal conflict between the goodness of the soul and the supposed badness of the body has led to an appalling awareness of our potentialities. She believed man cannot endure permanently half soul and half body. "I yield to no one in my admiration for the character of St. Paul," she said, "but I have ever profoundly disagreed with his attitude of spirit versus the life of the senses. His doctrines, spread over the Western World, have led to such a contempt for the body and its functions that we have a divided and disintegrating consciousness regarding our total personalities."

To be total, to be whole is to live in faith with understanding, in tradition with progress. She was just as far from denying the necessities of life as she was not willing to concede an inch of her principles. "Unless we are willing to do what we preach, we will not be believed nor obeyed," she said. Standing there on a platform, feeling how the audience was with her, she was apt to preach about the great mission of the dancer to better mankind, about the highest function of the dance as ennobling man's concept of himself, or about the wisdom of the world that has never been caught in the meshes of man's pettiness, however tightly knotted they may be—and then, almost in one breath, she could turn around and sell a rug for exercises ("It comes in all kinds of attractive colors"), an illustrated booklet, and the idea that anyone's duty towards himself is to keep his body rustfree. Ruth St. Denis could do both, could combine the sublime and the plain matter-of-fact as, to her, all roads were good roads that led to truth and the totality of body and soul. It seems that her translation of "mens sana in corpore sano" was "a flexible body will keep your soul cleaner." You cannot let your body rust, nor your mind rest. The rug and the booklet describing the exercises and the photos showing how she did them, the splits and headstands at the age of eighty and odd years, were packaged and to be had as "Vita Nuova." New life.

For her, the new life began at the doorstep of each day. The adventure of living, however, remained only half fulfilled without the pauses that accentuate the living. Only through those moments of meditation, feeding, replenishing his world within, can the artist (or anyone for that matter) bring self-realization to its highest point of expression. Only then can the dance become symbol and language for the communication of spiritual truths.

The spiritual truth begins with man himself. He will continue to disintegrate, she admonished us, as long as he takes from without instead of giving from within. This was the key to her Cathedral of the Future in which one day, she hoped, her dream of the sacred dance might become reality. But this is the key to the growth of any creative mind, to any human being who wants to extend his mere existence into the realm of conscious living.

Her rhythmic choir, the free flow of lyric movements, the visualization of hymns and psalms, the devotional gesture, whatever its choreographic form may be, must be judged as the realization of an urge to praise God, to praise Him neither with prayer nor with song but with the limited and limitless instrument He gave us, our body. As the personal feeling, the honesty of our faith that goes into our prayers varies with each devotee, as the church organist playing Bach reaches every one of us in a different mood, we can accept or reject Ruth St. Denis's sacred dancing, but we cannot doubt her emotional honesty, her artistic integrity on whatever level it may seem to move. Her entire life was a one-woman's crusade against all darkness and ugliness, against disorder and disharmony.

"The artist of today is the prophet of tomorrow," she said,

and her arms moved up and up, the sleeves bared her arms which were now straight and strong, sparse in outline as columns of an early Gothic church. Suddenly her arms trembled almost imperceptibly and came slowly down. She made a few steps backwards as if pulled by an irresistible force.

"Ruth Dennis," she heard a voice calling her which, at her age, did not come too unexpected.

"No one less than David Belasco canonized me when he gave me a five-year contract at the turn of the century," she snapped back. "And no one can erase the Saint Denis any more. It has been shield and battle cry for too long."

"One day time can cease to be." It sounded like the echo of an echo.

"Rubbish, I say. Nobody knows my exact age, not even I am sure of it as there is no birth certificate to be found. But I was born all right, and you can say I started to live when I came across that cigarette poster which by now has become dance history. Yes, the Egyptian goddess Isis on that poster awoke the dream of a new dance in me. There was hardly anything I hadn't done before: From high kicks and rollovers to modeling and taking part in a six-day bicycle race at Madison Square Garden. Admitted, I couldn't help being in a show in toe slippers after having had a measly three ballet lessons. But that poster had the power of making me take another road. Or it just happened to make me aware of what I needed to do. It was there to shout: 'Ruthie, forget those innane things you are doing! There must be meaning to every step and turn. Reveal the spiritual powers through movements of the body, free, flowing, daring enough to set your feelings afire.' Stop those silly routines, stop, I said to myself, stop!"

"Stop!" It came back to her.

"There were weeks and months and even years in my life

when the magic of my moon was eclipsed, but it never stopped me to search within, to search without and to work. And no one can stop me now as no one could stop me then. I had to turn to the East with its rich tradition, its wonder-woven language symbols, to Oriental themes, for there—there your belief in God lives in movement, your soul dances on your skin. I began to tour Europe. It was in 1906. It lasted three years. With bare feet, a bare waist, but with glittering garments I conquered the Europeans for three years. What did it matter that the Oriental trappings captivated them and not my message? A beginning was made. A beginning to find myself. And in the process of it I found Ted Shawn. Together we went on searching for the ultimate in the immediate. We dared the gesture that led from now to then, from here to there. We toured and stopped in the smallest hamlets in the States, in the biggest cities overseas. Nothing could stop us."

"But time—" The voice sounded more determined, and Ruth St. Denis cut it short.

"So they say. They also say I've born a child. In revolt against me it began to live. They called it modern dance, the Grahams, Humphreys and Weidmans. As if not everything that comes were modern, and everything that is old-fashioned, and everything that lasts modern again. Yes, my children turned against me, and they did not know they had my blessings. As decade breaks away from decade, we must go on. Don't you see, I have no time. So much is still undone to be rebelled against one day again—"

"The time has come, Ruth Dennis!"

"Yes, it has indeed to do our exercises." With two, three movements her white gown came down, and there she stood in her practice clothes for all people to see how she does her daily exercises. "You're all bone, my good man, and you rattle and clatter in your clothes that it cries out to God for mercy. Now, take this rug—you know, they come in all kinds of colors and I sell them with this booklet almost at a bargain price if you consider how they will help you begin a new life at any age, vita nuova—now, down on your back and slowly up with your legs, with your torso until you can stand on your head as the yogas do—and don't despair if it isn't perfect today or tomorrow. It's only a beginning. A beginning that leads to the end. Did I say tomorrow: There is no rush. Just let me pray and meditate and make my plans for the next ten years or so."

Margaret Lloyd

At Pearl Lang's recital I saw her last. The night before, at Paul Taylor's. There at the aisle, not far from where I sat, I could see her little figure, almost leaning out of her seat, a bit fidgety, fighting with herself and the obstruction in front of her, trying to secure a full view, ready to see.

Then with the houselights being dimmed, her forefinger would whisk over her lips and she would clear her throat as if to remind herself that now, now the circle of creativity would unfold before her eyes, she would be permitted to enter the kingdom of the dancer's soul.

There she sat, pleasantly tense, intensely eager to catch every movement on stage, to retain each image, to follow the flight of imagination with hers, to embrace the dancer's fleeting presence.

Margaret Lloyd was a high-strung person. The fact is that she did react emotionally to any artistic presentation. On the tangent of her heart she was a poet. Art mattered with her. It was priesthood, not pastime (to speak with Cocteau), if something was bad, she felt personally insulted. If something was good, she relived it, participated in the artist's achievement as if she had been involved from its beginning. But in spite of her unique enthusiasm she never lost sight of the critical aspect. Her judgment was sincere and clear. She tried to understand the dancer's reason for doing what he did, to sense his motivations.

For her, the dance had the poetic power of a personal statement with universal meaning. "I've always wanted to meet you," she addressed me across the table when, one summer, we finally met in New London. "You aren't a frustrated dancer, nor am I. You approach a dance work from a purely aesthetic-literary viewpoint, and so do I." I agreed but said I was afraid people might disapprove of it or misunderstand it. "It doesn't really matter," she replied, "as long as we know what we're talking about." She had an independent mind and a strong will of her own.

She was frustrated, though. She had within her a thousand and one stories hidden. She wanted to write, she could feel how, one day, her characters and their fates would take shape on the empty white paper in her typewriter. "The joy of seeing something come alive," she told me over a cup of tea in her Boston home, "to come alive what hasn't been alive before! You know how very much I love to write about the dance. But it isn't all, it does not fully satisfy me. I want to do something that lives and is a part of me. I write many stories, but I haven't sold them yet. Perhaps they aren't good." The telephone rang. When she turned to me again, she said with a helpless gesture and resigned annoyance: "That people will never get it into their heads. I'm Mrs. Sloper and Miss Lloyd. Margaret Lloyd is a fictitious person, the writer!"

She wanted to write because art mattered with her. Perhaps, because she loved people. Because she wanted to understand them. Because she wanted to know what makes them tick. She could talk to people with the same sensitive intensity with which she could watch a performance. She loved to go to parties to get the vicarious feeling of being a part of the whole. But suddenly, like an impatient bored child, she could become disgusted. "I want to go home," I heard her once say on such an occasion. "These people have nothing better to do but to gab. But I have to write!" she added as an explanation.

She never wore a mask. She was always herself, utterly herself. Kind and impatient. Demanding and giving. As no one else, she could leave a dance recital in a daze, as if holding on to images she did not want to lose, as if trying to piece them together again, limb by limb, movement by movement. "Don't tell me now what you think about it!" and a moment later: "It was great, wasn't it? The kind of thing that gets under your skin and into your heart!"

Louis Horst*

On January 23 Louis Horst left us.

I have deliberately chosen the words *left us* because they mean more than one thing. Louis has left us with a heritage of American modern dance, for it was he who helped give life and shape to it. He has left us, too, the tremendous task and awesome responsibility of continuing where he left off. He was a living symbol to four generations of modern dancers, and he will remain a symbolic reality for those to come.

Louis, as he was known to all, liked to call himself a grammar-school boy. Yet he was proud to receive an honorary doctorate from Wayne State University in Michigan this past December. I saw him at his home in the East Sixties shortly after his

* From a lecture delivered at Columbia University early February 1964.

return from the railroad station. He showed me the gown he had worn and the citation which honored him. It read: "As musician, artistic advisor, teacher, editor, critic and author, Louis Horst has influenced immeasurably the careers of leading dancers who have set out on new paths of creativeness in this age-old art."

I looked at the citation and then at the newly proclaimed Dr. Horst: "You must go to bed immediately, Louis, you look tired."

"Yah," he said, "we had engine trouble. It was a bad trip. I'm pooped. It's almost noon, now, and Doris (Rudko) will be by for me soon. I've got a one o'clock class at the Neighborhood Playhouse. And you've got to finish the editorial. I want to take it to the printer."

Louis was stubborn. You could not easily make him change his mind. So I sat down in the cubbyhole of the apartment which served as the office of the *Dance Observer* (a small monthly magazine devoted to modern dance which Louis had kept in continuous publication for thirty years). A few weeks away, on January 12, Louis was going to celebrate his eightieth birthday. The typewriter keys plunked: "THIS IS A MONTH OF CELEBRATION." (We did not know it would become a month of mourning.) "The *Dance Observer* and Louis Horst are one. The editors wish to congratulate him for being thirty years young at the age of eighty."

Louis drove off with Doris to teach the student actors at the Neighborhood Playhouse. He could not, would not stop. He always had a heightened feeling of responsibility, as if he personally carried the modern dance on his shoulders. And, in some ways he did. He had taught for decades not only at the Playhouse, but at Bennington College (twelve summers), at Connecticut School of Dance (sixteen summers), Columbia Teachers College, at Mills, Barnard, Sarah Lawrence, The Juilliard School of Music, and the Martha Graham School. There is hardly a modern dancer in the country who has not gone through his classes of preclassic and modern dance forms and has not learned the ABC—that is, the ABA—of dance composition from him. All this, plus what remains in the minds and hearts of those thousands of students and scores of leading dancers, plus his two books, are among the things he has left us.

Not long ago Louis became very angry with one of his *Dance Observer* reviewers: "If you have to write an unfavorable review," he scolded, "I demand constructive criticism. We are here to keep the modern dance going." I asked Louis: "Can you tell me where it's going?" Louis shrugged: "When Petipa was called to Russia, when Diaghilev asked Fokine to choreograph for him, did they know where they were going? Did we know it in the late Twenties when we felt we had to find a new way of expressing ourselves? What difference does it make where the new dancer is going as long as he is going!"

In 1915, Ruth St. Denis engaged him as accompanist for a two-week tour with her company. They liked the way he played for them, and he liked to play for them. Two weeks turned into ten years of close collaboration. In the Twenties Louis encouraged some of the young dancers to break away from Denishawn to find their own personalities and to find what they wanted to dance about. He went with them. He was ready to compose for them, to play for them, to help them to their self-fulfillment. They went out into a wilderness that meant artistic freedom, or into a freedom which was an artistic wilderness. Louis had gone to Vienna for a while to study at the *Konservatorium*. There he saw what the German *Ausdruckstänzer* were doing: Laban, Wigman, Kreutzberg. He saw the artistic world in Europe up in experimental arms. He returned to the New World, ready to inspire, to guide, to help. He was determined to give the new dance the same freedom and originality that the other arts were enjoying. He was determined also to give it structure and discipline.

"The new dance does not depend on beautiful line, unearthly balance, or sexual titillation." His lectures have always been quotable. "The movement is abstracted to express, in aesthetic form, the drives, desires and reactions of alive human beings." Or: "An idea is touched upon in the briefest fashion, like an insect which lights briefly on a leaf before flying on to the next. It is suggestive."

Louis was much loved. He was also feared, usually because of his sarcasm. He could not tolerate phoniness. After a concert at the "Y" he said: "These kids take toilet-flushing for music and structureless immobility for dancing. To rebel, to be way out is fine. But they don't know how far they can go and still be with us!"

That was Louis. He blended acute sensitivity and aesthetic creativity with sound horse-sense and biting wit. "He was terrible today, you can't please him," said a young dance composer, leaving his composition class in New London. Next week she reported: "He made me rewrite it three times. Now I know I've got it right." While Louis asked for the artist's utter dedication, he also warned him not to take himself too seriously. Robert Sabin tells of a visit to the ballet. Louis watched a famous ballerina swooning through a performance and then asked with a gleam in his eye: "Don't you think she ever gets tired of playing the Grand Duke's mistress?"

What infuriated him most was to see a former student give a bad performance. Then he would say: "Did you see that? And she took my classes!" or, if he was satisfied, but not completely, he would say: "It's not enough to be good. I've always told them, a great work of art reveals itself through its mystery."

Somehow I think of Dylan Thomas's lines:

Do not go gentle into that good night,
Old age should burn and rave at close of day;
Rage, rage against the dying of the light.

Louis may well have raged before that hour after midnight on January 23 when he closed his eyes. Going from class to class, from deadline to deadline, he never tired of youth, of music, and of dance. He and we too are forever angered at the dying of the day.

Part two

DANCE
& PAINTERS

POETS OF
PALETTE & CHISEL

THE PAINTINGS of early man have a sculpturesque quality. The visual artist in the days of artistic awakening worked with limited objects which were in the main the body of humans and animals. The most intriguing facet to him was the body in movement. Long before the advent of history and civilization man was caught in the magic of rhythmic movement which he observed in nature and himself.

It has often been said that the dance is the mother of all arts, but one should add that there is ecstasy in all art, however toned down, and that the ecstatic expression began with the dance. The visual artist in ancient Greece glorified the human body which to him was a gift of the gods in ecstasy. The concept of the creation of the world by the gods in a dancing mood, well-established in Eastern religion, is also an underlying thought with the Greeks who saw in the human body the ultimate of the creative will.

The nude body in ecstasy also is a symbol of rebirth in many cultures. Throughout history the ecstatic movement of the body has been related to the resurrection motif, from the solemnization of fertility on the sarcophagi to Michelangelo's drawings of the *Resurrection*. The Bacchic ecstasy found endless variations in the hands of Greek artists and has reached our own age in the great decorative painting *Dance* by Henri Matisse. Although he maintained to have been unimpressed by Isadora Duncan, her ecstatic movement is unmistakable in Matisse's painting. Goya's *Dance of Men and Women* with castanets shows not only the grotesque intensity characteristic of his work but almost a furioso expression in the satyrlike movements of the men and in the maenadlike poses of the women.

There are probably as many reasons for a painter to be inspired by the dance as there are for a poet to write about dancing and dancers. But the painter, far more than the writer, is preoccupied with shape and movement of human forms, with color, light and shade which can give the body a feeling of living reality. As a matter of fact, it is strange that not more painters have devoted more of their time to the dance.

Before photography came into its own, we badly needed the painter's and engraver's interest in the dance. For every generation over three centuries we would have needed a Jacques Callot enamored with the dance scene. The tremendous scope of his work on *commedia dell'arte* scenes and figures with their extraordinary movements afforded us great insight into the clowning and gaucheries of these improvised theatrical spectacles.

Nicolas Lancret, known for his paintings of Maria Camargo, conveyed to posterity how much she had shortened her skirt, and Jean Honoré Fragonard's Portraits of Madeleine Guimard, which betray his personal involvement, brought this ballerina closer to us as a human being. What contrasting views offer us Breughel's peasant dancers and Watteau's playful Rococo scenes!

Edvard Munch used the dance as an allegory and emotional symbol when he created *The Dance of Life,* portraying three stages of woman: to the left, innocence waiting for life to unfold; at the center the knowing, experienced woman; to the right woman in an attitude of disillusioned resignation. Auguste Renoir knows no such introspection. When he painted his *Dance in the Country* or *Le Moulin de la Galette* in 1876, he was interested in seeing the effect of bright colors and sunlight on the moving crowd. His feeling for rhythm is vividly expressed, but this rhythm of carefree existence and joy of life is a rhythm related to dance only as the painter subjects the dance to his purposes. Georges Rouault, on the other hand, does not change his heavy wild strokes and emphasized outlines when he approaches dance and dancers. Of his *Clown and Dancer, Dancer Lacing Her Slipper, Bal Tabarin,* done at the beginning of the century, and his much later created *Russian Ballet,* not one has any of the expected grace associated with balletic art. Rouault, who, with anger and fury and slashing strokes of color, has always presented suffering man, also focused on the personality in his specific environment whenever he approached the dance. He remained true to himself with an un-Rouaultlike *sujet* as much as Paul Klee, whose artistic essence is akin to the floating lightness of the dance and whose *Square Dance* or *Group de Ballet* express the same lyric abandonment and innocence as any of his other paintings.

There are painters like Klee whose realization of their form and color dreams have an inherent quality of dancing ease. In this context one cannot help thinking of Botticelli. Aside from his well-known *Primavera,* his painting *The Birth of Venus* is characterized by graceful movements and melodious lines, with the windswept hair of Venus and the other floating figures creating the image of seaborn beauty, an image which was often re-created on stage in the spectacular masques and ballets of the seventeenth century. But, in this play of contrasts, there is also an awareness of movement in design and color scheme of a painter such as Van Gogh, whose roads, cypresses, and infuriated skies have the dramatic power of passionate movement, even though they know no dance except the all-embracing rhythm of nature.

Pablo Picasso was attracted to the dance long before he did sets, costumes, and curtains for Diaghilev's Ballets Russes. His conviction to remain true to himself ("Whenever I had something to say, I have said it in the manner in which I have felt it ought to be said") and to any style he felt like choosing ("I have a horror of copying myself") can also be seen in his different approaches to dance and dancers.

From a Toulouse-Lautrec-influenced ball scene in 1900 he moved through a "pointillist" technique in his *Dwarf Dancer* a year later and reached his Negro period in 1907. *Dancer,* painted at that time, shows the sculptural beauty of African masks in the oval face of the dancer. Increased emphasis on physical distortion is reflected in the *Negro Dancer* of the same year. During his realistic-classic phase towards the end of World War I he drew a few lovely dancing figures before he entered a period of sudden violence in the mid-Twenties, taking as a cue surrealist André Breton's dictum, "Beauty must be convulsive or cease to be." By then, Picasso had also gone through his marriage with ballerina Olga Koklova when he painted *The Three Dancers* with the expression of emotional distortion and agonizing tensions in the dancers' faces and gestures.

While this painting foreshadowed a radically new Picasso whose released energies would strike out in as many disturbing or calming realms of form as he has been able to think of, his other drawings of *Four Ballet Dancers* and *Three Dancers Resting,* done during the same year as *The Three Dancers,* are marked again by realistic classicism, by spontaneity and a contagious sweep of movement. No form is alien to Picasso because no picture is intellectually reasoned out by him in advance but created while forced upon the artist during the process of creation.

The list of painters and sculptors drawn to and inspired by the dance is endless. Before looking at two of them in greater detail, however, I must mention Edouard Manet, because it is very likely that his dance paintings have had some prompting influence on Edgar Degas to make him plunge into the world of ballet. Manet's fascination with the dance was far more incidental than was Degas's. *The Spanish Dancers* and *Lola de Valence* were painted in 1862 when Mariano Camprubi's company performed at the Paris Hippodrome in a ballet, *Flor de Sevilla*. Manet made sketches during the performance and then had the company pose in a studio. He achieved a casualness in the accidental grouping of his figures within an intricate compositional structure which became the essential features of Degas's dance pictures.

Degas and decadence

When Edgar Degas found his inspiration in ballet which became the great love of his life, the art of the theater dance had achieved a virtuosity with a touch of the sterile and stereotype. Unimaginative repetitions of well-known patterns and figures were created by uninspired minds. At that moment of its history ballet showed little more than glimpses of its past greatness, satisfying the aging balletomane. The exciting events, however, took place outside the Opéra in cabarets and dance halls where the spirit of the *fin de siècle* in its mood of gay despair was embodied in the cancan.

Degas saw no great dance personality on the stage of the Opéra. Even Mlle Fiocre, whom he painted in 1866 as she appeared in the ballet *La Source* (choreographed by Arthur Saint-Léon) was a poor facsimile of the great ballerinas of the mid-century. Degas saw only those little girls in their tutus who sweated behind their makeup to create the illusion of a dream world and of fake glamor. Degas ended one of his sonnets with the lines:

> In spite of your so common looking face,
> Move boldly—all you goddesses of grace!
> The Dance gave you an otherness of sheen.
> And you must know from your own stagebound view
> That paint and distance make you seem a queen.

Of his many drawings of dancers only four have names inscribed, and they are names of no consequence in the history of the ballet. In 1895 a group of Russian dancers performed at the Folies-Bergère, and Degas made several drawings and pastels of them. Erroneously, these dancers were often thought of being from the Ballets Russes, but, in 1909, when Diaghilev came to Paris Degas's poor eyesight no longer permitted him to do such work. No other identifiable dance scenes or ballerinas can be found in his works. When Rodin and other contemporaries of his became caught up by the enthusiasm that raged around Isadora Duncan and Loie Fuller, Degas refused to see the promise of the future. Moreover, in keeping away from the Bohemian life and the excitement in the Moulin Rouge, he kept himself apart from the currents of the time.

All his life Degas was a conservative recluse. He greatly valued the past. He read Virgil in the original as long as his eyesight permitted. He believed that an artist must educate his taste and cultivate his memory, that he must know the old masters as well as his craft. Degas admired classical grandeur and a nobility which he thought mankind had reduced to nineteenth-century ordinariness. He deeply felt what he said about the age of Louis XIV: "They were dirty perhaps, but they were distinguished; we are clean, but we are common."

Movement as such fascinated him. He saw in it the manifestation of life. Whether he surprised a nude washing or combing herself, whether he painted race horses or ballerinas, his was a clinical study, a burning obsession with movement. In addition, his concern with color, light, and space helped create what he demanded from a painting: "A certain mystery, vagueness, fantasy."

His popularity rests upon his many ballet scenes which by now have become cliché, the picture-postcard idealization of romantic ballet. "They call me the painter of dancers," he once said explaining his real interest in the dance. "They don't realize that for me the dance has been a pretext for painting pretty materials and delineating movement." When his interest began to turn to the ballet, the dance meant little more to him than the horse races he had previously used as subject matter. Gradually the ballet world captured him completely. He painted the ballerina as a contorted body. Over and over again we see the same stereotyped elements of an animal nature in these dancing creatures. The total impression of light, movement, and color captivates, not the dancer as a human being. In action the dancers seem like marionettes directed by unseen strings; when relaxed they seem to move like tired racehorses being led away to the stable.

His jockeys, too, were always nondescript, a part of the horses which he recorded with dedication. He depicted the jostling of the horses at the start, the last minute excitement before the signal, all the moments before and after the race, the fatigued horse, the fiery horse that awakes to the joy of battle. But there is no emotion for the incidents described. Essentially, the horse remained an object with four legs, bred and trained to run, an object of study for the painter of motion.

In the late 1860s Degas began to tire of doing historic pictures and racehorses. A few years before Manet painted his Spanish dancers, Degas became interested in theater painting.

Manet's dancing pictures may have influenced him to some extent, but the influence of Japanese art certainly led Degas to look for other *sujets*. His first important theater painting was *The Orchestra of the Paris Opéra* which he painted in 1868 as a group painting of musicians, using at the same time musical instruments as a decorative theme. In the background onstage we see the legs and tutus of four or five ballerinas. This foreshadows his interest in the ballet. A few years later, in 1872, he finished *The Dance Foyer at the Opéra, Rue le Peletier,* the first informal rehearsal picture, showing the ballet-master Moraine working with some dancers. Degas reveals a certain disdain for realism when his dancers, at a rehearsal or in a class, do not appear in practice clothes, but are in costume with sashes and bows. ("Even in front of nature one must compose," he said.)

What made him turn from the horse race to the ballet stage? Both offered the excitement of movement. But horse races took place in the open air and needed the frame of a landscape. Degas added the landscape in his studio to suit them to the various sporting subjects, and he wearied of them. Degas was a perfectionist who, in his later years, would look for his earlier paintings in the home of collectors to take them back to his studio to paint them over again. The perfectionist in Degas—"I have never done with the finishing off of my paintings and pastels," he wrote to his friend Henri Rouart in 1873 at the height of his creativity— became dissatisfied with his sporting pictures and blamed their weakness on the landscape.

In the movements, in the poses, and relaxed positions of the little ballerinas he discovered a replica of his horses; there he found again the flawless function of the limbs, the synchronized motion of groups. In the classroom, on the stage, in the wings, and more so in his own studio his master hand triumphed. When an American collector of his work once asked Degas why he did so many ballet pictures, he was supposed to have replied: "Because there, Madame, I find the combined movements of the Greeks."

We know little of Degas's relationship to women. He was an eccentric misanthrope. For hours, he could sit at a party without saying a word, but, when his ire was aroused, his wit would become sharp and caustic without mercy. His brilliant bon mots were often repeated on the Parisian boulevards and in the cafés. He bluntly admitted once that perhaps he treated "la femme too much as an animal." On another occasion, while speaking of his artistic approach to the female, he exclaimed: "I show them stripped of their coquetry, in the state of animals cleansing themselves." This remark obviously referred to sketches on the one theme, women at their toilet, of which he did innumerable variations, particularly at the end of his career.

His models did not have an easy time with him. He liked to draw two or three ballerinas at the same time, making parallelograms out of arms and legs which pointed in one direction. He looked for the postures which intimated movement. He treated the arms and legs of the dancers as though they were parts of marionettes and not the extremities of human beings. For him they were the tools which created motion. He made the dancers stand with one leg raised at the barre. He twisted their heads, made them crouch down to the ground, contort their bodies. The arrested movement was his favorite choice. He was merciless in his passion for his art. One of his maxims was: "Do it again and again, ten times, a hundred times. Nothing in art must seem to be an accident, not even movement."

Edmond de Goncourt tells us in his *Journals* about one of his visits to Degas:

The painter shows you his pictures, from time to time adding to his explanation by mimicking a choreographic development, by imitating, in the language of the dancers, one of their arabesques, and it is really very illuminating to see him, his arms curved, mixing the dancing master's aesthetics with the aesthetics of the painter.

To Degas the dancer remained a pretext for the design, or, as Paul Valéry said: "No matter how great his interest in dancers, he captures rather than seduces them. He defines them."

The not-so gay nineties

Toulouse-Lautrec adored Degas and, like him, was obsessed by the joy of movement. But unlike Degas—who was his senior by thirty years and outlived him by more than half a generation —Lautrec saw people as human beings, moving, dancing, gesturing, living, and caught them on paper or on canvas in their most expressive moments. Arthur Symons said of him: "He desires beauty with the rage of a lover; he hates ugliness with the hatred of a lover; and to him sex is the supreme beauty."

Although of an old aristocratic family, he felt at home in dance halls, cabarets, and brothels. His attitude towards the depravity surrounding him seems to have been a cynical acceptance. Moreover, he found the vigor to survive the drabness and dirt of poverty. Yvette Guilbert said of Henri Toulouse-Lautrec: "Imagine a big brown head like the Guignol Lyonnais, set on the body of a dwarf, a high-colored black-bearded face, thick oily skin, a nose that might garnish two faces."

La Goulue, *one of many lithographs and paintings by Henri de Tou-louse-Lautrec of this famed dancer. This lithograph, dated 1894, shows La Goulue partnered by Valentin de Désessé, nicknamed the Boneless.* Collection The Museum of Modern Art, New York. Gift of Abby Aldrich Rockefeller.

This dwarfed cripple became a giant of pencil and brush. He had the creative power of Daumier without the irate indignation of the reformer. He did not want to improve people or conditions, nor did he try to beautify life. He loved life and painted it the way he saw it. He was a part of the world which embodied the final decade of the last century, which created and stimulated the big bubble of laughter, carefree joy, the floating clouds of petticoats in smoke-filled dance halls; he was among those whose days were so short because the nights were all they lived for, those little people who had to attend to their businesses during the day and who, in the evening, became great dancers. Toulouse-Lautrec was a part of the world of these dancers, singers, actors, prostitutes, and clowns, and he preserved their faces for us and the atmosphere in which they lived.

The night life of cheap dance halls centered in the Élysée-Montmartre when Lautrec appeared on the scene in the already gay mid-Eighties. "Montmartre," Léon Daudet wrote at that time, "is a Paris within Paris, a city apart." Lautrec was fascinated by its music and misery, by its noisy dancing and gaiety. The anticipation on the men's faces, the charming smiles and provocative glances of the women under the tremor of the gaslight were magic to him. There the crippled man sat until early dawn and made his sketches.

The *quadrille réaliste,* a variation of the *chahut,* or cancan, was the most popular dance at that time. A kind of square dance usually done by two couples, it was performed with dramatic accents and faster than the cancan. The climax was a rivalry between the women to see who kick the highest and show the most. The female dancers outraged even Montmartre taste and a censor, who became only an object of ridicule, was appointed to guard the public morals.

Le Quadrille de la Chaise Louis XIII a l'Élysée-Montmartre, a Lautrec painting of that period, shows two women dancers kicking their right legs skyward from a cloud of raised skirts and petticoats. One of the women in this picture was the famous La Goulue whom Lautrec painted many times.

The quadrille became increasingly intricate, a virtuoso feat, edging out amateurs. The Élysée-Montmartre where this dance became famous lost appeal as the professionals took over. When the Moulin Rouge was opened, the best performers moved there, and with them, Lautrec, whose name and work is irrevocably associated with this dance hall. His posters and paintings helped establish the fame of the dancers and singers of the Moulin Rouge.

He not only painted dancers, but those he painted are known today only because of his interest in them. In one of his earlier paintings (1890), called *Au Moulin Rouge: La Danse,* we see Valentin de Désossé in a quadrille. All the dancers of that time and genre were nicknamed by their audiences or partners, and because of his incredible agility Valentin was called the Boneless. He had complete control of his body and could jump, turn, and twist without visible effort. He was also an inventive choreographer of complex steps and intricate figures for his quadrille and waltzes. But there was nothing romantic about him. Terribly tall and thin, with a sad-looking face, sunken eyes and almost no lips, which he always kept drawn in and down as if he were about to cry, and with a big lower jaw and drooping chin; he was, indeed, grotesque. But one forgot all this when he danced. He came from a respectable bourgeois family and made his living by running a little coffee house near the Halles Centrales. At night he turned dance performer.

La Goulue was his partner. Valentin discovered her, a sixteen-year-old laundress, and a year later she was a famous nightclub dancer, becoming one of the best-known dancers in the Paris of that time. Her enigmatic mixture of dancing goddess and fishwife attracted Lautrec, and he made fifteen or more portraits of her, with her partner and alone, dancing and in repose. The best description of La Goulue can be found in Yvette Guilbert's book, *La Chanson de Ma Vie:*

La Goulue, in black silk stockings, with one foot shod in black satin held in outstretched hand, made the sixty yards of lace on her petticoats swirl and showed her drawers, with a heart coquettishly embroidered right in the middle of her little behind, when she bowed her impertinent acknowledgments; knots of pink ribbon at her knees, an adorable froth of lace falling to her dainty ankles, now disclosed, now concealed her beautiful legs, nimble, adept, alluring. The dancer sent her partner's hat flying with a neat little kick, then executed a split, her body erect, her slim waist sheathed in a blouse of sky-blue satin, her black satin skirt spread like an umbrella five yards in circumference.

It was magnificent! La Goulue was pretty and attractive to look at, in a vulgar way—blonde, with a fringe of hair hanging over her forehead down to her eyebrows. Her chignon, piled high on top of her head like a helmet, sprang from a single strand tightly twisted at the nape of her neck, so that it would not fall down when she danced. From her temples the classic *rouflaquette* (a ringlet) dangling over her ears, and all the way from Paris to the Bowery in New York, via the dives of Whitechapel in London, every hussy adopted the same style of hairdressing and wore a similar colored ribbon round her neck.

But after a few years La Goulue lost her supple figure, her face became flabby and ugly. She was no longer dancing at the Moulin Rouge. She had to make her living by performing at suburban fairs. Indulging in food and drink, she grew more and more shapeless. Her life ended sadly. She became destitute, lost her mind and died, in 1929, alone and forgotten, a charity patient, at a Parisian hospital.

In the fall of 1892 the Folies-Bergère announced the debut of an American dancer: Loie Fuller. At thirteen, she had made her debut in public as a temperance lecturer, later becoming a minor actress. She discovered the startling visual effects created by light on moving drapery in a play in which she wore a voluminous skirt:

My robe was so long that I was continually stepping upon it, and mechanically I held it up with both hands and raised my arms aloft, all the while that I continued to flit around the stage like a winged spirit.

There was a sudden exclamation from the house: "It's a butterfly! A butterfly!" I turned on my steps, running from one end of the stage to the other, and a second exclamation followed: "It's an orchid!"

Her *Skirt Dance* was born, followed by the *Serpentine Dance*.

She went to France, and *La Belle Americaine,* as she was called, made the Folies-Bergère almost a temple of art as she became the idol of Paris. Light effects fascinated her, and she usually worked on stage with forty electricians. She even asked Madame Curie, who had just discovered radium, to help her make "butterfly wings of radium" as she knew radium emitted a pale ethereal light.

Loie Fuller had only a few dance lessons in her youth and she cannot be called a great dancer. But she is important for her discovery of a new aspect of the stage dance which was fully developed more than half a century later by Alwin Nikolais. She embodied her time in her search for the new and in her effort to crack the sterile and rigid dictatorship of ballet. Before Isadora Duncan freed the dance from ballet and Michel Fokine gave the theater dance a badly needed new face, Loie Fuller experimented with the artful manipulation of draperies in the new miracle of electric light. It was still a novelty on stage. Directors, electricians, and audiences became wildly enthusiastic over this new toy.

It meant more to Loie Fuller. She became an expert electrician. "I am the only person known as a dancer . . . who has a personal preference for science," she admitted in her book *Quinze ans de ma vie* (to which Anatole France wrote the preface). "It is the great scheme of my life. In Paris I have a laboratory where I employ six men. Every penny I earn goes to that. I do not save for my old age. I do not care what happens then. Everything goes to my laboratory."

Toulouse-Lautrec painted Loie Fuller several times in 1893, and his portrait of her in the *Dance of Fire* turned out to be one of his best lithographs, a whirling image of flames blurred by light smoke. This dance was particularly popular because of its enchanting light effects of flame and smoke directly from underneath the dancer, who performed on a pane of glass. Auguste Rodin, who loved Isadora Duncan, considered Loie Fuller a woman of genius.

Whatever one may think of her dancing, one must grant that "La Loie" was a unique experimental artist. She was as well a woman of great heart, not only devoted to her mother all her life but ready to help any artist in need. She helped a young American pianist-turned dancer, Maud Allan, when she was still quite unknown, and in 1902 she went out of her way to introduce Isadora Duncan to all the influential people she knew, particularly in Berlin and Vienna. She managed to further the cause of her rival in many ways and with surprising self-denial.

Isadora seemed to have retained a strong impression of Loie Fuller, the artist, and especially of the innovator of stage effects. She described these impressions in her autobiography, *My Life*, with the words:

Before our very eyes she turned to many-colored shining orchids, to a wavering flowing sea-flower and at length to a spiral-like lily, all magic of Merlin, the sorcery of light, color, flowing form. What an extraordinary genius. . . . She was one of the first original inspirations of light and changing color—she became light.

Lautrec was always enchanted with the subjects of his brush and pencil, and in the years between 1893 and 1896 his attention was focused on Marcelle Lender, an operetta star, famous for her dancing, acting, and decolleté wardrobe. During this period he made more representations of her in all media than of any other dancer. One of his most elaborate paintings is called: *Lender Dansant le Pas du Boléro dans Chilpéric,* Chilpéric being an operetta by Hervé. Lautrec came to see her in this role innumerable times, interested only in seeing her move, in observing her figure. Repeatedly he was supposed to have exclaimed: "I come only to see Lender's back! Look at it, you will hardly see anything so wonderful again!" A great many of his sketches of her concentrated on her back and its gentle play of muscles.

He was intrigued also by the airy grace and pale delicacy of Jane Avril, who it was said had "the beauty of a fallen angel." Of course, she was far from being an angel. However, Jane Avril in contrast to La Goulue, whose sensuality and lack of refinement were clear in feature and gesture (Lautrec did not try to conceal anything of her coarseness in his portraits of her), was the ideal image of a dancer: she gave a feeling of floating lightness. In life as on the dance floor her gentleness and innate grace distinguished her from her colleagues.

Jane Avril's youth was one of uninterrupted neglect and misery which she escaped by running away from home. When she arrived in Paris, a penniless girl of seventeen, she became friendly with a medical student, who took her to the Bal Bullier, one of the gay nightspots in the Latin Quarter. Carried away by the music and almost in a trance, she began to dance by herself, inventing steps and movements, having never been taught any. That night decided her future: she wanted to be a dancer. She was gifted with a fine sense of rhythm and natural grace and continued to improvise throughout her career, but never received any formal training.

She not only danced her improvised solos, mostly waltzes, or joined her famous colleagues in a quadrille but became a star in the legitimate theater. She appeared as Anitra in Ibsen's *Peer Gynt,* dancing to Grieg's music and was also seen in musical comedies such as the world success *La Belle de New York.* In the ballet *L'Arc-en-Ciel* at the Folies-Bergère she danced the part of Pierrot with inimitable delicacy.

For a dancer of her background and time she was an unusual character. She tried to make up for her poor education by reading as much as she could, and her wit, her good taste and tact helped her over many a gap in her knowledge. Among her best friends were writers, painters, and composers with whom she seriously discussed their problems, and she was often present at the literary get-togethers at the Chat-Noir.

Jane Avril stood at the peak of her fame—she was not more than in her middle thirties—when she took voluntary leave from all the splendor and excitement which was part of such a dancing career. At that time she decided to marry one of her admirers who came from a rich bourgeois family and offered her a suburban home, security and the adoption of her son. Before long, her son left and never got in touch with her again. Her husband died in World War I, her income dwindled to almost nothing, and she took refuge in a home for the aged.

She lived with her memories the last four decades of her life and published them in Paris-Midi in 1933. In it she paid tribute to Lautrec: "It is undoubtedly to him that I owe the celebrity I have enjoyed, which dates from the appearance of his first poster of me." But Lautrec, too, had paid his tribute to Jane Avril by not only drawing her portrait for the Moulin Rouge and Jardin de Paris, but also by using her as a model for many more paintings and lithographs not concerned with the dance. She was his last model for a poster which was never used. Shortly afterwards, in February 1899, Toulouse-Lautrec suffered the severe breakdown from which he never recovered.

Movement in stone

Dance is sculpture in movement. The human body, sole instrument of the dancer, is an eternal theme of the sculptor. His work, like that of the dancer, exists in the three dimensions of space, defined by light and by its own inherent movement.

Both dancer and sculptor attempt to create the illusion of movement rather than movement itself, the essence of an idea; to capture a mood, a feeling, a thought within limited but well-arranged forms and designs; to catch the inexpressible, a fleeting impression of life in a gesture, in a pose, in the rhythm of motion.

Sculpture is the plastic fulfillment of one great moment out of many; it lacks the flowing grace of the dance, its constant change in uninterrupted continuity. On the other hand, the dance—though it has the advantage of moving in time—is wedded to the instant of its execution and can only be retained by our memory, sometimes supported by the eye of the camera. Sculpture, however, keeps the one chosen moment imprisoned in imperishable stone.

We expect from plastic balance and flow an aesthetic pleasure similar to the one felt when the human body floats through the air. The feeling of solid immobility disappears when the intensity of inner expression and the harmony of an apparently frozen line give the impression that only magic could have halted all motion and that, in utmost concentration, this motion is reduced to its final artistic formula.

Man has lost the sense of movement to a great extent and does not easily perceive the struggle with space and within space which takes place in solid forms. We are too much inclined to see everything only from the outside, since we cannot quickly enough visualize ourselves as the center of form and space. It is therefore difficult for us to recognize movement in the static, quiescent figure. We see the tree. But are we conscious of its constant growth, minute by minute, its inner drive to reach out within space for its own limits? There is tension, well controlled, in everything that seems immobile; there is an arrested impulse in it to move.

This apparently contradictory idea of "movement in repose" which sculpture actually represents, and represents in so many variations through the centuries and all cultures, seems to be most expressive in Eastern art. Though the movements and gestures of the East are far more formal and stylized than those of Western man, grace and lightness are inherent in most of their figures, a tacit gesture conveying the idea that the body is only the visible form underneath which dances its soul. It is grace infused with a seemingly profound spirituality. It is the inimitable lightness closest to a spin or leap in the classical dance. In the East the dance is basic to the concept of the gods, of the creation of the world and man's existence. Painting and particularly Eastern sculpture are essentially motivated by movement and the dance.

Western man's sculpture is different in conception and approach; less stylized and more human, more earthbound. One can feel how the artist wrested the human body from stone and marble. Lifelikeness, style, the laws of beauty and harmony may have varied in the course of time, but man's desire to create his images in plastic form has remained.

In the very beginning sculpture had something rigid and

helpless about it, even though the archaic sculptor was already fond of movement. These early figures are most often represented in groups, moving in a circle. Having learned to see through the eyes of such contemporaries as Henry Moore, we have come to recognize many modern aspects, including the nonnaturalistic, symbolic form, in these archaic figures. Their incompletion in no way detracts from their intensity of expression. "A work of art," Baudelaire said, "need not be finished to be complete, and a work, though finished, is not necessarily complete."

We find surprising realism in early Egyptian sculptures, but it was left to the ancient Greeks to discover the way to nature and harmony. This sculpture is more than innate movement, it gives our eyes not only the inner vision of a maiden, imbued with joy, ready to meet and to embrace the world but also, as Rainer Maria Rilke says, "an eternal picture of Hellenic wind in all its sweep and splendor."

Isadora Duncan was struck by the simplicity of these movements. "When I dance barefoot on the ground," she said in *The Dance of the Future*, "then I am compelled to use the Greek pose, for Greek poses are nothing but the most natural in the world."

The ancient Greeks had an unrestrained affinity to the human body. Mimetic, gymnastic, and expressive movement of the body was the primary inspiration for the Greek sculptor. The Dionysian motives influenced him to create poses and movements which suggested physical abandonment which, in turn, expressed spiritual liberation. The channels between body and mind were open, flowing into one another, feeding each other with their energies released. There is joy of life and vitality expressed by every gesture of Skopas's *Maenad* or in earlier friezes and reliefs portraying fighting or dancing warriors. The rhythm of movement is always that of the dance. ("Those who pay homage to the gods by dance, in battle are the first to hurl the lance," Socrates said.) Certain rhythms of movement, as caught by the Greek sculptors, had stylized and legible meaning: vigor and determination, for instance, were shown through a figure striding forward, one leg bent while the other forms a straight line with the figure's back.

The Greeks also knew how to choose the one right moment just before the dramatic climax, the moment in which all the preceding and following events are focused. We can hardly imagine a greater drama, expressed through movement in stone, than the group of *Laocoön* and his sons. The drama in this group moves on two different levels. On the one, it is the pure play of muscles on trunks, arms and legs, muscles wrestling with gigantic snakes which the Olympian gods, in their unjustified cruelty, sent from the sea to punish the priest and his sons for having spoken the truth. It is more, however, than the mere physical aspect of pain and the vain effort of the three men to free themselves as we see them struggle, man against beast, a dynamic drama of bodies. There is the higher level on which their silent suffering grows out of the movement itself. The movement alone—arrested at a point where the realization of defeat and death seems inevitable —pictures all human limitation through their inability to understand how right can be wronged, how the gods can approve such horror for the innocent. In this movement, not alien to expressive dance, human despair found its classical expression.

The Gothic gesture is born of a different temperament and cultural climate. The undulating line of harmony, the rounded-off beauty is missing. There is a Martha-Graham-like terseness and tension, the groping, hesitant gesture, the angularity of movement. The self-restrained, elongated expression of Gothic art satisfied the religious and emotional feelings of the Middle Ages just as the revitalized Greek form of the Renaissance was indicative of the reawakened joy of life in the fifteenth and sixteenth centuries. Even religion was humanized; angels could be full of inner vitality and dramatic force. The beauty of the human body was revered again, and the mysterious strength of life lived in its forms and movements, especially through the towering genius of Michelangelo. The famous Mercury of Giovanni Bologna has a ballet-like sweep of movement which gave Carlo Blasis the inspiration for the position of the *attitude*.

Flamboyant Baroque, the seventeenth and even more so the eighteenth century, no longer celebrated the beauty of the body as such: the pathos of passion was forced into a tight corset, it moved in dignified small steps to the music of the minuet. But more than ever were the painters and sculptors of that period attracted by dance and movement. It was a gay and yet tired world, toying with itself, engaged in frivolous flirtations; the shepherds were again playing and dancing in the meadows; the pruned gardens had hidden pavilions with statuettes—Cupids and Venuses inviting the couples to rest in their suggestive shade. Claude-Michel Clodion, whose charming terra cottas could be seen in all Parisian salons, translated successfully in his group of Bacchantes the Dionysian joy of antiquity into the playfulness of his period.

Characteristic of the early eighteenth century with its feminine touch, later to be followed by a cult of the heroic, was the Meissen porcelain portraying groups in ecstatic or delicately sweet movements. Greek mythology in Baroque attire was *le dernier cri* of a dying world. It was through the eyes of romanticism that the nineteenth century saw mythology. Jean Baptiste Carpeaux' ecstatic dancers, who still stand before the Paris Opéra, are an example of its exuberance. The Victorians considered this daring, sensuous art. Rainer Maria Rilke said about this group that it was "merely an object of mockery until finally it became so accustomed a sight that it was passed unnoticed."

With the advent of our modern age, particularly since Auguste Rodin, the dynamic sense became predominant in the sculptor's work. It was no longer harmony nor natural expression that mattered. The sculptor became movement-conscious more than ever before.

George Balanchine, speaking of his method of creation, once said: "I approach a group of dancers on the stage like a sculptor who breathes life into his material, who gives it form and expression. I can feel them like clay in my hands."

The dancers, in the hands of this master of movement, begin then to feel the dormant power of their bodies and awake to the infinite possibilities of being in movement. In the sculptor's figures these infinite possibilities are limited by one form in space, they are concentrated in his static material, into which he "breathes life." His dynamic power has to come from within and has to be felt on every spot of the surface. Rilke, in his essay on Rodin says:

Rodin knew that, first of all, sculpture depended upon an infallible knowledge of the human body. Slowly, searchingly, he had approached the surface of this body from which now a hand stretched out toward him, and the form, the gesture of this hand contained the semblance of the force within the body. The farther he progressed on this remote road, the more chance remained behind, and one law led him to another. And ultimately it was this surface toward which his search was directed. It consisted of infinitely many movements. The play of light upon these surfaces made manifest that each of these movements was different and each significant. At this point they seemed to flow into one another; at that, to greet each other hesitatingly; at a third, to pass each other without recognition, like strangers. There were undulations without end. There was no point at which there was not life and movement.

Movement meant life to Auguste Rodin, as exemplified in his bronze statue St. John, the Baptist Preaching (1878).
Collection The Museum of Modern Art, New York. Mrs. Simon Guggenheim Fund.

Rodin realized more than anyone else that life is continuous motion, that Nature knows no rest, that even death and decay merely represent a stage of transition. He was aware that "the artist sees a great conscience like his own throughout Nature. There is no living organism, no inert object, no cloud in the sky, not a touch of verdure in the meadow which does not confide to him the secret of an immense power hidden in all things."

All great sculpture contains this secret of "immense power," of intrinsic movement that may seem to reach out into the infinite or come from far distances, but the vitality conveyed lies within the stone. When Rodin worked with a model, he never arranged for a frozen pose; he had the model walk and move and would suddenly stop him in a certain position when he thought it merited closer study. The quiddity of the problem remained for him how to capture the lifelike progression of movement within a static moment.

The photograph of a moving body—though a true mechanical reproduction of a single moment within a series of movements—shows the oddity of a petrified pose, a human utterly paralyzed in mid-air. What photography has done here is to violate life. In reality time has no stop; the eye that sees a body moving, unconsciously absorbs the transition from one position to the next, and in this transition lies the secret of the sculptor's work. Rodin's figures retain the two attitudes which flow into each other and thus produce the impression of movement. Art which roots in nature can only be true to it when it rises above it, when it does not copy nature, but gives us its inner truth.

"An artist," Rodin said, "should express . . . the inner truth. When a good sculptor models a torso, he not only represents the muscles, but the life which animates them—more than the life, the force that fashioned them and communicated to them, it may be grace or strength, or amorous charm, or indomitable will."

Rodin is a good example for a sculptor with a strong theatrical sense who, standing on the threshold of our modern age, combines the classical conception with the expression of the twentieth century. To him, movement meant life; his was an uninterrupted search for the new gesture, the only right gesture expressing the inner drama of man.

In the Sistine frescoes, his most complete work, Michelangelo shows us Adam awakened to life at the touch of God. He saw the climactic moment of this episode in man's awakening. But Rodin takes the act of creation for granted. His Adam just rises from the dust, lifts himself up from the soil from which he was fashioned, his head still painfully pressed against his left shoulder. His muscles stretch, he begins to feel his own body, the power of his being. But frightful aloneness is around him, and the inner truth Rodin has created here is the traumatic terror of man's awakening as man, the prelude to his lifelong drama.

In the high relief of his *Tempest* his sense of the theatrical in even more abstract topics is evident. The head and shoulders of a screaming woman—with streaming hair, her mouth agape, her wide-open eyes hypnotically terrifying—seem to tear themselves away from the marble. The impact of this relief is a feeling of helplessness, but also of inevitability. It is not so much the face as it is the apparent movement of breaking loose which gives this female head the power of personified fury.

St. John, the Baptist is Rodin's first work of a walking figure. This is no longer a position, it is the walk of someone who measures the distances, whose message does not let him rest, the message which lies in his right arm stretched forth in order to give, to spread the truth. His beckoning gesture makes us feel that this man is not walking alone, that he knows he is followed by people who want to measure wide distances with him. It is an ascetic body, tested and tried, used to endure. We can see that this man has no thought left for gnawing hunger, for the glowing heat of the desert to which his body is exposed. He is obsessed by his divine mission, and the burden of his bones, the fear of his flesh seems totally excluded from his awareness.

Herein lies the mystery of Rodin's creations: in his conception of the soul in man, in the interrelation between the spirit and body. His burghers of Calais—and each of them in his own way—are captured by the spirit of their great task leading to immortality, their dragging bodies bearing their martyrdom with silent cries. And, there can be no stronger triumph of man's mental capacity, of his higher aspirations through meditation than is exemplified through the position of *The Thinker,* through the contrast of his sensitive intellectual head forced upon a body of massive strength. In the thinker's endeavor to grasp the abstract, to penetrate the absolute, this head, in utter repose, bends, crushes, and conquers the athletic body on which it rests. There is no transition between two positions to give this figure its life and the pulsebeat of movement. The transition lies in the contrasting power between body and soul, in the drama of the two great forces in man, brought to the surface. Let us look, as well, at the one step his giant Balzac takes: the one step of the haunted genius who cannot stop, who must march on from page to page, from character to character, from idea to idea, the genius whose bloated body must take the punishment of sleepless nights, of restless days. Into this one step Rodin forced the ultimate sense of a giant with a vision, the inner truth of his greatness.

Rodin did not care whether his sculpture could be called beautiful. "Only that which has character is beautiful," he said. He could breathe life into stone and give character to this life which, at any moment, could awake, stone-turned-flesh. Even in stillness lay for him the "unrest of living things" and stillness "consisted of hundreds and hundreds of moments of motion that kept their equilibrium," as Rilke said. (Merce Cunningham and other dancers of the mid-century rediscovered for themselves stillness in movement and movement in stillness.)

Rodin studied the problems of space and the moving body in its relation to space. He was fully aware of the kinship of his art with that of dancers such as Isadora Duncan. He realized that, in essence, his task was to translate life into movement which is, after all, also the dancers' task. Their tools of work and expression differ, but their aim is the same.

Actual movement, consciously constructed as an organic and inherent part of a work of art, is nothing new. Kurt Schwitters and the artists of the Bauhaus flirted with kinetic art, then an outgrowth of cubism and a logical extension of the dadaist experiment. But neither in the mid-Twenties nor in the Thirties did this art gain momentum.

It was in the Sixties that kinetic sculpture made some progress. Inspired by the possibilities of a technological age, the artist reacted against the machine by borrowing its wits and making fun of a world in movement. In an age in which engineering feats surprise mankind with their imaginative beauty, the artist is tempted to join forces with the engineer.

Kinetic sculpture, with its precise and carefully controlled functionalism, was also a reaction to the time's veneration of spontaneity, chance, and accident as basis for artistic expression. Kinetic sculpture is no longer related to the beauty of man but to motor and mechanism. It tries to capture and imitate the heartbeat of the machine. The artist knows he arrived at a point to give new form to the old human truths, to the excitement that lies in man and movement.

The scene designer

The scenic design is the shell that houses the soul of the dance or of any theatrical performance for that matter. It is as essential for the straight play as it is for the dance, although the

Design for Rite of Spring. *Joan Junyer, Catalonian painter, created many designs for ballets and painted dancers and dance scenes. His designs stress the relation between performer and scenic environment, the integration of costume and movement.*

Photograph Susan Haller. Collection Gertrude and Walter Sorell.

word can more easily grow beyond its scenic confines than the dance. In its reliance on the human body, its movements and gestures, the dance is as suggestive as the design. Both speak the same aesthetic language of visualization. This makes it imperative that design and dance are carefully attuned to one another, are based on a oneness of purpose, and create a unified feeling of mutual inevitability.

The perfect design for a straight play is the poetic visualization in style, suggestiveness, and economy of the dramatist's dream and theme. Furthermore, it must serve functionally the stage director's interpretation of the play. Director and dramatist are usually one and the same person in the theatrical dance. This ought to narrow the possible margin for errors.

With the lighting effects gaining more and more prominence in our time, the scene designer will have to work very closely with the lighting designer and, in the most ideal case, will take over both functions.* A strictly realistic design for the dance is, more often than not, self-defeating. The elusive and illusive power that lies in the dance can best be served by the strongest components of suggestiveness. Many modern ballets, particularly in the field of the modern expressionistic dance, need few or no sets but primarily a good lighting plot. In the case of Alwin Nikolais's dance theater of motion, light, and sound, the use of lights, projections, props, and the moving body, inseparable from one another and from the sound, creates the impact of a total design.

Realistic stage designs seem to me inescapable in most classi-

---

* I strongly believe that lighting will become more important than the décors in the future development of the stage craft. I remember the first production of Arthur Miller's *The Crucible* taking place in a realistic setting, soon followed by another production, staged by the author, in which no setting at all was used, and the scenic version was far more impressive in its dramatic impact because the spectator's imagination was in no way confined by any visual image.

cal ballets and most appropriate in humorous works. Humor needs a very pointed, often satiric, exaggeration of reality, while the décors of a classical work demands poetic vision and a great feeling for style. However obvious it may seem, it must be underlined that unity of style is essential. A recent restaging of *The Sleeping Beauty* by the Royal Ballet had the prologue set in a Renaissance chamber, the second act in a medieval court yard, the third act in a fantastic canyon, and the last one in a strangely sumptuous tent. If a feeling of medievalism is intended, it is a mistake to approach it from the Victorian concept of medievalism. Similarly, how wrong would be the idea of recreating a Hellenistic stage image as seen with Winckelmann's baroque eyes!

A ballet like *Giselle,* of course, needs a realistic approach in the first act and quite a different one in its second act. The latter would need a daring setting with a fantastic, weird background to give the Wilis scene greater credibility. But, traditionally, we look at a misty clearing in the woods with the intimation of a lake upstage and a grave with a huge cross stage right. It would be interesting to deviate from the traditional *Giselle* designs in both acts and create a highly stylized décor—not for the sake of being different but to stress the drama of the first part and the feeling of other-worldliness in the second part. Since Théophile Gautier and his helpers concocted a contrasting world of realness and fancy shadows, the modern designer should let his imagination go on a rampage to lift the face of this classic. If there is a well-founded desire to give *Hamlet* and the scenic image of the play a new stage realization from time to time—even though the sensitivity of some traditionalists may be hurt—then I see no reason why some of the ballet classics should not be approached with a spirit of inner freedom. Some of the unnecessary pantomime may then also fall by the wayside.

Two facts should not be overlooked. Whenever the curtain

opens, it is the visual image of the stage set that hits our eyes first and creates the mood for the play to come. Style and color tonality give us more than an inkling of the ballet. In the theater all our senses are in a state of anxious anticipation. Our readiness and expectations are first confronted with the décor as if we were reading a prefatory page to a book.

Moreover, the demands of the audiences change constantly. Particularly after the cataclysmic experiences of the two world wars, the ballet audience has grown tremendously and, because of so much infusion of new blood and differently oriented eyes, taste has changed.* The inveterate balletomane may still be willing to accept everything as long as there is dancing, and dancing at its virtuoso best. Nowadays, however, we demand "a new theatricality and dramatic logic. . . . We are all more sophisticated in our demands," as Clive Barnes said.

The scene designer is an artist and as such cannot help being creative. In fact, we expect him to be creative. But he must not forget that he serves the ballet and the ideas of the choreographer which he ought to support and enhance, not overpower. He may be more imaginative than the choreographer is in his field, but, as no translator must ever prove to be a better writer than the creator of the original, the designer must not doom a ballet by imposing his genius on the entire production. He is called upon to be congenial, not genial. He must create some of the implements—as must the composer—to give total *Gestalt* to the visualization and theatricalization of an idea. Self-criticism and humility must then counteract the temptation to be "over-creative."

The ideal design for a ballet must be functional and, at the same time, poetically illusive. It must set the mood and extend

* Similar changes in taste occurred during the Renaissance and after the French Revolution when the aristocratic elite and the taste of the boxes made room for the bourgeoisie and the taste of the galleries.

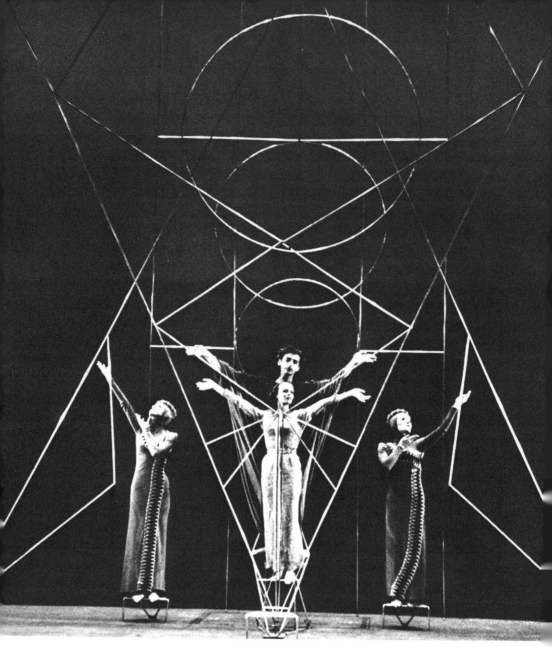

*One of the most theatrical and poetic stage sets in the American mod-
ern dance is Isamu Noguchi's design for Martha Graham's* Seraphic
Dialogue.

Photograph Martha Swope.

Henri Matisse is known for only two, but highly original, ballet designs which, like his costumes, display utmost simplicity and economy of means. He designed Le Chant du Rossignol *for the Ballets Russes in 1920 and* Rouge et Noir *for the Ballet Russe de Monte Carlo in 1939. The upper sketch, for the Curtain of* Le Chant du Rossignol, *reveals his almost self-effacing method of refinement.*

Courtesy Wadsworth Atheneum, Hartford.

Pablo Picasso designed décor and costumes for several Diaghilev ballets and later for Ballets des Champs-Elysées. The lower sketch, for the setting of Le Tricorne (The Three-Cornered Hat), *was done in 1919.*

Courtesy Wadsworth Atheneum, Hartford.

the dramatic idea. A plotless ballet needs less emphasis but more magic. Movable sets prove the closest collaboration between choreographer and designer. In Alwin Nikolais's dance theater, props grow into sets and sets may be used as props, and both are born as the total stage realization of a unified visual image which defies departmentalization in movement, décors, projection, light, and sound. Also the set is the brain child of the imagination of a painter-musician wedded to a dancer-choreographer.

The designer needs great insight into the choreographer's mind and poetic *Einfühlung* in his intentions in order to create sets which move with the dancers. Isamu Noguchi and Martha Graham come to mind. Noguchi succeeded more often than not in creating an emotional landscape with the most abstract images which became an inherent part of the dance. However, in Graham's *Alcestis,* Noguchi's sets lose their suggestive power and become strange looking pieces, endlessly moved across the stage, back and forth, by the dancers. These sets may serve symbolic purposes, but the choreography does not come to terms with their clumsy form. As little as these movable sets seem to help the dramatic dance image in *Alcestis,* all the more harmonious do they work in the *Canticle for Innocent Comedians.* Set and choreography speak the same poetic language, give form to a fleeting feeling here and there, or put an accent on the lyric notion of a phrase. Movable sets may be ideal for certain dances, but they are just as treacherous.

When John Martin could headline his review of *Firebird,* "Décor by Chagall Dominates Ballet," then something was decidedly wrong with the décor or even with the choice of the scene designer. Marc Chagall's way of seeing the world—I mean the world of make-believe which dwarfs reality—is so very personal and overwhelming in its suspension of everything real, in its defiance of gravity by creating an astronautic weightlessness that no dancer on stage can compete with his painted suggestiveness. Chagall is a characteristic case of a painting genius who, in his own metier, is the sole creator of a distinct allusive realism, of anything the stage can make poetically and dramatically valid. His creative imagination is theatrically self-sufficient, permitting no one else to trespass on his dream world.

The problem of collaboration and cooperation in the theater is of paramount importance. This impure art can rise in its purified greatness only if all contributors use their genius while renouncing it. The surrealist painter Kurt Seligmann created a variety of fantastically grotesque and imaginative costumes for Hanya Holm's *The Golden Fleece* through which the symbolism of each character was most colorfully expressed. But the costumes not only monopolized the attention, they were so weighty and unwieldy that they prevented the dancers from moving and defeated the choreographer's intentions.

Leonide Massine created the ballet *Bacchanale,* based on a scenario by Salvador Dali who did the setting and costumes for it. The hallucinations of the mad King of Bavaria, Ludwig II, were the theme and, as Massine said, "The bizarre subject exactly suited Dali's genius and inspired him to produce a series of weird hallucinatory images." Massine was overwhelmed by the design as was Hanya Holm. "As I had to sustain in my choreography Dali's bizarre atmosphere, without intruding on his scenic creations, I did not have in this ballet the scope of choreographic invention. . . . Also I found myself somewhat inhibited by the surrealist setting and costumes."

Do scenery and costumes get in the way of the creative theatrical process if the designer's personality as a painter is artistically too strong? Not necessarily. Pablo Picasso's designs for

*Georges Braque's Act Curtain (*The Naiad*) for* Les Facheux, *a Bronis-lava Nijinska ballet staged for Diaghilev's Ballets Russes in 1924. This is one of several versions (pencil, watercolor, gouache on paper) on the same subject.*

Courtesy Wadsworth Atheneum, Hartford.

For many years Eugene Berman was one of the most important stage designers for ballet, mainly between 1938 and 1956. He worked for many companies. The two scenic designs at right were done for Devil's Holiday *(1939), produced by Ballet Russe de Monte Carlo.*

Collection The Museum of Modern Art, New York. Gift of Paul Magriel.

*Parade,** *The Three-Cornered Hat,* or *Pulcinella* do not deny Picasso's personality while contributing scenic effects of visual richness and suggestiveness. The certainly willful and highly imaginative style of Joan Junyer, who designed scenery and costumes for ballets by Argentinita, Ballet Russe de Monte Carlo, and New York's Ballet Society, always worked towards an interaction of choreography and costume, enhancing the dancer's movements. ("I am driving towards a constructive place for painting, in association or rather as integrated with the other arts, by modern science and technique.")

All of Eugene Berman designs have the stamp of his genius. The decorative elements of the historic past in his work have a contemporary feeling and express a very personal note. He creates a sensuous dream world for the spectator while being "scenically discreet," as Edwin Denby said. His mysteriously blue and fantastically misty color schemes offset his architectural predilections and give his designs an eloquent quality without making them more articulate than the ballet. Berman saw in his contemporary, Christian Bérard, a paragon of the theatrical designer, who created the scenic image for Balanchine's *Cotillon* in 1932 and many Massine ballets.

Each period and style puts very special demands on the stage designer. What Jean Bérain did for Lully and Louis XIV, Léon Bakst and Alexandre Benois did for Diaghilev's Ballets Russes. And what a far cry is Jean Rosenthal's windswept and airy dance studio design for Jerome Robbins's *Afternoon of a Faun* from

---

* Gertrude Stein says about Picasso's set and costume designs for *Parade* in her book *Picasso:* "That was really the beginning of the general recognition of Picasso's work, when a work is put on stage of course everyone has to look at it and in a sense if it is put on the the stage everyone is forced to look and since they are forced to look at it, of course, they must accept it, there is nothing else to do."

Léon Bakst was one of the most prominent designers during the early period of Diaghilev's Ballets Russes. This is a portrait of Nijinsky in L'Après-Midi d'un Faune *for the cover of the souvenir program, 1912. (Pencil, charcoal, watercolor, gouache, gold on cardboard.)*

Courtesy Wadsworth Atheneum, Hartford.

Bakst's Oriental sumptuousness in his set for Nijinsky's *L'Après-midi d'un Faun!*

The contemporary scene embraces many different concepts and approaches, but essentially the designer no longer sees space from the spectator's seat, he "is more conscious of being within space," according to Reuben Ter-Arutunian. "It was Piet Mondrian, I believe, who conceived of 'being in art'—eventually living in art—within a controlled environment, shaped by a mind conscious of aesthetic relationships."

From Cecil Beaton's poetic playfulness to Ter-Arutunian's colorful creations of "the illusion of an illusion," most perfectly mastered by Pavel Tchelitchev, we find a striking economy in the use of material in the contemporary dance theater, a purgation of the unnecessary, and a balance of shapes and colors. Color and light are used with the minimum of a set in order to keep the stage open for the dance, in other words, simplicity with a maximum of suggestiveness. Many names come to mind—from Oliver Smith to David Hays, from Jo Mielziner to Peter Harvey, from Nicholas Georgiadis to Toer van Schack—who have found the poetic key to rendering unto the ballet the things which are the ballet's and to their own genius the things which are God's.

Jean Rosenthal designed the set for Jerome Robbins' 1953 version of Afternoon of a Faun, *produced by New York City Ballet. The dancers are Jacques d'Amboise and Allegra Kent.*

Photograph Fred Fehl.

Part three

DANCE
& ACTORS

TRENDS OF THE TIME

Why dance?

ALL FORMS of theater dance from classical ballet to ethnic dance, from representational to the nonliteral modern dance have assumed a leading and influential role among the arts in this century.

Dance played a paramount part in the latter half of the sixteenth century. Its social functions were blended with its incipient attempts at being theatrical in order to entertain an elite whose ambition was for almost a century to appear as patron, spectator, and performer. Until late into the eighteenth century dancing was in a losing competition with opera, although it had inadvertently helped the opera to make its first steps in a baroque and strongly stylized world of make-believe in which the theater dance was also at home. From Gluck and Mozart to Wagner, Verdi, and Strauss the opera remained blessed by the Muses. The drama was at a low point during the romantic era, and the well-made plays of the time gave the ballet an opportunity to shine in its fairy-tale glory. (Gautier fled to the ballet because the theatrical fares in the Forties and Fifties of the last century bored him.) It was only with the coming of Ibsen that the dramatic theater soared to new heights and the ballet lost the touch for the elusiveness of its poetic beauty.

The new century has been one of restlessness, revolutionary changes, and experiments. Like man during the Renaissance, twentieth-century man became more and more visual-minded. The moving pictures developed a heightened sense for everything pictorial. In their desperate attempt to give the world of losing and changing values the expression of their chaotic existence, the poets began to stammer expressionistically and dadaistically. The time-worn, tired look of the communicative lingo, the deterioration of the word into meaningless clichés, man's helplessness to make himself understood yielded all verbal brilliance to the brilliant world of pictures.

The word took on the appearance of a nineteenth-century apotheosis, while the mechanization of our daily life voluntarily surrendered to the visual and moving image. Moving, because the speed of the horseless cars and the realization of the Renaissance dream of man flying and overcoming all obstacles of nature gave man movement as a toy he progressively idealized; visual, because our passivity had grown with the growing mechanization which, on the other hand, has made us escape to our roots. In our longing for everything basic and primitive as a protest against an environment of a button-pushing oversophistication we discovered our folkloric past of which folk dance translated into theatrical terms has now become an essential element of the theater.

With the constant breaking down of taboos and the loosening of the established aesthetic laws an eroticizing trend started in the Twenties and, testing the border lines of permissiveness, triumphed in the Sixties. Since dance cannot escape being manifestly physical, our senses have come to associate—probably more than in any other era—erotic qualities with the dance, even though the trend towards total nudity has tried to discredit the illusionist's joy.

In any crucial period of transition man is as much aware of decay as he is desirous of youth, and with man's survival instinct being as strong as it is, the accent on youth must become increasingly pertinent the stronger the revolutionary changes become. Dance, limited to the young in body as performers and the young in heart as spectators, profits from the need of man to run after the bandwagon of those who try to escape the decay of the present and their inheritance of the past.

Movement per se has become a way of life in this century, whether it is the artistic expression through movement or movement capturing an environmental experience. The focus of life and art is on movement.

The ecstasy of non-art

There is no reason or need for having a non-art, except if you believe that zero times zero will make more than zero; or if you feel you have been overpowered by life and you must revenge yourself on life for your imagination's unconditional surrender by duplicating it, making an image of it; or if, temperamentally inclined to rage, you must rage by doing or nondoing whatever comes to your mind.

The trend to present off-stage activities on stage, to take art out of the museums in order to save it from the beauty of make-believe, or to write nonbooks is one step short of excluding the participation of the spectator, viewer, and reader. With this exclusion the ultimate of non-art is reached. Aristotle's concept of poetry as something emerging from nonexistence into existence is reinterpreted as "anything reduced from existence into existence."

Art, as a creative process has always been the consequence of man's search for himself, for his own identity, or the god in him, and his artistic accomplishments were man's only triumph over death. The pillar of all civilization is a creative feeling of permanence which man and the artist in man have lost. Non-art is the result of man's acceptance of futility and the fear of finality waiting around the corner. It is the result of man having lost his belief in posterity.

I can see the torment of the artists, even if they put on a hoax; I can see that all their mental somersaults are an act of despair because the artists' most private belief in the traditional notion of continuing to live through what the little god in them made them create was erased by the "bomb." I understand their compulsion to react to it like children that spite themselves in order to spite their parents, also with doubt, grim laughter, in a kidding mood, or with a nihilistic rage for chaos and nothingness. I know they feel as Dylan Thomas felt when he wrote: "Do not go gentle into that good night. . . . Rage, rage . . ." I only wish they had the strength of his poetry and his vision of despair.

I understand the contemporary artist's hate of the world and himself. But I cannot love his hate since I cannot help loving love.

Art has always been an attempt to unravel the mystery of life. Non-art begins with demystifying art. Merce Cunningham is a master craftsman at it. In *Walkaround Time* there is an intermission for the dancers, not the audience. You may walk out and around because the houselights come up. But who wants to miss the highlight of a non-dance when you can watch the dancers walk, squat, talk, lie around, massage their legs, rest on stage in a more leisurely way than during the actual performance? You are interested in the revelation of the private self, acting while pretending not to act. You do not expect any meaningful gesture in this intermission which is just one short step closer to the very reality of life than what preceded it. But you want to relax with the dancer-actors from having surrendered your thoughts and feelings to what they call "let it happen to you," whatever that may mean. In his book, *Changes: Notes on Choreography*, Merce Cunningham says:

Movement is an intrinsic part of the "total theatre" concept. The logic of one event coming as responsive to another seems inadequate now. We look at and listen to several at once. For dance it was all those words about meaning that got in the way. Right now they are broken up; they do not quite fit, we have to shuffle and deal them out again.

What happened is the realization that art as an experience is divested of its old meaning involving intellectual-emotional and kinesthetic reactions. You are invited to shed the various layers of your old skin (read: personality) and let the artist bombard all your senses with ear-puncturing sounds, non-dancers' dance movements, light effects, incoherent speech, and the like. If you cannot quite capitulate to the new laws of nonaesthetics, the experience is an apotheosis of nothingness, the mystification of bareness, that is, the demystification of art.

Merce Cunningham is a serious artist and, commenting on the inanity of life, the superiority of the commonplace, he re-creates inanity and commonplace, what all former artists throughout the centuries have replaced by an act of creativeness in order to make us forget or guide us across or give new meaning to these very same empty spots in our life. When John Cage stated that Cunningham "affirms life," he meant the life in its everyday look, drab, confusing, disconcerting, subject to irrational chance, sometimes with the touch of the poetic. Cunningham thus becomes the poet-dancer singing of the subordinary existence of man. Probably someone had to do it one day just to remind us of life being life being life, in case we had not noticed it. Cunningham being a great artist—God and Cunningham as well as Cage forgive me for using the word *art*—has done a superb job of it.

Art for the artist's sake

Much of what happens in the antitraditional sphere of creativity is to break through all barriers of established norms. The "isms," once having begun to run amuck, follow one another so quickly that they overlap and blur the image of any clear progression. The notion of experiment has become a shield for all the warriors of new "isms," fighting or kidding their way into the relevant indeterminacy of the future—to use the terminology of an indeterminate but relevant age.

Most of the "way-out" dancers have thrown overboard the concept of choreography. They have kept a semblance of dance only behind calisthenic movements. In an essay in the *Tulane Drama Review,* Yvonne Rainer says:

No to spectacle no to virtuosity no to transformations and magic and make-believe no to the glamour and transcendency of the star image no to the heroic no to the anti-heroic no to trash imagery no to involvement of performer or spectator no to style no to camp no to seduction of spectator by the wiles of the performer no to eccentricity no to moving or being moved

What is created by the avant-garde (by now a misnomer) is not dance but explorations in which time or place are not necessarily defined or recognizable, and the dancer's experience of one movement determines the next sequence of movements. Chance often plays its game with the material and its performer, or a movement is repeated over and over again. Boredom, or graded monotony, is intentionally created to prove that boredom is a part of our life. The performer then does not mind—and is probably considering it as a part of his success—if you receive the message and respond by walking out.

The material itself determines what is happening, and the performer's own experience is really what counts most while it is happening. Everything would be wonderful and everyone happy discovering the beauty that *is* if, as John Cage says, we could "simply wake up to the very life we're living, which is so excellent once one gets one's mind and one's desires out of one's way and lets it act of its own accord." All this sounds and seems to be as simple as the creation of a work of non-art. If we would only not live in our mechanized and oversophisticated world! It is easy to hang oneself on the rope of one's fallacies.

The experiments of the early modern dance in the late Twenties and Thirties were as close to literature as its explorations in the Fifties and Sixties were to the world of the painter. In many ways the trials and errors of the painters and dancers moved in the same direction, particularly in surrendering to the environment, magnifying or minimizing its terms of reference. Dances are taking place in railway stations, gardens, museums, and on streets.

Meredith Monk intended to do the first installment of her three-part *Juice* in the Pan Am Building, but finally did it in the Guggenheim Museum. Her theater cantata—neither theater nor dance, but a spectacle of sorts—was about perspective, dispersal, and compression. The environment decided the three stages of her happening. Miss Monk does not think of herself as a dancer, nor was what she did a work of dance. There was singing, walking, grouping, crouching, miming, masking. The contemporary artists have learned that you can cross new frontiers any second Friday.

Leonardo thought that "small rooms discipline the mind; large ones distract it." But of course he was not a non-artist. Although he dreamed of the flying machine which became a reality in our time, he did not dream of art ever intending to aim at the effect of never really accomplishing anything. Let us not forget that he was the archetype of an artist who hardly ever finished what he set out to do. What he did not finish, however, was a masterpiece, not a "put on."

The destruction of form

Among the theater arts the dance has gone much further than the drama has in the destruction of form. Pinter's silences are dramatic punctures in the flowing cadences of his menacing dialogue. The orchestration of his characters' speeches is of today, but in his structural form he has remained traditional.

Ionesco's antics are themes and variations on the loneliness of man, and his inability to break through the artificial trivia of life. Ionesco is not too far from the choreographer's concept of letting chance dictate each movement. The clown in Ionesco easily juggles with man and the inanimate, with the interchange of events dominating our life. A Bergsonian disciple, Ionesco proves that everything in a living person that makes one think of an inanimate mechanism has a comic effect, and so has the entire apparatus of mechanized life, particularly when presented upside down or even horizontal but magnified through repetition or distorted at a certain angle. In Ionesco we find parallels to the repetitive movement of the dancer, the deliberate emphasis on inanity and boredom of the experimental choreographer.

Ionesco underlines effects to the utmost, he tries "to push the theatre beyond that in-between zone that is neither theatre nor literature." In doing so, he again parallels what in choreographic terms is nonliteral and nontheatrical material. This is even more easily translated into dance terms as when Ionesco, describing his concepts of theater, emphatically declares:

no dramatic comedies any more, but a return to the insufferable. To push everything to paroxysm, to the point where the sources of the tragic lie. To create a theatre of violence—violently comic, violently dramatic.

The dramatist closest to the dance of the absurd is Samuel Beckett. He is a poet of few words, who prefers to create visual images on stage. As in the *modern* modern dance his stage visualizations are reduced to their most minimal essentials while being strikingly vivid and suggestive. It seems as if Beckett relies on the fact that we have become visually oriented and have learned to translate a stage image quickly into the reality of our emotions. In the theater, Beckett is the most vehement form-smasher. ("To find a form that accommodates the mess is the task of the artist now.") His plays have become progressively more cryptic, more reduced to nothingness. The precepts of Yvonne Rainer, as quoted, with their violent *NO*s to traditional theater are similar to Beckett's approach to drama which began first with the destruction of conventional form. There is only a faint semblance to a two-act structure in *Waiting for Godot,* with the dialogue cut into movement phrases in the same absurd, non sequitur form as we find them with Rainer and her confrères. The non-dancer's dance movement has its equivalent in Beckett's dialogue of inconsequential consequence.

The contemporary experimental dancer has been as radical as the visual artist in creating a world beyond imagination and in going outside the traditional framework. Self-reflection, the explanation of the puzzling mechanism of man, our truly Christian heritage, is seemingly out of place in our nuclear age. The wayout artist has no longer the time to stop to look inward. He feels compelled to turn against the inner man of man.

Youth has always been committed to the process of destroying the yesterday for the sake of its own tomorrow. In its fear of facing no tomorrow, form and order are destroyed.

In former days the genius went his own way and extended time-worn symbols, creating new content within the framework of the old. Isadora Duncan threw off the paraphernalia and the yoke of classical ballet, but, essentially, she remained a romantic, and her undulating movements echoed the spirit of balletic grace. She rebelled against ballet tradition, not against its expressive spirit; otherwise, Michel Fokine could not have translated so truly her principles into his barefoot ballet, *Eunice*. Isadora did for the twentieth-century dance what Cezanne did for the painters. Cezanne did not rebel against nature but against the tradition of how painters saw nature. Those who took off from where he stood, denied nature its image, and mocked it. Still later, Tristan Tzara could say that, if God can permit himself not to be successful everywhere and all the time, Dadaism must have the same privilege.

Unedited reality or eroticism in disguise and nudity

The ecological challenge facing man is probably more total and crucial than we are aware of. In the process of our traumatic experiences with which we enter a new age we may continue to be frightened into new "isms," and very likely we will embrace a new brand of neoromanticism whose propelling force was set into motion by the hippie movement. Undoubtedly, we are now about to create a new myth of man, and a future generation of comprehensivists will be able to accept the challenge of the "metaphysical mastering of the physical," as Buckminster Fuller expressed it.

One of the many byplays in our groping to understand ourselves in a time still frighteningly new to us is nudity in dance and even more so in dramatic experiments. Only when literature and the theater arts are no longer concerned with the revelation of the inner man, will the display of man in utter nakedness become flamboyantly obvious. There is a legitimate place for nudity in all art forms, not only in painting and sculpture. Nudity on stage must serve a choreographic purpose, for it is monotonous and boring if not justified by any dramatic urgency. It must be there to enhance our feeling of being human, to heighten our awareness of man's inner strength and outer beauty, or, in other words, to create a feeling of humility as much as pride in the humanity which we all share.

Nudity in painting and sculpture has been with us since antiquity and the days of the Renaissance in great abundance and variety, and it was never considered questionable or in bad taste. If the Museum of the Vatican clothed its statues with fig leaves, it made nakedness "most offensive and conspicuous," as Mark Twain said and taught us the difference between being naked, that is, undressed, and being nude, that is, in the natural beauty that God gave us, with genitals and all. The nude is always marked as naked by the fig leaf.

In spite of his visualization of nudity in the visual arts Renaissance man never liberated himself from his medieval heritage of shame and guilt. The ancient Greeks, however, saw in sexual desires a natural impulse. Their zest for life included a love for the beauty of the human body. Nobody was ashamed of being naked. When Athens celebrated its victory at Salamis, a procession of naked youth was led by Sophocles. Dancing in the nude was implicit during their symposia and the Kordax, the antic dance in comedies. These experiences were accepted with the joyful innocence that lies in beauty, not with the ambivalent satisfaction of eating again from the apple of the Biblical tree.

It is only now at the very end of Renaissance man's triumphant daring that he tries to free himself from puritanical remnants, from fear, guilt, and shame. Unfortunately, this revolutionary act made possible by the breakdown of all ethical codes together with formerly established values comes at a time of confusion, with man caught in a maze of anxieties. As is the case with most revolts and revolutionary ideas, they are misunderstood, misused, and exploited. There is a difference between an orgasmic wilderness and the freedom of taking delight in yourself as the being you are.

Without condemning nudity right out the point may be made that man has lived with his fiction of himself rather happily. As long as people are dressed, they can maintain that all men are born equal. The moment they undress it becomes obvious that the statement of equality among men is only a half-truth, and this in spite of the face that a naked body is a familiar shape. A naked woman is a naked woman, whereas a half-dressed woman is everything we can dream of.

When art is denuded to look like life, it may be there to be accepted and used. John Cage once said that art is not there to be enjoyed but to be used. The utilitarian has lost the dream. He goes to the other extreme of the romantic's disdain of everything utilitarian. I realize the weaknesses hidden in extreme romanticism. But how quickly have we exhausted naked reality! How minimal, in the truest sense of the word, art can become! Throughout the centuries man's story has been mirrored in the reflection of his dream of himself. He cannot exist without it. Give him nothing but reality in the raw and, without his dream, he will finally drown in a mirror without reflection.

In defense of the cult of nudity on stage it can be claimed as one of the many protests against our overmechanized society, as a desperate attempt to return to primitivism in which sophisticated homo sapiens offers his naked body for public display as a ritualistic sacrifice. In showing or intimating the functions of the human body in a possibly most realistic manner the artists do not intend to dull our senses so much as to juxtapose the carnal act to our button-pushing society. Thus, the body's functions are downgraded as another mechanical process to unromanticize art. But, at the same time life is humiliated.

In many instances the display of nudity is directed against eroticism in disguise or, as Yvonne Rainer said, against the "disguised sexual exhibition of most dancing." As she proves, you can rage against it with the same fanaticism with which Puritanism caused the adverse situation. Nakedness introduced as shock, as a weapon of spite is self-defeating. Where does disillusionment lead if you discredit the very thing you disrobe and if you nauseate your public with pubic exhibition? (Charles Baudelaire started his essay on the erotic subject in art with this statement: "Has it ever been your experience, as it has mine, that after spending long hours over a collection of bawdy prints, you fall into a great spell of melancholy?")

In Ann Halprin's *Parades and Changes* the dancers undressed on stage, put their clothes on again only to take them off. So far, the act of disrobing would have had little meaning, but then masses of paper were brought on stage, and the stark naked dancers started romping in the paper. Beautiful shapes of moving bodies and paper emerged as if from nowhere, growing into sculptural forms, flesh-colored and paper-hued, ever-changing into a variety of fascinating shapes. There were no longer naked bodies, but nude images in joyful unconcern about their bare skin, wading through the mounds of paper, conveying a feeling of innocent ecstasy. It became obvious that they could never have accomplished the same liberating sensation in practice clothes as in the nude. Or, in such a multisensual theater experience as in the musical *Hair,* the five boys and three girls appearing nude on the dim-lit stage in the last few seconds of the be-in scene suggests a poetic curtain line.

I am not opposed to nudity nor even against showing life in its nakedness, as long as this action is dramaturgically or choreographically justified, adding meaning and, in its heightened meaningfulness, a new dimension to my existence. The function of morality in art is primarily an aesthetic one. The presentation of the nude body must express and visualize an image at its most poetic. The replica of life will never do. We must live with unedited reality day in, day out. If the creative mind dictates the introduction of a nude body, then the editing of reality is more crucial than in the creation of any other material.

Great art—whether it involves nudity or not—has always stimulated the spectator's mind by leaving a margin for his own imagination to continue the creator's dream. When Romeo realizes that it is not the nightingale but the lark, nothing would be added for us to have seen the two lovers naked in bed, where undoubtedly they were a few minutes previous to the scene. We know about it, and we do not have to be shown. A close-up of the two lovers in carnal union would destroy the very essence of their innocence in which we truly believe. Their fate would be tragic but not the play. This is only one example speaking for eroticism in disguise which will survive the trend of nudity. The voluptuary can make an art of sin, the puritan always makes a sin of art.

Creativity is man's only proof of and testimony to being a child of God. By the same token, his creativity betrays the tools hidden in the subliminal, the incessant interplay of body and soul, flesh and spirit, the mingling of the *sensual* and *sensuous* in him. The spectator ought to live up to the artist's promise by desiring the experience of utter union with the presented work. He ought to have the opportunity of becoming one with the spirit of the artist, re-creating with the help of the staged image the beauty of life and the life of beauty, both visualized in their poetic realities.

Nudity has played an important part in its iconoclastic task of overcoming the taboos of the past. If it should turn out to have been little more than spite resulting from anguish or a mere fad of a confused time, then it will go the way of all flesh. But if it came to us with a sense of liberation, then it will remain an expression of social significance and a part of the artist's tools and means towards a heightened awareness and meaningfulness.

Towards a nonverbal theater

With the breakdown of all norms artistic perfection lost its values. The spontaneous, improvised, creativity-while-the-action-lasts performances established themselves as a new trend in the Sixties. This tendency was directed towards restoring the very beginning of the theater, the ritual in which everyone is actor and spectator alike.

The new theater tries valiantly to get the audience back into the act.* The actors undress and challenge the audience to follow suit. They touch and address the spectators in an attempt to have a dialogue with them, all improvised, of course. Through choral

* Some thirty years ago Walter Gropius argued in a monograph called "The Total Theatre" that goal and purpose of the modern playhouse was to "abolish the separation between the 'fictitious world' of the stage and the 'real world' of the audience . . . to draw the spectator into the drama . . . to coerce him into participation in the play."

movement and chant the actors hope to mesmerize the public into participation.

The dancers have never felt the same compulsive urge to invite audience participation as those experimenting in the theater. It is a curious phenomenon which can be explained by the very fact that the experimental actor-director suspects his audience to have lost its sense for listening and its sensibility for words— something the dancer-choreographer never has to contend with. But Ann Halprin, among a few other dancer-choreographers, invited her audiences to share in such experiences as, carrying one another down a passageway and standing in silent atonement for an unduly long time. There were attempts at breaking down the traditional barriers between dancers and the audience. The audience, at one point, was even invited to compose graffiti and given paper and magic markers for this purpose.

Originally, spectators were created out of orgiastic fellow worshipers. The trend to make coworshipers out of spectators is similar to going from a state of high sophistication all the way back to the primitivism of the ritual. Our mind may yield to emotional hypnotism, we may whip up an ecstatic feeling, but there is a great deal of pretense and rationalization as well as make-believe in reverse. With everyone busy doing his thing, nothing is accomplished. What the participatory craze achieves is to deprive us of one of the greatest assets of what the theater has come to offer: stimulation, food-for-thought, enlightenment, and innocent enjoyment.

Since theater has been mainly verbal through the last two thousand and five hundred years, the concept of the theater as a part of literature has dominated. Drama is literary, evocative, and provocative, an instrument with which a playwright tries to reach his audience. But, drama is not necessarily theater. The actor preceded the dramatist, and what is now happening in the theater—

at least in its radical and most influential wing from Antonin Artaud in the Thirties to Jerzy Grotowski in the Sixties—is a total return to the actor and actor-director. In the actor-director's rage for new ways of communication, the word was crucified and the literary image of the theater burned at the stakes of their belief that, according to Peter Brook, "all through the world in order to save the theatre almost everything of the theatre still has to be swept away." With the diminished role of the word, the significance of stage movement rose.

Such revolt against the established theater happened before in history. At the end of the Renaissance, more precisely during the first half of the sixteenth century, the *commedia dell'arte* was a violent reaction to a highly sophisticated, literary theater in which the humanists indulged themselves in an "in" theater with plays of polished verses and meticulous meters. Like our own time, it was a socially restless period in which the Reformation movement was only one, even though major, expression of the changing scene.

The coarse and crudely improvisational theater of the commedia came into being as the result of the actors' despair and disgust with the poetically hollow phrase of the court theater and their own alienation from the populace. It would be erroneous to assume that the *commedia* actors did not use many words, although, in the main, they were improvisations and essentially entrance and exit lines. The *concertatore,* or manager, informed the actors of the scenario which was a bare outline of the major phases in the plot. The actors had to invent their lines, and whenever they were at a loss for words the comic business, the *lazzis,* kept the audience amused. Whether the actors spoke or not, they relied heavily on gesture and bodily movement.

The influence of the *commedia dell'arte* on the European theater was unique. *Commedia* types metamorphosed and became a part of theater tradition. Pedrolino, for example, turned into Pierrot, Pulcinella became the English Punch, Arlecchino emerged as the German Hans Wurst and Kasperl, and Columbina reappeared as our musical comedy soubrette. Far more important was the *commedia*'s influence on the playwrights of the seventeenth and eighteenth centuries, on Molière, Goldoni, and Gozzi, to mention three master craftsmen of the verbal theater, even though the *commedia* was a nonliterary adventure.

Very similar to the *commedia dell'arte*, Jerzy Grotowski treats the literary products of the playwrights as raw material for his theater of external poverty. He creates his stage around and with the audience, using no scenic or lighting effects. He rearranges the text to serve as orchestration of action and mood. Grotowski's is an antiliterary or an actor's theater of a weird sophisticated *and* ritualistic theatricalization, cutting deep into our nervous system, to the thin edge of our mental capacities.

He comes closest to fulfilling Antonin Artaud's dreams of myth and detachment in the theater where poems are no longer declaimed but lived, where the stress must lie on the physical expression of the actor, on gesture, and movement. Artaud said that there are "attitudes in the realm of thought and intelligence that words are incapable of grasping and that gestures and . . . a spatial language attain with more precision." Artaud, with his concept of a theater of purgation and cruelty, contributed essentially to the destruction of the word and gave stage movement and the expressive gesture a vital function in the new theater.

The theaters all over the world are full with little Grotowskis or with those who have used his concept and daring as a point of departure for their own stage adventures. Joseph Chaikin's experiments with the actors of his "Open Theatre" is movement-motivated. Tom O'Horgan, who gave the world *Hair,* thinks of his approach to directing as "kinetic sculpture." Peter Brook's staging of *Marat/Sade* was based on a detailed study of each character whose most intrinsic and psychodramatic features were translated into a pattern of expressive movements, and all characters, similar to instruments in an orchestra, were rhythmically attuned to one another in an over-all choreographic image. Richard Schechner explained his theories underlying the staging of *Dionysus in 69:*

Language is a species of action. It is a tool of immense power. The question for the new theatre is not whether language will be used, but who will control its use. Furthermore, what is the relationship between verbal and nonverbal language? The actors I work with want to articulate their bodies as well as their heads and hands. . . . Everyone who attacks the new theatre defends the playwright. His authority is said to be the final one. But he is often a dead or absentee or theatrically ignorant landlord. And where he is alive, on the spot, and knowledgeable, the traditional, commercial theatre usually treats him with contempt.

It is more likely that the nonverbal theater will be absorbed by the traditional theater than vice versa. In *Marat/Sade* Peter Brook adapted Grotowski's ideas which are always absorbing but often unendurable, to the commercial theater. Although the *Marat/Sade* experience unnerved some traditional minds and drove them out of the theater, Brook's staging combined experimental shock with such polished perfection of acting that the resulting theater experience was high-powered and, in its constant bombardment of all our senses, inescapable.

The influence created by the *commedia dell'arte* on the literary theater of its time will be paralleled by the influence of the nonverbal experiments on the established theater in our electronic era. The imaginative use of movement, music, and lighting will give live theater a new lease on life.

"When a man," Chekhov wrote, "spends the least possible

number of movements on some definite action, then that is grace-fulness." It has always been economy, the purgation of the unnec-essary that marked the greatness of a work. The disbelief in the word and artistic perfection have led to the director's emotional cornucopia indiscriminately machine-gunning the stage with ama-teurish excesses in the use of movement in order to create stage images. With the accent on the purely visual, movement on stage can become a dangerous toy. Blinded by its effect for effect's sake, the director may overlook the need for all movement to be dra-matically integrated.

In many ways the experiments of the Sixties fulfilled the promises made by the experiments in the Twenties. Alexander Tairov's and Vsevolod Meyerhold's theater experiments in Russia in the first half of the Twenties are among those that have discov-ered the importance of movement in order to create an expres-sionistic and constructivistic stage image. Meyerhold declared that "words in the theater are only a design on the canvas of motion" and that "We must put the body back."

Now that stage movement has been reclaimed by the stage directors as a vital means of giving a theater experience its physi-cal backbone, movement, reduced in an appropriate measure to its poetic potentialities, will remain a propelling impulse and the visual realization of a theatrical dream reality.

The nondividing line

The disbelief in the word has not come about through exis-tentialist feelings or frantic despair as the expression of the Six-ties. The word was already looked at with great doubts by the lyric and dramatic poet Hugo von Hofmannsthal as early as the 1890s, and, when Gordon Craig began to publish his periodical,

The Mask, in 1908, he tried to reorient concepts of theater split up into departments. "The ideal theater would focus all the arts in a magnificent over-powering unity of impression." He took up the slogan: "I know of but one art"; turned against the playwright: "I have parted company with the popular belief that the written play is of any deep value to the Art of the Theatre. . . . It is the actor and the fury of the actor (that creates drama). He creates it by taking a story and inventing what dialogue is necessary as he goes along."

Jean-Louis Barrault once said that the theater and actor must regain what seems to have been lost: "the sense of movement, the rhythm that lies hidden in man and of which the gesture is the outward manifestation, the dance its artistic fulfillment."

Jerome Robbins proved the existence of an intimate relationship between dancer and actor in *West Side Story* and has shown that the theater is the dancer's as well as the actor's legitimate world. When asked about their interrelationship, he said:

Dancers and choreographers are already working *in* the theatre, thus I actually never feel they have turned toward it. Every actor should have a vigorous dance training and vice versa. Every dancer must act and every actor must dance. I find no great separation in the approach to either.

"I relate to the theatre in its totality," Anna Sokolow said,

no matter whether I work with actors or dancers. For me the theatre is in no way limited, certainly not to any form of expression. It is a world open to all possible experiences and only waiting for the miracle to happen that we always expect from it.

It makes no difference to me what you do on stage. What matters is that it be truthful—truthful to your own self as well as to your time. This is the essence, the life breath of the theatre. For only through your truth can the mystery of reality be revealed.

It would be wrong to approach actors with the notion that as non-dancers they cannot be expected to do certain things. On the other hand, there should be no persistent drill to make the actor become a perfect dancer. Essentially, the teacher's approach should not be far from the one that is usually applied to dancers. It makes no difference which method of movement is used as long as the body is trained to be well placed, is expressive and in its expressiveness meaningful. Anna Sokolow explained:

Movement is like a language. I believe that there is beauty in emotion when it finds its true expression. This is important for the actor whose business is to create an emotional climate with the immediacy of his physical appearance. In this respect I see no difference between actor and dancer. The difference lies only in the degree of intensity with which each uses his body.

My first aim is to free the actor from his self-consciousness. I help him to stop worrying about what he is to do with his hands. I make him forget about the clichés of having to smoke, to touch or handle something. It is amazing to see how this freedom from artificial contrivances conditions the quality of his face, how it colors his acting. It may seem to the actor that he is learning how to move and how to use the body, but what he really learns is to be simple, honest and human.

Great teachers utilize the ideas coming from their students and experiment as much as possible. While actors recite a Greek classic or recite passages from the Bible, they should move like modern dancers. Verbal expression and body movement ought to create contrasts and a dramatic mood on which the future actor must thrive. Stress should also be put on the physical relationship between the actors on stage so that each body can function in this group work as does an instrument in an orchestra. Preclassic dance forms, when freely applied, best prepare the actor to play in period pieces.

"The various possibilities and the possible variations of how a teacher creates in the actor an awareness of his body," Anna Sokolow stressed,

an awareness of which he can eventually make unconscious use, are endless. They may be improvised or emerge from a given situation. I feel I have really achieved my aim when the actor can create, through merely being and moving on stage, the intangible poetic atmosphere from which his spoken words can honestly come forth. And I am gratified, too, when he has learned to stop thinking and dares react like an animal. I suppose these two are not self-exclusive and are only two sides of one and the same coin.

Conventional misconceptions of how to move and gesture on stage have prevailed for a long time. The worst that can happen to an actor is for him to equate the function of the gesturing hand with certain predetermined movement patterns. Then, such a great actress as Helen Hayes can be misled in her rationalizations of what she thinks she ought to do on stage to the statement that "In comedy, I have found that I must keep myself up, arms must be held higher, gestures must be of an upward nature. In tragedy just the reverse." Dancers-turned-actors, on the other hand, may be tricked into an unconscious reaction. The story has it that such an actor suddenly found himself standing in ballet's second position when the director called to him: "What are you doing with your feet?"

"Modern dancers, used to thinking in abstractions, are good acting material," Alvin Ailey remarked. "They are expressing feeling. Unlike most ballet dancers, they don't think primarily of steps. The modern dancer speaks without words all the time."

There are notable exceptions, among them Moira Shearer and Robert Helpmann, who both came from ballet to acting.

"Everything in dancing is style, allusion, the essence of many thoughts and feelings, the abstraction of many moments. Each movement is the sum total of moments and experiences," Alvin Ailey continued.

In acting you don't condense that way, you have to live every moment, you are there to make that moment a living reality. Of course, there are certain things which you can say better with a few movements, perhaps an inner experience which might need lengthy speeches to express verbally with the same poetic precision. On the other hand, there are many things you simply cannot dance, for example, intricate human relationships. You can only express basic relationships through movement.

As to the difficulties a dancer meets in switching to acting, Ailey said:

You have to learn to walk again. Every step a dancer makes is different from an actor's. But the real difficulty for me is that, like a choreographer, I visualize everything in its totality. When I played in *Tiger, Tiger, Burning Bright* I insisted on being told what will happen to the man I portrayed. I had to know his final fate—beyond the actual play—before I could act the part. I have to see the whole structure of a human life and the many threads leading from him to the world in which he exists. I find that the hard discipline you learn as a dancer helps you while acting. I gradually realized that as an actor I had great freedom to contribute. I was, so to speak, my own choreographer—and the director fitted the choreographer's image I had of the human being I played into his stage concept. In other words, the director selected from my attempts to find myself.

The dancer in him profited from acting as much as the actor learned from the dancer:

I have learned a great deal from method acting. Through the sense memory exercises, such as touching or tasting, I found expression of images through movement that have universal meaning. I have learned to abstract what is real and to make it bigger than life. I still derive the greatest satisfaction from choreographing, from creating with other people. I like to help mould a performer and get him to that point which I call "room for error," where he is good, just right, but not yet perfect. This is the moment in which his personality fully unfolds, when he is able to communicate something vital of himself.

Valerie Bettis has danced, acted, and choreographed. From the very beginning when she started to dance she thought in theatrical terms. Most of her dance works have, beyond the sheer excitement of the theatricality, a feeling for the drama. For example, she staged William Faulkner's *As I Lay Dying* as a dance-drama, a meaningless term if it does not indicate that dancers interweave spoken words in their movement patterns.

The dance-drama, or dance with spoken words, has a long history, particularly among the American modern dancers, with some notable accomplishments. The word has often been used as an extension of the musical score, as Martha Graham did with Emily Dickinson's words in *Letter to the World,* or like a percussion instrument in Doris Humphrey's *Lament for Ignacio Sanchez Mejias* in which Federico Garcia Lorca's line, "At five o'clock in the afternoon," whips the movement pattern to rising crescendos.

As early as 1917 when Jean Cocteau tried to convince Serge Diaghilev that the cubistic imagery of *Parade* needed the spoken word as well, ballet attempted not only to visualize a poetic concept but also to have its verbal sound accompany the action. Diaghilev, who certainly embraced the idea of the *Gesamtkunstwerk,* saw in the spoken word a dangerous intruder. In his opinion, all other art forms supported the expressiveness of stylized movement, while verbalization, that is, spoken imagery, can more readily reach the receptivity of the spectator and reduce, instead of enhance, the projected power of the dance.

Cocteau experimented with words accompanying the dance in his ballet *Les Mariés de la Tour Eiffel*, but the dancers themselves did not speak—an essential feature of the dance-drama. The words were uttered by two narrators dressed as phonographs, commenting on the danced action, reciting the parts of the characters. The structure of this comedy-ballet has the quality of a documentary with on-the-spot reporters telling us what is happening. Cocteau introduced the word without integrating it into the ballet.

Since Noverre declared ballet an independent art form, essentially liberating it from the opera, there has been a tendency to keep the spoken drama separated from ballet, a schism thas has never occurred in the East. It is a sociocultural phenomenon that the choreographer's desire to incorporate the word in his works should have come at a time when the word had lost most of its value.

Total integration of word and movement was experimented with by American choreographers mainly in the late Forties and during the Fifties. It seems that they are temperamentally predestined for such experiments if for no other reason than they are never as tradition-bound as the European dancers. Ruth Page has always had an affinity for the drama and tried to emphasize the dramatic purpose of the drama in her ballets.

Ruth Page blended speech and dancing, acting and pantomime in her ballet-play *Billy Sunday,* in which she portrayed this colorful American personality. Her attempt at a ballet-play was preceded by Eugene Loring's *The Great American Goof,* which had scenario and words by William Saroyan. In the late Fifties Donald Saddler's *This Property Is Condemned,* the Tennessee

Williams play, achieved the smoothest integration of word and movement. He skillfully used the two theatrical elements of drama and dance in order to create a poetic mood of dramatic intensity.

At that time—at the end of the Fifties—the dance-drama had become common currency among the modern dancers. The works of the poetic dramatists, Lorca, Williams, Yeats, and Synge attracted the young choreographers of that period, foremost Mary Anthony and Valerie Bettis, to move symbolism and imagery out of the confines of the representational modern dance, which was under heavy attack by those who refuted all literalism. From an historic viewpoint it now seems as if many choreographers recognized the need to give the modern dance a new impetus, a new form. Merce Cunningham, Merle Marsicano, Erick Hawkins, and Alwin Nikolais led the revolution and turned towards the nonliteral. A hard core of literally- and literary-minded choreographers hoped to stem the tide by moving closer to the word. But the simultaneous trend in the theater towards the prevalence of nonverbal imagery stopped the dance-drama from properly unfolding.

The modern dancer being as articulate as he is has often felt close to the word which never ceased being a part of his artistic sensibilities. Mary Anthony, an actress-writer, besides having made the dance her career, became convinced that the theater was once a spectacle in which the actors spoke as much as they moved when she saw a Greek production of *Electra* with Katina Paxinou in the leading part. Some of her experiments with words and the dance followed this experience. Yeats's *At the Hawk's Well* failed since the danced imagery was expressive in itself, the poetic words hovering heavily above the moving bodies. Tennessee Williams's *The Purification* succeeded in creating an integrated poetic image of the word as extending the movement which, in turn, became an extension of the word's symbolism.

Some of the successful creations in the dance-drama genre came from Valerie Bettis, who likes to refer to directing as choreography, echoing Tyrone Guthrie, one of the stage directors obsessed with the idea of movement. Of course, one cannot be an effective director unless one is concerned with movement since movement is as inherent a part of acting as is speech. If movement in a play would only be of similar importance as silence is in music, its role would be indisputably of major proportion. Valerie Bettis staged a series of dances as much from a theatrical viewpoint as she choreographed plays.

A milestone in the development of a theater dance was her contribution to the New York production of James Joyce's *Ulysses in Nighttown* for which she was billed: "stage movement by." What in such a case becomes the highest ideal and most necessary reality was achieved: a flawless fusion of the dancers acting and the actors dancing. The actors conveyed a total physical awareness of rhythm, and the rhythms of the bodies followed the rhythms hidden in Joyce's prose, which functioned like a music score demanding its very own hallucinatory and highly stylized visualization.

One would not immediately associate Joyce's work with dance, and yet the uniqueness of his concept of stream-of-consciousness and his free-flowing imagery, not confined by any boundaries, trespassing on yet undiscovered lingual lands, has a rhythmic sweep that moves ecstatically, intoxicated by its own being. After almost ten years of work on a dance creation centered on Anna Livia Plurabelle, one of the characters in James Joyce's *Finnegans Wake,* Jean Erdman finally conceived a theater experience—drama as much as dance—which she called *The Coach With The Six Insides.*

The more she worked on it, the more she realized that narration to the dance would not do justice to her idea, that the words had to become a part of the dance. When she auditioned dancers for the various parts, she found them limited by their metrical feeling. She became convinced that an ametrical rhythm would better serve her purpose and decided to try out actors who could feel, while moving, the underlying pulse in pace and rhythm.

"I found that the actor's imagination is inspired by the director's words," Jean Erdman said,

while a dancer in the same situation would simply ask: "And what step shall I make here?" Actors may lack a certain movement quality which I expect to find in dancers. But the actors were not asked to dance, only to move in a certain defined rhythm. I tried to extend my own craft rhythmically to find a common platform with the actors and to lead them from an expressive realization to a more expressive stylization. Every actor had his shade of stylization which was not whimsically chosen. It was achieved through a long and subtle process of trying and eliminating with the purpose of showing the real personality of the characters. In juxtaposition, they created a very realistic stage image.

Whatever the process, Jean Erdman achieved the creation of a nonplay whose words were as intoxicating as its rhythm was revealing. The action remained one step removed from reality, and yet everything was there: Joyce's enigmatic words; eerie music accentuating the flow of action and underlining the unreality of the real; the movement in its filmy magic of remoteness. One word led to another movement, one motion to another word. The rhythmic pulse and poetic image became one.

"For a long time our theater lacked something," Jean Erdman said.

The directors had lost interest in movement. But the visual image of the actor's body is our very first experience when watching a play. I think the theater of the absurd has, if nothing else, taught us new uses of the theater, of the irrational element on stage in which there is a great deal of magic.

It may be paradoxical—after all, so is our entire age—but it seems that, in our jet age, we begin to move as if in a *Coach* with many insides towards a total unification of word and movement in a theater that may soon wish to wipe out any difference between drama and dance.

Part four

DANCE & POETS

THE LITERARY IMAGE

THERE WAS HARDLY a great mind in antiquity that would not have reacted to dancing in one way or another, from Homer to Euripides, from Lucian to Socrates, from Plato to Vergil. They have discussed its aesthetic and ethic principles, they have recorded dances performed in their midst as a part of religion or entertainment, and they gave dance its creative image on their stages. The great dramatist-poets were directors, actors, dancers, and choreographers. Sophocles did not find it beneath his dignity to appear as a dancer in a ball-juggling act in his own play *Nausicaa*. He also wrote a prose work on the tragic chorus and the dance. If this work, presumably written in dialogue form, had not been lost, we would, without doubt, know precisely what and how the Greek chorus danced.

The three dramatists in ancient Greece held a progressively different attitude towards the dance. Aeschylus saw in it a possibility for heightening the dramatic means. For Sophocles dance had all the potentialities to express and underline decisive characteristic changes in a dramatic situation. And, for Euripides the dancing chorus had to express through pantomime the feelings evoked by a play, that is, he used the dance to re-create the es-

241

sence of the drama through movement. Euripides, it seems, was the first dramatist-choreographer to have staged solo dancing.

It is an interesting phenomenon that writers who thought highly of the dance have invariably felt compelled to defend their attitude by defending the dance against those who slighted and dragged it into the mire of their questionable minds. From Cicero to Savonarola, from many ecclesiastic and secular personalities, from antiquity far beyond Oliver Cromwell and the seventeenth century poured forth abuse of the dance. Cicero was persuaded by political reasons, and Savonarola made a last desperate attempt to turn the Renaissance clock back to medieval standard time. They all had their moral motivations, no doubt, and the writers, positively attuned to the dance, had to pirouette their refutations.

In *The Dialogues of Lucian* we find Lycinius as Lucian's spokesman pitted against the cynic Crato who derided "dance and the dancer's art itself," saying in his haughty philippic:

Is there an educated man, having the slightest acquaintance with philosophy, who can give up striving for betterment and his association with the wisdom of the aged in order to sit down to listen to a flutist and to watch effeminate men imitating wanton women accompanied by lewd songs . . . all this really stupid stuff becomes you little.

Lucian of course realizes that the origin of the art of dancing has much to do with the creation of the world, one of the concepts borrowed from the East, and that the cosmic Eros finds its symbolic manifestation in the dance. Lucian says:

Then, too, all the rest are activities of one or the other of the two elements in man, some of them are activities of the soul, some of the body; but in dancing both are combined. For there is a display of mind in the performance as well as expression of bodily development, and the most important part of it is the wisdom that controls the action, and the fact that nothing is irrational. . . . Indeed, Lesbonax of Mytilene, a man of excellent parts used to go to see them with the expectation of returning a better man. Timocrates, his teacher, one day by chance, saw a dancer and said: "What a treat for the eyes my reverence for philosophy has deprived me of!"

The benefits of the dance are manifold, but Lucian lets Lycinius stress:

Herodotus says that what is apprehended through the eyes is more trustworthy than hearing, but dancing possesses what appeals to ear and eye alike. Its spell is so potent that if a lover enters a theatre he is restored to his right mind by seeing all the evil consequences of love; and one who is in the clutch of grief leaves the theatre in brighter mood, as if he had taken some potion that brings forgetfulness and surcease from sorrow and anger.

The writers inspired by the dance and, in turn, inspiring the creative dancer are so many and manifold that a sizable pocket encyclopedia could be compiled to do justice to all of them. To serve "the Muse of the many-twinkling feet," to use Lord Byron's phrase, and to realize "the poetry of the foot," as Dryden said, many writers desired "to dance with the pen," keeping Nietzsche ecstatic company. The relationship of the writers to the dance have varied from a nodding acquaintance to a casual flirtation to gentle courtship to passionate love.

There are writers who went into literary history with the dance as their brides, and I am trying to give them the space and place they duly deserve. I do not doubt that some may not have found the key to my heart nor the keys to my typewriter, but exclusion of certain writers has become unavoidable, while my own surprise in finding someone unexpectedly in Terpsichore's company may have induced me to include him here, even though his acquaintance with the dance was more than peripheral.

An example of the latter is William Makepeace Thackeray, who could write as well as he could draw, although he maintained a condescending attitude towards having to make one's livelihood with brush or pen. He went to Paris as a young man and mingled with the Parisian artists and fellow expatriates with whom he enjoyed a dolce-vita existence for some time. Thackeray often went to the Opéra. He cared little for the opera and Rossini, who then was the most talked-about composer, but he was charmed by Marie Taglioni "(Will the young folk ever see anything so charming, anything so classic, anything like Taglioni?") and took dance lessons with the famous Coulon ("a little creature four feet high with a pigtail").

As the other extreme we recognize Aleksander Sergeevich Pushkin who became an impassioned balletomane at the time when the Frenchman Charles Didelot established the Imperial School and gave the Russian ballet a consistent foundation of classical instruction. In characteristic romantic exaggeration Pushkin reacted to Didelot's ballets by exclaiming that there was more poetry in them than in all the French literature at that time.* He also declared that "Didelot's ballets are invested with a rich imaginative quality and an amazing charm."

Pushkin was amply rewarded for his interest in the ballet by many choreographers who translated some of his works into the language of movement. The Soviet ballet has produced his *Prisoner of the Caucasus, The Fountain of Bakhchisarai, Mistress into Maid,* and *The Captain's Daughter.* Michel Fokine's *Le Coq d'Or* is based on Pushkin's satirical poem of the same name and

* It is interesting to compare this ecstatic pronouncement with very similar exclamations found in Stendhal's reactions to Vigano at the very same period. We must also be aware of the fact that at that time in France such major figures as Victor Hugo, Alfred Musset, Alphonse Lamartine were only beginning to scribble their very first poems on the margin of their school copybooks.

Leonide Massine used his narrative poem *The Gypsies* for his ballet *Aleko.*

The great Russian ballerina of the second decade of the last century was Avdotsia Istomina, who, according to Serge Lifar, ought to be credited with the introduction of the toe shoe and toe dance. She is mentioned here because Pushkin sang her praise in his *Eugene Onegin:*

> The house is crammed. A thousand lamps
> On pit, stalls, boxes, brightly blaze,
> Impatiently the gallery stamps,
> The curtain now they slowly raise.
> Obedient to the magic strings,
> Brilliant, ethereal, there springs
> Forth from the crowd of nymphs surrounding
> Istomina, the nimble-bounding.
> With one foot resting on its tip
> Slow circling round its fellow swings
> And now she skips and now she springs
> Like down from Aeolus's lip,
> Now her lithe form she arches o'er
> And beats with rapid foot the floor.

Anatole Chujoy called our attention to a less familiar passage from *Eugene Onegin,* showing the poet's balletomania:

> . . . But now it's time for the ballet.
> The theatre's wicked legislator,
> Who unto every fascinator
> In turn his fickle flattery brings,
> And boasts the freedom of the wings,
> Onegin flies to taste the blisses
> And breathe the free air of the stage,
> To praise the dancer now the rage,
> Or greet a luckless Phèdre with hisses,

Or called the actress he preferred
Just for the sake of being heard.

Wherever religion is a significant part of life, so is dance and is at once worship and prayer. Lucian already remarked that "you cannot find a single mystery in which there is no dancing; in fact, most people say of the devotees of the mysteries that they danced them out." To a certain degree, all dance is a ritual. D. H. Lawrence realized this when describing the Quetzales whose mesmerizing dance is mentioned in his *Mornings in Mexico:*

All the men sing in unison, as they move with the soft, yet heavy bird tread which is the whole of the dance, with bodies bent a little forward, shoulders and heads loose and heavy, feet powerful but soft, the men tread the rhythm into the centre of the earth. The drums keep up the pulsating heartbeat and for hours, hours it goes on.

How different, and still a ritual, is the chapter in Nathaniel Hawthorne's story, *The Marble Faun.* The visualization of a Sylvan Dance conjures up the spirit of the Golden Age:

"Dance! dance!" he cried, joyously. "If we take breath we shall be as we were yesterday. There, now, the music, just beyond this clump of trees. Dance, Miriam, dance!" . . . It might be that there was magic in the sound, or contagion, at least, in the spirit which had got possessed of Miriam and himself, for very soon a number of festal people were drawn to the spot, and struck into the dance, singly, or in pairs. . . .

Here, as it seemed, had the Golden Age come back again within the precincts of this sunny glade, thawing mankind out of their cold formalities, releasing them from their irksome restraint, mingling them together in such childlike gaiety that new flowers sprang up beneath their footsteps.

Innumerable are the poems to which the dance inspired the poets. They are most often ecstatic expressions trying to verbalize the jubilant feeling of rejoicing—tripudiate is the archaic word for rejoicing and dancing—to catch the excitement of turning and leaping. Sometimes the fleeting image of the dance is used to philosophize, as Edna St. Vincent Millay did in her sonnet, *The Dance:*

> How stealthily their feet upon the floor
> Strike down!—these are no spirits, but a band
> Of children, surely, leaping hand in hand
> Into the air, in groups of three and four!
> Wearing their silken rags as if they were
> Leaves only and light grasses, or a strand
> Of bleak elusive seaweed cozing sand,
> And running hard, as if along a shore!
> I know how lost forever, and at length
> How still, these lovely tossing limbs shall lie,
> And the bright laughter and the panting breath;
> And yet, before such beauty and such strength,
> Again, as always when the dance is high,
> I am rebuked that I believe in death.

Poetry in prose done to perfection was created by Isak Dinesen when, in her story, *The Poet,* from *Seven Gothic Tales,* she depicts an old man looking through a window into a room where a young girl danced a Pas Seul:

The young mistress of the house stood on the tips of her toes in the middle of the room. She had on the very short diaphanous frock of a ballet dancer, and her little heelless shoes were fastened with black ribbons laced around her delicate ankles and legs. She held her arms over her head, gracefully rounded, and stood quite still, watching the music, her face like the placid, happy face of a doll.

As her bar of music fell in, she suddenly came to life. She lifted her right leg slowly, slowly, the toe pointing straight at the Councilor, higher and higher, as if she were really rising from the ground and about to fly. Then she brought it down again, slowly, slowly, on the tip of the toe, with a little gentle pat, no more than a fingertap upon the table.

The spectator outside held his breath. As before, on watching the ballet at Vienna, he had the feeling that this was too much; it could not be done. And then it was done, lightly, as in jest. One begins to doubt the fall of man, and not to worry about it, when a young dancer can thus rise from it again.

Standing upon the tip of her right toe now, she lifted her left leg, slowly high up, opened her arms in a swift audacious movement, whirled all around herself, and began to dance. The dance was more than a real mazurka, very fiery and light, lasting perhaps two minutes: a humming top, a flower, a flame dancing, a play upon the law of gravity, a piece of celestial drollery. It was also a bit of acting: love, sweet innocence, tears, a *sursum cordae* expressed in music and movement. In the middle of it there was a little pause to frighten the audience, but it went on all the same, only even more admirably, as if transposed into a higher key. Just as the music box gave signs of running down, she looked straight at the Councilor and sank down upon the floor in a graceful heap, like a flower flung stem upward, exactly as if her legs had been cut off with a pair of scissors. . . .

. . . she had got up, but remained as if irresolute, and did not turn on the box again. There was a long mirror in the room. Pressing the palm of her hand gently upon the glass she bent forward and kissed her own silvery image within it. Then she took up a long extinguisher, and one by one she put out the candles of the chandelier. She opened the door and was gone.

This passage is quoted at such length because it proves the close kinship of poetry and the dance, the major theme of this book. This is one more example of how only poetic power can capture the elusiveness of the dance, how such a felicitous phrase as "a piece of celestial drollery" can capsule a visual impression and give it the finality of an exclamation mark. The Isak Dinesen quotation should be read and reread in this light which also falls on the beautifully visualized allusion of the dancer in love with herself.

At the age of fourteen Hans Christian Andersen participated in the production of a ballet, and his first part was to be "an anonymous goblin in a corps of goblins." Shortly afterwards he was in the ballet *Armida,* in which he had a small part. He was a spirit, he relates in his autobiography, and saw his name in print for the first time. He already visualized himself immortalized: "I was continually looking at the printed paper. I carried the program bill of the ballet to bed with me at night, was lying there and read my name by candlelight—in short I was happy!"

Afterwards he did not give up his attachment to the dance. Very early in his life he developed a special gift. He could cut out things in paper with a pair of scissors, and in almost all his paper cutouts little dancing figures play a major part. Even trees are gracefully bent and non-dancing figures are always in motion. Moreover, it is not mere coincidence that Andersen's first book with *Fairy Tales* was published in 1835, at the height of Romanticism, when the choreographers thirsted for the kind of material that was hidden in Andersen's stories. At that time he influenced them far more indirectly than in our own era when his story of *The Red Shoes* became a climactic point in cinematic ballet and Stravinsky found inspiration in *The Ice Maiden* which turned into *Le Baiser de la Fée,* and *The Nightingale* which reappeared in the form of opera and ballet. George Balanchine's advice to parents who wish to prepare their children for a dance career was: "I would suggest reading the child fairy stories . . . by all means read the stories of the great Hans Christian Andersen. I don't mean Andersen's stories, or any others, as they are watered down, especially translated and condensed for children. Good fairy stories were always written for intelligent people."

When Théophile Gautier thought that the divine Carlotta Grisi could do no wrong, Andersen became enamoured with Fanny Cerito, who made her debut in 1835. "There must be youth," he exclaimed, "and that I found in Cerito. It was something incomparably beautiful, it was a swallow flight in the dance, a sport of Psyche." In 1846, two years before Marie Taglioni retired, he saw her in *La Pas des Déesses* and wrote about his impression in the *Story of My Life:*

Before she appeared I felt a throbbing of my heart, which I always have when my expectation is raised for something excellent and grand.

She appeared as an old, little sturdy, and quite pretty woman; she would have been a nice lady in a salon, but as a young goddess— *fuimus Troes!* I sat cool and indifferent at the graceful dancing of that old lady.

Then he broke out into the cry for youth he found in Cerito and the feeling of a flight she gave him and which he no longer saw in Taglioni. Understandably, Andersen felt more than a passing infatuation for his compatriot ballerina Lucille Grahn, who was also in London at that time

and was highly admired of all, but she had a sore foot and did not dance. One evening when *Elisire d'Amore* was given, she sent for me to see her in her little box, where she disclosed for me with liveliness and fun the world behind the scenes, and gave me an account of each of the actors.

On his various journeys Andersen realized how great the accomplishments of the Danish Ballet at the Copenhagen Theatre was. Seeing the ballet in Vienna, he could not help drawing comparisons and wrote in *A Poet's Bazaar:*

The theatre "Nächst dem Kärnthner Thor" has, besides the opera, a ballet; but though there is a large stage here, with plenty of pomp and show, yet the ballet department will not bear any comparison with that of the Copenhagen Theatre, which, at this time [about 1845] stands very high, and our ballets surpass in taste and poetry all those I have had an opportunity of seeing in Germany and Italy. Paris and Naples, without doubt, excel us in the number of their dancers and in their splendid decorations, but not in composition.

When the Italian Galeotti died in Denmark, Terpsichore wept. Who was there that could supply his place as ballet composer? No one took his place; but a new one was born, who, like every true genius, made his own way—and that is Bournonville.

The phenomenon of movement is basic to all experience in life from birth to death; it lies in all growth, in man's changing feelings and gaining thoughts. Its conceptual transformation into an art form has invariably and in varied ways fascinated the poet, but so has its purely abstract *Gestalt* in all its facets. One of them is the seemingly constant circling, the whirl and turn which appears manifested in the planets. Dante saw in the cosmic Reigen the holy mystery and power of love which lies behind the fulfillment of our existence. The microcosmic experience of man in the sweep of the turn reveals a mysterious center of stillness, the movement that lies in stillness, the quiet that is the heart and secret of movement. In *Sonnets to Orpheus* Rainer Maria Rilke looked at the revelation of this secret when he said:

> Dancer, O you who is the postponement
> of all that fades in eternal flow: how you gave us yourself.
> And then the final whirl, this tree growing out of movement,
> did it not take total possession of the accomplished year?

The reflection of the dance in the literature of the late Middle Ages and the Renaissance is not as impressive as it might have been, measured by the dance consciousness of that time. But there was hardly any great writer who would not have treated the dance as the self-evident experience and daily occurrence it then was.

Dance has always been an essential part of courtship. What still passed for dancing in the eleventh century was a pretext for uncouth wooing. The participants walked, stepped about, and jumped from time to time. This went on for hours, chain dances which were in no way defined nor ruled by any feeling for etiquette. During the twelfth century the pendulum swung to the other extreme. The motives of romantic love and chivalry became predominant, sex was subordinated to symbol, and etiquette became the guiding rod to living. The knight was inspired by the myth of Tristan and Isolt which made passion triumphant over conjugal union. The myth of love as escape and dream, as suffering and death became a characteristic product of the time and characteristic of the complex nature of courtly love. It had its reflection in literature and the dance.

Already in the eleventh century we find courtly wooing through dance expressed in a Latin poem of Roodlieb, who wrote about a couple that never touched each other while dancing: he danced around her in the manner of the flight of a falcon and she imitated a pursued swallow; he tried to seize her, and she glided away—one of the favored pantomimic dances of the time. In the first half of the thirteenth century we find the verbal tapestry of a choral dance woven in Guillaume de Lorris's *Roman de la Rose:*

> And then a dance you might have seen,
> The maidens and the men in joy have been
> To tread a measure and to turn their rounds
> On grassy green of spring, and to the sounds
> Of flutists and of minstrels with a strain
> They sing of beautiful Lorraine. . . .
>
> Then came two damsels, young and neat,
> Their kirtles showed their forms sweet.
> In gaiety the two began to dance

With queenlike leaps and furtive glance;
Their bodies, lithe and limber, now advance
And give their lips to kiss but half a chance.
And then once more did they retreat
To turn a dancing measure with their feet.
What more could I describe and tell
Of all their dancing, done so well.

Dancing was one of the few emotional outlets for the people when visited by the bubonic plague. Giovanni Boccaccio, writing about 1350, described a scene of rich people who meet in a country house to escape the plague:

Breakfast done, the tables were removed, and the Queen (or elected story-leader) bade fetch instruments of music; for all, ladies and young men alike, knew how to tread a measure, and some of them played and sang with great skill; so, at her command Dioneo (this is Boccaccio himself) having taken a lute, and Fiametta a viol, they struck up a dance in sweet concert; and the servants being dismissed to their repast, the queen, attended by the other ladies and the two young men, led off a stately carole.

Such scenes are repeated in Boccaccio's *Decameron*. The seven ladies and three gentlemen spend, for instance, the evening of the seventh day "now dancing to the music of the hornpipe of Tindaro, and now caroling to other sounds."

Although Dante's work is imbued with the extremes of the medieval spirit, his lofty thoughts embraced the dance in sublime similes time and again. The bearing of a woman dancing was usually prescribed as chaste, modest, and stately, and Dante said in his *Purgatorio:*

As a lady who is dancing turns her round
with feet close to the ground and to each other,
and hardly putteth foot before foot,

she turned toward me upon the red and upon
the yellow flowerets, not otherwise than a virgin
that droppeth her modest eyes; . . .

Leonardo da Vinci, who wrote the stunning aphorism, "Movement is the cause of all life," once composed a ballet, an astral dance, in which the entire astronomic system was depicted. His idea echoed Dante's visualization of a round dance of the sun in *Paradiso* of *The Divine Comedy:*

Soon as the blessed flame had taken up the
final word to speak, began the sacred millstone
to revolve,
and in its rolling had not turned full round
ere a second, circling, embraced it and struck
motion to its motion and song to its song. . . .

And lo! around, of lustre equable, upsprings
a shining beyond what was there, in fashion
of a brightening horizon.
And as, at the first rise of evening, new
things-to-see begin to show in heaven, so that
the sight doth, yet doth not, seem real;
I there began to perceive new-come existences
making a circle out beyond the other two
circumferences.

What seemed to many scholars a rather childish indulgence on Leonardo's part is the composition of pictographs. Words are represented by animals or objects and sometimes letters are added to complete them. These pictographs have puzzled the researchers. There is one drawing, now at Windsor Castle, a mysterious allegory in which various objects fall down from the clouds. This allegory very likely refers to the occupations which are forced upon man by fate. Leonardo, who designed many Trionfi, may have sketched a figure choral in which many dancers were supposed to participate. This dance entertainment developed at an early stage of the court ballet, and its various arrangements and movement of lines, forming letters in significant succession, offered great visual joy and satisfaction for observers and participants. This dance of letters must already have been known in Dante's time since he uses the same concept in his *Paradiso:*

> And as birds, risen from the bank, as though re-
> joicing together o'er their pasture, make them-
> selves now a round, now a long, flock,
> so within the lights the sacred creatures flying
> sang, and in their shapings made themselves now
> D, now I, now L.
> First singing to their note they moved, then as
> they made themselves one of these signs, a little
> space would stay and hold their peace.

The foundation to theatrical dance was laid in the early Renaissance with the growing importance of the dancing masters. A vocabulary of steps and a choreographic pattern or design was needed for the creation of a dance art. The dancing masters of that time were the first ballet masters *and* choreographers composing a sequence of steps, striving towards elegant movements. They created theatrical dancing for certain stage effects, though the stage was the ballroom floor of princely courts. Guglielmo Ebreo of Pesaro, a contemporary of Lorenzo de Medici, was one of the more important dancing masters. He had an extraordinarily creative mind and the ability to articulate his concepts of what dancing should be. His endeavor to put down basic rules for the dance was in keeping with the growing scientific trend of the time. The esteem in which he was held by his contemporaries is substantiated by the fact that his work on dancing was used in

several places at the same time. It also contained a couple of
dances by Lorenzo de Medici, most of whose canzoni were written
with the explicit purpose of having dancers move to the verses; in
fact, Lorenzo's verses appear to be so constructed as to fall in with
the different movements and pauses of the dancing.

The dancing masters were respected artists, the masters of etiquette, and often the confidants of the princes and dukes. Curt
Sachs mentions that "at Venetian weddings, where it was the custom to present the bride first in a silent dance, [the dancing mas-
ter] might appear in place of the father." It was said of Guglielmo Ebreo that he "excelled all men in the dance" and
contemporary poets wrote flattering verses to his agility as a dancer and his skill as a musician. Giovanni Mario Philelfo, poet lau-
reate at the court of Duke Federigo of Urbino, composed a long
poem in honor and praise of Guglielmo. Here are a few lines of
it:

So gentle and angelic is the harmony
  In the sweet music of Guglielmo, the Hebrew,
  So much grace is in his beautiful dancing
That Maccabeus would lay down his arms,
  Solomon forget all his wisdom as would King David,
  And he would make cruel Eurystheus feel ashamed of himself.

The famous Medicean Trionfi and the entire craze for the arrangement of Trionfi and Carri were inspired by Petrarch's
Trionfo d'Amore. (The idea of celebrating the triumph of something with a pageant has survived to our days in the Mardi Gras
festivities, Thanksgiving Day observances, and the New Year's
Day "Bowl" parades.) Petrarch is the only case of a Renaissance
poet who contributed creatively, though unconsciously, to the
dance. Undoubtedly, the painters and architects of the Renaissance had the greatest influence on the dance. Also the develop-

ment of the scientific concept of perspective has led not only to foreshortening in painting and to a new approach in scenic design but also to the revolutionary idea of "turn-out" in the theater dance.

Nota Bene: Ballet history could be written from the viewpoint of the use of subject matter. One could rightly claim that, like ballet, the drama has also leaned heavily on Biblical, mythological, and historical material, but the theater dance has in its own movement language interpreted many a drama. The fact remains that ballet and particularly the modern dance owe a great debt to the literary word. On the other hand, I know of no dramatic play whose inspirational source had been a dance experience.

National characteristics and the sociocultural background of a country have decisive influence on the choice of subject matter and on the choreographer's closeness to the literary word. One can only register one's surprise at the interest of the greatest names in French literature with which they actively contributed to the ballet, from Paul Claudel to Marcel Proust to Jean Cocteau. This collaborative trend is undoubtedly based on the century-old ballet tradition in France. The writers of the Anglo-Saxon or German world have never been exposed to ballet as intensely as their French counterparts have and therefore have never acquired the same taste and flair for it. The Russians fall in between these two extremes.

It is difficult to assess whether the choreographers of the twentieth century have become increasingly literary-minded. The literary story element was far more pronounced in the eighteenth- and nineteenth-century ballets than it is now, since the *ballets géographiques* and Noverre's *ballet d'action,* followed by Viganò's *choréodrame* and the fairy-tale world of Romanticism depended on literary prototypes. The modern ballet choreographer, it seems, has learned to rely on the music for inspiration. Since the days of Diaghilev the dancer has, to a great extent, become the patron of the composers, and music has often shaped many balletic ideas.

The modern dance, by its virtue of externalizing personal experiences, has been literature-prone from the very beginning. If it did not rely on a literary work, it received its inspiration through a poem or a line of poetry; and when it expressed its own feelings, it invariably told us the whole book, or a chapter from that one book with which we all run around: the story of our life. In its psychodramatic existence the modern dance was not only literal, it was mainly literary. Its latest offspring, the nonliteral dance, is neither inspired by music (which it usually tolerates, but prefers sound effects instead) nor owes its existence thematically to literature. It has attained a new nowness, has become an environmental dance striving towards the creation of a new myth (which may easily reveal itself as a nonmyth) and the folklore of rootlessness.

This new trend of the extremism in modern dance must exert some influence on the established ballet within a short time. As much as science already now longs for the poetic touch of humanness, these extreme trends will have to find back to the poetic image of life. The inspiration for the choreographer may no longer come from the Bible and mythology, from Shakespeare or Garcia Lorca. But it will have to come from the provocative persuasion of life, from an evocative image of what life may be to us, or an allusive notion of that secret that makes living worthwhile. For all we know, the choreographer may find inspiration in a composite of all the beauty and horror that has always been our heritage, however much we want to deny that we are yesterday's children.

THE ENGLISH SCENE

THE ENGLISH, on whom the French have always looked down as a mercantile and sober people and whom the Germans consider *amusisch,* have, since the days of the Renaissance, produced many writers and poets who have taken issue with the dance. They were inspired observers, even though they have thrown their creative imagination into the dancing ring less actively than their French counterparts have, particularly during the nineteenth century.

Sir John Davies gave us *Orchestra,* published in 1597, a lyric companion piece to Arbeau's *Orchésographie.* He verbally notated in detail the various dances known and practiced in the late Renaissance with an often contagious enthusiasm and engaging naïveté as shown by two stanzas chosen at random:

Dauncing (bright Lady) then began to bee,
When the first seeds whereof the world did spring,
The fire, ayre, earth, and water—did agree,
By Love's perswasion,—Nature's mighty King,—
To leave their first disordred combating;
    And in a daunce such measure to observe,
    As all the world their motion should preserve.

259

Behold the world, how it is whirled around,
And for it is so whirl'd, is named so;
In whose large volume many rules are found
Of this new Art, which it doth farely show;
For your quicke eyes in wandring too and fro
From East to West, on no one thing can glaunce
But if you marke it well, it seemes to daunce.

More than in his being a poet, his importance lies in having recorded the dances of his time with as much accuracy as feasible in rhymes; his description of the courante may serve as an example:

What shall I name those current travases,
That on a triple dactyl foot do run
Close to the ground with sliding passages,
Wherein that dancer greatest praise hath won,
Which with best order can all order shun:
For everywhere he wantonly must range,
And turn and wind with unexpected change.

At the beginning and the end of the seventeenth century, dance played a magnificent role in the entertainment at the royal court and the festivities of the nobility, but its use, intent, and influence varied greatly. Queen Elizabeth and the Stuart queens rivaled with the splendor of the French, Danish, and Florentine courts, and the means of entertainment became trump cards in a state's political propaganda. The lavish gesture on a festive occasion was a measure of prestige in those days. The English crown loved to display the power of its throne and the riches of its realm in productions of Masques and Anti-Masques. The artistic culmination of the many forms of ballet-mascarades developed during the Renaissance into a splendid social diversion. More will have to be said about it when we speak of Shakespeare, but it should be mentioned that his dramatic rival, Ben Jonson, had also accepted the challenge to give the dance and scenic splendor their poetic motivation and background.

After having written twenty of the thirty-seven masques presented at court during the reign of James I, Jonson's collaboration with the scene master Inigo Jones, whom he called "a maker of properties . . . whirling his whimsies" in his anger, came to an abrupt end in 1631. The people of the early seventeenth century were captivated by visual magnificence whether it was the most stunning stage pictures and magical scene changes, with miraculous effects achieved by cloud machines, or whether it was in the movement design of the many richly or anticly costumed figures who danced through these masques. They offered Ben Jonson an opportunity to write an integrated work for the theater in which the poetic image was composed of drama, music, movement, and color. Thus, the Masques and Anti-Masques were the first consciously created ideas for a total theater effect.

Ben Jonson must have been delighted to come upon the notion of contrasting the beauty of his verses and the flourish of visual exhibitions with the humor of the Anti-Masque, whose grotesque potentialities lay mainly in the dance. When he wrote his court masques—most of which were epithalamia—he thought not only in dramatic-poetic terms but in terms of dance. His sense of dramaturgy had to proportion the spoken or sung word and dance movement. The visual images, mostly of mythological nature, emerged logically from his lines, even though his stage directions describe his visualizations. Jonson left the dancing itself to the dancing master, but besides saying in his direction, "They danc'd their maine Dance," he often meditated about the dance as in the sung stanzas that follow from *The Vision of Delight, a Masque presented at Court in Christmas, 1617:*

In curious knots and mazes so
The Spring at first was taught to go:
And *Zephire,* when he came to wooe
His *Flora,* had their motions too,
And thence did *Venus* learne to lead
Th' *Idalian* Braules, and so to tread
As if the wind, not she did walke;
Nor prest a flower, nor bow'd a stalke.

On occasion Jonson also introduced the dance with a couple of lines:

Advance, his favour calls you to advance,
And do your (this nights) homage in a dance.

This was then followed by the entry of the dancers. There is nowhere any indication of difficulties Ben Jonson might have had with the dancing masters. His masques fully show Jonson's understanding for the dance which never crossed and rather furthered his poetic inspirations. When he realized that the parade of visual sumptuousness, however impressive in itself, overwhelmed his dramatic and poetic intentions, he parted company with Inigo Jones and stopped writing masques. He had no harsh word for the dance. His fury was directed against "painting and carpentry," which finally had become "the soul of masque."

Pepys: and so to bed

The era of Charles II, who loved life and pretty girls, the theater and dance, had an astute observer in Samuel Pepys whose diaries are a valuable and entertaining record of the scene. In 1660, Charles returned from exile in France and brought with him the gusto for being entertained and for entertaining his court. Very soon two theaters were opened, the Duke's House in Lincoln's Inn Fields and the King's in Vere Street.

In contrast to the Elizabethan and Tudor periods—before citizen Oliver Cromwell took over the reign—the theater fare was rather lightweight. The Shakespearean plays were bowdlerized, musical shows were the hits of those days, and even *Macbeth* and *The Tempest* were performed with music and dance. Pepys recorded for us in his Diary in 1668 that he saw a seamen's dance in *The Tempest,* and he had nothing but praise for a *Macbeth* production, "one of the best plays for a stage, and variety of dancing and musique that ever I saw."

The straight plays, in the main, light comedies and bloody revenge plays, were not performed without dancing. The custom of the Elizabethan period to end each play with a jig and to show a dance in the intermission was continued during the Restoration period and long into the eighteenth century. An incidental dance in the course of the action was always a welcome and expected addition. *Macbeth* was probably presented not as a musical in our sense but as a play with some music and choreography for the scenes of the witches.

The two London theaters, opened again after more than two decades, were not very comfortable, not more comfortable than some of our off-Broadway theaters. This may have been one reason for playwright and actors to try their best to entertain their audiences who, after so many lean years, were hungry for the spectacular and thirsty for the hot, bawdy stuff. The king and his court were often seen in the theater, in the first tier boxes. The king did not even mind a bad play, as long as he could look at the beauties in the boxes and the pretty wenches on the backless benches in the pit, whose faces seemed even more exciting in the candle light which lively flickered outshining the bit of daylight coming through the roof. There the king must have noticed Nell

Gwyn, "pretty, witty Nell," with her flaming red hair and dim-
pled cheeks, who began her theater career selling oranges and ap-
ples to the gallants and men about town before becoming a star
and finally the concubine of the king. The middle class sat in the
galleries.

For quite some time the theater was mainly frequented by an
elite, aristocratic and intellectual; by women who wanted to be
noticed but not really seen and usually wore masks for the purpose of greater excitement; by sluts—an epithet often found in
Pepys's Diary—for whom the theater was more than stimulation.
Still for many years after Puritan domination the bourgeois citizen kept away from the theaters and King Charles's sinful entertainments.

Samuel Pepys, Clerk of the Acts, was a very devoted civil servant, who put in many hours of work. In his Diary we often come
across the phrase: late at the office . . . so weary and late to
bed." But, sometimes it so happened that he passed the theaters
on a business errand or after lunch and was tempted to see what
his king saw. Like the majority of the middle-class citizens, Pepys
had a puritanical attitude towards the theater in the first couple
of years, but then he seemed to have quickly adjusted to the *joie
de vivre* of the Restoration period. On September 11, 1661, we
still read that when

I to Dr. Williams to talk with him again, and he and I walking
through Lincoln's Inn Fields observed at the Opera a new play,
"Twelfth Night," was acted there, and the King there; so I, against my
own mind and resolution, could not forbear to go in, which did make
the play seem a burthen to me, and I took no pleasure at all in it; and
so after it was done went home with my mind troubled for my going
thither.

Two months later, on November 11, he wrote:

Captain Ferrier carried me the first time that ever I saw any gaming house . . . folly of men to lay and lose so much money. . . . And thence he took me to a dancing school in Fleet Street, where we saw a company of pretty girls dance, but I do not in myself like to have young girls exposed to so much vanity.

Then he was still guilt-ridden and fought the temptations of dance and theater which, however, did not keep him from seeing shows. Before his puritan conscience was silenced, he may have comforted himself with the thought that he did what the king did and, in a way, to please him and to be au courant. On the last day of 1662 he noted:

Mr. Povy and I to Whitehall; he taking me thither on purpose to carry me into the hall this night before the King . . . and so other lords, other ladies; and they danced the Bransle. After that the King led a lady a single Coranto; and then the rest of the lords, one after another, other ladies; very noble it was, and great pleasure to see. Then to country dances; the King leading the first, which he called for, which was, says he, "Cuckolds all awry," the old dance of England. Of the ladies that danced, the Duke of Monmouth's mistress, and my Lady Castlemaine and a daughter of Sir Harry de Vicke's were the best. The manner was, when the King dances, all the ladies in the room, and the Queen herself, stand up; and indeed he dances rarely, and much better than the Duke of York. Having stayed here as long as I thought fit, to my infinite content, it being the greatest pleasure I could wish now to see at Court, I went home, leaving them dancing.

Pepys had seen dancing in the theater that year since he commented on the then famous dancer John Lacey, who appeared in the title role of *The French Dancing Master* and whom he considered "the best in the world."

In his long diary entry about New Year's Eve at Whitehall, there was no mentioning yet of himself as a dancer. On May 4, 1663, he watched his wife taking a dancing lesson:

The dancing-master came, whom standing by, seeing him instructing my wife, when he had done with her, he would needs have me try the steps of a coranto; and what with his desire, and my wife's importunity, I did begin, and then was obliged to give him entry money 10s, and am become his scholar. The truth is I think it is a thing very useful for any gentleman.

Four days later he went to the theater:

The play was *The Humorous Lieutenant,* a play that has little good in it. . . . In the dance the tall devil's actions was very pretty. . . . We home by water. . . . At supper comes Pembleton/the dancing master/, and afterwards we all up to dancing till late. They say that I am like to make a dancer.

The ice was broken. He and his wife took lessons with Pembleton, his wife was a bit clumsy. It actually all began on April 19, 1663:

To church, where the young Scotchman preaching, I slept awhile. After supper fell in discourse of dancing, and I find that Ashwell hath a very fine carriage, which makes my wife almost ashamed of herself to see herself so outdone, but tomorrow she begins to learn to dance, for a month or two.

There are innumerable entries in his Diary telling us that on coming home from his work he finds his wife with a few friends dancing: "and here I danced with them, and had a good supper and as merry as could be" or "and after supper to dancing and singing till about twelve at night . . . and then to bed."

What were they usually dancing? "After the bransles, then to a corant and now and then a french dance; but that so rare that the corants grew tiresome, that I wished it done. Only Mrs. Stewart danced mighty finely, and many french dances, specially one the King called the New Dance."

With the years Pepys had become quite a man about town and learned to dance until late at night. January 6, 1668:

and after supper to dancing and singing till about twelve at night . . . by the coming in of young Goodyer and some others of our neighbors, young men that could dance, hearing of our dancing, and anon comes in Mrs. Turner. . . . And so to dancing again and singing, with extraordinary great pleasure, till about two in the morning . . . and so away to bed.

All this does not indicate that Samuel Pepys neglected his duties as civil servant or that his personal pleasure in dancing overshadowed his interest in the theater, even though he reproached himself for having spent so much time and money in the theater. He was neither a drama nor a dance critic. He never analyzed nor described in detail what he saw; he recorded his impressions and was most interested in personalities. At this time there were not any newspapers. His Diary is an intellectualized gossip column which affords us to piece together little details. As a chronicle of the social scene his Diary is invaluable.

There were very few great actors or dancers in England at that time. The influence of the *commedia dell'arte* was still great —Molière's influence reached all over Europe in those days—and the stress in dancing and acting lay on bravura and skill, not on a refined interpretation. The comedy of manners created types more than human beings. The theater-going public felt like humans in type's cloth, identified with them and enjoyed laughing at themselves. The acrobatic skill of the Italians was felt even more in dancing than in acting. Pepys was bored by the play *The Sullen Lovers:* "But a little boy, for a farce, do dance Polichinelli, the best that ever anything was done in the world, by all men's report."

The spectacular feats and the king's favor led to the hearts of the audience. Jacob Hall was a famous rope dancer who advertised his art as "Excellent Dancing and Vaulting on the Ropes; with Variety of Rare Feats of Activity and Agility of Body upon the Stage; as doing Somersets, and Flipflaps, Flying over Thirty Rapiers, and over several Men's heads; and also flying through several Hoops." Pepys thought that it was such action as "I never saw before, and mighty worth seeing."

The two great dancer-actresses of the time were Nell Gwyn and Moll Davies. The "little Nelly," as Pepys called her, seemed to have been the more acrobatic and flexible dancer who conquered her audience with the challenging pertness of her personality. Even though Mrs. Pepys, quoted by her husband, spoke of Moll Davies as "a most impertinent slut," Samuel Pepys was "mightily" pleased by her dancing in a shepherd's clothes and quoted his wife's friend, a certain Mrs. Pierce, as having said that "she is a most homely jade as ever she saw though she dances beyond anything in the world," the world rather confined to the London stage.

It seems that Pepys could not make up his mind as to whom of the two he should consider the greater dancer. Nell, in male attire, also delighted him when he saw her dance a jig in *Secret Love* or the *Maiden Queen:* "so great a performance of a comical part was never, I believe, in the world before as Nell do this . . . best of all when she comes in like a young gallant; and hath the motions and carriage of a spark the most that ever I saw any man have. It makes me, I confess, admire her."

Nell Gwyn's personality must have been ravishing to make Pepys more eloquent than usual. Pretty, witty Nelly was also clever. She left the theater career at the peak of her fame for the good—and probably better—fortune of becoming the king's paramour. Pepys's comment: "Poor girl! I pity her; but more the loss of her at the King's house." And so to bed.

Shakespeare and the dance

A feeling of spiritual and physical awakening, of inhaling a new vigorous air and exhaling the joy of life, long suppressed but always dormant in man, swept over Europe in the fifteenth and sixteenth centuries, and it did not stop at the Channel. The English, then on the eve of becoming the world's greatest merchants and destined to rule the waves for a long time to come, had more frequent contact with the peoples of Europe than we now imagine. In the sixteenth century, in spite of the hazards of travel, journeys to Denmark, the Netherlands, and Germany, but particularly to France and Italy were undertaken by merchants and the nobility, by adventurers and actors. While French dancing masters and Italian actors often crossed the Channel, entire companies of English players went to the continent. As a matter of fact, a great many of them felt obliged to go abroad since there were always more players than parts to be had in the London theaters, and they were all excellent dancers besides being proficient actors.

Dancing was a necessary accomplishment for all actors, for they were often called upon to dance in a play. Shakespeare and his contemporary playwrights indicated through such laconic notes as "Dance" or "They dance" in their stage directions that they took the actors' dancing ability for granted. At that time no director of any company had to worry about finding an actor who could also dance or a dancer who could also act. He who was not a good dancer and fencer was not considered a good actor. This was the spirit of the *commedia dell'arte,* and the very same spirit dominated the training of the English actor. The demands on the actors' versatility of the *commedia dell'arte* staggers our imagination today; the best of them were excellent mimes, acrobats, accomplished musicians and dancers, men of superlative swordsmanship, and of no slight education. The English actor abroad faced comparison with his Italian colleagues and, on the whole, fared pretty well. His skill as a dancer especially was mentioned time and again.

In Elizabethan, though no longer in Jacobean, days a play performed at court entertainments was often followed by a mask. On the public stages the playgoers after the play expected to see a jig or one or two of the company's members conclude the spectacle with a dance, as borne out by the closing lines in *Much Ado About Nothing:* "Strike up, pipers. Dance"; or when in *As You Like It* the banished Duke announces to the happily united couples:

> Play, music! And you, brides and bridegrooms all,
> With measure heap'd in joy, to the measures fall.

This invitation to the "measures," a stately, pavane-like dance, mostly followed by livelier steps, culminates in the Duke's last words:

> Proceed, proceed: we will begin these rites,
> As we do trust they'll end, in true delights.
>   A Dance.

The playgoing public usually considered the epilogue a natural lead into a dance or jig. Even amateur performances, of which there were many at that time in England, ended with dancing. Shakespeare, parodying amateurs in *A Midsummer Night's Dream* with the artisans' performance, has Bottom ask Theseus, Duke of Athens, in his malapropos way: "Will it please you to see the epilogue, or to hear a Bergomask dance between two of our company?"; whereupon Theseus asks for a Bergomask, or more correctly, a Bergomasco, a then popular Italian round dance.

Our present-day conception of the theater is essentially different from that of the Elizabethan playgoers, whose participation in whatever was spoken or shown on the stage was intense. There was a mental kinetic reaction to it, often passionate and violent, but an experience which electrified both players and spectators. It may have something to do with the Elizabethan stage being thrust into the audience, with no separating curtain, with greater physical contact between the giving and receiving end. I am inclined, however, to think that it is far more a difference in attitude toward what we call entertainment. We pay our entrance fee and want, as much as the Elizabethans, to be entertained, but deep within, we do not care to become too much absorbed by and concerned with what we are shown. We actually fight it, we want to remain detached, we lean back in our seats, figuratively speaking. Most of us have lost the quality of losing ourselves in the magic of word and movement. The Elizabethan still knew the innocent joy of being a part of it. In fact, he had no choice, he had to give himself up completely to the play and players if he wanted to get something out of the performance, since the greatest demands were made on his attention and imagination. Although the acting was more often realistic than not, there was no, or scarcely any, scenery; the auditor depended entirely upon the word to identify the location of each scene, and it was the word and the poetry which painted the emotions of each character and mounted the events of the play. Words alone had to create the magic of love-making, because younger boys played the parts of the women. Moreover, the listener's ear was subjected to a rapid delivery of the lines.

Therefore, it becomes more understandable to us that so much stress was put on dancing and that, as relief for the audience, musical interludes were scheduled between the acts, and not seldom a boy came forward to dance. In Fletcher's *Faithful Shepherdess* we find the lines:

> Nor wants there those who, as the boy doth dance
> Between the acts, will censure the whole play.

And, seen in this light, it is quite conceivable that the audience demanded to stay a short while longer after the play to see a dance. It may seem unpardonable to us to add a dance number to a tragedy, but it was a physical and emotional necessity for the Elizabethan audience. The dance was as well prepared as the play itself, "a thing studied and rehearst as a Iigge after a play." Sometimes, as in the Second Part of *King Henry IV* the epilogue was even spoken by a dancer. When, today, we should hear him say toward the end of his speech, "my tongue is weary; when my legs are too, I will bid you good night," it would make no sense to us who expect the curtain to fall after his last word. In those days, he then began to dance until his legs were actually weary.

Statistical minds have found that out of 237 Elizabethan plays 68 call for dancing in their actual text. Music and the dance are close to the heart of most poets, and they figure prominently in Shakespeare's writing. About 500 passages—in one form or another—deal with musical matters. Shakespeare mentions 12 different dances in his dramatic and poetic works, altogether he concerns himself 50 times with dancing in his plays and poems. As Shakespeare so often used the simile of life being a stage and felt that a play held a mirror up to nature, we can safely assume that the music- and dance-minded stage of the Elizabethans was the true reflection of their life.

This era carries rightly the name of England's Queen, for she was the incarnation of all we associate with her time. The assertion of man's emancipation from the fetters of the medieval past came to full fruition under her leadership. She gave her country the renaissance of mind and body, the adventurous spirit, the triumph over the Spanish Armada, stability, and the iron reign so necessary at a time in which the political game was dangerous and full of intricate intrigues and plots. Nevertheless, her subjects worshiped her, the Virgin Queen, and "when foreign ambassadors enquired the secret of it, she danced before them."

The daughter of Henry VIII and Anne Boleyn was accomplished in most of the arts. Not only did she speak six languages fluently and translate from Latin and Greek poets but she wrote her own poetry, and, as one of her contemporaries phrased it, "her learned, delicate, noble Muse easily surmounteth all the rest . . . be it in ode, epigram, or any other kind of poem heroic and lyric." However, Elizabeth had the good taste to keep her work from circulation. She liked the theater and had a sound instinct for what makes a play; she must have been quite a critical audience when Shakespeare's company played for her. Elizabeth was also an expert musician and was sometimes heard playing her own compositions, but her great passion was dancing. She was an experienced dancer, with a strong sense of rhythm. It is said that when she watched a dance she followed "the cadence with her head, hand and foot".

Love of the dance endured with Elizabeth to the verge of her grave. Her share in the Twelfth Night revels of 1599 was reported to Spain by its ambassador with biting sarcasm: "the head of the Church of England and Ireland was to be seen in her old age dancing three or four gaillards." About a year later she was still dancing "gayement et de belle disposition" at the wedding of Anne Russel, and in April 1602 she danced yet two galliards with the Duke of Nevers. This passion for the dance seemed to have run in the family, since Henry VIII was described by a foreign ambassador as a "truly indefatigable" dancer who particularly liked the lusty, gay, and amorous type of dance.

The Londoners considered Queen Elizabeth as one of themselves since she was "descended of citizens." She was loved and feared, praised and imitated. The Queen liked the theater, and thousands of Londoners went to see the plays. The Queen loved music, and people would sit around the table after supper and sing madrigals. Even while a barber shaved, the customer was entertained with music. The Queen had a passion for dancing, and the Londoners became passionate dancers. In 1587 a Puritan writer complained that "London is so full of unprofitable pipers and fiddlers that a man can no sooner enter a tavern than two or three of them hang at his heels, to give him a dance before he depart."

London was full of dancing schools, frequented by the nobility as much as by the citizens. The Duke of Bourbon declares disdainfully in *Henry V* (III.v), "They bid us to the English dancing schools/and teach lavoltas high and swift corantos." Of course, he who could afford it went to France, which was the mecca of the dance. Thus we read of George Villiers, first Duke of Buckingham, that "his chief exercises were dancing, fencing, vaulting, etc." and that, after a sojourn in France where he went to finish his studies, he returned to England in 1613 "with the distinction of being the finest dancer in the country." Nobody at the English Court could then afford not to dance, as can be seen from a report of the Spanish Ambassador, Juan Fernandez, who tells of a ball at Whitehall Palace on August 19, 1604, during which "the Prince"—Prince Henry Frederick who died in 1612 —"was commanded by his parents to dance a galliard and they pointed out to him the lady who was to be his partner; and this he did with much sprightliness and modesty, cutting several capers of the dance—con algunas cabriolas."

The dances then in vogue were not easy, and the many dancing schools in London profited from the fact. The taste of the time was for the theatrical, the spectacular, dances with intricate steps, with leaps and lifting of one's partner, as we are now used to see on the stage rather than on the ballroom floor. The French dances dominated the English scene and, in spite of their intricacies, won more and more popularity after the middle of the sixteenth century. A visitor to one of the London dancing schools in 1585 watched a performer do a galliard and remarked how "at our entring hee was beginning a trick as I remember of sixteens and seuenteens, I do not very wel remember, but wonderfully hee leaped, flung and took on." The London citizenry did as well in these French dances as the courtiers. Of course, the surprised visitor was watching an amateur practicing for his own pleasure. And if nonprofessionals were such excellent dancers, we can imagine what expert performances were expected from the actors on the stage.

We get the best conception of the Elizabethans' craving for the dance, and their indulgence in it, from those who opposed this rage and from the writers who satirized it. Most outspoken, weaponed with the fury of fanaticism, were the Puritans, the preachers and self-appointed moralists, and the London Council, which always used the specter of the plague as a pretense for its antitheatrical actions and which eyed any diversion of youth with disapproval, fearing for its morals as well as its industry. Once the London Council went so far as to ask Archbishop Whitgift's help to save the city's youth, whose way of life became "infected with many evil and ungodly qualities by reason of the wanton and profane devices represented upon the stages."

It seems that any occasion called for dancing. In 1577, Northbrooke, a puritan zealot, described his contemporaries as dancing "with ordinate gestures, and with monstrous thumping of the feete, to pleasant soundes, to wanton songs, to dishonest verses." He was particularly bitter when thinking of how grave women were caught by the craze: "it is a worlde to see, nay a hel to see, howe they will swing, leape, and turne when the pypers and crowders begin to play."

Philip Stubbes, another moralist, echoed Northbrooke, when railing against the dancing madness in his *Anatomy of Abuses,* published in 1583:

Some haue broken their legs with skipping, leaping, turning and vawting . . . men and women together . . . in publique assemblies and frequencies of People, with such beastly slabberings, bussings & misdemeanors . . . every leap or skip in dance, is a leap toward hel.

The record of the Middlesex Justices shows that, in 1612, they made a special order for "Suppressing Jigs at the end of plays on the ground that the lewd jigs, songs and dances so used at the Fortune led to the resort of cutpurses and other ill-disposed persons and to consequent breaches of the peace." The Puritans, of course, were most concerned with the many women who indulged in those dances which demanded agility and acrobatics rather than dignity, though to them, with their medieval sense of sin, all dancing led to hell. But even Arbeau, the French priest, who gave the world the invaluable description of the Renaissance dances in his *Orchesographie* and who certainly cannot be accused of disliking the dance per se, fully agreed with the Elizabethan Puritans in disapproving of leaps and kicks by the ladies.

No doubt, the then so popular galliard was often danced with almost acrobatic tricks. A deaf person, unable to perceive the music, watched a galliard dancer in one of the London dancing schools and thought "verily that hee had been stark mad and out of his wit." These extravagances were satirized by Samuel Rowlands in "My fine Dauncer" with these lines:

You nimble skipiacke, turning on the toe,
As though you had Gun-pouder in your tayle:
You that do leape about and caper soe,
Esteeming our old Country Daunces stale.
You that do liue by shaking of the heele,
By hopping, and by turning like a wheele.

Innumerable are the references to the delight the English people took in dancing and the manner in which it probably was overdone by a great many. The pictures painted by those people who tried to stem the tide of a dance-mad time may be exaggerated, as a matter of fact it must be exaggerated, as all satiric descriptions are. But they point to the important role dancing played in the social life of the people.

The dances mentioned in Shakespearean texts were the favorite dances of the age. However, it is difficult to define precisely how the various dances were done, for there seems to have been general confusion in the use of the dance terms in the late sixteenth century in England. In fact, even as late as 1728 Soame Jenyns wrote in *The Art of Dancing:*

Long was the Dancing Art unfix'd and free:
Hence lost in error and Uncertainty:
No Precepts did it mind, or Rules obey,
But every Master taught a different Way.

Moreover, there are a great many indications that the good dancers varied their steps and may have devised their own variations. Thomas Morley, one of the foremost composers of the age, mentions in his discussion of courtly dances in *Plaine and Easie Introduction to Practicall Musicke,* that dancing had "come to that perfection that euerie reasonable dauncer wil make measure of no measure, so that it is no great matter of what number you make your strayne." Richard Brome, a Stuart playwright and disciple of

Ben Jonson, made fun of this state of confusion in his play *The
City Wit* (IV.i), in which one of the characters speaking of the
dance asks his friend, "I prithee teach me some tricks," whereupon his friend answers:

Ha! Tricks of Twenty: Your Traverses, Slidings, Falling back, Jumps,
Closings, Openings, Shorts, Turns, Pacings, Gracings—As for—
Corantoes, Lavoltoes, Jigs, Measures, Pavins, Brawls, Galliards, or Ca-
naries.

The lightfooted and nimble Elizabethans took great pride
and delight in their many homegrown country dances, but also
willingly surrendered and succumbed to the then fashionable con-
tinental imports. The fondness of the English people for their
country dances developed during the Middle Ages and has a long
history. The gay Absolon in Chaucer's *The Miller's Tale* was already an expert dancer, since

> In twenty manere coude he trippe and daunce
> After the scole of Oxenforde tho,
> And with his legges casten to and fro . . .

Many of the country dances, whose popularity can at no time be
doubted, went through stages of refinement and sophistication to
become acceptable to the nobility. They must have been taught
in the dancing schools along with the imported French dances, although they were, or could be, danced with simple steps. In their
refined stage they invaded the court time and again. In 1602, the
Earl of Worcester wrote to the Earl of Shrewsbury these characteristic lines: "We are frolic here in Court; much dancing in the
Privy Chamber of country dances before the Queen's Majesty,
who is exceedingly pleased herewith." They were often preferred
to the French dances which needed far more practice and, above
all, talent. A courtier could easily cut a bad figure in a French

dance, and one of the courtiers during the reign of James I made the sarcastic remark that it was easier to put on fine clothes than to learn the dances of the French and that therefore "none but country dances" were seen at the Court.

This, of course, was an exaggeration, but it only goes to show that we cannot draw a clear line of demarcation and that the English country dances as well as the French court dances constantly crossed the social border lines. On the stage we naturally find the same confusion.

In his *Orchestra* Sir John Davies has a poet's explanation. He said, "Love taught men to dance rounds and heys, meaning country dances. But as men grew more civil, Love framed the measures, the galliards, etc." We can just as well say that with the ascent of the Tudors, the French influence in manners and fashions became more and more pronounced in England. Henry VII, who had spent some time in exile in Paris, had acquired a taste for what he had observed in France, particularly for the court entertainments of masquerades and moriscoes, those mimed and danced spectacles. French players were invited to London, and the Christmas Revels and Royal Progresses on the first of May were welcome occasions for both English folk dances and French dances. His son, Henry VIII, liked a lusty life, wanted England to share Europe's Humanism, the grandeur of the Italian Renaissance, the splendor of the French court. We find a passage in Hall's *Chronicles of the Reign* that speaks of an Italian "masquerie" that took place in 1512:

the kyng with XI. other wer disguised, after the maner of Italie, called a maske, a thyng not seen afore in Englande . . . these maskers came in, with six gentlemen disguised in silke bearyng staffe torches, and desired the ladies to daunce, some were content, and some that knewe the fashion of it refused, because it was not a thyng commonly seen. And after thei daunced and commoned together, as the fashion of the

Maskes is, thei toke their leave and departed, and so did the Quene, and all the ladies.

This kind of entertainment, in which the dance was an essential, if not the main part, became more and more the favorite courtly spectacle. It develops into full artistic maturity in Jacobean times, with poets of the rank of Ben Jonson writing the most magnificent masques. The dances were arranged by the dancing masters, who were the choreographers of that time and who drilled the dancers. The rehearsals for such a masque usually lasted many weeks, and in one instance the record speaks of no less than fifty days. The dancing masters tried, of course, to please His Majesty, and it was known of James I that he favored vigorous and sustained dancing at such masques.

At a certain point of the entertainment the masquers "took out" the guests of the opposite sex to dance. It is said that, in 1532, Anne Boleyn led the first recorded masque in which women took out the lords to dance with them. This "commoning" between masquers and spectators was one of the highlights of these spectacles. At first, of course, there was dancing on the stage, the masques and antimasques performed. Then the masquers left the stage and took the spectators out to dance "the measures," which often lasted an hour. A song, or another stage dance, followed, whereupon lavoltas, galliards, and corantos were again danced by everyone.

Masques, originally only masked dances, were not always such costly and elaborate affairs with stage spectacle, rich costuming and profuse scenery. But these courtly masques were imitated on many occasions, with far more modest means, by the lower nobility and the London citizenry. How common the masques became is reflected in the many plays which made them part of the plot.

Shakespeare has a masque in *Romeo and Juliet* (I.iv.5) and in *Henry VIII* (I.iv.). In *Timon of Athens* (I.ii) during the banquet in Timon's house, pleasure is promised him by Cupid "to feast thine eyes." Cupid then exits only to re-enter with "a masque of Ladies as Amazons, with lutes in their hands dancing and playing." When Apemantus, speaking the poet's mind, says:

> Hoy-day, what a sweep of vanity comes this way!
> They dance! They are mad women.
> Like madness is the glory of this life,
> As this pomp shows to a little oil and root. . . .
> I should fear those who dance before me now
> Would one day stamp upon me: 't has been done;
> Men shut their doors against a setting sun,

the "commoning" begins; "The Lords rise from the table . . . each singles out an Amazon, and all dance, men with women, a lofty strain or two to the hautboys, and cease." When the dance stops, the host expresses his gratitude and the prevailing sentiment of the time about this kind of entertainment:

> You have done our pleasures much grace, fair ladies,
> Set a fair fashion on our entertainment,
> Which was not half so beautiful and kind:
> You have added worth unto't and lively lustre,
> And entertained me with mine own device;
> I am to thank for it.

When Shakespeare intimates that men and women are dancing to a "lofty strain or two," it is not very descriptive, but we can harldy go wrong when we have them at first dance a "measure" that turns into a galliard. This would imitate the customary procedure of courtly masques, and the fact that Shakespeare presents Timon's guests with a short spectacle in which Cupid leads boy actors disguised as Amazons to a dance is an intimation of a Court

Masque. Ben Jonson says in his famous *Masque of Queens* that after the masquers' second dance "they took out the men and daunc'd the *measures,* entertayning the time, almost to the space of an hower, with singular variety."

In *Timon of Athens,* however, there is no place for a dance that long. As a matter of fact, these little masques, and all other dances, within Shakespeare's plays must be brief or they will keep the plot from moving. They must never be done for the sake of the dance or dancer, and they should try to approximate the style and manner in which they were probably done on the Elizabethan stage. The modern touch and flavor which, of course, cannot be avoided ought to be in relation to the change a Shakespearian play has undergone as far as the entire conception of direction, acting, and elocution is concerned. In other words, it would seem "out of character" to have Cupid and the Amazons perform a ballet on toes or a modern dance à la Martha Graham when dancing for Timon and his guests.

As the sword dance was one of the favorite folk dances of the time, it seems appropriate that they perform some variation of sword dance. Socrates said that the best dancer is also the best warrior, and since Shakespeare introduces the masquers as Amazons, a war dance would be logical. It is doubtful that Shakespeare and his fellow actors thought of having the Amazons dance as the ancient Greeks might have performed a weapon dance. They most likely danced the then popular sword dance. As a figure folk dance it bears the influence of its ritual origin and was often used in masques as well as on the stage. Arbeau mentions a sophisticated sword dance to his pupil, the young Capriol. Sir John Harington in his *The Metamorphosis of Ajax,* published in 1596, proves that the sword dance was quite common on the stage in England and France when he says, "Such as I haue seene in stage playes when they daunce Machachinas." Machachinas is an older form of Matachin, a sword dancer wearing a fantastic costume and mask. When we have the Amazons wear fantastic costumes and masks and do a sword dance, we are close to the spirit in which Shakespeare conceived this scene.

The "commoning" always began with a measure which, in Elizabethan days, took the place of the pavane. The measure, along with the jig, is the word most often used in reference to the dance in Shakespeare's plays, and Beatrice in *Much Ado About Nothing* (II.i) describes it as "full of state and ancientry." John Davies says in stanzas 65 and 66 of his *Orchestra:*

> He did more graue and solemne measures frame,
> With such faire order and proportion trew,
> And correspondence euery way the same. . . .
> Not. . . .
> Atlas. . . . Prometheus. . . .
> Which on the starres did . . . looke,
> Could euer find such measures in the skies,
> So full of change and rare varieties:
> Yet all the feete whereon these measures goe,
> Are onely spondeis, solemne, graue, and sloe.

In contrast to the simple pavane, it seems that the Elizabethans worked out a great variety of elaborate designs for this stately dance. The measure was always followed by a galliard— literally meaning 'merry'—a gayer, quicker dance whose basic unit is the cinquepace, which Shakespeare often calls *sinkepas,* probably the bowdlerized form of the French *cinque pas* then used in England. The galliard also had many variations, but, according to Thoinot Arbeau, is composed of four movements of the feet, a "cadence," climaxed by a leap ("sault majeur"), and a posture, or assiette. Arbeau describes the many variations of the galliard which, in the main, consists of four small kicks, a leap during which the front foot is swung up and out the side, then brought back to the floor behind the other foot, so to speak into the fifth position, and one foot is at once put behind the other with the toes turned out. There are variations of backward and forward kicks which give the galliard its characteristic hopping motion.

It is quite a vigorous and lively dance, termed a dance for young men by Arbeau, who does not forget to admonish his young pupil to soften the leaps and perform them barely off the ground when he should hold a girl by the hand. This gentler version of it, "as a damsel might do it," is called tordion. Sir John Davies saw the sun and earth dancing a galliard, for they move "both back and forth and sidewaies." The leap was the main feature of this dance. Sir Andrew Aguecheek boasts in *Twelfth Night* (I.iv) that he delights "in masques and revels sometimes altogether," and when Sir Toby Belch asks him facetiously: "What is your excellence in a galliard, knight?" he proudly proclaims: "Faith, I can cut a caper."

This, of course, would put Sir Andrew into the class of the most skillful dancers of his time who could easily do "caprioles," beating the legs together in the air. We can see that the Elizabethans were not too far from the skill of today's ballet dancer in their social dances when done to perfection. Sir Andrew may have only dreamt of being able to cut a caper, but after the performance, he himself may have become the actor-turned-dancer who showed his audience that he could do it.

In our own staging of the masque and dance scene of *Timon of Athens* we can have any dancer among Timon's guests perform a vigorous "sault majeur." The "fair ladies" who gave "lively lustre" to the short entertainment must be excellent dancers to recreate the atmosphere of an Elizabethan masque. However, we must by no means feel induced to approximate those elaborate

Court Masques, for Shakespeare and his colleagues must have been well aware that the mere allusion to a masque would suffice to show Timon as the lavish patron of the arts and extravagant entertainer whom the playwright intended to introduce to his playgoers.

In *Henry VIII* we also have a masque at the banquet of Cardinal Wolsey, at which the king appears masked as a shepherd. Here we face a different situation. We must not lose sight of Henry VIII's predilection for lusty, amorous dances; the more indecorous they were, the better he liked them. When the maskers took out the guests, it was customary to kiss one's partner and King Henry says to his chosen maid, Anne Bullen:

> Sweet heart,
> I were unmannerly to take you out
> And not to kiss you.

Shakespeare underlines the fact that King Henry would not want to miss an opportunity such as this.

Arbeau speaks of lavoltas as wanton and wayward dances. "In dancing them," he says, "the damsels are made to bounce about in such a fashion that more often than not they show their bare knees unless they keep one hand on their skirts to prevent it." The volte was such a wild dance that it was banned from the French Court during Louis XIII's reign because of its indecency. This only proves the popularity of the dance. It was danced with violence and passion, and, it is said, the ladies of the Court worked up such a perspiration that they had to change their underwear during court festivities.

That we would do best to choose a volte for *Henry VIII* is also borne out by the following bit of dialogue:

Cardinal Wolsey: Your Grace,
         I fear, with dancing is a little heated.
   King Henry: I fear too much.
Cardinal Wolsey: There's fresher air, my lord,
         In the next chamber.

Shakespeare speaks, in *Henry V*, of "lavoltas high and swift corantos," both favorite dances of the English aristocracy. Sir John Davies is also quite enthusiastic about the volte and stresses the close
embrace of the two dancers:

> A lofty jumping, or a leaping round,
> When, arm in arm, two dancers are entwined,
> And whirl themselves, with strict embracements bound.

The English courant which apparently came from Italy, is,
on the other hand, best characterized by its speed "close by the
ground, with sliding passages." Thomas Morley calls the "swift"
corantos "trauising and running" dances. Moreover, the volte and
the courant were among the favorite dances of Queen Elizabeth,
and, as Shakespeare wrote *Henry VIII* to honor the Queen, it
can be assumed that these two dances were used for this scene,
and we are on safe ground in following suit.

When Capulet, Juliet's father, invites his friends for supper,
"this night I hold an old accustomed feast," we find, of course,
musicians and maskers there. Capulet welcomes the guests and
then says:

> Come, musicians, play.
> A hall, a hall! give room! and foot it, girls.
> [Music plays, and they dance.]
> More light, you knaves; and turn the tables up,
> And quench the fire, the room is grown too hot.

The musicians could hardly have played a slow, stately measure; it simply would not fit the text. On the contrary, a dance as swift as a coranto or, at least, as gay as a galliard must have set in at once. The necessity to quench the fire because, due to the dancing, the room had grown too hot, speaks for passion and vigor, and Capulet's guests might have done a canary.

Canaries seem to have been the symbol for vigor, because Lafeu in *All's Well that Ends Well* (II.i) offers the King of France a medicine he knows about

> That's able to breathe life into a stone,
> Quicken a rock, and make you dance canary
> With spritely fire and motion.

Arbeau describes the canary as a lively, strange, and bizarre dance, marked by stamping and a heel-and-toe movement. It allows the dancer a great deal of freedom to invent steps as long as the dance keeps its "gay but nevertheless strange" character and remains "fantastic with a strong barbaric flavor." This dance, in which very high leaps were quite common, came either from the Canary Isles or "from a ballet composed for a masquerade in which the dancers were dressed as kings and queens of Mauretania" (what is now Morocco and western Algeria), "or else like savages in feathers dyed to many a hue." Should any modern producer wish to use the canary for this scene, he will find Arbeau a free consultant on the costumes of the masquers.

Although Romeo tells us that, as soon as the "measure [is] done," he will try to get close to Juliet, I do not think that this remark was meant to identify the dance. If they had done a stately measure, even old Capulet might have been able to join in the dance, and certainly his thought, "for you and I are past our dancing days," would not have stood in sharp enough contrast to a slow dance. In accordance with Arbeau's description of the

masking for a canary as exotic or savage-like, Romeo's image of
the dancing Juliet,

> It seems she hangs upon the cheek of night
> Like a rich jewel in an Ethiope's ear,

may have some weight in reference to the kind of dance and
masks used.

In *The Merchant of Venice* Shylock warns his daughter Jessica:

> What, are there masques? Hear you me, Jessica:
> Lock up my doors; and when you hear the drum
> And the vile squealing of the wry-neck'd fife,
> Clamber you not up to the casements then,
> Nor thrust your head into the public street
> To gaze on Christian fools with varnish'd faces,

a reference to either a morris dance or a canary, but we are never
shown the masque. *Love's Labour's Lost* is another one of Shakespeare's plays in which a great deal is said about dancing, although the actors get no chance to prove their dancing skill.
There is considerable masquerading though, and when Rosaline,
one of the ladies-in-waiting to the Princess of France, asks the musicians (V.ii) to play, she suddenly decides, "no dance: thus
change I like the moon."

Among the many references to dancing in this play are two
that name the favorite dances of the time. When the village
schoolmaster and the curate (V.i) discuss their pageant of the
Nine Worthies, which they prepare for presentation before the
sophisticated ladies and gentlemen, Anthony Dull, the constable,
who "hath never fed of the dainties that are bred in a book," suggests as his contribution to the entertainment: "I will play on the
tabor to the Worthies, and let them dance the hay."

Hay, also spelled hey and haye, is an old country dance, which, Dr. Johnson says in his dictionary, may have been so called because it was originally danced around a haycock. It is one of the round dances mentioned among the 104 popular dances in John Playford's *The English Dancing Master: or, Plaine and easie rules for the Dancing of Country Dances, with the tunes to each dance,* published in 1651. Basically, all dancers join hands in this dance, begin a circular movement, the ladies turning left, the gentlemen to the right, and all wind through the circle until the original couple come together again; or, as Cecil J. Sharp describes it, the hey is "the rhythmical interlacing in serpentine fashion of two groups of dancers, moving in single file and in opposite direction."

It seems that round dances were popular in England long before the Elizabethan period. A passage in an early dramatic interlude of the *Four Elements* speaks of people

That shall both daunce and spring,
And torne clean above the grounde
With fryscas and with gambaudes rounde,
That all the hall shall ryng.

Masked as animals and other grotesque appearances during folk games, the dancers often gave the hay an antic character which was later used to great advantage in the antimasques at Court festivals. Gavestone, in Christopher Marlowe's *Edward the Second* (I.i), plans to please the king and suggests Italian masques by night, comedies, and pleasing shows: "And in the day . . . my men, like satyres grazing on the lawns, shall with their goat feet dance an antic hay."

The antic hay was often shown on the Elizabethan stage, and I think that it is perfect dance material for *The Winter's Tale* (IV.iv), in which Shakespeare has twelve satyrs dance. Dances in

Shakespearean plays come necessarily out of the plot, are carefully planned and prepared for. Moreover, Shakespeare likes to introduce them with descriptive words which, in this case, are put into a servant's mouth

Master, there is three carters, three shepherds, three neat-herds, three swineherds, that have made themselves all men of hair [i.e., probably clad in skins], call themselves Saltiers, and they have a dance which the wenches say is gallimaufry of gambols, because they are not in't; but they themselves are o' the mind, if it be not too rough for some that know little but bowling, it will please plentifully. . . . One three of them, by their own report, sir, hath danced before the king; and not the worst of the three but jumps twelve foot and a half by the sqier.

This scene is preceded by a dance of shepherds and shepherdesses, for which a country dance, less grotesque and wild than the antic hay, would seem appropriate. When during this dance Polixenes remarks that Perdita "dances featly," that is, gracefully, the choreographer must give her a chance to do so. Here, some of the many variations of the French brawl would serve our purpose best. That many variations of it were danced, is implied by Sir John Davies when he says that of the seven motions in nature, namely up and downward, forth and back, to this side and that, and turning around, Love compounds a thousand brawls. Arbeau devotes much time and effort to the brawl, or branle. In his talk with young Capriol he mentions almost a score of different brawls. In his opinion it is easy for those who master the pavane or any basse dance to dance a brawl, if they remember that in a brawl one moves sideways and not forward. This dance is full of dramatic features and borrows steps from the galliard as well as from many country dances. Of one form, the "Haut Barrois" branle, Arbeau says that it is "danced by lackeys and serving wenches, and sometimes by young men and damsels of gentle birth in a masquerade, disguised as peasants and shepherds." This would justify the choreographer of any modern production of the *The Winter's Tale* in introducing a branle in this scene. Of course, he may also use, as basic material, the "Branle de la Haye," which takes in the interweaving movement of the hay.

The popularity of the brawl in Shakespeare's time is implied also by Moth's question, "Master, will you win your love with a French brawl?" (*Love's Labour's Lost,* III.i.) Another dramatist of the age, John Marston, comments on the brawl in *The Malcontent* (IV.ii)

Enter Mendoza supporting the Duchess; Guerrino. The ladies that are on the stage rise. Ferrard ushers in the Duchess, and then takes a Lady to read a measure.

Aurelia:	We will dance; music! We will dance.
Guerrino:	"Les quanto," lady, "Pensez bien," "Passa regis," or Biancha's brawl?
Aurelia:	We have forgot the brawl.
Ferrard:	So soon? 'Tis wonder.
Guerrino:	Why, 'tis but two singles on the left, two on the right, three doubles forward, a traverse of six round; do this twice, three singles side, galliard trick-of-twenty, coranto-pace; a figure of eight, three singles broken down, come up, meet two doubles, fall back, and then honor.
Aurelia:	O Daedalus, thy maze! I have quite forgot it.
Maquerelle:	Trust me, so have I, saving the falling-back, and then honor.

This scene will not have failed in its humor with Marston's audience so familiar with the brawl. Even Sir Philip Sidney mentions in his unfinished prose romance *Arcadia,* written in 1590, a dance by two groups of shepherds "as it were in a braule," which only confirms that we cannot go wrong with a brawl in the shepherd's scene of *The Winter's Tale*.

      The stage director and choreographer of *The Tempest* face almost the same grave problems as would those of *A Midsummer Night's Dream,* which has always lured, and usually trapped, both the director and choreographer. Through the magic of the word more than through any magic of action, Shakespeare created in these two plays a mood which is full of dancing, whether or not stage directions clearly pronounce: "They dance".

      Both plays have an atmosphere of the dance about them. When dancing is a symbolic art, reduced to the most essential, to the allusion rather than to the spelling out of an idea; when it transcends existence, carrying us on wings of illusion out of the world of every-day life and "transports reality onto a higher plane," as Henri Bergson says; when it gives us the sublimation of action, emotion and thought, probes the depths of all things and still remains more suggestive than expressive, then *The Tempest* as well as *A Midsummer Night's Dream*—each in its own way—is dance wrapped in poetic words.

      Mark van Doren says about *The Tempest* that "its meaning is precisely as rich as the human mind, and it says that the world is what it is. But what the world is cannot be said in a sentence. Or even in a poem as complete and beautiful as *The Tempest*." But it is inherent in the verbal music and movement that is the play's real *Gestalt,* in which all desired things can be brought about through magic. What is theater if not make-believe, and dance its most elusive form? The play is there, ready to yield to any interpretation, to any meaning the eyes and ears, the thoughts and feelings will be able to find in it. As in any dance, it borrows means of expression which must be factual, as words or steps.

These are only the means to the end which rests in our perception, our imagination.

Ariel, like Puck, is an angelic messenger, who, restive, impatiently waiting for his complete freedom, becomes mischievous under the burden of being the extended arm of a great magician. Ariel is light as music and moonbeams, fast and colorful as a rainbow. He must move through the entire action of the play, must dance without really dancing. Apparently the difficulty lies in conveying the feeling of constant movement without moving constantly. On stage intensity of projection need not be acted out to be there. It actually rests in restraint. Only if Ariel can unlock the language of his body, will he be able to match the magic of Shakespeare's poetry.

When in the third act, Scene 3, "several strange shapes enter, bringing in a banquet; they dance about it with gentle actions of salutations; and, inviting the King, etc. to eat, they depart," it would seem that Shakespeare thought of a very short and, as he says, gentle dance of free rhythm. But the King's party is only being mocked by Prospero and Ariel with this banquet. The moment they try to eat, the banquet "vanishes in thunder; then, to soft music, enter the shapes again, and dance, with mocks and mows, and carrying out the table." This must be a gay, wanton dance, a counterpart to the gentle movements of the previous dance action, no doubt, contrasting with it with particular stress on mimicry and mockery.

We find another dance in Act IV, Scene 1, of *The Tempest*, when Iris says:

> You sunburnt sicklemen, of August weary,
> Come hither from the furrow and be merry:
> Make holiday; your rye-straw hats put on
> And these fresh nymphs encounter every one
> In country footing.

Then "enter certain reapers, properly habited: they join with the nymphs in a graceful dance."

It is quite obvious that the nymphs and reapers join in a country dance which is "to celebrate a contract of true love." The dance is the climactic event of a prenuptial pageant of nymphs and reapers enacted by Prospero's spirits in the guise of Iris, Ceres, and Juno. In essence, it is a Court Masque on the occasion of a wedding, transposed into the airy atmosphere of *The Tempest*.

Curt Sachs explains that a wedding dance is always a round dance and that it matters little around what it is danced. "The specific meaning is a charm for fertility," he says, and, after all, the Maypole dance, a favorite country dance of the Elizabethans, is nothing more than a fertility dance. Since Shakespeare speaks of "temperate" nymphs and a "graceful dance," the choreographer would best use a Maypole dance in its refined stage, as it probably was done at the Court during spring festivals. In choreographing this dance, we may also use the morris and jig, both of which are often mentioned in connection with this dance.

The Tempest was written in 1611, at a time when William Kempe, "the head master of the morris dancers" was no longer with Shakespeare's company. The tradition lived on and it is very likely that, on stage, they made use of the morris dance. Its figures are quite elaborate. While the whole body was little used, the feet, often carrying jingling bells, were doing complicated steps, changing and replacing each other rapidly and precisely.

Beatrice in *Much Ado About Nothing* (II.i) describes the Scotch jig as "hot and hasty and full as fantastical." As in the Scottish dances the trunk was held erect, the heels beat the floor, and the toes pointed once right, once left.

Whatever dances we try to work into this pastoral scene, we

must not overlook that essentially they must correspond to the airiness and lightness of the play.

In *A Midsummer Night's Dream* we have the Bergomask dance of the artisans in the last act and as the finale of the play within the play. By many it is considered a clown dance, and in most performances it is danced by Bottom in a grotesque and clumsy way to underscore the humor of the situation and the comic of the comedian.

The Bergomask was well known in England as an Italian country dance. As such it was a round dance of couples in which the dancers execute little entrechats after every sixth or ninth step. Since William Kempe created the role of Bottom we can well imagine that, being the comedian he was, and an excellent dancer as well, he probably put in the Bergomask acrobatic and clownish features. In our specialized age in which an actor rarely is a good dancer, the clownish part of it is usually overstressed and the acrobatics omitted.

This is the least of the choreographic problems of *A Midsummer Night's Dream*. One that seems insurmountable to many is the fact that in 1826, at a time when the Romantic age was at its peak, Mendelssohn wrote a beautiful score for this play. His music is still closely associated with the play, and to leave it out would be called an unpardonable sin by many a critic. The music was written more than a hundred years ago and, since it caught the spirit of the play and was, by the same token, the very expression of its time, it was then acceptable. It is no longer so today. Now we must have the courage to decide whether we want to serve Shakespeare or Mendelssohn.

His score also lures too many directors and choreographers into the trap of an elaborate dance production overshadowing the plot. Thus it has more often than not blurred the "airy nothing-ness" of this sweet nonsense woven out of verbal wonderment into the finest gossamer design. Using this music poses a great problem for the choreographer. Should he match Mendelssohn's score with the classic ballet steps of his era? The ballerina on her toes sym-bolizes, no doubt, flight and ease which Shakespeare seemed to have wanted expressed in this summer night's dream. One might think it would stand in wonderful contrast to the rustic quality and reality of Bottom.

The classic toe dance within the ballet program lives its own rightful existence, but Titania and Oberon on toes, being lifted and holding an arabesque cannot capture the enchantment of night and dream. Sylphidine ballerinas with their constantly wav-ing *port de bras* negate exactly what the choreographer wants to show: the flight from gravity, the oneness of the aerial spirits with the dreamlike quality of the moon. The buoyant lightness and artless merriment of the play must come from the acting, and no superimposed ballet will do.

The choice of music determines the approach to the produc-tion and, therewith, the dancing, whether it is Carl Orff's score weaving into its texture madrigals and contemporary tunes or Henry Purcell's music for *The Fairy Queen* which has its roots in the spirit of the Elizabethan age and gives the choreographer a great chance to enhance the poetry of the play. However, let us make no mistake: the intrinsic music lies in the lines correctly spoken. Where Shakespeare envisioned song and dance as in the fairy scenes and in Oberon's and Titania's finale, Elizabethan music, used incidentally, or such modern equivalent as Carl Orff's score, will add, through their flavor of remoteness, to the moonlit night and its many dreams. Then these fairy toys, held against the footlights with a loving and knowing hand, will turn into stage reality and make a great dream of a great poet come true.

Peter Brook's staging of *A Midsummer Night's Dream,* produced by the Royal Shakespeare Company in Stratford-on-Avon in 1969 and in New York in 1970, is light-years away from any previous stage version of this play. It mocks Mendelssohn's music in its incidental, rock-type accompaniment and takes place in a circus atmosphere with firemen's ladders instead of trees, with Oberon swinging on a trapeze and Puck, dispensing the love potion with a juggler's trick, hanging on ropes and running on stilts.

The style chosen is an elevated, sophisticated level of the *commedia dell'arte.* Ideas are mingled, roles doubled in order to unify all the lovers in a common dream. Startling surprises enhance the illusion while demystifying conventional concepts. Not a single word of the Shakespearean text is omitted or tampered with, and every line is spoken with the lilt of its most lyric value. The playfulness of the mixed-up lovers suddenly makes sense on a brightly lit stage in a clinical atmosphere of circus tricks. "The lunatic, the lover, and the poet" become unified in the acrobat, a skillful stage magician who seems to reveal all his tricks while performing them. So far Peter Brook's *Dream* has, in all its dramatic and poetic terms, best translated Shakespeare's magic of true make-believe into a twentieth-century stage realization.

The case of William Kempe

The most popular actor-dancer on the Elizabethan stage was William Kempe, the uncontested master of the morris dance. He is exemplary proof of the dance craze of his time and the dancing skill of its actors.

Kempe was an exceptional personality, who might have made his name immortal by a "publicity stunt," dancing for nine days from London to Norwich, had he not been the great comedian in Shakespeare's company which he joined in 1593 and with which he stayed until 1599.

As early as 1590 he was already known as "that most comical jestmonger," a sharply profiled clown, a clown at any price, who would sacrifice anything without scruples for a laugh. The clown demands and commands a great deal of independence. He plays directly to the audience. Inspired by their reaction he reacts with impromptus. He lives on laughs, and the shortest way to it leads over the extempore. Kempe was the loudmouthed, vulgar jester, full of practical jokes with which he harassed the other characters.

Kempe also took a great deal from the country lout, the loutish servant of the popular Italian comedy, and transformed the *commedia dell'arte* style into silly clowning with perfect mimicry and any gestures or stage movement that would produce a laugh. How very much he was inclined to extemporize can be seen from the fact that a play of the year 1594, *A Knack to Know a Knaue,* was published with the additional phrase, "With Kemps applauded Merrimentes of the men of Goteham." In reading the play, however, we find no particular "merriment" at all, except a brief scene of a perhaps funny dialogue between three foolish villagers preparing to receive their king. "Kempe's merriments" would certainly not have been put into print if people had not talked about them and been thoroughly amused. All that can be assumed is that it was not in the lines, but in Kempe's sure-fire impromptus.

He wore enormous slippers and had funny feet. He not only loved to forget the script and make the cracks that came to his mind, he would also start moving around on stage, with his feet being acrobatically involved in some kind of jig. He must have been a very headstrong personality which asserted itself time and again and often gave occasion for offence. As he was so sure of having the laughs on his side, the company had to cater to his many whims and very likely to his overbearing wishes. But since the days of Aristophanes most any producer of a play has done anything to put his audience into a good mood. Even if we read that Kempe played for the groundlings, we also know that laughter is contagious and that, moreover, no one less than Queen Elizabeth preferred comedies to tragedies. And Kempe was able to please Her Majesty more often than not.

However, he does not seem to have pleased Shakespeare very much who, when writing parts for the actors of his company, was forced to give Kempe his due. Time and again, the poet in Shakespeare must have been annoyed by Kempe's stepping out of character and playing for a laugh. Shakespeare could not afford to ignore him. Kempe was a powerful figure and just as beloved as Richard Burbage or Edward Alleyn.

How very much Shakespeare resented Kempe's impromptus has come to the fore in *Hamlet* (III,ii,42), written after the rift with Kempe, when he says:

And let those that play our clowns speak no more
than is set down for them; for there be of them that
will themselves laugh, to set on some quantity of
barren spectators to laugh too, though in the
meantime some necessary question of the play be
then to be considered.

Shakespeare must have been well aware of Kempe's personality and his own feelings toward him. Creating the character of Bottom, the weaver, for him in *A Midsummer Night's Dream,* he expressed his unconscious, if not conscious, rejection of the comedian by having Bottom admit that he desires to be the whole show. No doubt, Kempe not only wanted to be the lion too, he wanted to have the lion's share in a play. Teamwork was the key word for the actors at that time as it is now. Grave difficulties often arise from star behavior, and Kempe seemed to have called forth this protest of the Bard, wrapped in the tissue of softened satire.

We get a fairly good idea of Kempe's favorite stage business in the part of Launce of *The Two Gentlemen of Verona,* the first role Shakespeare envisaged for the comedian. Shakespeare knew the kind of foolery Kempe loved best, and at that time he seemed to have still been eager to please him. In the second act he comes in leading his dog Crab on a rope and begins with a verbal confusion: "I have received my proportion like the Prodigious son and I am going with Sir Proteus to the Imperial's Court" (II,iii,). With his wooden shoes, his hat and staff he prepares for his big clowning act in which he parodies a serious scene of leave-taking which preceded his. "This hat is Nan, our maid. I am the dog. No, the dog is himself and I am the dog. O, the dog is me and I am myself" (II,iii.). The confusion in his mind corresponds with his complete entanglement in his stage properties, an act that must have become very funny when he wanted to extricate himself to come to the next line.

The stress on the physical involvement is most important with Kempe since, no doubt, he leaned more and more to dancing and acrobatics. As Grumio in *The Taming of the Shrew* he must have had his field day as far as mere physical stunts are concerned, because the wringing of ears and the knocking of heads come natural to Petruchio and his servants.

We know that Kempe played Peter in *Romeo and Juliet* and Dogberry in *Much Ado About Nothing,* and both parts, as clownish servant and pompous official, gave him plenty of opportunity to show his art as a mime. In *The Pilgrimage to Parnassus* the clown calls out: "Now if I could but make a fine scurvey face, I were a Kinge! O nature, why didest thou give mee soe good a looke?" As this clown was meant to be Kempe, we can imagine how well he must have used facial expressions. Pantomime, gestures, and dance were the means which the *commedia-dell'-arte*-acting employed for its clowns, and they were Kempe's means throughout.

It is very likely that Kempe extemporized a great deal in an earlier court play, *Love's Labour's Lost*, but in *Much Ado About Nothing* he must have overdone it and things came to a head. It is assumed he took liberties with the part, which seriously offended Shakespeare. The facts speak for Kempe's necessitated departure from the company.

In Lent 1600 the Globe was closed in obedience to the authorities. Lent began on February 6. On the tenth, four days later,

Will Kemp the clown hath wagered that he will dance from London to Norwich, and this morning before 7 of the clock is set forward from the Lord Mayor's toward the Mayor of Norwich, accompanied by Thomas Sly his taborer and George Sprat that is appointed for his overseer.

The great comedian Will Kempe sold his share and was never seen on Shakespeare's stage again. He probably did not realize that it was the end of his acting career. Or did he, when he wrote that he had "daunst him selfe out of the world"? *

After his "Nine daies" dance he went to Europe to cross the

---

* The World is Ben Jonson's name for the Globe and it was probably often referred to as such by other people too. Whatever Kempe may have meant, the use of this phrase attests to his literacy and wit.

Alps with his morris dance and then returned to London in the summer of 1601 when he joined a rival company, the Worcester's men. But it was a kind of swan song for him. Although the date of his death has not been determined with certainty, it is generally believed that he fell victim to the plague and was buried on November 2, 1603. At least one does not hear about him after this date.

In the Quarto (III,i,26–43), Hamlet's reference to "Let not your clowns speak more than is set down," we find the unabridged version which closes with the lines: "blabbering with his lips and thus keeping in his cinque pace of jests, when, God knows, the warm clown cannot make a jest unless by chance, as the blind man catcheth the hare, Masters, tell him of it."

The phrase "keeping in his cinque pace of jests" shows the dance playing quite a part in Kempe's course of jesting. A man who could not stand still, who knew the value of gesture and mimicry and the impact of the dance, William Kempe wrapped his clownery into movement. He must have felt drawn to the dance even more than to acting, or loved best to mix them as in his famous jigs.

There are frequent allusions to his jigs, and four, now lost, were entered in Stationers' Registers during 1591–95: "The thirde and last part of Kempe's Jiggs"; "a pleasant newe Jigge of the broomeman," ascribed to Kempe in the margin; "Master Kempes Newe Jigge of the Kitchen stuffe woman"; and "Kemps newe Jigge betwixt a Soldiour and a Miser and Sym the clown."

John Marston refers to his satiric play *The Scourge of Villanie* to "wanton jiggin skips" with the words:

A hall! a hall!
Roome for the spheres; the orbs celestial
Will daunce Kempe's jigge!

To his own report on *Kemps nine daies wonder,* published in 1600, is added a contemporary woodcut which depicts him dancing, accompanied by his taborer. On that picture, he is shown with a beard, long hair and a pleasing face. He does not seem tall on it, rather stockily built. At that time he was probably close to his forty-fifth year, if not slightly more. And for a man of that age it was certainly a strenuous exercise to dance from London to Norwich.

Kempe was called the headmaster of the morris dance. It is not uninteresting that he, a most independent and willful individual, should have chosen to master this dance to perfection. It is one of the few dances which show total absence of a love motive from all its movements. It can be danced by a single person and was originally danced by men.

Cecil Sharp tells us about the morris dance:

The Morris, f.i., is a ceremonial, spectacular, and professional dance; it is performed by men only, and has no sex characteristics. The many curious customs—as well as the extra characters, e.g., the squire or fool, king, queen, witch, cake and sword bearer—which are commonly associated with the dance, all indicate that the Morris was once something more than a mere dance; that, originally, the dance formed but one part of what may very likely have been an elaborate quasi-religious ceremony.

Kempe uses in his book phrases such as "I leapt," "and to our iumps we fell," "I tript forward" which are not very expressive. Kempe certainly holds the world's long-distance record in dancing, and the nine days were in many ways a triumph for him in spite of the fact that not everyone who was willing to accept his wager, paid the debt.

People like Will Kempe have many enemies, and he was much maligned and attacked. It was also often said that he was illiterate which is refuted by the fact that he had a ready wit and sat down to describe his nine days' dance in a literary manner. He did so mainly to "reprocue the flounders spred of him: many things merry, nothing hurtfull."

He was also known for his wanderlust which brought him early to the continent, to Denmark, Germany, and the Netherlands, where he acted and danced. His fame in Europe did not stand too much behind his reputation at home where his name was, no doubt, far more frequently on the people's tongues than Shakespeare's name. After his nine days' dance, finding the doors of the Globe closed to him, he decided to jig over the Alps to Italy, although this venture was not successful.

From that time on things did not go well with him. There are several references to the fact that he had to borrow money after his return. His fame was declining and so was his strength after 1601. Two years later his feet no longer "daunst" nor "jigged." In *Remains after Death* R. Braithwaite wrote an epitaph:

UPON KEMPE AND HIS MORICE

Welcome from Norwich, Kempe! all ioy to see
Thy safe returne moriscoed lustily.
But out, alasse, how soone's thy morice done!
When Pipe and Taber, all thy friends be gone,
And leaue thee now to dance the second part
With feeble nature, not with nimble Art;
Then all thy triumphs fraught with strains of mirth
Shall be cag'd up within a chest of earth:
Shall be? they are: th'ast danc'd thee out of breath,
And now must make thy parting dance with death.

The choreographer and Shakespeare

. . . when you do dance, I wish you
A wave o' the sea, that you might ever do
Nothing but that . . .

Florizel says these words to his beloved Perdita in Shakespeare's *The Winter's Tale* when he asks her to dance. Not only here, but in many of his works Shakespeare has created an elusive magic which has become an inspiration to choreographers. Sometimes it is in the plot and character. Sometimes the inspiration may come from a line only, from one of those powerful metaphors that shine in bright colors and make meaning meaningful.

Can it be that a familiar figure, a well-known action, or the mysterious beauty of a verbal image prompts the choreographic mind to move? Pearl Lang—who, as early as 1943, created a lyric solo suggested by *The Dark Lady of the Sonnets*—thinks that it may appear as if a plot, a character, or the writing had attracted the dancer. "But it is far more than that," she says.

With Shakespeare it is the indescribable something, removed and yet there, the edge of meaning, the veiled depth of what he says that matters. How can the dancer, should he ever really find and absorb the mystery of it, translate this mystery? It is painfully treacherous. When I worked on *The Dark Lady of the Sonnets* I did not intend to exploit the dramatic angle of the theme, I only tried to follow the rhythm of Shakespeare's thoughts, the elusiveness of his lyricism.

The *Sonnets* have remained the most baffling background for a dance creation. Their theme is love, but not love alone. They encompass loneliness, loss, waste, and doom. The abstractness and intellectualization of their topics will—if at all—attract the modern dancer more than the ballet choreographer. Sophie Maslow put her own images inspired by the *Sonnets* into a dance sequence of the same title. "Although the original impetus came from Shakespeare's *Sonnets*," Sophie Maslow explains, "the connection with them became more and more tenuous while I went along. I created a dance in four movements which illustrated various feelings of love."

Next to the *Sonnets*, *Hamlet* is open to the most divergent interpretations. The play can be accepted on many levels. Its dramatic dimensions are all-embracing. As a human being Hamlet is an actor of many tongues. He is real and yet unfathomable. He is universal in spite of, and yet because of, his unique personality. He is masculine in his thoughts and feminine in his feelings. More than any other, this male figure has attracted actresses and ballerinas.

Antony Tudor's *La Gloire*, a dramatic ballet in one act (first presented by the New York City Ballet in 1952), tells of a famed actress and dancer whose career has overwhelmed her personal life. This figure is a composite of Sarah Bernhardt and Anna Pavlova. She appears in several roles, and Hamlet is the culmination. As her greatness fades with Hamlet's death, the shadow of youth, in the shape of a young actress—the new generation—hovers over her.

The German mind, with its strange convolutions, is particularly drawn to the intricate psyche of the Danish prince. The versions of *Hamlet* danced in Germany after the last World War were surprisingly numerous and experimental, all of them attempting to reveal hidden facets through movement action. There was Tatjana Gsovsky's *Hamlet* at the West Berlin Staedtische Oper. ("To do *Hamlet* was one of my wish dreams. It is ideal stage material, with all five figures having their conflicts.") In Munich one saw another *Hamlet* by Tatjana's former husband, Victor Gsovsky. Some time later, Helga Swedlund choreographed her conception of *Hamlet* at the Hamburg Staatsoper and Yvonne Georgi in the Landestheater Hannover. All these Hamlets were done to the score of Boris Blacher, which was also used for the same theme by Erwin Hansen at the Staatstheater in Oldenburg and by Herbert Freund in Frankfurt.

Many choreographers have attempted to do justice to this play in balletic form. When Bronislava Nijinska formed her company in 1932 and called it *Théâtre de Danse,* she made quite clear through its title that she intended to stress theatricality in her repertory, and one of her attempts at theatricalization of the ballet was a *Hamlet* version in 1934. The most memorable danced *Hamlet,* however, was Robert Helpmann's dramatic ballet in one act. He danced the title role opposite Margot Fonteyn's Ophelia in the Sadler's Wells 1942 production. Helpmann did not retell the story, scene by scene. His was rather a kaleidoscopic image of the dramatic events in Hamlet's life, as if in nightmarish recall. He chose as a point of departure the motto: "For in that sleep of death, what dreams may come/When we have shuffled off this mortal coil/Must give us pause." A revival of Helpmann's work at Covent Garden had Rudolf Nureyev in the title role. Richard Buckle, writing of the maverick Russian as Hamlet, found him "tremendous, dead right."

The Russians have a one-act Hamlet version, called *Soliloquies,* choreographed by Nikita Dolgushin to Tchaikovsky's *Ouverture Fantasie,* in the repertory of the Maly Theatre in Leningrad. One of the more recent full-length ballets on the Hamlet theme was staged by Konstantin Sergeyev for the Kirov Ballet in 1970. The choreographer used music by Nikolai Chervinsky and relied on a scenario written by Nikolai Volkov in 1965. It was a seemingly overlong ballet with some effective scenes, such as Ophelia's death and Gertrude's tortured solo expressive of her inner turmoil, or the queen's duet with Hamlet in which her psyche bares her sexual ambivalence, her more than maternal feelings for the prince. The attempt at intricate psychological revelations and a balletic recreation of the quintessence of Hamlet's motivations rather than the telling of a known story demands dramatic insight and intensity expressed through convincing choreographic inventiveness. The critical reactions indicated that the goal set by the choreographer for himself and the artistic fulfillment of his dream were not evenly matched.

The role of Ophelia, too, exerts great fascination. Pearl Lang intended to dance Ophelia—and she is still toying with the idea —as the central figure of the dramatic conflict. "I feel," she says, "that Ophelia could be liberated from the cliché-image we have of her and that her real humanness could be shown in relation to the various images of Hamlet."

"While exploring movement of disintegration," Jean Erdman has said,

I created a female figure who had to face an experience put upon her from the *outside* that was more than she could bear or assimilate. I choreographed it without realizing that the figure I had created had all the features of Ophelia. After the title had been set, I analyzed what I had done from the viewpoint of Ophelia, and none of its dynamics or movements had to be changed. Unconsciously, I must have had Ophelia in mind. I also did *Four Portraits From Duke Ellington's Shakespeare Album* and my subtitles, *In Search of the Moor, Lady Mac, Sonnet for Sister Kate,* and *She Died a Queen* indicate that, inspired by Ellington's delightfully humorous jazz, my approach was a satiric comic one. I was hard put to it to find a way to *kid* poor little Desdemona, but I had great fun with the hands of Lady Mac in jazz style. Cleopatra had her oversized asp on a golden leash, and this wonder monster is now serving a new duty in Joyce's *Coach.*

Many modern dancers have been drawn to the guilt-ridden figure of ambitious Lady Macbeth. Valerie Bettis was one who realized "the theatricality of the theme as well as the opposite dynamic of the changes wrought between Lady Macbeth and her husband." In 1948, Mary Anthony created her Lady Macbeth, and Doris Hering wrote in *Dance Magazine:*

Cast in an angular, tense vein, the solo depicted Lady Macbeth in the progressive states of ambition and guilt. There were props and a heraldic symbol for the king to elucidate what was really very clear dance acting.

Ten years later, of May O'Donnell's *The Queen's Obsession*, based on the sleepwalking scene, Walter Terry commented:

Miss O'Donnell has created an exciting, graphic compression of Shakespeare's guilt-obsessed queen. Beginning with the eerie prophecy by the three witches of the crown to come, the dance proceeds to the anguish of Lady Macbeth following the bloody deeds necessary to obtain the kingship and ends with her death.

Pauline Koner was Lady Macbeth in José Limón's *Barren Sceptre* in 1959. She saw the two different aspects in her personality,

the ruthless, driving force in a woman obsessed, the evil leading to the deed. But the intense strength in her is basically as little normal as the guilt feelings which bring about her insanity as expressed in the sleepwalking scene. The difficult and most important thing is to make her obsession clear and yet to arouse sympathy for her.

"I am very much interested in violent human emotions and in magnificent form," says José Limón. "And I find both, in their ultimate expression, in Shakespeare. What Bach has been to me in music, Shakespeare is in the conception of characters and plots." Mr. Limón's masterpiece is *The Moor's Pavane* which tells, within the very solemnity and stately form of the pavane, the violent story of Othello's jealousy. Eric Bentley once said that, asked what he would send to Europe and Asia as a show piece of American art, he would choose *The Moor's Pavane.*

History has often put the accents on the wrong syllables in its unfairness towards the genius. No one will ever quite know what and who ignites the spark of genius, but we can often recognize the crossroads of trends and the interaction of influences. David Garrick, the famous English actor, appeared in Paris in 1751 and pantomimed scenes of Shakespearean plays. At that time the Parisian intellectuals, the encyclopedists, were eager for new ideas which could replace the artificialities of their Baroque past. Such men as Denis Diderot welcomed David Garrick, among whose admirers was a twenty-four-year-old dancer: Jean-Georges Noverre.

The meeting between Garrick and Noverre strengthened the revolutionary convictions of the man who was destined to reform the art of the ballet and who history rewarded for his deed much too late with too little. Noverre resolved that technique and virtuosity, the logical consequence of the dancers' achieved elevation and the fashion of the day, were insufficient. He realized that the stress had to be shifted to pantomime which then was the term used for expressiveness. But expressiveness was what Noverre meant, dance drama or the danced play. Noverre told David Garrick about his ideas, and Garrick carried his approval to the point of calling him "the Shakespeare of the Dance."

In creating his dramatic ballets, Noverre mainly reworked such themes of world literature which seemed to contain dance-worthy material. In a Shakespearean manner he took the themes from other works and the most divergent sources, but he knew how to give them the final stamp of his personality. It is ironic that the Shakespeare of the dance went twice only to Shakespeare as source material. It was about or after 1761 that he staged *An-*

toine et Cleopatra and *Les Amours d'Henry IV*. One of his disciples, Francesco Clerico, choreographed a ballet based on *Hamlet*. His *Amleto* was produced in Venice in 1788 to music he himself composed. To put Shakespeare on the dance stage successfully, however, was left to Salvatore Viganó, who, as ballet master and choreographer of La Scala in Milan, created the first *Othello* ballet in 1818. It was preceded by a *Coriolano* ballet, which Viganó had choreographed as early as 1805.

History recorded Viganó's *Otello* as the first great Shakespearean ballet. This play, next to *Romeo and Juliet* as well as *Hamlet,* seems to contain basic dance material. Noverre defined that, above all, passions which render man "speechless," such as love (*Romeo and Juliet*), madness (*Hamlet*), and jealousy (*Othello*) have all the necessary dramatic and lyric ingredients for ballets.

Stendhal fell into a paroxism of enthusiasm about Viganó's *Otello*. It seemed to have been highly theatrical. Viganó's opening program note says: "With jubilant shouts and cannon shots. . . ." It is not difficult to see how little of the real Shakespeare was left considering the changes he made. Viganó was less interested in re-creating the Shakespearean drama of jealousy than in creating the fury of jealousy as one of the dramas of man. In Shakespeare, Othello's jealousy is gradually fanned in seven stages and heightened into the rage which finally paralyzes the mind's control. In Viganó's ballet, Iago whispers the poisonous secret once only, and Othello's heart, feeling deceived, begins immediately to burn with rage. This probably worked with the audience of the early nineteenth century which, by 1818, was accustomed to Viganó's choreodramatic technique which made use of the pantomimic overstatement. It was *ballet d'action* in its purest form and ideal as late manifestation of classicism.

It seems that Limón's *The Moor's Pavane* influenced many

choreographers to take up the challenge of this drama. A Prague version in the choreography of Jiri Nemecek with music by Jan Hanus was done in 1956 and the Moscow version by Alexei Matschawariani a year later. Both were realistic full-length ballets with strong socialistic connotations.

In Vienna, Erika Hanka choreographed *The Moor of Venice* to Boris Blacher's score in 1955. Hanka intended "to limit the best-known drama of jealousy to its essentially human content in balletic form. . . . It must not be a danced imitation of Shakespeare's unique spiritual and literary message—it should be Othello as a symbol, the man who is 'you and I,' the general fate which has general meaning." This is why she had the ballet drama unfold in flashbacks, in loosely connected scenes after she had shown the actually fatal and climactic moment of the drama in the Prologue. Furthermore, she enlarged intellectually on the theme by creating abstract reflections after each scene, a "ritornelle" following each phase of Othello's visions as a kind of refrain or danced aria, "as an extension into the all-too-human." Hanka called these dance abstractions *About the Lust of Love, About the Compassion of Kind Women, About the Deception of Women, About the Torments of Jealousy, About the Cruelty of Disappointment, About the Power of Evil.* The Epilogue returns to the scene of murder. Othello realizes his delusion and kills himself. Iago runs into the spears of the soldiers. The Moor dies by the side of Desdemona. Hanka wrote:

The essence of the art of dancing lies in the realm of the soul and heart; it is not the intellect but the emotions from which the dance takes off. . . . It is not Othello's fate only, it is the passion by which each feeling creature is hit with equal consequences.

Of Shakespeare's tragic heroes the role of *King Lear* is at least as tempting as *Hamlet,* but so far very few choreographers have dared tackle this task. Lear, in an incipient state of senile innocence, grows into an awareness of shattering truth. To make the constantly deepening effect of his tragedy visually effective is particularly difficult since, from the very beginning, when he throws away his power and bans those from his heart who are closest to it, he plunges into raging and wailing. His is a single cry, however heartbreaking and lasting it may be. His "O let me not be mad, not mad, sweet heaven!" is the howling music that accompanies him on his descent into the hell of his own making.

"It would be necessary," says Ted Shawn who was *King Lear* in Myra Kinch's choreography,

to dance Lear so often that you forget you are dancing, and Lear becomes you or you Lear. When I attempted to do this role I felt it was suitable to my age. You must have lived a long time to do Lear, you must have survived many challenges in life. This is why I don't think a young man can ever do full justice to Lear. This part enriched me as an artist, it gave me the reassurance that growth is the important thing, the inner growth that comes with the experience of this character. And we must grow whatever age we are in.

Erick Hawkins was no longer a young man, but much younger than Ted Shawn, when he appeared as Lear in Martha Graham's *The Eye of Anguish*. He would not dispute the need of maturity which this part demands. But, he feels, maturity is not necessarily determined by years alone. The intent was not to retell the story, but to distill and reveal the essence of the play in the brief span of the dance. "Perhaps from studying Lear," he says,

I learned what a true tragedy is. Of all Shakespeare's plays, *Lear* is the most perfect tragedy, for the end of the play shows the hero's insight into his error and therefore his rebirth even though he is about to die. The error most modern playwrights and choreographers fall into is mistaking the tragic for tragedy. Merely to report the tragic, the neurosis of our time, I feel, is worthless. Only when the dancer rises to the understanding of the ritual of tragedy will it be good enough and will dance audiences be moved and enlightened.

To the Shakespearean plays which successfully resist being turned into ballets belongs *The Tempest*. A very poor concoction of a ballet, based on *The Tempest,* was staged at the Paris Opéra in 1834 under the title of *La Tempête*. Gautier said, it is a "ballet, the best of which can be said of it is that it is a ballet." It was choreographed by Jean Coralli with Pauline Duvernay in the leading part. It is of historic interest because Fanny Elssler made her debut in it, which marked the beginning of her great rivalry with Marie Taglioni. Fanny Elssler appeared mysteriously veiled. When she dropped the veil, a storm of applause greeted her. It is said that even Taglioni felt forced to applaud, making the rise of her rival unmistakable.

A Midsummer Night's Dream has a "weak and idle theme," as Puck apologizes at the end of the play. It is full of sublime artificiality expressed in the fun of mistaken identities, the sweet touch of the fairy tale. It has the atmosphere of romance and poetry at its most innocent, and, therefore, is ideal for balletic treatment. Puck is a figure that demands a dancing approach from the actor even in the play. Max Reinhardt, a stage director of genius, cast Harald Kreutzberg as Puck in the dramatic version he also presented in New York in 1928.

Michel Fokine made it into a one-act ballet in 1906, still in his old style, at the Maryinsky Theatre, and he came back to the same theme in 1925 when he worked on it at the Drury Lane Theatre in London. In the early Thirties David Lichine based his ballet *Nocturne* on *A Midsummer Night's Dream*.

Isadora Duncan's first stage appearance was in that play with the Augustin Daly Company. He engaged her to be one of the fairies, but she was already at that time interested in expressing her feelings and, dancing to the *Scherzo* by Mendelssohn, impressed the audience and displeased Daly who is supposed to have said: "It is unheard of to have a dance number in a Shakespearean play. This isn't a music hall." It happened in 1897. (Shortly after, Isadora appeared in a solo program at the small Music Room of Carnegie Hall, where she also impersonated Ophelia, probably the first danced Ophelia as a solo characterization.)

A strange version of *A Midsummer Night's Dream* was planned by Jean Cocteau shortly before he came up with the startling scenario for *Parade*. Nothing came of Cocteau's idea, but he intended to collaborate with several composers, among them Edgard Varèse, Igor Stravinsky, Claude Debussy, and Erik Satie. He asked them to contribute incidental music for a circus version of *A Midsummer Night's Dream*. Oberon was to have made his entrance into the ring of the Cirque Médrano to the strains of Tipperary.

George Balanchine's lavish full-length version of *A Midsummer Night's Dream* was, according to the consensus of critical opinion "filled with dances and delight." Doris Hering commented:

What is so distinctive about Balanchine's *A Midsummer Night's Dream* is its swiftness—the way it reflects the atmosphere of the Shakespeare play and yet, through the special fluidity of ballet, is able to glide deftly between reality and fantasy.

Frederick Ashton's shorter version, called *The Dream,* was staged on the occasion of the quadricentennial celebration of Shakespeare's birth. Ashton choreographed it with a profound feeling for the airiness of its theme which, in his hands, never becomes literal or sidetracked into too much obvious detail. The ballet has a flow of its own by being mainly concerned with the magical happenings in the forest and achieves, among all versions shown so far, the most poetic blending of comedy, lyrical love, and the gossamer touch of the inexpressible.

While *A Midsummer Night's Dream* builds its world out of music and joy, *Twelfth Night* builds it out of music and melancholy. This play attracted Andrée Howard, who recreated its atmosphere in balletic terms for the International Ballet in 1942. Antony Tudor's first creative effort in the ballet world was *Cross-Garter'd* which was based on the "affection'd ass" Malvolio in *Twelfth Night*.

Of all of Shakespeare's plays none has found its way into dance more often than *Romeo and Juliet*. From Yugoslavia to Argentina, from Moscow to San Francisco, it has been presented in ballet form. Even such a sophisticated mind as Jean Cocteau could not help trying his hand at this story. *Romeo and Juliet* is the epitome of romantic love. Whether the characters speak of it, or not, the play is saturated with passion. It opens up a world as complete in itself as its characters. Shakespeare creates an excitement of feeling into which we are helplessly drawn.

The list of those who have translated this play into the ballet idiom is almost endless. There have been elaborate full-length productions, such as Leonid Lavrovsky's 1940 production for the Bolshoi, which was later shown in a cinematic version with Galina Ulanova in the title role. He also did condensed and simplified versions in pas de deux form. Ulanova wrote about her thoughts of dancing Julia:

There is much unexpected, unusual in Prokofiev's music, something uncomfortable for the dance. For example, the frequent change in rhythm creates difficulties for the performer, handicaps him. I remember when we all—performers, régisseurs, and the composer—met after the first performance, I could not help saying:

I bet there are no more difficult ways
than to dance to Prokofiev's music for ballets.

. . . In spite of all its novel intonation and feeling for our *Zeit-geist,* this work does justice to the spirit of Shakespeare's tragedy to a surprising degree. . . . As Julia I had to reveal the eternal, deeply human theme which Dante best expressed when he wrote: "Love which compels the return of love." . . . Shakespeare prompted me the serene unconcern of the first scene, surprise and bewilderment in the ball scene, the blissfulness of the first rendez-vous, the chaste purity at the wedding ceremony, the brave overcoming of horror in the tomb scene.

There have been several ballet versions of the play: Bronislava Nijinska staged her *Romeo and Juliet* as a non-*Romeo and Juliet* ballet, "a rehearsal in two parts without scenery," for the Diaghilev company in 1926. The surrealist sets were by Max Ernst, Joan Miró designed a curtain, and the costumes were by both artists. To music by Constant Lambert, Karsavina and Lifar appeared as two dancers in love who are expected for a rehearsal of *Romeo and Juliet.* They arrive late and escape before the end by plane. Two years previously, Jean Cocteau created a theater piece with dancing, not strictly speaking a ballet, a fascinating and perplexing version of the play. The staging was strongly influenced by the then much-talked about stage experiments of Tairov, Meyerhold, and Vakhtangov.

Shorter versions were staged by Birgit Cullberg in Stockholm in 1944, by Serge Lifar at the Paris Opera in 1955 (this was preceded by a more successful ballet on the same theme by Lifar done to Tchaikovsky's fantasy-overture of *Romeo and Juliet* in 1942 for the debut of Ludmilla Tcherina); the Tchaikovsky score was also used by George Skibine for his *Tragedy at Verona,* presented by the Grand Ballet du Marquis de Cuevas in 1950; in the

same year and with the same music Birger Bartholin choreographed his *Romeo and Juliet* at the Royal Theatre in Copenhagen with Erik Bruhn.

The most impressive of all short versions was Antony Tudor's one-act *Romeo and Juliet,* staged for The American Ballet
Theatre in 1943 with Alicia Markova and Hugh Laing in the
principal roles. Edwin Denby wrote about it: "It does not sweep
through the story. It is, so to speak, a meditation on the play. But
it is strangely moving. Its strength is that of an intensely and consistently poetic attitude." John Martin denied its balletic elo-
quence and spoke of "a play without words rather than a ballet." Mr. Tudor has said, "I was inspired to do the ballet while
listening to Prokofiev's music, but then I waited and when I began to work on it I chose a score of selected pieces by Delius."

Frederick Ashton staged *Romeo and Juliet* to Prokofiev's
score in a romantic style with a great deal of pantomime for the
Royal Danish Ballet in 1955. The action was extended over three
stage levels. Svend Kragh-Jacobsen reported on it:

Ashton has chosen to form it as a psychological version of the two lover's personal development and tragedy, rather than the powerful Renaissance painting of the feud between two families. . . . He has focused attention on the leading characters while the great ensemble
scenes, which in the Russian ballet film are almost predominant, are
most conventional in Ashton's treatment.

As a matter of fact, he concentrated on the two lovers with such
glowing warmth that his version makes the impression of an eve-
ning-long pas de deux, full of wonderfully detailed tenderness, although we completely lose sight of their environment, so decisive
for their tragedy.

Clive Barnes pointed out that Ashton's *Romeo and Juliet*

"has its roots in the Petipa tradition, while the Bolshoi's Lavrovsky is a fully developed dance-drama all in accordance with Fokine's Five Principles." Barnes stresses "the debt Ashton owes to the influence of Petipa . . . In him, as in Balanchine, can be seen elements both of the old Imperial Russian Ballet and the Diaghilev Ballets Russes." As if to demonstrate the difference between the older and younger generation of choreographers, Ashton asked Kenneth MacMillan to stage a new version of the play for the Royal Ballet. While MacMillan lost nothing of the consuming passion and tragedy of the star-cross'd lovers, he created at the same time the drama of their environment.

There were earlier productions of *Romeo and Juliet:* In 1785 Eusebio Luzzi, soloist and choreographer, staged a *Giulietta e Romeo* in Venice; in 1811 Vincenzo Galeotti choreographed his dramatic ballet about the two lovers in Copenhagen. Undoubtedly, this theme has a strong hold on the imagination of choreographers since it so conveniently combines the most intimate passion with the spectacular elements of the environment. In 1955 the de Cuevas company presented probably the most opulent production of the drama in the Cour Carrée of the Louvre and employed no less than four choreographers: Taras, Skibine, Golovine, and Skouratoff. The use of Berlioz music characterizes this sumptuous display. I am certain that there will be many more productions of *Romeo and Juliet* as there have been many more than I can mention here.

The play has also served as inspiration and model for Jerome Robbins's musical *West Side Story,* a successful blending of the Shakespearean theme with the gang warfare in the big cities of mid-twentieth-century America. Leonard Bernstein wrote the score. Robbins achieved a unique theatrical totality by remaining faithful to the ballet and pantomime concept in the course of telling the drama, by characterizing the actor-singer-dancers through gesture and movement taken from everyday life but heightened through stylization.

Other plays by Shakespeare were turned into musicals: Rogers and Hart based *The Boys from Syracuse* on *The Comedy of Errors,* and who will ever forget the charm of Hanya Holm's dances in Cole Porter's *Kiss Me, Kate,* which was inspired by *The Taming of the Shrew.*

That our time has grown closer to Shakespeare cannot be denied. But this cannot be the only reason for our preoccupation with his work. It may be difficult to define what inspires a choreographer or which literary source prompts his creative urge most and best. That Shakespeare leads all dramatists as source material for the dancer, however, is not difficult to prove.

Shakespeare is as quotable as the Bible, and it may also be that his work penetrates the mystery of existence and reveals more of its uniqueness more deeply than any other writer's work. In his plays, lyricism does not hinder or halt the flow of action, on the contrary, it holds it tighter together; his images have the sweep and sweetness of poetry; he knows how to give *Gestalt* to the inexpressible and new dimensions to the expressible; there is an unmistakable universality about his characters; sometimes there is a basic fairy-tale quality in his plots which is so meaningful that its obviousness is a matter of no concern; and everywhere, unrestrained, theatricality prevails, in good taste, and in both its gayest and most somber moods.

It seems that all this, or some part of it, must also go into the making of dances.

In an age of essays, letters, and journals

An entire age rushed to find solace in reason and hope in enlightenment. Voltaire, its foremost spokesman, said of himself, "I have no sceptre but I have a pen," while the past was guillotined. Carried by the modest beginning of the Industrial Revolution, the bourgeois moved up on the proverbial rungs of the social ladder. The quest for knowledge could no longer be stopped or slowed down, historical and critical dictionaries preceded the encyclopedists. Descartes's dictum of "I think, therefore I am," bore its scientific fruits in the eighteenth century.

Rousseau who had turned against the principles of the Enlightenment and romanticized the state of nature, while condemning the established institutions for corrupting man, prepared the world for its romantic age which was then around the corner of a new century. In the old one the stress was on the individual who began to search outside and within himself. He began to travel and wrote journals as James Boswell had done. With the introduction of the postal system, people began to write letters which inundated literature. Whenever one had something to say, particularly something unorthodox, one used the form of letters as Jean-Georges Noverre did in his *Lettres sur la Danse et sur les Ballets*. Since the eighteenth century also introduced the novel, many novels were written as letters.

The first newspapers and periodicals appeared at the beginning of the century, among them *The Tatler* from 1709 to 1711, followed by *The Spectator* from 1711 to 1712. Joseph Addison and Richard Steele are identified with them and can claim to have perfected the essay as a literary type. Dancing in its historical, allegorical, social, and theatrical forms was often of concern to

The Spectator. We can hear reason in the beginning and feel the touch of a rational homily at the close of an entry such as:

> It would be a great improvement as well as embellishment to the theatre if dancing were more regarded and taught to all the actors. One who has the advantage of such an agreeable girlish person as Mrs. Bicknell, joined with her capacity of imitation, could in proper gesture and motion represent all the decent characters of female life. An amiable modesty in one aspect of a dancer and assumed confidence in another, a sudden joy in another, a falling off with an impatience of being beheld, a return toward the audience with an unsteady resolution to approach them, and well-acted solicitude to please, would revive in the company all the fine touches of mind raised in observing all the objects of affection and passion they had before beheld. Such elegant entertainments as these would polish the town into judgement in their gratifications; and delicacy in pleasure is the first step people of condition take in reformation from vice.

In another entry we are told of someone's daughter taking lessons with Monsieur Ridagoon, a dancing master in the city, who advises her to go to one of his balls. The observing father reports that the first dance which they called Hunt the Squirrel was full of modesty and discretion. But "as the best institutions are liable to corruptions," we are told by the writer of this letter, "I must acquaint you, that very great abuses are crept into this entertainment." Then he tells of a dance back to back and how a dancer after two or three capers whisked the girl round cleverly above ground in such a manner that he, "who sat upon one of the lowest benches, saw further above her shoe than I can think fit to acquaint you with." This is followed by the moral:

> I must confess I am afraid that my correspondent had too much reason to be a little out of humour at the treatment of his daughter, but I conclude that he would have been much more so, had he seen one of

those kissing dances in which Will Honeycomb assures me they are obliged to dwell almost a minute on the Fair one's lips, or they will be too quick for the musick, and dance quite out of time. I am not able however to give my final sentence against this diversion . . . so much of dancing, at least, as belongs to the behaviour and handsome carriage of the body, is extremely useful, if not absolutely necessary.

As for country-dancing, it must indeed be confessed that the great familiarities between the two sexes on this occasion may sometimes produce very dangerous consequences; and I have often thought that few Ladies hearts are so obdurate as not to be melted by the charms of musick, the force of motion, and an handsome young fellow who is continually playing before their eyes, and convincing them that he has the perfect use of all his limbs.

But as this kind of dance is the particular invention of our own country, and as everyone is more or less a proficient in it, I would not discountenance it; but rather suppose it may be practised innocently by other, as well as myself, who am often partner to my landlady's eldest daughter.

Any attempt at serious dancing, usually imported from France, found little response in England at that time. Some of the great French dancers—Jean Ballon, for instance—appeared at Lincoln's Inn Fields for an exorbitant fee. Less distinguished guests were seen in vaudeville programs together with dogs trained to dance a minuet on a tight rope. *The Spectator* raised the question why "dancing, an art celebrated by the ancients in so extraordinary a manner, be totally neglected by the moderns, and left destitute of any pen to recommend its various excellencies and substantial merit to mankind?" The answer to its own question was:

The low ebb to which dancing is now fallen, is altogether owing to this silence. The art is esteem'd only as an amusing trifle; it lies altogether uncultivated, and is unhappily fallen under the imputation of illiterate and mechanick: And as Terence, in one of his prologues, complains of the rope-dancers drawing all the spectators from his play, so may we well say, that capering and tumbling is now preferred to, and supplie the place of, just and regular dancing on our theatres. It is therefore, in my opinion, high time that someone should come to its assistance, and relieve it from the many gross and growing errors that have crept into it, and overcast its real beauties; and to set dancing in its true light, would shew the usefulness and elegance of it, with the pleasure and instruction produc'd from it; and also lay down some fundamental rules, that might so tend to the improvement of its professors, and information of the spectators, that the first might be the better enabled to perform, and the latter render'd more capable of judging, what is (if there be anything) valuable in this art.

When this Cassandra cry appeared, *The Spectator* was not aware that a certain John Weaver was about to break "this silence" and enter into a serious discussion of the art. John Weaver, ballet master at the Drury Lane Theatre, was a rare exception, an intellectual oasis in an artistic desert as far as the ballet in England was concerned. In 1717 he staged a dramatic pantomime, *The Loves of Mars and Venus*. In it he came close to creating a *ballet d'action*. The well-known critic of that era, Colley Cibber, wrote about it:

The fable of Mars and Venus was formed into a connected presentation of dances in character, wherein the passions were so happily expressed, and the whole story was so intelligibly told, by a mute narration of gesture only, that even thinking spectators allowed it both a pleasing and rational entertainment.

Early eighteenth-century England did not produce any striking dance personality except Weaver. Perhaps Hester Santlow, known as an actress and dancer, should be mentioned. She made her dancing debut in 1706 and later seemed to have combined both arts with great dexterity, appearing, for instance, on one evening in 1710 as Ophelia in *Hamlet* and in a dance sketch, called *Dutch Skipper*. Weaver referred to her in his *Anatomical Lectures* saying that in her "Art and Nature have combin'd to produce a beautiful Figure, allow'd by all Judges in our Art to be the most graceful, most agreeable, the most correct Performer in the World." Also, the activity of John Rich at Lincoln's Inn Fields should not go unmentioned because he created a bridge between the pantomime of the *commedia dell'arte* and the art of ballet.

What interests us here most is John Weaver's writing, which, though not being a literary achievement, has great merit as an essay of recorded theories that heralded some of the basic ideas for which history credits Noverre. It was in the year 1712, when *The Spectator* ceased publication, that Weaver's *Essay towards an History of Dancing* was issued. He discriminated between "serious" dancing, that is, the genteel French school, and the Italian style of dancing, which he called "grotesque," rejecting the former as insufficient for the demands on ballet and giving the latter its due as serving a purpose, particularly in opera dancing. Weaver projected a far-reaching idea which he described as "scenical" dancing. It was nothing else but the ability of the choreographer to unfold a whole story by action. Nine years later, Weaver published his *Anatomical and Mechanical Lectures upon Dancing* and, in 1728, *The History of the Mimes and Pantomimes*.

The whole age was caught in a feverish thirst for knowledge, for investigating the laws of nature and theorizing about the arts as based on investigation. Irreverence for the classics and scriptures, as well as a curiosity for the reasons behind all being, was characteristic of the time. The systematization of knowledge in the sciences and arts led Weaver to theorize about the dance, which, for him, could only have the complementary effects of di-version *and* instruction. What he tried to achieve was the estab-lishment of an anatomical base for proper dance instruction.

It is also indicative of this era that the satiric painter Wil-liam Hogarth, who, on his canvases, caught life in its very act of being, wrote a treatise, *The Analysis of Beauty,* on his quest into the laws of nature. Hogarth insisted on an intimate relationship between nature and the creative artist, extolling "the beauties of nature unimproved." He dealt with a new method of acquiring easy and graceful movements of parts of the body from a painter's viewpoint, but in one chapter he also talked about dancing. He used dancing to illustrate and fortify his concepts of ideal beauty which he saw in the pyramidal and serpentlike form, the economy of simplicity, the gracefulness of the undulating line, and the im-portance of variety.

Hogarth singled out the minuet—not for its being the favor-ite dance of his age but for containing a variety of movements in the serpentine lines—as a fine composition of movements.

The ordinary undulating motion of the body in common walking (as may be plainly seen by the waving line, which the shadow of a man's head makes against a wall as he is in walking between it and the after-noon sun) is augmented in dancing into a larger quantity of *waving* by means of the minuet-step, which is so contrived as to raise the body by gentle degrees somewhat higher than ordinary, and sink it again in the same manner lower in the going on of the dance. The figure of the minuet-path on the floor is also composed of serpentine lines varying a little with the fashion. . . . The other beauties belonging to this dance, are the turns of the head, and twist of the body in passing each other, as also gentle bowing and presenting hands in the manner be-fore described, all which together, displays the greatest variety of movements in serpentine lines imaginable, keeping equal pace with musical time. There are other dances that entertain merely because they are composed of variety of movements and performed in proper time, but the less they consist of serpentine or waving lines, the lower they are in the estimation of dancing-masters.

We learn from Hogarth's reminiscences how strongly he was influenced by the theater when he said that he was determined to "compose pictures on canvas similiar to representations on stage," expecting them to be tried

by the same test, and criticized by the same criterion. . . . Let the figures in either pictures or prints be considered as players dressed either for the sublime—for genteel comedy, or farce—for high or low life. I have endeavoured to treat my subjects as a dramatic writer: my picture is my stage, and men and women are my players, who by means of certain actions and gestures, are to exhibit a dumb show.

And theatricality remained Hogarth's trademark as a painter.

Also accustomed to seeing dancing from a theatrical viewpoint, he recognized a greater consistency in the dances of the Italian theater than of the French, even though "dancing seems to be the genius of that nation." He visualized humor as an inherent part of the movements indicative of the *commedia dell'arte* types: "The attitudes of the harlequin are ingeniously composed of certain little quick movements of the head, hands and feet, some of which shoot out as it were from the body in straight lines or are twirled about in little circles." Speaking of country dances in this essay, he praised the variety of lines and their intricacy. Again, the serpentine lines "interlacing or intervolving each other" fascinated him most, particularly those in the hay.

The importance of Hogarth's writing lies in the fact that his was the first attempt to define beauty in empirical terms and to make formal values the basis of an aesthetic system. Standing between the Baroque and the Rococo, he tended towards the more restless, mobile, and wanton expression of the new form, leaving behind him the voluptuous and dramatic solemnity of the Baroque.

Macaulay's attitude towards James Boswell notwithstanding, his *Journals* and biography, *The Life of Samuel Johnson,* provide us with invaluable knowledge of the temper, mores, and events in the eighteenth century. Boswell may have been a person of loose morals, but this did not prevent him from being an astute observer and skillful diarist. Certainly Casanova cannot put too high a claim on morality, but his *Memoirs* are a wonderful source of the world he lived in, and, for instance, his description of Louis Dupré, whom he saw in *Les Fêtes Venetiennes* in 1750, is one of the best records we have of Dupré and this ballet.

Boswell was chided by his critics for being a fool who was clever enough to ride to fame on the shoulders of a great man. So must this be said then of Eckermann, who preserved for us some of the best thoughts of such a giant as Goethe. Of course, it is of little interest where, with whom, and how well Boswell dined or with whom he danced well on what occasion; what matters is the image we perceive of the arts and life of his time. While traveling in Germany he saw a French comedy one night, the next an operetta which did not amuse him, and then again a German comedy. Two days previously, on August 13, 1764, he had dinner and then went to see "the noble entertainment of rope-dancing at which was the Duke and all the Court." We also learn that he attended several balls within the interval of a few days and that he was interrupted in a minuet when "the fiddlers struck up a country dance which the Hereditary Prince was to begin."

Another passage of his *Journals* tells us that Sheridan, during a dinner party, came to speak about acting at the Drury Lane Theatre. "Without propriety of speech," said Sheridan, "all the powers of acting are nothing. It is just like time in dancing. And let a dancer play never so many tricks and feats of agility, he will not be applauded if he does not observe time." Even though Boswell thought that this comparison was not just, we learn from it that dancing was on Sheridan's mind, who also wrote poetry inspired by dance. Or we are informed about what Dr. Johnson thought of dancing through an entry on March 30, 1781:

I ventured to mention a ludicrous paragraph in the newspapers, that Dr. Johnson was learning to dance of Vestris. Lord Charlemont, wishing to excite him to talk, proposed in a whisper, that he should be asked whether it was true. "Shall I ask him?" said his lordship. We were, by a great majority, clear for the experiment. Upon which his lordship very gravely, and with a courteous air, said: "Pray, sir, is it true that you are taking lessons of Vestris?" This was risking a good deal, and required the boldness of a general of Irish Volunteers to make the attempt. Johnson was at first startled, and in some heat answered: "How can your Lordship ask so simple a question?" But immediately recovering himself, whether from unwillingness to be deceived, or whether from real good humour, he kept up the joke: "Nay, but if anybody were to answer the paragraph, and contradict it, I'd have a reply, and would say, that he who contradicted it was no friend either to Vestris or me. For why should not Dr. Johnson add to his other powers a little corporeal agility?"

G. B. S., dance critic

As music and drama critic George Bernard Shaw saw and reviewed ballets. The man who championed Wagner and Ibsen saw the dance with literary eyes. Perhaps he knew enough of dance history to realize that what he demanded from the ballet in terms of aesthetic tenets had been asked for by Jean-Georges Noverre a hundred and thirty years previously.

In almost all his dance reviews Shaw iterated that only the

dance drama had any right to exist ("I have had enough of mere ballet: what I want now is dance-drama.") and comdemned the apparent need of a principal dancer "in order to get even a very conventional round of applause" to "spoil her solo by a silly, flustering, ugly teetotum spin, which no really fine dancer should condescend to." He also echoes the defender of the *ballet d'action* when Shaw shouts in one of his reviews, on February 8, 1893, warning against "the detestable bravura solos which everybody hates":

Move us; act for us; make our favorite stories real to us; weave your grace and skill into the fabric of our life; but don't put us off for the thousandth time with those dreary pirouettes and entrechats and arabesques and whatd'yecal lems. That is the cry of humanity to the danseuse, the ballet master, and the manager.

What Shaw looks for is "poetic color and motion." He cannot write often enough that "the monotony and limitation of the dancer's art vanishes when it becomes dramatic." He put up a target which he calls "teetotum spin" and at which he sends his verbal arrows in desperate repetition. It is to him the symbol of empty display, of mere technical tricks.

On January 24, 1894, he wrote again:

The danseuses were still trying to give some freshness to the half-dozen *pas* of which every possible combination and permutation has been worn to death any time these hundred years, still calling each hopeless attempt a "variation," and still finishing up with the teetotum spin which is to the dancer what the high note at the end of a dull song is to a second-rate singer. I wonder is there anything on earth as stupid as what I may call, in the Wagnerian terminology, "absolute dancing"! Sisyphus trying to get uphill with the stone that always rolls down again must have a fairly enjoyable life compared with a ballet master.

Although Shaw reviewed operas too and was a frequent guest at Covent Garden, there is no mention in his reviews of any dancing in *Faust, Carmen, Aida,* or *Tannhäuser*. Rather early in his career as a music critic, on November 12, 1890, he refers to the ballet in Gluck's *Orpheus* saying that he "will not chide Katti Lanner's maidens for being no more able than the chorus to move as gods to the noble measures of Gluck, which baffled 'the many twinkling feet' even in the times of the old order in France, when the grand school was much grander than it is now."

The place where most ballet was seen in London in the early Nineties was the music hall. The programs were less selective in the Alhambra and the Empire than they were in the great opera houses on the continent. The quantity was more impressive than the quality in their two nightly performances which then took place. As early as October 4, 1889, Shaw declared that

At one point of my chequered career I made a point of seeing every ballet produced at the Alhambra in order to study one of the most remarkable artistic institutions of the time. The virtuosity of the principal dancers was the result of a training of a severity and duration unknown among singers. . . . Even the rank and file were skilled to a degree unkown in opera choruses, and by no means common in orchestras. The grouping and coloring were thought out by real artists. A ballet called *Yolande* . . . reached a standard of technical perfection which would have been received with astonished acclamation in any other art. Yet nobody of any intelligence cared two straws about the Alhambra. The brainless artificiality of the ballets was too much for the public. People went and stared; but the quality of applause was always poor. I gave it up at last as a hopeless affair.

He would not have been Shaw had he not analyzed, dissected, and attacked in his reviews. Even though he was not a dance expert, he knew exactly what he wanted. As a person of penetrating intellect, verbal facility, and a high aesthetic standard he could have written about any art form with the same clear judgement and revealing spirit as about music and the drama. In discussing the dancing at the Alhambra, he explained what ballet was to him. For example, on August 27, 1890:

The ballet, wherein we passed at a bound from the Utter Popular to the Ultra Academic—from the toe and heel crudities of the step-dance to the classical *entrechats* of the grand school—was dramatically weak. A ballet without a good story and plenty of variety and scene and incident is much like one of Händel's operas, which were only stage concerts for shewing off the technical skill of the singers. Now the deftest shake and the most perfect roulade soon pall unless they are turned to some dramatic purpose: we put up even with the nightingale only by giving it credit for poetic fancies that never came into its head. It is the same with dancing when somebody else is doing it: we soon weary of the few *pas* which make up the dancer's stock-in-trade.

We demand, first, a pretty dance (and composers of good dances are no more plentiful than composers of good songs); and, second, a whole drama in dance, in which the *pas seul* shall merge, as the aria and cavatina have at last merged in the Wagnerian music-drama.

On February 21 of the same year Shaw had been even more explicit about his concept of a great ballerina:

Many a première danseuse holds her position in spite of a neck and wrists which are, dancingly considered, dead as doornails. But the dancer who dances to the tips of her fingers and the top of her head: that is the perfect dancer; for dancing being a sort of pulsation of grace in the limbs which dance, the perfect dancer is all grace; and if she has, to boot, a touch of tragic passion in her, it will find instant and vivid expression in her dancing. To such a nonpareil you would unhesitatingly give, if she asked for it, the head of Adelina Patti or Sarasate in a charger. So perhaps it is just as well that she is the rarest of rare birds.

In the same review Shaw made it quite clear that his approach to the dance was literary. He did not even admit that it might be good to know all the technical details of the dance, the vocabulary of the *danse d'école,* only to dismiss them when seeing the dance unfold. With the famous Shavian insistence and exaggeration in order to make his point stick, he exclaimed: *

I care not a jot about the technology of the art of dancing. I do not know, and, what is more, I positively refuse to know, which particular *temps* is a *battement* and which a *ronde de jambe.* If I were equally ignorant of the technical differences between a tonal fugue and a quadrille, I should be a better musical critic than I am; for I should not so often be led astray from the essential purpose of art by mere curiosity as to the mechanical difficulties created by certain forms of it. All that concerns me is how beautifully or how expressively a dancer can dance, and how best I can stop the silly practice of ending every solo with a teetotum twirl like the old concert ending to the overture to Iphigenia in Aulis.

It seems that Shaw was also exposed to a great deal of skirt dancing, and in reviewing a musical farce he hailed one of the actress-dancers. In doing so, he did not forget to hit the tediousness of the endless divertissements and variations he encountered in classical ballets (November 22, 1893):

The success of *Morocco Bound* centres round a single artist—Miss Letty Lind. Sarasate's playing is not more exquisite than her dancing; it is a delight to see her simply march across the stage in time to the

* *Dance Magazine*'s Doris Hering, who cannot be reproached for not being a balletomane with a thorough knowledge of the art's technique, reviewed the Leningrad Kirov Ballet in the November 1964 issue: "Time and again I found myself actually assigning its proper French title to a particular *pas* or *enchaînement* and being oblivious of the context into which the steps were set. While lexicography can be an absorbing game, this also means that the choreography is not calling forth a total response."

music. She is no mere skirt-dancer: if she were invisible from the waist downwards, the motion of her head and wrists would still persuade me to give her anybody's head on a charger—and this is the test of the perfect dancer as distinguished from the mere step dancer. She gives us all the grace of classical dancing without its insufferable pedantry and its worn-out forms.

Many years later, he wrote for the *Saturday Review* about a musical, *A Man About Town,* that he had seen at the Avenue Theatre on January 2, 1897. In this musical farce of no significance there must have been inefficient skirt dancing which prompted Shaw to set up rules and formulas for criticizing a dancer:

The formula for criticizing a dancer is simple enough. At the two extremes of the art are the step dancer who dances with the feet alone, with spine rigid, shoulders pushed up to the top of it and nailed hard there, fists clinched, neck stiff as iron, and head held convulsively as if only the most violent effort of continence on the dancer's part could keep it from exploding. At the other you have the perfect dancer along whose limbs the rhythmic stream flows unbroken to the very tips of the fingers and root of the hair, whose head moves beautifully, whose nape and wrists make the music visible, who can flex the spine at each vertebra more certainly than an ordinary person can flex his finger at each joint, and who is the personification of skill, grace, strength, and health.

If Shaw had continued to write reviews instead of becoming one of the greatest playwrights of the century, he would have been a staunch defender of the modern dance and its wide range of meaningful expressiveness. An excerpt of his review on April 6, 1892, testifies to it:

The *entrechats* of Vincenti at his entry in the ballet *Asmodeus* were worthy of Euphorion: but the recollection of them rather intensifies the boredom with which I contemplate the ordinary danseuse who makes a conceited jump and comes down like a wing-clipped fowl without having for an instant shown that momentary picture of a vigorous and beautiful flying feature which is the sole object of the feat. In short, I am as tired of the ballet in its present phase as I became of ante-Wagnerian Italian opera; and I believe that the public is much of my mind in the matter. . . . Under such circumstances, a development of the dramatic element, not only in extent but in realistic treatment, is inevitable if the ballet is to survive at all.

Shaw once confessed that his "own weakness is neither medicine, nor law, nor tailoring, or any of the respectable departments of bogusdom. It is the theatre." He was so much a part of the theater, even though he used it as a pulpit for his entertaining sermons, that one cannot help believing his honesty and sincerity in whatever dictum he could lay down as "his" gospel truth. He seemed to have been worried about the art of dancing—at least, at his time—being far removed from reality. Art being divorced from life was immoral to him. In the course of reviewing a ballet he wrote on January 24, 1894:

Another result, with which I am more immediately concerned, is that the ballet, being the acme of unreality in stage plays, is by no means unpopular on that account—quite the reverse, in fact. Unfortunately, it is so remote from life that it is absolutely unmoral, and therefore incapable of sentiment or hypocrisy. I therefore suggest thay by getting rid of the dreary academic dancing, the "variations," and the stereotyped *divertissements* at the end, and making the ballet sufficiently dramatic throughout to add the fascination of moral unreality to that of physical impossibility, it might attain a new lease of life.

No one can say that George Bernard Shaw approached the dance in a condescending way. He was well aware of the historic role of the dance as a most essential and primary form of human expression. He saw the limitations of the classical dance and, as a theater man and the man he was, he could not help being frank about it. He saw ballet at the time of its lowest artistic ebb and at a place where one could not even comfort oneself with the thought of facing a well-founded tradition which will always create out of its midst a rebel who would save the tradition by giving it "a new lease of life" of which Shaw spoke.

In 1888 a conflict arose between the Bishop of London and the Reverend Stewart Headlam as to the godliness of dancing, a struggle which "ended practically in the excommunication of the dancers and the inhibition of the popular clergyman." It was the first time Shaw wrote about the dance, and it seems self-evident that Shaw would defend the Reverend's attempt to have his flock dance in his church instead of going to the pubs to drink.

This is shocking, no doubt, to our insular conception of a church as a place where we must on no account enjoy ourselves, and where ladies are trained in the English art in sitting in rows for hours, dumb, expressionless, and with the elbows uncomfortably turned in. But since people must enjoy themselves sometimes, why not in their own churches . . . ? "Dancing is an art," says Mr. Headlam. "All art is praise," says Mr. Ruskin. Praise is surely not out of place in a church. We sing there; why should we not dance?

A year later, when he began to see more and more dance performances at the music halls he still harked to the propriety of the dance and, at the same time, anticipated what should become his basic attitude toward ballet when he wrote on October 4, 1889:

Pious people who are not ashamed to confess that they have never been to a theatre think the ballet indecent. Would it were! . . . The Ballet indecent! Why, it is the most formal, the most punctilious, ceremonious, professor-ridden, pigheaded solemnity that exists. Talk of your fugues, canons, key-relationships, single and double counterpoint, fifty orthodox resolutions of the chord of the minor ninth and the rest of it! What are they to the *entrechats, battements, ronde de jambes, arabesques, elavations,* that are the stock-in-trade of the art of theatrical dancing?

The dance was still on his mind towards the end of his career as a professional newspaper and magazine critic. When, on September 21, 1895, he saw in the Lyceum Theatre a performance of *Romeo and Juliet* with his beloved Mrs. Patrick Campbell in the leading role, he rose to impartiality—for Shaw art was art was art —and to the realization of the irresistibility of the dance:

As to Juliet, she danced like the daughter of Herodias. And she knew the measure of her lines to a hairsbreadth. . . . Mrs. Patrick Campbell . . . as Juliet . . . still fits herself into the hospitable manly heart without effort, simply because she is a wonderful person, not only in mere facial prettiness . . . not even in her light, beautifully proportioned figure, but in the extraordinary swiftness and certainty of her physical command. . . . This physical talent, which is seldom consciously recognized except when it is professedly specialized in some particular direction . . . will, when accompanied by nimbleness of mind, quick observation, and lively theatrical instinct, carry any actress with a rush to the front of her profession, as it has carried Mrs. Patrick Campbell. Her Juliet, nevertheless, is an immature performance. . . . Nothing of it is memorable except the dance—the irresistible dance.

What price dancing?

The literary minds and ballerinas found to one another in their spiritual and visual exaltations in nineteenth-century France and carried their demonstrative love affair into the early twentieth century. The English men of letters, however, had only a nodding acquaintance with the dance. Some of their poets brushed Terpsichore in passing, Shelley and Byron dropped a poem or two into her lap, as did John Keats, Arthur O'Shaughnessy, and Dante Gabriel Rossetti.

It was only from the turn of the century on that the English poets took to the dance, and the excitement which it generated in the Western World did not elude them. Poems on the dance became more frequent, and particularly dancers such as Isadora Duncan who had the ability to create their own legends during their lifetime challenged a host of minor poets to set the fleeting image of such immortal greatness a verbal monument.

However, the lyric outpouring remained minor and accidental in comparison to the dramatists who felt drawn to the dance. Of course, there were moments of philosophic-mystical ecstasy, as in T. S. Eliot's *Four Quartets:*

> At the still point of the turning world,
>   neither flesh nor fleshless;
> Neither from nor towards; at the still
>   point, there the dance is,
> But neither arrest nor movement. . . .
> Except for the point, the still point,
> There would be no dance, and there is
>   only the dance. . . .

or the pirouettes of verbal contortion in James Joyce's *Finnegans Wake:*

—Dawncing the kniejinsky choreopiscopally like an easter sun round the colander, the vice! Taranta boontoday. You should pree him prance the polcat, you would sniff him wops around, you should hear his piedigrotts schraying as his skimpies skirp a. . . .

—Crashedafar Corumbas! A Czardanser indeed! Dervilish affection through his blood like a bad influenza in a leap at bounding point?

—Out of Prisky Poppagenua, the palsied old priamite, home from Edwin Hamilton's Christmas pantaloonade, *Oropos Roxy and Pantharhea* at the Gaiety, trippudiating round the aria, with his fifty-two heirs of age! They may reel at his likes but it's Noeh Bonum's shin do.

Loie Fuller in her *Fire Dance* in which she created the image of standing in blazing flames without ever burning, projecting life-in-death and death-in-life, inspired many poets and philosophers; among them was William Butler Yeats, who must have thought of her image when writing in his *Byzantium:*

. . . blood-begotten spirits come
And all complexities of fury leave;
    Dying into a dance,
    An agony of trance,
An agony of flame that cannot singe a sleeve.

All his life Yeats fought a losing battle with the theater. He wanted to achieve poetic purity, well-knowing that such theater contradicts the very essence of theater as a communal experience. Particularly at the time when he thought to have found a point of departure in the esoteric Noh play, the dance, in its physical immediacy and spiritual elusiveness, became a means of connecting his poetic images with reality when he embarked on writing *Four Plays For Dancers*. While Bertolt Brecht, about ten years later, also experimented with the Noh play, he used its structure mainly for the purpose of instruction and enlightenment. Brecht divested the Noh play of its esoteric connotations in order to make its didactic intent clear. Yeats, however, heightened the feeling of a unique remoteness from reality with his poetic depth and playfulness.

In *At the Hawk's Well,* the best of his *Four Plays For Dancers,* Yeats used dance in a dramaturgically decisive moment, but without indicating what the dance should be. To say, "the Guardian of the Well has begun to dance, moving like a hawk," would make a mediocre choreographer use movements of birdlike kitsch and an expert choreographer forget what was said. The story tells of Cuchulain approaching the fabled Hawk's Well in the hope of gaining immortality by drinking from it. There he finds an old man who has been waiting his entire life at the well in order to drink from it, but whenever the water runs he is asleep. A woman guards the well. Her cry of a hawk is the signal that the water is about to flow. The old man cannot stand her gaze and, as if hypnotized, he falls asleep again. The young man cries out:

> Why do you fix those eyes of a hawk upon me?
> I am not afraid of you, bird, woman, or witch.
> Do what you will, I shall not leave this place
> Till I have grown immortal like yourself.

But the woman's dance has magnetic power, and it casts a spell on him. "The madness has laid hold upon him now," the Musician says, "for he grows pale and staggers to his feet." The dance captivates him more and more, the woman leaves for the mountains, and he follows her in a trancelike state. "He has lost what may not be found," the Musicians sing in lieu of a Greek chorus. When Cuchulain returns the well is dry again.

It is a story simple in its symbolism, haunting in its rhythmic poetry, and failing in its dramatic projection. It suggests the eternal quest of man for the higher things in life, his desire to overcome the seeming impossible, the hope with which he is left, challenged time and again in order not to miss the moment when the water fills the well.

Yeats introduced the dance arbitrarily as if it were a *dea ex machina,* as if he could have turned it into a dramaturgic device of theatrical effectiveness. The introduction of the dance at the most crucial point of the story charges the choreographer with a tremendous task. The dance—however expressive in itself with all potentialities of allusive drama—can hardly create the drama which the words and dramatic situations lack. Dance is also the focal point in Oscar Wilde's *Salome,* but there it is the motivating force from the very beginning of the play and its natural climax.

Yeats himself claimed that drama "shows events" and does "not merely tell of them." But all his plays lack dramatic narrative in contrasts and conflicts, a climax in which worlds clash. His *Four Plays For Dancers* rely unduly much on dance and music to make words and story dramatically workable. He was aware of this weakness when, in rewriting *The Only Jealousy of Emer* for a public presentation, he admitted:

I rewrote the play not only to fit it for such a stage but to free it from abstraction and confusion. I have retold the story in prose which I have tried to make very simple, and left imaginative suggestion to dancers, singers, musicians. I have left the words of the opening and closing lyrics unchanged, for sung to modern music in the modern way they suggest strange patterns to the ear without obtruding upon their difficult, irrelevant words.

Out of such self-irony speaks his frustration with not being able to write for the legitimate or even experimental theater. His text would never lend itself to the composition of an opera, but a choreographer may under certain circumstances take Yeats's verbal allusions as an inspiration for a ballet leading into a new poetic and dramatic atmosphere. From his viewpoint Yeats rightly rebelled against an insensitive public, saying in a note on *Four Plays For Dancers* on the occasion of their first production:

In writing these little plays I know that I was creating something which could only fully succeed in a civilization very unlike ours. I think they should be written for some country where all classes share in a half-mythological, half-philosophical folk-belief which the writer and his small audience lift into a new subtlety.

Such a dream of such a country can only be found in the mind of a child burdened with the wisdom of a sage. Its nonexistence perhaps explains the beautiful dramatic dream of a nondramatist. The fact that Yeats relinquished dramatic power as a poetic writer of the drama and called on the dance to help him create the climax and on the music to paint the needed mood, he virtually renounces his being a dramatist.

Sir James M. Barrie was famous for his whimsies which he served with chocolate icing and for sugar-coated satires. An uneven dramatist, he loved to prick balloons with which the adult world likes to play, and he often escaped into a land of fantasy that shows the mind of a child spiting the make-believe of reality.

In 1920, the success of Diaghilev's Ballets Russes challenged Barrie's fantasy to deal with *The Truth About the Russian Dancers* as they collide with the British aristocracy. Measured by the yardstick of *Peter Pan* or *The Admirable Crichton,* this short and flimsy one-act play belongs with many other forgettable plays Barrie wrote. Seen from the balletomane's viewpoint, however, it gains charm and the fanciful lightness which is associated with certain classical ballets. Barrie spoofed the ballet while declaring it his love.

Karissima, who is no one else but Tamara Karsavina, is the central figure. In quick succession she is married and dies and experiences a funny resurrection when the Maestro, who is Diaghilev, decides at the last moment to make the supreme sacrifice in dying in her stead. Karissima is overcome by the nobility of his action, and everyone on stage gets on his toes and dances wildly.

A great deal of naïve fun is made of the pun that the Maestro "makes" the dancers, an allusion to their unreal being. Karissima who has no speaking lines but dances her reactions and bits of conversation, carries the burden of humor which lies in the mechanical seriousness of her balletic movements. In the context of the playlet they border on the ridiculous.

Barrie was a Scot, and there may have been something parsimonious in his whimsical humor. Although the Scots came originally from northern Ireland, the Irish have an innate and boisterous humor. The Irish have a way of being closer to poetry than any other dramatists. They cover the whole universe with their verbal gestures and rage passionately between the most realistic realism and the gossamer dream of fancy flights. Because of their poetic feeling they are drawn to the dance. Yeats felt the need to engage the dance to help him dramaturgically. Sean O'Casey, his opposite in *Weltanschauung* and literary temperament, unbridled in his word-music or broad humor, tossed dancing into his plays whenever the spirit moved him.

In the New York Sunday *Times* of October 21, 1934, he expressed that modern dramatists

have pilloried drama too long to the form of dead naturalism, and all fresh and imaginatively minded dramatists are out to release drama from the pillory of naturalism and to send her dancing through the streets. . . . We're out to put dancing and song back again where they belong and make the movement of the body express something quite as well as the sound of the voice.

O'Casey began as a realistic writer, with his anger and sadness recreating the antiheroic life of the little people in its tragic and comic aspects, and he excluded dancing from such plays as *Juno and the Paycock* or *The Plough and the Stars*. In his middle period, however, when he began to experiment with expressionism and created the powerful morality play *Within the Gates* and, some time later, when he celebrated the vital life force in a curious blending of comedy and fantasy, the dance became an integrated and meaningful part of the play. In Act IV of *The Silver Tassie* the gay dancing in the background is used as a counterpoint to the tragic experience of the crippled hero.

In the wayward comedy *Purple Dust,* dance becomes the action itself when in the opening scene the two destined to become lovers meet and find each other while dancing. The entire mood is one of singing and dancing when the play opens in the dilapidated Tudor castle which, at the end, is drowned together with man's illusions in the rising waters. The castle as well as the illusions harking to yesterday have no longer any meaning in our time which dances into tomorrow, however precarious this morrow may be. Again, the dancing done by the working-class people only serves to underline the affirmation of life and the future.

In *Cock-A-Doodle-Dandy* the dancing fits the joyous fantasy and symbolic meaning of the comedy which strikes at bigotry and intolerance. Like a flower of light rises the dance in *Red Roses For Me,* out of the miseries of the unemployed and the flower girls, out of the splendor of their strength. "Praise God for th' urge of jubiliation in th' heart of th' young," says one of the characters when the dance comes to an end.

O'Casey knew how to send his plays dancing through the streets.

GERMAN DREAM
& AMBIVALENCE

DANCE HISTORY has been made in Italy, France, and Russia, and only recently in England and America. An explanation for the absence of any vital German contribution to the art of the dance cannot easily be found, if not totally obscured, by the temperament and mentality of the people as a whole.

There never was a dearth of opportunity for the growth of the dance in Germany. Interest in the ballet was not negligible in Stuttgart under Charles-Eugène, the lavish Duke of Württemberg, nor at the courts in Vienna or Potsdam in the eighteenth and nineteenth centuries. At that time the ballet was dominated by French and Italian masters. The only ballerinas of international stature to come out of the heart of Central Europe were Anna Heinel and, some time later, Fanny Elssler. Theatrical dancing was in a pitiful state in the German lands when compared with the incredible riches the German and Austrian people brought forth in the musical field at about the same time. From the very beginning of the eighteenth century intense music criticism played a great role in fostering a readiness of, and receptivity for, the coming of the musical genius. On the other hand, utter lack of dance notation and of serious critical writing on the ballet as

345

an art form, as well as the acceptance of ballet as "foreign" entertainment were indicative of the German attitude and mentality in regard to dancing.

Enumerating the major or even minor giants produced by the German-speaking people in the field of dance runs little risk of boring readers. Mentioning the great creative dancers of Germany, we find isolated, even though exceptional, cases, and with some of them we encounter ethnogeographic difficulties. The scholar and great theoretician Rudolf Laban was Hungarian-born, although he began his career in Germany. His disciples Mary Wigman and Kurt Jooss are German. Harold Kreutzberg, often associated with those three, was born in Bohemia and lived in Switzerland. True, Emile Jaques-Dalcroze reigned in Hellerau near Dresden, but his parents were French-Swiss and his influence on the dance was peripheral. One of his students was Hanya Holm who became Wigman's assistant. Holm is a German who established herself in America. One could mention another Wigman disciple, Dore Hoyer, or the Viennese dancers Wiesenthal and Rosalie Chladek, but they are neither pioneers nor of international caliber.

The Germans have always had an ambivalent attitude towards the dance, as if suspicious of an art demanding light-spiritedness and inner grace. They took Isadora Duncan to their hearts and helped her to her triumph. They sympathized with her revolt against the ballet, because of or despite the fact that ballet had never taken root with them. It was in Germany, through Mary Wigman's accomplishment, that the modern dance added the disciplined ecstasy of the body to Isadora's ecstatic spirit.

The sudden orientation towards the classical ballet in the post-Hitlerian era is an interesting sociocultural phenomenon. Does it imply that the nation tried to deny its immediate past and needed to embrace something that had been alien to them?

German men of letters have always viewed the dance from a safe distance emotionally. They were never—with the exception of a few isolated cases—practically involved in dance creations as were their French counterparts. They have been rather inclined to approach the dance in a scholarly manner, even where their verbal enthusiasm borders on the sound of ecstasy, as in Nietzsche's case.

I call Johann Wolfgang Goethe as my first witness. Since he is considered a Renaissance genius of Olympian stature, undoubtedly one of the last polyhistorians interested in and knowledgeable of everything, and one of the first great modern men, his attitude towards the dance must be relevant and revealing.

Goethe, the historian, held the dance in high esteem and saw in it the primordial and universal art it is. His acquaintance with dancing reached back to his early youth. In his autobiographical writing, *Aus meinem Leben,* he tells us that he took dancing lessons from his father and that he "instructed us most precisely in the positions and steps, and when he had brought us far enough to dance a minuet, played some pretty thing in three-four time on his *flûte-douce,* and we moved in time as best we could."

At that time the waltz, originally a German peasant dance, broke through the defenses of bourgeois society. It retained a certain rustic roughness. The physical closeness of the couples, the endless gyrations of the dance were frightening to many and had a revolutionary effect on the minuet-minded people. Goethe and Lotte were accustomed to dancing the minuet together, but he tried to persuade her to dance the English *contre* and waltz with him. A student in Strassburg, Goethe felt obliged to learn the waltz because, without its knowledge, he did not think it possible to enter the higher social circles. But the waltz had its difficulties, it seems, because as they were "rolling around together like spheres are rolling around each other, it was certainly a little rough to begin with, because so few knew how to dance it." In whatever Goethe endeavored, perfection was as important for him as the process of learning. Goethe was apologetic for having made slow progress with the waltz and in his defense he cited the daughters of the Strassburg dancing master, who also had quite a hard time with this new dance while they were always "willing to dance a minuet to their father's little fiddle."

A few years later, in 1774, Goethe must have mastered the intoxicating turns of the waltz when he admitted in *The Sorrows of Young Werther* that he has never "moved so lightly. I was no longer a human being. To hold the most adorable creature in one's arms and fly around with her like the wind, so that everything around us fades away." Goethe realized that the images of the dance defy verbal description, a feeling he strongly expressed even in verse:

> How much, indeed, can be expressed in words,
> In speech we show this as in poetry;
> But graceful movement, as we have beheld,
> We dare not render in descriptive terms;
> The sight itself gives us the sense of value,
> The lovely dance must be its own sole herald.

On one of his journeys to Italy, in 1787, he saw Emma Hamilton, muse of Lord Nelson and Romney's favorite model, in a series of expressive poses based on Greek sculpture and described his impressions in his journal:

[Sir William Hamilton] has had a Graecian robe made for her which becomes her extremely well. She puts it on, lets her hair down, drapes a pair of shawls around her and then assumes such a variety of attitudes, postures and expressions that you think you are dreaming. . . . One moment she is standing, then she is seated, then reclining, then kneeling at your feet. Now she is solemn. Now she is sad. Now she is teasing, now enticing, bashful, alluring, reproachful or shy. . . . One follows upon the other and the one emerges out of the other. She drapes her shawls to suit her every pose and changes them about to enhance it. She can make a hundred kinds of headdress out of those two shawls.

As a humanist and lover of Greek and Roman art, he was also intrigued by a similar experience when he had the opportunity of observing Henriette Hendel—whom Lillian Moore called the eighteenth-century Isadora—in her dance poses. After such an evening with this great mime he wrote in her *Stammbuch:*

> To the dear, incomparable, feminine Proteus
> Henriette Hendel-Schütz
> with thanks for very beautiful, only too
> short hours.

In his essay *On Art and Antiquity* Goethe made the remark that

the mimic art of dancing virtually ought to destroy all the visual arts, and rightly so. Fortunately, the sensuous enchantment it creates is but fleeting, and the dance must go to extremes in order to entrance. This, fortunately, immediately frightens away all the other artists; but, if they are clever and circumspect, they can learn from it a great deal.

Used to a balanced and measured manner of analysis and comparison, he not only realized the potentialities of the dance but also saw its shortcomings. When he wrote about the law of necessary changes, he again referred to dancing: "We have dances which please us to a high degree because 'major' and 'minor' changes in them, whereas dances on a major scale or a minor one alone would tire us at once."

His *Faust* attracted choreographers as much as composers,

350 DANCE AND POETS

and Filippo Taglioni based his ballet, *Le Dieu et la Bayadère,* on Goethe's poem, *Gott und die Bayadere.* In his novel *Werther,* in *Poetry and Truth* and such essays as *The Roman Carnival* he used the dance as a simile or introduced it to underline a point. From time to time dancing became the focal point in his poems. In *Dance of the Planets* four winds make room for the twelve zodiacs which bring Love, Life, and Growth with them. Mercury calls on all the planets which follow his invitation, and a solemn dance begins, accompanied by beautiful verses. Probably inspired by some tarantella dancers he saw in Italy, Goethe wrote his *Quadrille of Italian Dancers* which, however, is in its mood and poetic power far from any description of the dance itself.

His poem *Antiphony for a Dance* visualizes an indifferent and an affectionate lover, both in their own ways requesting to dance with their beloved. The indifferent lover stresses the point that those who are very much in love cannot really dance well together, and the affectionate one feels that love is already a heavenly dance. This poem, juxtaposed to his *Werther,* in which dancing plays an active and integrated role, illustrates the contrast between the young Goethe, a captive of the dance craze of his time, and the Olympian, detached attitude of the older Goethe towards the dance.

Two of the older German writers who had decided influence on the course of German literature were Christoph Martin Wieland and Johann Gottfried von Herder. They touched upon the dance peripherally only and mainly in the context of their aesthetic studies. Wieland was a versatile and fertile writer with fifty-three volumes to his credit testifying to the variety of his talents and his diligence. His most brilliant work was the epic *Oberon,* characterized by lightness and wit. He discussed aesthetic principles in *The History of Agathon,* which he published in 1773.

Today we may find a touch of naïveté in the way he developed man's rise from a state of primitivism to one blessed by the Graces. True beauty, in the most spiritual sense, could only be attained through the wholesome influence of the Graces. In order to render his similes and images as plastic as possible, Wieland used the dance as a means of mirroring the mores and attitudes of man and his society. Moreover, dancing was the most immediate association with the Three Graces.

He assumed that nature is full of harmony which, by no apparent plan, is forced upon it and that human society in its original state has no grace, being "free of laws, needs and grief." These people—he conjured up an ideal picture of the Arcadians—did not know evil per se, nor were they good in any ethic sense. They were simple, and in their simplicity wild and sensual. Days were eternal feasts for them and "the hours of circling dances seemed to them like a single blissful moment."

Only after the Graces appeared to man, was man's nature tamed. Wild wantonness turned into naïve gaiety, and a spirit of harmony elevated them to social human beings. The dance illustrates the effect of the Three Graces when it seems like

the unprepared inspiration of a naïve joy which gave their feet and arms a soul or rather breathed into them a communal soul through all their movements like the Reigen of Latona's daughter who danced with the Graces and Muses in the delphic grove.

This dance created the necessary harmony between men as well as between man and nature. Thus man rose from his near-animalistic state to the state of being human. Wieland intimates that not even the philosophers can do well without the Graces' favor. Through their influence and guidance "wisdom and virtue lose their bloated and exaggerated appearance, all that is harsh, stiff, and angular." The philosophers must learn from the gods who also have changed their crude customs as prompted by the Three Graces. What are their essential gifts? Joy, love, and harmony. Without them beauty is empty and sterile. Grace, therefore, is "the beauty of the soul," the composite of characteristics which are very much our own, our eyes, smile, voice, and walk. The Graces are movement incarnate and thus the beauty of our soul is in motion. But only those movements are graceful that have "that appearance of unconstrained lightness, that splendor of perfection," a gift of nature rather than a work of art.

Herder, a theologist came early in his career under the influence of Kant and later sought to find a common denominator for what Kant divided, namely mind and nature, the individual and society. In his essay on *Die Plastik* Herder said that the human body was by nature a manifestation of life and vigor and, therefore, beautiful. He realized the significance of the gesture, exclaiming: "How mighty is a gesture! Convincing, exciting, lasting." To him movement was the sensuous annunciation of life, and life the annunciation of the soul. "In this way and in this way only the soul speaks through the body."

His was an evolutionary approach to history. He visualized mankind in all spheres of its existence—physically, morally, and politically—in a continuous progress. He thought euphorically that perfectibility was no deception, but only a means and final purpose to create a humane being. Movement, or the dance, aims at the same totality of human happiness, of the beautiful, the true, and the good.

In the nineteenth century the German writers were particularly far outdistanced by their French colleagues in their interest in the dance. Only Heinrich Heine played a unique part, and Nietzsche's voice came back as a philosophic echo of the romantic spirit.

Richard Wagner had an ambivalent attitude towards the dance. He violently rejected the artistic expression of the dance as presented by the ballet, essentially the French ballet. Strangely enough, he considered theater dance as an intrusion on his *Gesamtkunstwerk*. He loathed the idea of dancing in his operas. His first work, *Rienzi,* contained a ballet, but Wagner disliked the idea of senseless pirouettes and cabrioles dragging his operas down dramatically at that point. (He was even more infuriated that "it was at this moment that the theatre always burst into roars of applause.") He vowed never again to give ballet a chance to slip into his works. But when *Tannhäuser* was scheduled for its premiere in Paris he was forced to write a ballet into it since the patrons, members of the Jockey Club, were accustomed to seeing a ballet in the second act. Wagner interpolated a bacchanale in the opening scene, however. The Paris premiere was a fiasco. (The gentlemen of the Jockey Club had the habit of coming to the Opèra after the first act only.)

But Wagner did write that

The most genuine of all art forms is the dance. Its artistic medium is the living human being and not merely one part of it but the whole . . . body from the soles of the feet to the top of the head. For anyone completely sensitive to art, music and poetry can only truly become comprehensible through the art of the dance-mime.

The dance he accepted was dance-mime. He asserted that

Mime is the immediate expression of the inner life, and it is not only the sensual rhythm of sound, but the spiritual rhythm of the word which gives its law. . . . The harmonized dance is the base of the richest masterpieces of modern symphonics.

More than anything else Wagner feared to find the structure of his music-dramas interrupted by such visual entertainments as a divertissement. On the other hand, he never tried to give pure mimic expression a dramatic place in his operas. He maintained that an artist must be at once dancer, poet, and musician. All this was sound theory, but he never made any serious attempt at including the dance-mime in his *Gesamtkunstwerk*.

Two writers, if not relegated to footnotes, should at least be honorably mentioned in the manner of a postscriptum. Baron Friedrich Melchior Grimm was born in Regensburg, Germany, but lived most of his life in Paris from where he wrote his informative series of periodical letters, his *Correspondance littéraire*. Writing at a climactic and crucial period when ballet had become an independent art form and fought a valiant battle between virtuoso dancing and expressiveness, that is between 1753 and 1774, Grimm's reports about ballet productions and his descriptive accounts of certain dancers have great value as source material. Moreover, they are first-rate writing. Grimm's wit developed a Gallic flavor when, for example, he wrote of the dancer Charles Le Picq that "If he does not dance like God the Father, at least he dances like the King of Sylphs." Or what ironic esprit lies in his important observation of Maria Camargo:

Camargo was the first who ventured to shorten her skirts. This useful invention, which afforded connoisseurs an opportunity of passing judgment upon the lower limbs of a *danseuse,* has since been generally adopted, although at the time, it promised to occasion a very dangerous schism. The Jansenists in the pit cried out heresy and scandal, and refused to tolerate the shortened skirts. The Molinists, on the other hand, maintained that this innovation was more in accordance with the spirit of the primitive Church, which objected to *pirouettes* and *gargouillades* being hampered by the length of petticoats.

Wilhelm Busch, the painter-author of some nasty, mordant verse stories for the enlightenment of the young and partly as encouragement to cruelty, also wrote *The Temptation of the Holy Antonius,* a humorous and whimsical story in rhymes, as a ballet. The devil in disguise of a ballerina dances around the saint and tries to tempt him with promises of unknown pleasures. But when sitting on his knee and kissing him, she does something to his saintly equanimity. To save his body and soul he rushed to the cross on the wall and unmasked the ballerina as the devil who then escaped through the chimney. The six pastelles that go with the verses show us the twirling devil as an enticing danseuse, and Busch's visualizations of her are surprisingly balletic. Wilhelm Busch, an inveterate bachelor and not too fond of women, put an obvious touch of contempt into the drawing of a saint's dilemma and of Terpsichore's devilish daughter.

It is very unlikely that Busch knew of Heinrich Heine's ballet scenario of *Faust* in which Mephistopheles appears as a ballerina. After all, it was a very romantic and, at the same time, satiric idea. Both Heine and Busch were satirists with a more and less romantic bent, even though they were spiritual light-years apart.

Heinrich Heine's Faust Ballet

Heinrich Heine is best known to the dance world as the poet who inspired Théophile Gautier to help create a ballet that is one of the great classics: *Giselle.*

A week after *Giselle's* premiere at the Théâtre de l'Academie Royale de Musique in Paris on June 28, 1841, Gautier wrote a long letter to Heine in which, among other things, he said:

My dear Heinrich Heine,

When, a while ago, I reviewed your fine book *De L'Allemagne,* I came across a charming passage—one has only to open the book at random to find many—where you speak of elves in white dresses whose hems are always damp; of nixies whose little satin feet patter on the ceiling of the nuptial chamber; of snow-colored Wilis who waltz pitilessly; and of all those delicious apparitions you have encountered in the Harz Mountains and on the banks of the Ilse, in a mist softened by German moonlight; and I involuntarily said to myself, "Wouldn't this make a pretty ballet". . . .

Since the state of your health has prevented your being present at the first performance, I am going to attempt, if a French journalist is permitted to tell a fantastic story to a German poet, to explain to you how M. de Saint-Georges, while respecting the spirit of your legend, has made it acceptable at the Opéra. . . .

The second act is, as nearly as could be done, an exact translation of the page I have taken the liberty of extracting from your book. I hope when you return from Cauterets, fully receovered, you will not find it too misinterpreted. . . .

And the letter closed with the words: "So, my dear Heine, your German Wilis have succeeded completely at the French Opéra."

Although Heine was then living in Paris, we are not certain when he saw a performance of *Giselle*, but about half a year after its premiere, on February 7, 1842, he wrote in one of his letters on the political, artistic, and social life of France:

I shall speak of nothing but Carlotta Grisi, who distinguishes herself in a brilliant and delightful manner in the venerable company of the rue Lepelletier/the street in which the Opéra was situated/, rather like an orange among potatoes. It is pre-eminently Carlotta who is responsible for the unheard-of success of the ballet of *Les Wilis,* the fortunate subject of which has been borrowed from a certain German author of whom you have heard.

At that time Heine was deeply preoccupied with himself, his illnesses, and with a nasty, scandalous affair which resulted from his vituperative attack on Ludwig Börne, another German writer.

In Heine's book *On Börne,* all the stored-up bitterness of many unhappy years misled him into slandering the lady to whom Börne was emotionally attached. Although Heine's health was then in very poor condition, the lady's husband sought revenge.

It will never be proved whether Heine's or the husband's version of the famed incident in a Parisian street was correct— whether, at their meeting, Heine was slapped by the husband and fled to the Pyrenees to escape the duel or whether Heine told him he was about to leave for Cauterets in the Pyrenees and left his address. The former seems unlikely, as Heine, on his return to Paris ten weeks later, had trouble in finding his adversary, whose version of the story had meanwhile been taken up by the papers. It would seem plausible that the husband's feeling for revenge was cooled by then, in fact satisfied by the well-circulated, slanderous reports of Heine's "cowardice." Whatever the truth, it was now Heine's turn to demand a duel. This duel took place on September 8, 1841. Heine wrote about it:

The day before yesterday at seven o'clock I had at last the satisfaction of meeting Mr. Straus. He showed more courage than I had credited him with, and he was remarkably favored by circumstances. His bullet struck my hip, which is at present still very swollen and as black as coal. I have to stay in bed and shall not be able to walk properly for some time. The bone was not injured, but has suffered a bruise which I still feel. The affair has gone off well for me—physically, not morally.

He remained in a miserable state of mind from then on. A week before the duel, he married his mistress, the shop girl Mathilde, in order to secure her legal rights in case of his death. Not immediate, but slow death was waiting at his door. "The horrible thing is dying, not death," he wrote in 1846. On his "mattress grave" he spent another ten years in waking agony, fighting re-

lentless pain and the even more relentless demands of his landlord, the physicians he needed and despised, and his extravagant
young wife.

Between 1846 and 1851 Heine wrote a whole volume of
verses, the *Romancero,* which proved to be the crowning point of
his poetic achievement. During these agonizing years he also
wrote a few works in prose, among them *Gods in Exile* and his famous *Confessions:* "Ah! God's mockery weighs heavily upon me."
It was in this desperate mood, in 1847, that Heine fashioned a
ballet scenario which has the stamp of his genius. Perhaps it was
the success of *Giselle* that prompted him to embrace Terpsichore.

In his introductory remarks to the libretto, he writes that
Benjamin Lumley, Director of Her Majesty's Theatre in London,
had asked him to write a ballet libretto for the Theatre of Her
Majesty the Queen, and that *Doctor Faustus, a dance poem,* was
the result. As Lumley seems to have been in a hurry, Heine finished the script within four weeks. (He remarks in the preface
that Goethe took a lifetime for *his* Faust.)

Heine's ballet story was not put on its dancing feet, however,
by Lumley, who paid Heine for the prompt delivery of the libretto, but, oddly enough, prevented its production. For a
hundred and one years it gathered dust as a little noticed chapter
in Heine's collected works.

On June 6, 1948, a Faust ballet in five scenes, *Abraxas,* was
premiered at the Bayrische Staatsoper München, Prinzregen-
tentheater. Marcel Luipart choreographed this ballet for which
Werner Egk wrote the music and scenario. Although the title—
Abraxas is an occult symbol from the Kabbala, representing the
number 365 and power—and the names of the characters were
changed, Egk's scenario is based on Heine's idea and also adheres
to its plot. A different setting was chosen for some of the scenes,
such as the Spanish court of Charles IV in the second act and the

period of the *fin de siècle* for the scene of the pandemonium. Egk's version kept Heine's anticlerical coloring, "the scornful mockery of clerical asceticism." The Bavarian clergy took offense, and the question of the ballet's amorality became a political football. After six performances *Abraxas* was banned. This made it a very popular ballet, and it was produced in many other German cities. The most successful production was the one in Berlin at the Municipal Opera in 1949 with choreography by Janine Charrat. In 1963 Ruth Page used Heine's scenario as a point of departure for her ballet *Mephistophela,* which she choreographed for the Chicago Opera Ballet.

The legend of the learned Doctor Faust, or Faustus, who surrendered his soul to the devil in exchange for youth, knowledge, and magical power is supposedly based on the life of one Dr. Johann Faust about whom fantastic tales were told in the sixteenth century. They were used for many puppet shows all over Europe, and Christopher Marlowe based his Faust play on these sources. But ever since Goethe wrote his philosophical play on man's dualistic—the Faustian—nature, this legend has become an innate part of the Western World's mind and especially of German *Kultur.* Heine's dance-poem is, in contrast to Goethe's version, based on the original source material reissued in Scheible's *Kloster* in 1846.

Many operas deal with Faust. But there was only one memorable ballet on this theme in the nineteenth century. This was *Faust* choreographed by Jules Perrot and premiered at La Scala in 1848 with Fanny Elssler and, on the second night, with the American ballerina Augusta Maywood. This ballet was inspired by Goethe's play; Perrot knew nothing of Heine's dance-poem.

What probably attracted Heine most was his idea of turning Mephistopheles into a Mephistophela. Based on his claim that

"Mephistopheles not only has no real Gestalt, but has also never become popular in a definitely set shape," he decided that the devil could easily be shown as a woman, who, moreover, seen with balletic eyes, could enchant the audience as a prima ballerina.

When Faust, the erudite scholar, at the very beginning of the ballet practices his magic art and attempts to conjure up the devil, he is at first stunned that "the devil could not find a more horrible shape than that of a ballet dancer," but being the male he is, he finally takes a liking to this graceful girl, this devil in tutu. The first thing she does—with the instinct of the female to change the looks of a room—is to transform everything in his study with her magic wand. Everything becomes somehow more enjoyable and beautiful, but without completely losing its former reality—a female trick to ingratiate herself to the doctor. Then she presents Faust with the ominous parchment that proposes the exchange of a year of youth in exchange for his soul, while assuring him of her friendship.

But Faust is not yet ready to sign and demands to make the acquaintance of the other princes of darkness. These frighteningly ugly figures of Hell appear. Even as they dance before Faust they turn into charming dancers. This is our introduction to the corps de ballet. Presented in clear innuendo, the spectator sees beauty where in reality there is hellish ugliness.

Although Faust enjoys looking at these devilish girls, he finds that none really satisfies his taste, but Mephistophela seems to know what he wants. In the mirror on the wall appears an enchanting woman dressed like a duchess. Doctor Faust feels admiration, desire, and love at first sight, and he approaches the mirror and makes his longing known to her. She rejects him. He kneels down before her, imploring her to accept his love. She gestures in contempt.

Distressed, he turns to Mephistophela for help, and she, who has waited for this moment to teach him and the audience a lesson, conjures up a handsome male ballet dancer who gains the lady's favor by dancing a few fairly insipid steps.

Now Mephistophela indicates that Faust can be just as successful with the lady of his desire if he signs the pact. Faust, without a moment's hesitation, signs with his blood. The male dancer disappears. Mephistophela and the entire corps de ballet give Faust his first lesson. His stiff limbs become suppler and suppler until he, too, dares to dance in front of the mirror for his lady love. She begins to respond. However, the beginning bliss of love is rudely interrupted by Mephistophela, who finds that Faust is not yet skillful enough as a dancer to deserve such happiness. The lady disappears again, and Faust must continue to practice his entrechats and tours en l'air until the curtain falls on Act I.

The second act takes us to a square in front of a castle. It seems to be a festive occasion. Gentlemen of the aristocracy are courting their ladies, and on a dais we find "the woman in the mirror" seated in the center, only this time she is very much alive as the duchess of the castle and the wife of an elderly duke, whom we see at her side. The duchess wears a golden shoe on her left foot.

A bucolic scene in Rococo style is enacted for the enjoyment of the assembled courtiers. The performance is interrupted when Faust and Mephistophela enter with their demonic, yet sweet-looking corps de ballet. Faust and his partner greet the duke and his wife ceremoniously. Then Faust dances his praise of the duchess' beauty, and all four dance together, Faust with the duchess, Mephistophela with the duke. The enraptured passion which Faust shows in his dance with the duchess has its satiric counterpoint in the awkward movements of the duke, who becomes enamoured with Mephistophela's charms.

Heine now makes the duke demand to see a few tricks of

Faust, the great magician. As a test, the duke suggests the scene in which King David danced before the Ark of the Covenant. Faust complies with his host's wishes, and the audience on stage is enthusiastic about this interlude, which is followed by another pas de quatre in the course of which Faust becomes more daring in wooing the duchess. A kiss on her neck leads to the discovery of a devil's mark on her fair skin. The duchess a witch? She protests vehemently. But in the heat of her denials, she forgets about her golden shoe, another proof, of which Faust now becomes aware. He demands a rendezvous at the next Witches' Sabbath. She promises to meet him there.

To give the choreographer another chance to prove his mettle, Heine has his Duke ask for more magic tricks. And now the poet again overlooks technical difficulties and demands that Faust turn the corps de ballet back into the same frightening creatures of hell which they were when they first entered the stage in Act I. Moreover, in a boisterous, wildly comic scene Heine would like to see them disappear in flames. In the ensuing pas de quatre for the two leading couples, he pictures their passions as becoming more and more intense, ending with Faust kneeling before the duchess, who does not hide her feeling towards him. At the other end of the stage we see the duke on his knees like a "wanton, though doddering, Faun" and Mephistophela putting huge horns on his head. As Heine imagines it, the duchess rushes towards the duke and holds him back by his horns, while in the general bewilderment among the courtiers, Faust and Mephistophela escape.

The third act unfolds as the nocturnal scene of the Witches' Sabbath. It is a highly bizarre affair. Creatures of the underworld are dancing with prominent figures of various countries and epochs as if this were a timeless and international costume ball. An altar stands in the center of the stage, a he-goat ensconced on it.

The dancers often turn toward the altar, showing a kind of facetious and lascivious homage.

Faust finds his duchess, who, Heine says, should appear as naked as possible. Their wild dancing is in contrast to whatever Mephistophela and her partner do. She and the duke, in a black Spanish coat and a blood-red feather in his beret, dance in extremely slow measure, full of empty gallantries—of the gentle lie. Faust and the duchess reach the climax of their ecstasy and leave the stage while the group performs a round dance in which the dancers move back to back without ever seeing their partners.

According to his annotations, Heinrich Heine attached great importance to this circle, and explains that, as a measure of precaution, none of the creatures of the underworld wants to see the face of his or her partner. Witches, who may later face their judges, want to make sure not to be able to identify the person they have met at the Sabbath dance.

There is then a scene which might be called The Adoration of the Goat. A great many of the most prominent personalities of yore come to kneel before the altar, after some fast turns or exaggerated polka steps. Meanwhile, nuns and monks have appeared, dancing grotesquely. Faust and the duchess return, but he has changed. While she still pursues him with her caresses, he is annoyed and makes clear that he is no longer interested in her.

The goat steps down from the altar and dances a stately minuet with her. As this pas de deux unfolds, Faust tells Mephistophela of his disgust with the duchess and with the Witches' Sabbath. She realizes that Faust has reached the point where he desires the purity of beauty. With the help of her magic wand, the spirit of Helen of Troy becomes visible. This is obviously the ideal of antiquity, Greek harmony, pure beauty.

Faust escapes with Mephistophela to find the Hellenistic ideal, and the duchess, aware of his flight, falls into a state of uncontrolled fury and then faints. She is carried around in mock triumph. Church bells and organ music sound like an infamous parody of holy music. Then everyone turns toward the altar, where the he-goat disappears in flames. After the curtain has come down, thought Heine, the audience should still hear the "gruesome, outrageous sounds of this satanic Mass."

The fourth act brings us to a Greek island of Homeric beauty. In his letter to Lumley, Heine calls it "Achillea" and places it somewhere at the estuary of the Danube. This is an island where Trojan heroes live together with Helen, their queen. When the curtain rises she dances with her maids in front of the temple of Venus. The dance is "chaste and solemn."

It is an island of untroubled happiness. Faust and Mephistophela arrive there on black horses which carry them through the air, and are deeply impressed by the sight of this "Ur-beauty," as Heine describes it. The islanders greet them with grace, invite them to stay, to eat, to share their happiness. Faust and his partner reply with gay dances which turn into a procession leading into the temple of Venus. When Faust and Mephistophela reappear they have exchanged their medieval garb for the "simple magnificence of Greek clothes." A "mythological" pas de trois is danced by Faust with Helen and Mephistophela.

Then, while Helen and Faust rest at the right of the stage, Mephistophela leads a group of bacchantes in a lively dance. They are joined by young men fighting mock battles, and by amoretti. Suddenly the madly jealous duchess appears and brings an end to this playful, innocent dance. She reproaches Faust violently, then harangues and attacks Helen, whom Faust tries to protect. During this struggle she succeeds in getting hold of Faust's magic wand. She swings it wildly around and suddenly the stage darkens, the noise becomes unbearable.

When the light comes on again Faust finds Helen changed into an old woman. Enraged and desperate, Faust stabs the duchess. The islanders are furious at what has happened to Helen and threaten Faust and Mephistophela, who flee the scene.

The poet gives this episode a characteristically Heinesque twist as he writes of the portentous meaning of the beautiful Helen in the Faust legend. It explains, he feels, the epoch of Faust and gives certain clues to the saga itself. This flowering ideal of grace and beauty, symbol of harmony, stands for the Hellenistic dream emerging in the heart of Germany at the time of the Renaissance. But in Germany it was also the time of the Reformation when Luther translated the Bible, and Heine says that "the rebellion of the realistic, sensual joy of life pitted against the spiritual, old-Catholic asceticism is the actual idea of the Faust legend." Faust knew by heart his Homer as much as his Lutheran Bible, and, according to the oldest Faust sources, the devil's intention was "to keep Faust from entering matrimony and to force him into the hellish, abominable net of whoredom when he gave him Helen as concubine."

The last act takes place in a square in front of a Gothic cathedral. We are among burghers somewhere in Holland. Costumes are those of the sixteenth century. It is a typical noisy fair, with tables, gay groups, musicians, and puppet shows. Some villagers drink and eat heartily; others play games.

Doctor Faust, standing on a cart, and clad in the kind of flamboyant costume that befits a medieval quack, is pulled on stage. Mephistophela, also garishly dressed, leads the horses. She praises the fame of the great doctor, who is soon surrounded by the people and sells them little bottles and wonder drugs for much money. Some people bring him a specimen of their urine. He is also kept busy pulling teeth. He performs miracles by curing cripples who then express their joy through dancing. He sells vials, the content of which heals all wounds, frees everyone from ills, and makes them spin and turn.

The festive crowd is seized by an irrepressible desire to dance. Faust has meanwhile approached the mayor's daughter, and, charmed by her unaffected demeanor and simple beauty, he declares his love. Pointing to the church, he asks her to marry him. She takes him by the hand and brings him to her parents, in whose presence he repeats his request. Blushingly she says yes, and they both receive the parental blessings. Church bells begin to ring, and they receive flowers. Forgotten are all dreams of greatness and adventure. Faust has finally found his happiness in the cozy and modest love of a simple girl.

The bride and bridegroom, with a solemn group behind them, move in the direction of the church. But on their way Mephistophela stops Faust. She commands him to follow her. He resists. Mephistophela lifts her hand, and the bells stop ringing. She lifts her hand again, and hellish noise mingled with sarcastic laughter is heard. The villagers flee. Mephistophela takes a parchment from her bosom and shows it to Faust. It is his agreement with the devil, signed with his blood. His time of borrowed youth is over.

Faust wants to flee, but wherever he turns devilish monsters bar his way. He kneels down and implores Mephistophela's mercy. She laughs. She makes him get up and dance with her a macabre pas de deux in which she turns into a snake and strangles him. He dies in her arms while dancing. Then she triumphantly dances around his dead body, supported by some of the underworld creatures. When this dance reaches frantic intensity the curtain falls.

The poet defends the creation of Mephistophela, the devil as a woman, in his letter to Lumley, pointing out that the devil must not be seen as an ordinary hellish blackguard, but a "subtle spirit." Moreover, "the devil loved to disguise as a woman," as the oldest Faust book tells:

When Faust was alone and wanted to meditate on God's word, the devil would come to him in the shape of a beautiful woman, embrace him and indulge in lasciviousness with him, so that he soon forgot the word of the Lord and, disregarding it, continued in his libertinage.

Heine's dance poem contains the most essential material of the old legend of Doctor Faustus. Heine not only used its major ideas as he knew them but constantly referred to books about Faust which he remembered reading when he was a boy and saw enacted in puppet shows. Although the writing of this scenario took only four weeks, including the research that went into it, it remains a fascinating document of a highly literate mind, a daring step of a poet into the gossamer world of the ballet.

The ballet scenario of Faust was preceded by a briefer attempt to outline the idea for a ballet. In 1846 Heine responded to Benjamin Lumley's wish "for a ballet *sujet* which would permit the magnificent unfolding of décors and costumes." Heine suggested *The Goddess Diane,* a ballet in four tableaux which offered a great deal of stage magic for the scene designer. The first tableau shows the ruins of the temple of Diane, well-preserved, with only a few dilapidated columns and a hole in the roof through which the night sky with a half moon became visible. The third tableau presents a wild mountain region with a fantastic wood and lake to the right and the steep wall of a rock with a gate-like opening to the left. Both settings have all the earmarks of romanticism with their wild, nocturnal landscapes evoking a past mythological world which Heine pictures as fulfillment of inner freedom and ultimate rest.

In comparison to these two open-air scenes the second and fourth are their counterpoints and contrasts. The huge hall of a Gothic castle somewhere in Germany is juxtaposed with a subterranean palace, "magnificent in its Renaissance architecture and decoration, only far more imaginative and almost reminiscent of the sumptuous background of an Arabian fairy tale." Heine called this scene Mount of Venus and peopled it with "famous men and women of the ancient and medieval world whom people believe to find in the Mount of Venus because of their reputation as sensualists and eccentrics." Heine imagines seeing there anyone from the beautiful Helena, the Queen of Saba, and Cleopatra to Julius Caesar and Goethe. The music is supposed to evoke the feeling of a *dolce far niente* atmosphere which turns towards "voluptuous sounds of joy when Venus appears with her *Cavaliere servente* Tannhäuser." Both are scantily dressed and dance a "sensuous pas de deux."

The visually beautiful stage image, as well as the opening pas de deux, sets the mood for the grand finale of this ballet whose story is characteristic of the romantic age, the German dream, and Heine as a living epitome of both. A young German knight is in search of the romantic flower of his longing, symbolized by the goddess Diane whom he follows, ready to sacrifice his life for her. She prevents his suicide and yields to his passion. Apollo and Dionysus dance around the two lovers, with the ecstatic promises of Dionysus being accepted by the knight and the goddess.

The second tableau presents the knight in his castle. A *ballet de cour* is opened by him and his wife who dance together "a stately German waltz." A wild torch dance follows, after which the castle is invaded by merry maskers. They dance their entrées until finally one of these masked figures forces the knight to follow her. The lady of the castle stops her whereupon the beautiful masked figure throws off her mantilla and unmasks. To no one's surprise it is the goddess Diane visiting her lover. She indicates he may see her at the Mount of Venus. "The lady of the castle expresses her fury and indignation through wild leaps, and we see a pas de deux between her and Diane, a contest between the Greek-pagan joy of the gods and Germanic-spiritualistic virtue of domesticity."

In the third scene the knight seeks to find his goddess and the Mount of Venus. He encounters undines, sylphs, gnomes, and salamanders until he finally runs into Diane, who intends to take him through the gate in the rock into the interior of "Mount of Venus, the seat of all lust and wantonness." Their triumphant entrance is cut short by an old warrior with a white beard. He is no one else but the "faithful Eckart who warneth everyone," also warning the knight of the dangers to which his soul will be exposed in the pagan Mount of Venus. The knight refuses to listen to him, and, in the ensuing duel, he dies at the hands of Eckart who "totters clumsily but content off scene, probably enjoying the thought of having saved at least the knight's soul. Desperate and desolate, the goddess Diane throws herself over his dead body."

The knight's body is brought into the Mount of Venus. Diane begs Venus to awake him from his sleep, but Venus is helpless in the face of death. Finally, Dionysus succeeds where Venus and Apollo fail by pouring wine over the knight's lips. The jubilation of everyone present is expressed through dancing, after the knight "reborn, jumps up and throws himself into the most drunken and daring dances." Then he and Diane kneel in front of Venus, who puts a wreath of roses on their heads.

The ballet closes with this "glory of transfiguration." It is an apotheosis of the German dream for classic antiquity, of the dream of man for the symbol of eternal passion. It also shows how Heine combined the thought of love and resurrection with Dionysus whose movements of ecstasy remain victorious over those of the other gods. Diane is not a luring, evil being. She is the Goethean image of the Eternal Feminine, the beginning and the end of man's dream. This ballet scenario contains everything that a classic-romantic ballet needs to succeed. It is difficult to understand how Lumley—best known to balletomanes as the impresario who arranged the celebrated *Pas de Quatre* of 1845—could fail to give this scenario its stage reality.

True to the romantic spirit of his time, Heine associated dance with the instinctive and uninhibited forces that characterize Dionysus, with the rhythmic expression of sensuality and the ecstatic state of emotionalism. Dance had something beautifully pagan for him, dotted with carnal and sometimes also satanic accents. Heine was very close in his conception of dance to Théophile Gautier. Whereas Gautier felt attuned to the colorful sensualism of the female body as poeticized through rhythmic motion, Heine discriminated between the natural impulses revealed through Dionysian movements of ecstasy and movements of satanic frenzy whose propelling impulses hide demonic intentions. The former, Heine felt, are close to magic, the latter to sexuality.

The sensual experience and erotic magic emanating from the moving female body were for Gautier as well as Heine a prelude to the awakening of all senses, a poetic substitute for the sexual act. Dance as an art form was in Heine's day only classical ballet at its most romantic. When he visualized Dionysian, pagan forces unleashed through movement, Heine's ideal image of the dance was closer to what Isadora Duncan tried to achieve half a century later than to the art of ballet he witnessed. In *Atta Troll* he spoke of the dance as "this art/Which should remain a cult." Undoubtedly, he had the dancer's spontaneous release of emotions in mind, translated into free movement. For him, the classical ballet did not permit of the genuine expression of personality, but confined, through its set vocabulary, the shaping of emotional experiences into Apollonian movement, a far cry from the powerful discharge of Dionysian ecstasy.

Heine also shared with Gautier the delight in the sensuous quality of a ballerina of Carlotta Grisi's stature when he wrote about her in *Lutezia:*

How deliciously she dances! Seeing her, one forgets that Taglioni is in Russia and Elssler in America, indeed, one forgets America and Russia, the whole world for that matter, and soars with her into the world of spirits, full of the magic of hanging gardens, where she reigns supreme. Yes, she truly has the character of those elemental spirits we always visualize dancing.

Heinrich Heine visualized the great dancer as the ecstatic apparition whose dreamlike unreality awakened in him the poetry and potency of his entire being.

Marionettes, gods, and silence

Heinrich von Kleist made a unique contribution to the dance with his essay *On the Marionette Theatre,* which belongs to the foremost essays of its kind. Kleist was a dramatic poet who, born in 1777, took his own life in 1811, unhappy and unsuccessful as it seemed to him. He left seven plays, among them the brilliant comedy *The Broken Jug* and his dramatic masterpiece *Prince of Homburg.* He wrote a powerful prose as proved in his essays and in such novelettes as *Michael Kohlhaas* and *The Marquise of O.*

On the Marionette Theatre deals with problems which still beset the dancers of today and probably more so than they could conceivably have mattered to the ballet dancer of the eighteenth century. Kleist speaks in it of "the purest and most innate grace" in man which makes the absolute dancer and comes to the conclusion that it can only be found in beings endowed with the highest degree of awareness, that is, in godly beings or in those who have no awareness at all, namely the marionettes.

In an either-or attitude Kleist groped throughout his life in the dark for the final truth, for *the* truth and not for the many little truths which so easily satisfy man. In his search for the absolute, Kleist came to the realization that "Every first impulse, all that is involuntary, is beautiful; and everything is crooked and cramped as soon as it understands itself." Therefore, grace "in its most exalted state" can be found in primitive instinctiveness (as Kleist illustrates with his story of the bear that outfences the best fencing master) or in the state of complete innocence.

Kleist was "fully aware of the disorder and destruction wreaked by man's intellect upon his native, god-given grace." This is why he contended in his essay that "if he could have a marionette built according to his specifications, he would be able to create a dance which neither he nor any other great contemporary dancer, including even Vestris, could duplicate."

Martha Graham once alluded to this state of innocence when, in one of her lectures, she spoke of how a simple movement can become inner reality. She told of a little girl who loved to pull one of her favorite toys behind her. She did so through many days. But once—either she could not find it or did no longer need the toy to enjoy the idea of pulling it behind her (or both) —she walked through the rooms in the exact replica of the movement with which she was used to pulling the toy. In her state of innocence and complete unawareness, this very movement, in all its phases, had become inner reality for the child.

Kleist expressed the idea of such total innocence at the end of the essay:

grace becomes ever more resplendent and predominant with our dwindling and darkening awareness. It is like this; the way in which two parallel lines meeting at infinity reappear on the other end, or the way in which the reflection in a concave mirror, after receding into the infinite, suddenly emerges again close before us,—so must our consciousness journey into the infinite before grace reappears in its most exalted state. Thus we find the purest and most innate grace in those human bodies endowed with an all-encompassing awareness or with those having no awareness at all, that is in the godly being or in the marionette.

When Kleist raised the question of the center of gravity or discussed that state of unawareness and innocence which creates the absolute dancer, he could have used Martha Graham's words as a motto:

I am certain that movement never lies. . . . The motivation, the cause of movement, establishes a center of gravity. This center of gravity induces the co-ordination that is body-spirit, and this spirit-of-body is the state of innocence that is the secret of the absolute dancer.

Kleist said, "Man is a god when he dreams, a beggar when he reflects." Friedrich Nietzsche dreamed even when he reflected. Kleist was all mental torture and continuous struggle to liberate himself from his own heaviness; Nietzsche was all lucidity and lightness, however penetrating his thoughts may have been. "Dancing in all its forms cannot be excluded from the curriculum of all noble education: dancing with the feet, with ideas, with words, and, need I add that one must also be able to dance with the pen?"

Nietzsche's writing has a poetic grandeur and a sensitivity through which one can hear his affinity to music. "My style is a dance," he said, and on another occasion: "Every day I count wasted in which there has been no dance." Havelock Ellis remarked that Nietzsche "showed himself possessed by the conception of the art of life as a dance in which the dancer achieves the rhythmic freedom and harmony of a hundred Damoclean swords."

Nietzsche's dance-mindedness has little to do with the dance as an art form. He used dance as a literary image. To him the ability to dance was one of the facets of the *Herrenmensch* who has freed himself from all slavish belonging, who defies gravity ("the devil is the spirit of gravity") as he defies the traditional morality of the weak, the heaviness of the *Herdenmensch*. Thus, the idea of the dance is used as a symbol of superiority, of the inner freedom of nobility, the dancing god and the dancing soul in man.

His accomplishments as a philosopher show him as one of the great philosophical psychologists of the last century. He arrived at a philosophy of life rather than at academic precepts. Life worth living must develop the strength, fearlessness, and integrity to overcome the unavoidable sufferings and misfortunes of existence without escaping into a fictitious world. In his greatest and most popular work, *Thus Spake Zarathustra,* he expresses his doctrine of the supremacy of power. To grow beyond one's ordinariness Nietzsche visualizes the need for inner lightness which is the lightness of the dancer.

In the opening lines he recognizes Zarathustra: "Pure is his eye, and no loathing lurketh about his mouth. Goeth he not along like a dancer?" Since the message of the work comes from the lips of a dancing Zoroaster, Nietzsche makes it quite clear that gravity has to be slain, and he exclaims: "I should only believe in a God that would know how to dance." He interpolated many dance songs which have a pastoral quality when Zarathustra meets dancing maidens in a forest ("Cease not your dancing . . . How could I, ye light-footed ones, be hostile to divine dances?"), or he describes a couple dance, man and woman circling around each other, attacking and fleeing in the course of courtship:

> Unto thee did I spring: then fledst thou back from my
> bound;
> And towards me waved thy fleeing, flying tresses round!
> Away from thee did I spring, and from thy snaky tresses:
> Then stoodst thou there half-turned, and in thine eye caresses.

In the Grave-Song Zarathustra complains: "Only in the dance do I know how to speak the parable of the highest things: —and now my grandest parable remained unspoken in my limbs!", and in The Cry of Distress: "But although thou shouldst dance before me, and leap all thy side-leaps, no one may say unto me: 'Behold, here danceth the last joyous man!'" Zarathustra explains in the section The Higher Man that he who comes close to his goal, dances. And then:

Better however to be foolish with happiness than foolish with misfortune, better to dance awkwardly than walk lamely. So learn, I pray you, my wisdom, ye higher man: even the worst thing hath two good dancing legs: so learn, I pray you, ye higher man, to put yourselves on your proper legs!

At the end of the eternal struggle between good and evil, between being human and super-human we hear Zarathustra's voice:

praised be this wild, good, free spirit of the storm, which danceth upon fears and afflictions as upon meadows! Ye higher men, the worst thing in you is that none of you have learned to dance as ye ought to dance—to dance beyond yourselves! What doth it matter that ye have failed!

Sporadically some minor dramatic pantomimes made their appearance in German literature at about the turn of the century, such as *Luzifer* by the poet Richard Dehmel, written in 1899. Of greater interest, however, is Frank Wedekind's fascination with circus life which resulted in his pantomimic ballet *The Fleas or the Dance of Pain.* This fairy-tale ballet in fourteen scenes features a professor, his circus, and three couples of lovers in comic situations. Moments of cynic eroticism, so characteristic of Wedekind's work, play a great part in it. The dramatist also wrote many dances into the script and not only for the chorus of peasants and noble ladies but for such humorous visualizations as a round and a victory dance for the fleas.

Even more revealing is Wedekind's ballet scenario *The Empress of Newfoundland.* The empress is told by her physician she must choose between marrying or dying. She decides on the first alternative of course, but rejects a great many of her wooers, a poet, an inventor, even Napoleon, and finally chooses an athlete whose physical potentialities electrify her. She asks for more and more proof of his strength and physical abilities until at last she charges him to lift a weight of two thousand kilos. In the process of getting him to do it, she gives away the fortune of her country. All warnings remain unheeded. The athlete finally lifts the demanded weight. The empress falling into a state of ecstatic rapture goes mad over this feat. The athlete squanders his fortune on whores, while the empress begs him for signs of love. But his strength has come to an end, he can no longer lift even fifty pounds. She escapes into self-destructive fury and finally strangles herself.

This dramatic ballet which was premiered in Munich by the famous literary cabaret *Die Elf Scharfrichter* (The Eleven Executioners) in 1902, foreshadows Wedekind's most important dramatic figure *Lulu.*

Hugo von Hofmannsthal was a romantic-symbolic poet and dramatist who stunned the literary world with his poems when he was but sixteen and who, later in his life, became well known for a series of libretti for Richard Strauss. He was a brilliant classic scholar and seemed to have adopted Calderon's *leitmotiv* of dreams being a higher form of reality and realities the foil of a true dream.

Hofmannsthal was the product of Old Vienna at a time when this city carried heavily the burden of its centuries-old culture to the cultural slaughterhouse of the twentieth century. The Baroque, a bit worn at the seams, still looked through the impressionistic and symbolistic writing of a few men whose wistful glance at the past and tired passivity became their most active manifestations. While the populace pretended to find solace in wine, women, and song, the men of letters expressed their unconscious realization and fear of decay with rare intellectual subtleness and a hedonism wrapped in melancholy. They escaped into irony, skepticism, and pessimism, even though they tried to reconcile their private dreams of past greatness with the realities of their time.

Hofmannsthal was one of them. His early poems and poetic dramas are characterized by poetic aloofness of a disillusioned and detached observer. With the exception of his opera libretti and his modern version of *Everyman,* his writing shows his concern with language by moving away from the rational language of everyday communication to symbolism which, in his opinion, was better equipped to unravel the mystery of life, to recreate the beauty of being, and to marvel at the wonder of the world.

Hugo von Hofmannsthal was one of the first writers to call language and consequently all human utterances into question. He was amazed at the fact that all things are different from what they appear to be and that the words we use to define and to describe these things are different again. At the age of twenty-one he wrote in a review of a book on the *Burgtheater* actor Friedrich Mitterwurzer: "People are rather tired of having to listen to talk. Words deeply nauseate them: Because the words have stepped in front of the things. . . . Therefore, a desperate love awoke for all the arts which are practiced in silence: music, dance, and all the arts of acrobats and jugglers." A year before his death, in 1928, Hofmannsthal wrote in the essay *The Egyptian Helena:* "I shy away from words. They deprive us of the best." In his imaginary conversation with Balzac, Hofmannsthal expresses the thought through Balzac's lips that in about half a century, that is around 1890, the poets will begin to realize their inability to express their thought-feelings with the existing words.

In 1906 Hofmannsthal saw Ruth St. Denis dance in *Radha* in Berlin and wrote about his impressions in the magazine *Die Zeit.* He was struck by the extraordinary immediacy of her poses and movements. He found the dream of the Orient crystallized into her "unforgettable gestures." She viewed the eternal things of the East

with eyes which were not at all ordinary. Whether she has lived among them for a year or for an hour—what has time to do with it? It is positively only a matter of a moment for the creative impulse to be fixed. Like a bolt of lightning, the chance of art strikes the few spirits born for it.

He recognized in this dance the presentation of something mysteriously strange in an unashamed manner without pretending to be

ethnographic or sensational. It is there simply for the sake of its beauty. I find this drama thoroughly imbued with the aroma of the single moment in which we are living. I feel that something here has, like a flame, penetrated the real and sensuous, something which for a few decades has existed only in the shadowy atmosphere of spiritual enjoyment. And then, suddenly and unexpectedly, it has become concretized, here and there, in incommensurate works of art, suffusing European imagination with Asiatic beauty.

Twice at different points of his essay Hofmannsthal declares that dances cannot be described, only the incidental such as the costumes, the sentimental, and allegorical. But then he succeeds in giving us one long paragraph revisualizing his impressions of the dance, as only a great poet can do:

The stage was the interior of an Indian temple. Incense rose up, there was the beating of a gong, priests were squatting on the floor, touching the steps of the altar with their foreheads, practicing some rites in the semi-darkness. The whole light, a strong blue light, fell on the statue of the goddess. Her face was a bluish ivory, her garments of blue-sparkling metal. She sat in the hieratic attitude of the Buddha on the lotus flower: legs crossed, knees wide apart, hands folded in front of her body, the palms pressed together tightly. Nothing in her stirred; her eyes were open, but her eyelashes did not move. Some untold force held together her entire body. This scene lasted fully one minute but one would have wished to go on viewing this motionless figure. It had no resemblance to a statue as imitated by a human being. There was no forced, artificial stiffness in it, but rather an inner spiritual necessity. From the depth of this seated girl, there flowed into these rigid limbs from that substance which lifted the great gestures of Eleanora Duse above the possibility of being imagined otherwise. And then she gets up from that position. This rising up is like a miracle. It is as though a motionless lotus flower were rising up toward us. She stands up, descends the steps of the altar, the blue light is extinguished, her face is brownish but brighter than her body, her garment flowing gold and precious stones. On the ankles of her handsome statuesque feet are small silver bells. Her motionless eyes continue to have the same mysterious smile: the smile of the statue of Buddha, a smile not of this world; an absolutely unfeminine smile; a smile that somehow is akin to the impenetrable smile of the paintings of da Vinci; a smile to which is impelled the soul of remarkable persons and which from the very first moment on and incessantly, alienates the heart of women and the sensual curiosity of many men. And now her dance begins. They are movements; they are movements which pass over into one another. It is the same as the tiny Javanese women have been observed dancing in Paris in 1889 and the female dancers of the king of Cambodia the same year. It is of course the same that all Oriental dances are aiming for: the dance, the dance as such, the silent music of the human body: the rhythmical flow of unceasing and true movement, as Rodin has put it.

The essay closes with a comparison of Isadora Duncan with Ruth St. Denis, the former being elegant, wise, and decorous; Ruth being grandiose, indefinable, and elemental. But he comes to the conclusion that there will be no reason to compare her with Duncan in whom there was something of "the professor of archaeology, very engaging and devoted to the beautiful," but her dancing an exhibition, a demonstration. "Ruth St. Denis is the Lydian dancer, just stepped off from the relief sculpture."

In his essay *On Pantomime* Hofmannsthal emphasized the significance and effectiveness of gesture in the theater and recognized the intimate kinship of gesture to dance. Wherever he intended to create a climactic moment in his own plays, he used in his stage directions a detailed description of gestures and miming or asked for a dance to heighten the dramatic expression. There is more movement and dance in Hofmannsthal's libretto *Elektra,* for Richard Strauss, than in Oscar Wilde's *Salome,* although in the latter the events are relentlessly directed towards Salome's dance which finally becomes a dramaturgic necessity.

In Electra's confrontation with Aegisthus and in anticipation of his death she first encircles the man whom she decided to send to his doom. Hofmannsthal's stage direction indicates that she "circles around him in a sinister dance," and Aegisthus asks: "Why do you stagger around with your light? What do you dance?" When Clytemnestra and Aegisthus are dead and Agamemnon's death avenged, Hofmannsthal writes: "She descends the steps. She holds her head thrown back like a maenad. She raises her knees, her arms are stretched out, it is an indescribable dance in which she moves forward." In the moment of human triumph, the inexpressible feeling can only be expressed through dancing. Her words with which she calls on Chrysothemis to join her in her dance are incidental: "He who is as happy as we are can do one thing only: be silent and dance."

In silence lies the consummate moment of existence which words can destroy. If there is happiness, then it is hidden in a gesture, in movement, in the dance. Hofmannsthal returned to this idea when he wrote the playlet *The Conversation of the Dancers,* in which two dancing girls, Laidion and Hymnis, givers of joy to men, receive a second mate from a merchant ship. He tells them of a miraculous island and leaves, rewarding Laidion richly for her kindness.

Laidion complains about her fate when she has to dance for twelve or twenty men,

among them a few rich old dodderers and the rest parasites. We dance and then we are tired and then everything turns ugly: everything crowds in on me, the faces of the men, the lights, the noise; like the beaks of greedy birds everything pecks me in the face. I would rather die than lie with them and drink and listen to their shrieks. Then I wish myself as far away as a bird can fly. I have always known that somewhere there is an island like the one he told me about."

The girls' dancing is held against the dancing of the people on that island. Are we ever really happy when we dance, Laidion asks herself, deep inside? Can we forget ourselves, "get rid of all fear, get rid of the shadow that darkens the blood in your veins . . . ? You have wishes, and wishes are fear." Hofmannsthal asks whether all dancing is nothing but wishing, fleeing from oneself when one jumps back and forth. If the dancers express gestures of animals in trees, are they ever becoming one with them, or in other words, can they ever get away from themselves and their fear? The people on that miraculous island can.

And nothing on the island defies the power of the dancers; at this moment they are as strong as the gods. . . . They are givers of birth . . . bearers of death and life.

At this moment Laidion hardly resembles herself any longer. Under her tense features appears something terrifying, threatening, eternal: the face of a barbarian deity. Her arms rise up and down in a frightening rhythm . . . her eyes seem filled with a hardly bearable tension of bliss. And there she lies already on the bed, breathing hard and short, surrounded by the small empty room, reality and Hymnis, who covers her with a small red rug.

Laidion opens her eyes after a while and sits up. She is very pale and says to Hymnis:

Here I lie and know it—and I have nothing! I want to scream . . . that such a thing exists in the world and I have none of it! . . . that man had to come and tell me that somewhere there is such an island where they dance and are happy without the thorn of hope! For that's it, Hymnis, that's everything, Hymnis, to be happy without hope.

Happiness without hope lies in the bliss of silence whose most articulate expression is the dance.

THE FRENCH
ESPRIT

IF ANY NATION was destined to give the dance, above all
the classical ballet, a philosophical basis and a literary profile, it
was France. Even though they borrowed a great deal from the
Italian Renaissance genius, they always had the necessary curiosity and a certain flair for notating the dance—from Arbeau, Beau-
joyeulx, Feuillet to Pierre Rameau. They were the first who felt
compelled to give this art form a more serious and durable foundation.

As early as 1570 Jean Antoine de Baïf established an academy and tried to formulate a harmonious relationship between
the measured rhythm of antique verse and the dancer's gestures
and steps. Political turmoil cut his endeavor short. Moreover,
with regard to the artistic and theatrical development of the
dance, Baïf entered the scene too early.

A hundred years later, in the late seventeenth century, with
its emphasis on scientific exploration and an ever-growing interest
in finding the aesthetic basis for the arts, the time was ripe for the
final solidification and codification of dance together with music
in an academic framework. Jean Baptiste Lully and Pierre Beauchamps made it happen. The *Académie Royale de la Musique et*

de la Danse not only established the principles of the classic ballet, it also put the dance in the same category with music. This was an important historic step. It reflected the interest the French had in the dance at that time which, about a hundred years later, occupied the great philosophers.

In Lully's time the French had their "musicals." The new theatrical form featuring the dance, music, and the spoken word was called *comédie-ballet,* and its principal representatives were Molière, Lully, and Beauchamps. In his preface to *Les Facheux* Molière spoke of the fusion of the three artistic disciplines into a whole as "new to our stage, but one might find authority for it in antiquity; and, as everybody was pleased with it, it may serve as a suggestion for other performances which can be worked out more at leisure."

Molière, as a direct descendent of the *commedia dell'arte* players, was very close to the concept of expressive movement and, knowing how much movement can mean in theatrical terms, gave it a prominent part in his comedies. In *Le bourgeois gentilhomme* M. Jourdain, a middle-class shopkeeper, who has amassed a small fortune, is determined to enter the world of society. He appears in dressing gown and nightcap in imitation of the aristocrats who held their morning levees in that fashion. He summons dancing- and music-masters, and the scenes between Jourdain and his teachers are examples of how Molière created dialogue to mirror the movements of the actors. The rhythm and motion of the masters during their lessons with Jourdain follow the rhythm of the speeches and illustrate how the actors' movements evolve from Molière's dialogue. An often quoted passage in this play proves Molière's preoccupation with the dance:

All the ills of mankind, all the tragic misfortunes that fill the history books, all political blunders, all the failures of great commanders, have arisen merely from lack of skill in dancing. . . .

J J
IL

:950331 :Status: PENDING 950331
cDate: :RenewalReq:
eDate: 95430 :NewDueDate:

nterpoints.
ess, 1971.

@N

ry/100 St. Anselm

:COPYRT COMPLIANCE:
:SHIP INSURANCE:

GV
1781
.562

```
SYNCO2-1JPRISM        JBLKJ      J         J              ILL

Entire record displayed.

ILL   Pending  950331
CAN YOU SUPPLY ?  YES    NO  COND  FUTUREDATE
:ILL: 7915940          :Borrower: SAC   :ReqDate
:OCLC: 205673          :NeedBefore: 950430 :Re
:Lender: *CYC,PSM,KNM,NHM,BNT
:CALLNO:
:AUTHOR:  Sorell, Walter, 1905-
:TITLE:   The dancer's image: points & cou
:IMPRINT: New York, Columbia University P
:VERIFIED: OCLC
:PATRON:  Hoffman/Fac/Fine Arts
:SHIP TO: St. Anselm College/Geisel Libr
Drive/Manchester,NH 03102-1310
:BILL TO: Same
:SHIP VIA: Library Rate          :MAXCOST
:LENDING CHARGES:                :SHIPPED
:LENDING RESTRICTIONS:
:LENDING NOTES:
:RETURN TO:
:RETURN VIA:
```

When a man has been guilty of a mistake, either in ordering his own affairs, or in directing those of the State, or in commanding an army, do we not always say: So and so has made a false step in this affair? . . .

And can making a false step derive from anything but lack of skill in dancing?

Paris remained the center of the classical ballet throughout the eighteenth and, to a great extent, the nineteenth centuries. Even though it was with the help of Russian genius, France again played a trail-blazing role in the ballet of the early twentieth century.

Among the consequences of the *Académie* was the idealization of clarity, regularity, and balance, even if bought at the price of rigidity. More and more the striving for technical nuances and bravura overshadowed expressiveness, naturalism, and vitality. Under these circumstances the *danse d'école* flourished as an instrument of technical proficiency. Creativity, under the yoke of any academic institution, suffers from self-imposed limitations. This soon became manifest in the productions of the Royal Academy, a fact which made a contemporary critic remark that one must not believe "in the creative power of artistic prescriptions."

Any establishment being by virtue or rather vice of its nature unresponsive to the demanding spirit of the time always generates its own countermovements which, in the eighteenth century, crystallized around the personalities of John Weaver, Marie Sallé, and Jean-Georges Noverre who strove for expressiveness and meaningfulness in the theatrical dance. At that time the lasting struggle began between those who believed in the dance for the mere sake of dancing, in pure dance in contrast to the expressive dance. Noverre was supported in his appeal for reforms in the direction of simplicity and meaningfulness by the philosophes. Denis Diderot, one of their spokesmen, rejected any ballet that lacked enlightenment or a moral subject matter. He defined in his famous Encyclopedia: "Ballet is an action explained by a dance." This attitude is not entirely new. It goes back to Aristotle who defined dancing as the presentation of "passions, actions and manners" which should avoid "fine steps which represent nothing."

The encyclopedists wanted to eliminate the capricious and fanciful world of make-believe, the Rococo atmosphere of sylphs and shepherds, the escape for escape's sake. In its stead they demanded to see a search for a human reality and human sentiment. Diderot went much further in his demands than did Noverre, who continued to deal with the mythological world and the *deus ex machina* concept. Diderot said: "The enchanted world may serve to amuse children. The *real* world alone pleases the mind." Everything was reduced to its reality, and in this spirit Voltaire defined dancing "as an art because it is subject to rules."

However, when faced with the reality of theater dance at its best, the artist in Voltaire got the better of the rationalist. Marie Sallé, the exponent of the expressive dance, had a rival in Maria Camargo, the most brilliant technician of the era, a dancer credited with shortening the skirt and the invention of the *entrechat quatre*. Voltaire expressed his feelings in a madrigal and made clear for all times that we may be enchanted by technical bravura as much as we may be intrigued by expressive meaningfulness:

> Ah! Camargo, how brilliant you are!
> But, great gods, how ravishing is also Sallé!
> How frivolous are your steps and how gentle are hers!
> The one is inimitable and the other so new.
> Only nymphs can leap as you do,
> But the graces dance like her.

Voltaire, as most of the eminent writers and thinkers of the eighteenth century, never gave up his interest in the dance and proposed to write a ballet scenario for Noverre on the theme of *Henriade*.

When Noverre said, "It is shameful that the Dance should give up her power over the mind, and strive only to please the eye," he did not propose to abandon the potentialities of beauty that lie in human movement. His *ballet d'action* wanted to preserve the continuity of a story told through dramatic action. It was as if on the threshold of romanticism he intended to prevent the classical ballet from going the way of all lyricism or from losing itself in passages of pure dancing similar to the aria in operas regardless of the action. Both the lyrical and dramatic potentialities of the ballet have inspired the French poets and philosophers during the nineteenth century who used the popularity of the dance, the most natural expression of the romantic ideal, as a point of departure for their poetic exaltations or philosophic speculations. Both the elusiveness and physical immediacy of the dance made it possible for the most divergent minds to recreate through its poetic image their own world. Each of these men of letters used the dance with either a tempest of passion or the finesse of thought for their own purposes—as we so often do with the object of our love without ever being aware of it.

The profane, sublime, and esoteric

POET-PHILOSOPHERS AND THE DANCE

On a visit to Italy in 1843 Paul de Musset passed Milan and Florence. He was puzzled by the dance craze of the Italians and compared the raging balletomanes at La Scala in Milan with those in Florence in a half-facetious report in his *Voyage en Italie:*

at Milan it was another story. The divine Taglioni and Mlle. Cerito took turns dancing at La Scala. Here was something to really get worked up about. The enthusiasm shown night after night surpasses the powers of imagination. . . . at Florence the public was divided between the two dancers, one tall, the other petite. It was another war of the Montagues and Capulets. Bouquets gave place to super-bouquets, then wreaths, and there was apprehension lest the two subjects perish —smothered under a deluge of flowers. Luxury ran riot; a follower of the tall dancer threw silver-wreathed leaves. Friends of the smaller hurled leaves of gold. One evening a bundle all tied up landed on the stage: it was a velvet robe. Nothing daunted the other faction which answered the next evening with a Cashmere shawl. It was already rumored in the city that a certain lord baron, leader of one group, was conniving ways and means of letting in upon the proscenium a four-horse coach with driver, which doubtless would have been countered with an actual castle complete with turrets and moats. The end of the dramatic year put a stop to this magnificent crescendo.

We find Gustave Flaubert among the travelers to the Orient who were deeply affected by their experience with Oriental dancers. Flaubert was so impressed by the personality and the manner of dancing of an Egyptian *almée* that he found it difficult to describe what he saw ("I spare you any description of the dance —it would not come off," he wrote to his poet friend Louis Bouilhet). Flaubert's letters from his journey to the East tell us a great deal about his personal experiences, but some of his observations have general validity. In the first half of the nineteenth century when Muhammed Ali exiled the public dancing girls from the Cairo area to create a better image of the city, the male dancers took their places providing most of the entertainment. Flaubert noted that the male dancers were often more audacious and salacious than the girls.

He carried a seemingly deep impression with him from his visit to the Orient. The Brothers Goncourt describe how he used to "sit in Turkish fashion on his divan." They also noted that "mystery and depravity fascinate him. Being a glutton of depravity and a collector of it, being happy, as he puts it, seeing a garbage man eating what he transports." A few years later an entry in *The Goncourt Journals* tell us of "Flaubert, his face flaming," proclaiming "in his booming voice that beauty was not erotic, that beautiful women were not made to be physically loved . . . he shouted that he never truly possessed a woman; that he was a virgin; that all the women he had had were no more than the couch on which lay the woman of his dreams."

In the light of these confessions we must see Flaubert being enamoured by Safiya, one of the great Oriental dancers, who called herself Kutchuk Hanem which means 'little princess' in Turkish. He wrote to Bouilhet about her. Flaubert was aware of her being a "very celebrated courtesan" and described her as "a regal-looking creature, large-breasted, fleshy, with slit nostrils, enormous eyes, and magnificent knees."

Before she danced for him, he went to bed with her.

When it was time to leave, I did not go . . . I went down to the ground floor into Kutchuk's room. A wick was burning in an antique-style lamp hanging on the wall. . . . Her body was sweaty; she was tired from dancing, and cold. I covered her with my fur coat and she fell asleep. As for me, I hardly closed an eye. I spent the night feeling profound, endless, dreamlike impulses.

Some time later returning from his trip along the Nile, he saw her again:

it was sad. I found her changed. She had been sick. The weather was oppressive and cloudy. . . . I stared at her for a long while to keep a picture of her in my mind. When I left, we told her we would return the next day, but we did not. I relished the bitterness of the whole thing; that was the main thing—it hit me hard.

In his travel notes Flaubert, the painstaking realist, was overwhelmed by the romanticist in him, when he wrote about the night he spent with the courtesan dancer: "How flattering it would be to the pride, if at the moment of leaving you were sure that you left a memory behind, that she would think of you more than of the others who have been there, that you would remain in her heart!" The image of this dancer was never darkened in his memory because years later he confided in the Brothers Goncourt his "great and continued desire to write a novel about the modern Orient, the Orient that now dresses in black."

There were a great many balletomaniacs among the French poets who succumbed to the attraction of the ballerina. In 1895 when ballet was at its artistically lowest level, François Coppée fell in love with Rosita Mauri and publicly confessed his feelings for her by reporting on *La Korrigane* in *Figaro Illustré* under the heading of *"A propos d'un Ballet"*:

La Mauri is divine, seen from the audience with or without the aid of opera-glasses. Indeed, I regard it as one of the greatest events in my life as a dramatist to have seen that extraordinary artist, that ethereal being who after a prodigious bound—I put it badly—after soaring in the air, returned to the stage so lightly, so delicately that you could not hear a sound, no more than when a bird descends and alights on a twig.

La Mauri is dancing personified. To the trials of rehearsal, so tedious and wearing for all the artistes, but particularly exhausting for the prima ballerina who must expend so much strength and dexterity, La Mauri brought a kind of physical enthusiasm, a kind of joyous delirium. You felt that she loved to dance for nothing, from instinct, for the love of dancing, even in a dark and empty theatre. She whinnied and darted like a young foal; she soared and glided in space like a wild bird; and, in her sombre and somewhat wild beauty, there is something of both the Arab steed and the swallow.

Jules Lemaître was born in 1853 when Gautier was at the height of his critical power. Lemaître's poetic sensitivities perceived the dance on an elevated level as if the soul were dancing in visible but scarcely carnal form. He found the classic ideal reexperienced in the precise and refined movements of the *danse d'école,* speaking the classic language of spirituality, harmony, and regularity. In contrast to Gautier he visualized the dance in terms of poetic purity and "chaste elegance."

As a critic Lemaître was a humanist and moralist, a traditionalist and chauvinist. Since ballet, in his eyes, was an artistic fixture of French culture, it could do no wrong when serving all four of his principles, singly or collectively. As a humanist he leaned towards the Greek conception of beauty as manifested in the perfect form of the human body. His demands on ballet as a "vision of accomplished feminine grace" were similar to those of Gautier. Lemaître considered the human body as a Greek sculpture and the most beautiful thing we know. When he played the part of the moralist, he easily contradicted himself. Gautier openly and often defiantly admitted his sensual excitation when viewing ballet. Not so Lemaître. The puritan in him defined the true purpose of ballet, "avowed or not, of this type of entertainment, is the exhibition, skillful shrouded and discreet, of the glorious feminine form."

He betrayed the moralist's fears in that he might find many arguments against the dancer's body "infused with beauty" if his senses were not immediately overwhelmed. ("If a ballet does not bewitch the eyes victoriously and without any possible resistance, it soon becomes almost painful.") When the humanist, moralist, and chauvinist combined forces, Lemaître felt compelled to condemn the dance of the East as being too utilitarian and to reject the use of the sole female figure dancing in which he saw an instrument of voluptuousness. He contrasted her dance with the theater dance of the West whose core, the pas de deux, goes back to medieval chivalry and the proper wooing of women. While implying sexually different and morally lower connotations with regard to the Eastern dance, he was ready to embrace and praise the dancing at the Folies Bergères, Chat Noir, or Moulin Rouge, the world of the can-can. ("Those slender legs moulded in black silk and shooting towards the ceiling in a frenzied pendulum-like movement, amid the flutter of snow-white petticoats, look so witty and contented.") The frolics of a La Goulue and Jane Avril have Rabelaisian characteristics for him and were thoroughly home-grown.

He was never consistent in his attitudes towards the dance. He could say, "I would readily admit that a ballet should dispense with a 'book,' should express nothing precise or coherent, and be only a succession of 'figures' pleasing to the eye." On the other hand, he thought little of virtuoso dancing which, essentially, was the kind of dancing favored in his time. ("But these wild leaps and whirlings are they then the whole of dancing?") He suggested that the ballet become "deeply expressive again" and ought to be provided with a scenario which, above all, must be poetic beyond all plastic pictorialization.

It could be said that Jules Lemaître—about forty years younger than Gautier—carried on as his literary heir. Yet Lemaître's interests were more strongly anchored in literature and in all the theatrical arts of which ballet was one phase only. He realized the importance of the male dancer, so much slighted by Gautier, probably because he had the opportunity of observing the general decay of the balletic art. He was also fully aware of Gautier's partiality and prejudices.

Time and again Lemaître stressed that a rejuvenation of the ballet had to occur. Being a literary-minded man, he looked to literature for comparisons when describing the need for choreogra-

phers of stature: "The choreographer would need the imagination of Victor Hugo and the intelligence of M. Renan." Although
knowing that the twentieth-century ballet would have to have
choreographers of penetrating intellect and daring imagination in
order to survive, he was too conservative even to spell out the
great need of that time for a total reorientation of the creative
mind. On his deathbed in 1914 Jules Lemaître must have been
aware of the sweeping changes revolutionizing the world, including the ballet. Unlike Gautier, neither the ballet nor the image of
a ballerina was then on his mind.

Charles Baudelaire was fascinated by the interrelation of the
arts, but as a critic mainly of the visual arts his perceptions were
visually oriented. He wrote in similes of visual power. His attitude towards criticism makes us understand why he felt close to
Théophile Gautier, who, like Baudelaire, took as a critical starting point the shock of pleasure as an immediate reaction. Baudelaire then proceeded to analyze the why and turned the shock of
pleasure into critical realization.

In his criticisms he may have relied on his instinctive reactions to a work of art, but as to the process of creation he did not
believe in being guided by spontaneity or inspiration. Thus he
recognized the classical ballet a foremost example of an art emerging from hard work and physical efforts. He was all the more impressed by the final product of grace and lightness as total denial
of the perspiration that went into it. He saw in the dance poetry
come alive, "poetry composed with arms and legs," with the ideal
and sensual being equally potent for him.

Despite its seeming legibility he found the clarity of the
physical line created by the moving body full of poetic elusiveness, and, in fact, he felt that the dancing revealed "all the mystery that music conceals." When Baudelaire transformed his inner
experiences into poetic images he painted his sighs and sobs as

much as the happiness of intoxicating pleasures with flaming colors within precise forms that gave his poetry its unique and convincing power. Whatever he perceived he saw in images and accepted music mainly as a means of inspiration. "Dancing," he said, "is far above music as the visible and the created are above the invisible and the uncreated. Those alone can understand to whom music gives ideas of painting."

In his analysis of Baudelaire Jean-Paul Sartre came closest to explain the poet's kinship to the dance in pointing out the virtually physical impact emanating from the rhythmic movement of his verses: "His poems are in themselves 'corporel' thoughts, not only because they come from the body, but because each of them has a rhythm that, hesitating and all-knowing, translates grace into words, a kind of fleeting existence, and the effect of an odor."

If no one else has proved the most innate relationship between poetry and the dance, the French poet-philosophers have, particularly Stéphane Mallarmé and Paul Valéry. Dream and illusion have always been the pillars on which the poets built their palaces, reality was to them a phantom which man has overcome day after day without ever mastering it. The poet knows how to transform the dream into words which create a world of allusion leading to many new dreams. Through this process poetry transcends the ordinariness of existence and "penetrates the mysterious world of essences," as Mallarmé said.

Since "ballet is preeminently the theatrical form of poetry," or "the plastic rendering, on stage, of poetry," it gives the immaterial and its dream the physical *Gestalt* which, through its silence, becomes expressive. In the dancer's movement the inexpressible becomes audible and more concrete than reality can ever be. In the gesture of the dance lies the key to the reality of all dreams.

Mallarmé was not interested in the story ballet. To tell a story through movement was to him comparable to ordinary prose. He neither believed in the dancer as a human being nor in any emotional or intellectual statement through dance. In discovering the power of symbolism, he attempted to free the poetic from the obvious and concrete, from syntactic arrangement at the risk of avoiding intelligibility and transferred this to the ballet.

The essence of poetry does not necessarily lie in the words themselves but between the lines and in the reflection of word images surrounding them. The inner relations, the threads of these relations, the metaphor that lies between two images and moves from one to another is also symbolic of the dancer who moves from the seeming reality of her being to the dream and the symbol of expression.

The dance was to Mallarmé a fleeting vision and lived, like poetry, on its power of suggestion. The dancer is only half human, with the other and more important half being a symbol. Mallarmé pleaded for the elimination of her humanness because the human factors only distract from the potential miracle that unfolds. In effacing herself, the dancer lets her motion create its own intrinsic meaning. The function of her reality is to be non-real, to be a link between reality and dream.

If Mallarmé was a philosophic poet, Paul Valéry was the poetic philosopher. Even though T.S. Eliot claimed that Valéry "will remain for posterity the representative poet . . . of the first half of the twentieth century—not Yeats, not Rilke, not anyone else," his poetry was to him an aesthetic exercise with which to demonstrate his philosophical speculations. "A poem must be a holiday of Mind," he said, obviously omitting its appeal to the emotions. "It can be nothing else. . . . The holiday over, nothing must remain. Ashes, trampled garlands."

As Mallarmé's disciple, Valéry found many points of comparison between poetry and dancing. The same ephemeral feeling, the fading into meaningful nothingness is common to both. He also expressed this thought in a poem, *The Exquisite Dancers*, which could easily have been inspired by the second act of *Giselle*. The poem opens with:

> They who are delicate as flowers are come,
> Figures of golden loveliness, minute and slim.

And it ends:

> Their hands are gracious to the cherished flower-cups,
> A thread of moonlight sleeps on their devoted lips,
> And their enchanting arms that move with dreamy grace
> Unravel lovingly, beneath the myrtle's boughs
> Their tawny tresses and the tree's caress. . . . But some,
> Less bound by the remoteness of the harps' strange rhythm,
> Steel on pointed feet towards the lake's shrouded fan,
> To drink the lily-dew of pure oblivion.

Dancing was to Valéry a key to flesh-turned-mystery, a road leading to truth and revelation, and he spoke of it as "the release of our bodies entirely possessed with the spirit of illusion and drunk with the negation of our empty reality." He built many of his similes around dancing. The thought of dance and the symbolic image of dancers run like a *leitmotiv* through his poems and prose, providing a playground for his thoughts and finding a climactic expression in his symposium *Dance and the Soul*, in which Socrates compares life with the dancer:

She is a dancing woman, who would divinely cease to be a woman, if she could pursue her leap up to the skies. But as we cannot go as far as infinity, either dreaming or waking, so she, likewise, returns always to being herself again; stops being a flake, a bird, an idea;—being, in a word, all that the flute has pleased her to be, for the same Earth that sent her out, calls her back and returns her, panting, to her woman's nature and to her lover.

Phaedrus discovers how much food for thought he can find in the moving images created by the dancer. Eryximachus watches the dancer Athikte: "This monumental walk . . . has no object but itself." The moment she is pausing in her "commensurable graces," Socrates maintains, "She is feeling herself become an event." And this moment itself is "of absolute virginity."

Complete rest is death, Pascal said, and Valéry believed that life is movement and movement life. The "most real in reality" is movement and rhythm, and dance is a climactic moment of existence achieved in a state of intoxication. Dance is a most innate form of life because it is in constant movement and opposed to immobility which, however lucid it may be, is a denial of action and negation of life ("to stop being clear in order to become light"). Then dance is liberation from finality, a joyous state of intoxication. Valéry lets Socrates say in his symposium that "amongst all intoxications, the noblest, the most inimical to ennui, is the intoxication due to action. Our acts, and particularly those of our acts that set our bodies in motion may throw us into a strange and admirable state."

To him, dancing is primarily a phenomenon of movement. Dance as an art form involves us the very moment we see such an "extreme dancer" as Athikte

who is moving so adorably before our eyes, this glowing Athikte, who divides and gathers herself together again, who rises and sinks, who opens and shuts so swiftly, who seems to belong to other constellations than ours—does she not look as if she were living quite at her ease in an element comparable to fire,—in a highly subtle essence of music

and motion, where she inhales inexhaustible energy, while she partici-
pates with her whole being in the pure and immediate violence of extreme felicity?

Valéry saw the dancer as a flickering creature, and "Dancing
seems to come from her body like a flame." The dancer's essence
was caught by Valéry in this one simile and elaborated on in poetic prose. The flame is the very moment itself, "the act of the
moment which is between earth and Heaven." Dancing is the liberation of our bodies which leap "like flame replacing flame," de-
vouring the moment there is, destroying "the very place where it
happens to be," the symbol of reality from which the body escapes. In the movement, like in the flame, lies purification and
the beauty of being that was and is no longer—which is "Doubtless, the unique and perpetual object of the soul."

The thought of this self-consuming existence of purity and
beauty is paralleled by Valéry's emphasis on the moment between
the "moments" when nothing as yet exists, but a nothingness
pregnant with the creative act. This moment "between the void
and the pure event," as he called it, is close to Aristotle's definition of poetry as something emerging from nonexistence into existence. As poetry springs from prose by destroying the superfluous,
so the dancer leaps from ordinary movement to the poetic image
of dance and from there into the ecstasy of movement which takes
her "outside of all things."

It is significant that Valéry quoted Degas's remark that in
the evening the Muses do not discuss, they dance.

Rouge ou Noir: Stendhal, a balletomane

After the downfall of Napoleon, on July 20, 1814, Stendhal
—at that time still Henry Beyle—left for Milan "on horseback in

the morning, alone, and rode for two or three leagues through a silent forest, a good occasion for reflection." He had much to think about. He had hoped that Napoleon would bring the destruction of feudalism, as begun by the revolution, to a final conclusion. "The sabre kills the spirit," he wrote in bitter disappointment.

On the one hand, he had been pleased that the despotic reign of Napoleon, "who had stolen France's liberties," had come to an end. On the other hand, he was so utterly disgusted with the Restoration, with man's corruptibility and venality, with the ease with which everyone turned about and swore allegiance to the restored Bourbon king, that his admiration for Napoleon was reawakened.

He could have done as the others did, stretched out his hand, asked forgiveness for the political folly of having admired Napoleon and followed him, and he would have been given a fair position. But, true to his romantic impulses, he chose to go into exile, to escape to Italy where he stayed for seven years. This was partly a pose—all the more since he knew he would be shadowed there by Metternich's police—and partly a sincere desire to "be himself." But even truer to this romantic side of his character was the probably unconscious longing to go back to Italy where he had been before and where the sensualist in him could find the life he yearned for: to plunge into the pleasures of soul and body, to give himself up to the sun of a blue sky, to the ever onrushing waves of artistic excitement, to the circle of congenial men and women who knew the secret of how to live. "If a man have a heart and a shirt on his back," he wrote later, "he should sell his shirt to see Italy."

Henry Beyle did so, to see the Correggios and Leonardos again, to be reunited with his beloved Gina Pietragrua, to be able to go nightly to La Scala. And in his enthusiasm he exclaimed:

"Canova, Rossini and Viganó—they are the glory of the Italy of today!"

Viganó is probably the least known of the three today, though the serious dance student is well acquainted with his creation of the choréodrame, the dance-drama, in which for the first time each dancer and each dance group was prompted to act according to their individual feelings. There was no longer any uniformity of poses to express emotion, and yet Viganó knew how to form a choreographic unity out of these individual animations and continually changing pictures. Noverre, who had tried to reform the dance shortly before him, was well understood by Viganó and put into practice. Pantomime, alive and natural, played the greatest part in his innovations. "It expresses with rapidity," he said, "the movement of the soul: it is the language of all peoples, of all ages and times. It depicts better than words extremes of joy and sorrow. . . . It is not enough for me to please the eye, I wish to engage the heart."

Salvatore Viganó was born in Naples in 1769. He came from an artistic family. His father was a dancer and so were his father's brothers. His mother was a dancer and the sister of the well-known composer Boccherini. In the beginning Salvatore showed no particular propensity for dancing, in fact, he was more interested in literature. Had he concentrated entirely on it, he would —as his contemporary, the poet and dramatist, Vincenzo Monti, said—have become a second Ariosto, or, with his creative mind and sense for the theater, a second Goldoni. But his love for music, inherited from his mother, seemed to have been stronger. At an early age he began to compose, and an intermezzo of his was performed in Rome when he was only seventeen. Finally, the music that was in him moved to his feet and decided his career.

He first danced in Rome, then in Madrid where he fell in love with the beautiful Spanish dancer Maria Medina whom he married. From 1790 to 1812 the couple danced everywhere in Europe with sensational success. Their performances in Vienna, then one of the major capitals on the continent, caused a furore. À la Viganó became a slogan. Beethoven who later wrote his *Prometheus* for him, composed a minuet à la Viganó, based on a theme from one of their ballets. Shopkeepers tried to profit from their popularity and styled their products à la Viganó, from clothes and hairdos to bonbons and cigars. This craze reached such an extent that when Maria Viganó was pregnant the society ladies wore false stomachs in imitation of her. It is said that the Emperor was so enchanted by her, that the jealousy of the Empress made it impossible for the court to go to see the ballet after opening night.

When Viganó became estranged from his wife with whom he had established his reputation as a dancer he went to Milan where he stayed until his death in 1821. There he composed more than forty ballets. He became *maître de ballet* at the Scala, decided to give up dancing and to concentrate on choreography. At the Scala he had all the facilities for the realization of his theoretical dreams.

For quite some time Viganó was as good as forgotten. Only Henry Prunières's research, in the main based on the Viganó biography by Carlo Ritorni (which was published in 1838), and André Levinson's work on him inspired by the notes and letters of Stendhal, have restored his historical importance.

At that time, the Scala in Milan was more than a sanctuary for opera and ballet, more than the best theater on the continent, it was a place of rendezvous where the women of society sat in their loges night after night indulging in amorous playfulness and where the men of the world flirted with them openly as though they were ladies of the demimonde. Stendhal's description of it is quite sarcastic: "At the Scala a woman's reputation was made or broken; it was made when she had her lover escort her to her box; broken when only a servant or her husband accompanied her."

Today we may discuss heatedly whether the theater ought to offer greater comfort for the spectators: lounge chairs or divans, permission to smoke, the facilities of a snack bar. But at that time the big loges of the Scala were used as salons where visitors came and went, where there was hardly ever a let-up in the most animated conversation and where card games in the background were a matter of routine. One played for high stakes in the half concealed privacy of the loges. One gambled at the card table as one gambled for love. Time and again, however, they would interrupt gambling and flirting and come forward to hear a favorite aria or to see a new ballet.

These privileges for the privileged people paved the way for the artistic productions. This was the case at the Scala in Milan as well as at the San Carlo of Naples. When gambling was forbidden, we hear Stendhal's warning and sober voice: "These two theatres will fall and with them the art of music. Viganó was only able to perform his charming ballets in Milan because of this gambling."

Music was more to Stendhal than only a mental stimulus, it pleased him as "an expression of love," he considered it "the language of the aristocracy of the heart." During his stay in Milan he would sit night after night with thousands of other entranced people in the balcony or the orchestra of the Scala. Stendhal needed the opera and the ballet—they were the very antithesis of his own mind, of his probing, cold, matter-of-fact thinking that wanted to get behind the motives of man's actions and desired to achieve "the knowledge of the human heart." Music and ballet were the sanctuaries of his romantic longings; here he found "the resources open to unhappy hearts"; here he could take his deep melancholy, his sadness "thoughtful, dry, without tears and consolation"; but it was, first of all, the place where his need for creative happiness found its gratification.

Time and again we find Stendhal in an ecstatic mood during his stay in Italy between 1814 and 1821. He himself expresses this mood best when he says in his book *Rome, Naples and Florence:*

I experience a sensation of happiness at my sojourn in Italy which I have found nowhere. . . . I feel a magic in this country that I can scarcely define: it is like love; and yet I am not in love with anyone. . . . Often, late at night, returning to my house [in Milan] . . . passing those great portals, my soul obsessed by the lovely eyes I have just seen, looking at those places in dense shadow, their masses outlined in the clear moonlight, it happens sometimes that I am choked with joy and exclaim to myself: "How beautiful it is!" . . . How well I have done to come to Italy.

He went to Italy as one goes to the temple of one's faith. The growing shadow of Metternich's police little disturbed his enthusiasm. That he was observed and listed as Bonapartist and bohemian with dangerous political ideas, given to undesirable philosophical speculation, only added, in his eyes, to the sensational feeling of being so utterly enwrapped in living.

Milan was the center of music and literature where, in hourlong discussions, Stendhal could sit in the cafés with the novelist Manzoni, the patriot Silvio Pellico, and Lord Byron. "Romanticism is all the rage here," he wrote to a friend in Paris. "I too am a wild romantic, that is to say, I am for Shakespeare against Racine, for Lord Byron against Boileau." The Scala became his headquarters, the galleries and cafés his outposts. "Italy pleases me, I pass each day from seven to midnight hearing music and seeing two ballets."

Stendhal's enthusiasm for the ballet and the "immortal Vi-

ganó" of the Scala was not based on a new experience. He must
have often seen the ballet in France, for he writes about it with
the assuredness of a connoisseur, and we find as early as 1804 a
note in his diary when he saw Pierre Gardel's *Psyche,* a ballet
that enjoyed a sensational success at the turn of the eighteenth
century:

I saw *Psyche* for the first time. I was enchanted by this ballet. Duport
is graceful, but indulges too much in pirouettes which he had at one
time sensibly abandoned but has taken up again, since that is what the
public applauds. Could he do without them, he would awaken a sweet
sensation in our soul, only akin to the one which Virgil's eclogue
arouses in us. More than once he has made that impression on me in
the charming part of Zephyrus.

Only one completely enamored with the art could have continued
with this entry in his diary, speaking in detail about various performers and concluding with the following words: "I was enchanted by *Psyche.* It is a marvelous work, I must go and see it
again."

At that time he not only showed enthusiasm, but also quite
some understanding of the ballet. He learned more about it in
those seven years in Milan, which turned out to be an important
period for the crystallization of his aesthetic theories, of his reflections on the arts and life in general. His analytical method, his
conception of the artist as being conditioned by the entire culture
whence he comes, by climate and customs of the society in which
he lives, took on a definitive form. This was then a revolutionary
thought, later taken up and defined more thoroughly by Hyppol-
ite Taine.

While turning against the academicians and Racine, their
idol, he placed Shakespeare on the highest pedestal. In his literary comparisons, but also in his opinions on the ballet, he would
always bring in the name of Shakespeare. Some of his utterances

and analogies seem strange to us today, but are symptomatic of romantic exaggeration, the disease of the time which even Stendhal could not withstand. In one of his discourses he went so far as to say: "I challenge all classical writers of the world to draw a single ballet from the entire *œuvre* of Racine which could be compared to the genial ballet *Othello* [one of Viganó's ballets]."

How very ballet-minded Stendhal must have been during his stay at Milan becomes obvious when we come across such sentences as, "the tragedies of my God Shakespeare actually are ready-made ballets." His enthusiasm knows no limits. Even his God Shakespeare has to be dethroned when he leaves the Scala after "having seen this ballet [Viganó's *Myrrha*] for the eighth or tenth time, still quite excited." Looking for images and comparisons to explain his exalted feelings, he exclaims: "I saw Kean as Othello and Richard III in London; then I thought the theatre could offer no stronger impressions; but Shakespeare's best tragedy does not impress me half as much as Viganó's ballets. He is a genius who will make his art grow with him and who has no equal in France."

When reading some of his remarks on the ballet, one begins to realize more and more how difficult it is to write on an art so visual and elusive as the dance, since even Stendhal—certainly a master of his craft—fails to formulate the impact of the absorbed images, his thoughts and feelings of overstimulation. He often escapes into rather empty exclamations. But we must not do him wrong. Sometimes he not only finds the right phrase, but remains also descriptive and poetically picturesque in his most ecstatic moments. Thus he writes in 1817 when he again sees the famous Duport dance:

Now as ever seeing Duport is a great delight to me. He amuses me like a kitten: I could watch him dance for hours. . . . He still has all the buoyant ease he showed as Figaro in Paris. With him one never feels any effort, gradually his dance becomes animated and then comes to a climactic end in a state of rapture and drunkenness of that passion he wants to present. This is the highest degree of expressiveness which this art can achieve, or, at least, I have never seen anything like it. Vestris, Taglioni as well as all other second-rate dancers do not understand how to hide their exertion and, moreover, their dance lacks the feeling for the gradual unfolding, for the development of movement. Thus they do not even achieve voluptuous gratification, the first aim of all art. The women dance better than the men. Enthusiasm and delight are the only achievements of this so limited art. The eye caressed by the beauty of the decorations, by the ever changing groups is supposed to make the soul receptive to a lively and loving absorption of the passions represented by the dances.

Stendhal was well aware of his strange role as a balletomane, at a time when his concept of Beylism began to take firm root in him. Time and again his mind seemed to curb the sensual romanticist in him who would have loved to put to paper his most ecstatic impressions about the dance had he not been afraid of appearing "ludicrous." Speaking of Viganó's *The Gypsies* he writes:

Noverre has, if one may believe rumors, achieved sensations of carnal lust. Viganó developed the expressiveness in all directions. The instinct for his art led to his discovery of the real genius of ballet which is predominantly romantic. . . . The soul, enraptured by the joy of the new, remains, without interruption, in a state of delight for one and a quarter of an hour and, although it is impossible to express such enjoyment through the written word because one is afraid of appearing ludicrous, nevertheless one must still think of it many years later.

He realizes that the dance, more than any other form of art, demands from its audience a participation in which all the senses are involved. He does not yet know of the unconscious kinetic reaction of the dance viewer and thinks that "everyone's imagination, if stimulated by music, becomes more alive and makes these dancers, who never speak, in their way articulate."

Stendhal has seen so many ballets in Milan that he has learned to discriminate between good and bad. Though it is obvious that his emotions mostly have the better of him when he is at the Scala, his critical faculties have not forsaken him. On December 1, 1817, he dares to censure Viganó for having done *Psammi, King of Egypt,* "quite an amusing ballet," but one that remains a "mediocre work of a great artist." He can be even sharper in his criticism when writing about the ballet *The Three Oranges:* "The beginning of this ballet is wonderful, the middle —passable, the end—miserable; this is a third-rate Viganó!"

It was through music that he came to the dance. In those years he wrote his first book *Haydn, Mozart et Metastase,* and became intimately acquainted with Rossini. This friendship culminated in his *Vie de Rossini,* a book in which he also spoke a great deal about the dance. In it he gave an example of an Italian opera performance in those days:

On February 1, 1818, the show at La Scala contained the first act of "The Thieving Magpie" played from 7 to 8:15, followed by Viganó's ballet "The Vestal" from 8:30 to 10, then came the second act of "The Thieving Magpie" from 10:45 to 11:15 and finally Viganó's little ballet buffoonery "The Shoemaker's Wife" which was booed by the public—as though it felt it had to uphold its own dignity. But the same public saw it again performed with great pleasure, for it had meanwhile found out that there was something new in it. The performance closed with this little ballet which reached its end between midnight and one o'clock. Each week these little ballets show a new *pas.*

One of Rossini's pupils, a wonderful soprano, was Elena Viganó, the choreographer's daughter, known among her friends as the "mad Nina." After the performance at the Scala, Stendhal, would often go to her house and sit in Nina's salon with her friends (many of whom were also his), and the hostess or one of her guests would sing and play the piano until the early morning hours. There Stendhal was enchanted by the artistic atmosphere, intoxicated by music. All his hidden unhappiness could be submerged in it, and he himself followed the advice he gave to the unknown reader in his *Histoire de la peinture en Italie:* "Surrender yourself freely to the arts. Their study . . . will bring you, out of the depths of your misery, a most splendid consolation."

Undoubtedly, in Nina's home he became personally acquainted with her father, the silent poet, as he often called this great dancer and choreographer. Stendhal had not only the opportunity to admire his finished productions on stage, Viganó must also have invited him to rehearsals where he could see the master at work. He was greatly impressed, as he tells us, to have seen him surrounded by eighty dancers on the stage, with an orchestra of ten musicians at his feet, and keeping his patience, which Stendhal considered one of the facets of his genius. Viganó apparently did not come with a ready outline of his choreographic conceits, he seemed to have relied more or less on his intuitive feeling during the rehearsals. For Stendhal says, "there he composes his dances and, if he feels the need for it, has, time and again, the artists repeat a few bars which do not quite satisfy him."

Viganó must have been one of those artists who cannot stop changing, redoing, and polishing his work before showing it to the public. Stendhal must have been struck by Viganó's method because he again mentions on the third of January 1818 that "this genial person does not know how to work on paper." For instance, Viganó worked on his ballet *Daedalus and Icarus* almost five full months and rehearsed daily from ten o'clock in the morning until six in the evening and continued to rehearse from ten at night until four in the early morning.

Although this ballet was booed at opening night, it seems to have had a great deal which Stendhal liked, for he again finds it comparable to the Shakespearean historical tragedies. In spite of the fact that he realizes its weakness he cannot refrain from another literary reference in writing about it. "Neither Racine nor Voltaire could have created anything similar," he says and enjoys grading his fellow writers as he so often has done in his diaries and letters. With the years he changed the sequence of his favorites somewhat, but Shakespeare remained on top. All the more significant is the fact that whenever he wants to put Viganó onto the highest pedestal he knows no better way than to liken him to Shakespeare. So we read, "he has an imagination of Shakespearean range, although he may never have heard of Shakespeare at all; he unites a musical genius with that of a painter. If he cannot find a musical motif which expresses what he has in mind, he himself creates it."

Stendhal was captivated by Viganó's work and particularly admired his inventiveness in arranging the corps de ballet in endlessly varying patterns and his ability to shade the facial, pantomimic expression of his dancers. In this connection, Stendhal's comparison would turn to painting, and he proclaims that even "an eye used to the highest beauty in painting must recognize the genius of this great artist."

Through the years we find Stendhal preoccupied with the ballet and with Viganó in particular. But already in 1813 while on a short trip through Italy—at a time when he had not yet had any contact with the dancer—he wrote in his diary on September 14 of that year:

Seven or eight major facts confirm me in the opinion that this land is that of the arts. At Paris, the people are eunuchs who in several art varieties don't create or won't let others create, for instance, the ballet like that of Viganó.

Five years later, with his almost daily visits to the Scala, he had become an expert on the dance. He writes with conviction and an authoritative tone on the ballet. But his enthusiasm about the choreographic theater of the time and his many outbreaks into ecstatic exclamations, so completely out of key with genuine "Beylism," must be attributed partly to his excitable temperament, partly to the contagious Milanese atmosphere of intellectualized sensualism or sensualized intellectualism. In the course of the years spent in Milan Stendhal often reports to his friend in Paris, Baron de Mareste, about his artistic and emotional adventures. Sometimes Stendhal seems to be fully aware that he is carried away by his emotions, when he remarks at the close of one of his letters in which he went overboard with praise for Viganó: "I could bet—you will think I am exaggerating. But if you had never seen a painting by Raphael what would you think of the fame which is attributed to him?"

In general Stendhal's remarks about and descriptions of Viganó and his contemporaries give us a rather clear picture of his choreodrama which combined emotional expression through pantomime with pictorial visualization through movement of groups and solo dancers; the music not only served as stimulation but was first of all vigorously translated into movement patterns and gestures. Viganó demanded from his miming dancers the then unconventional "natural" gesture and movement, laden with intent, full of meaning. The great advance of archeological research at that time in the wake of Winckelmann's *Geschichte der Kunst des Altertums* and the classic revival that followed it, furnished Viganó with the image of many wonderful Greek and Roman sculptures on which he could base some movements for the classical themes he mostly chose.

One must not think that Stendhal is easily victimized and trapped by his own romantic notions. Unquestionably, he knows what he wants. He realizes how empty a ballet can be when it does not strive for some kind of theme and emotional expressiveness. Though he flatly states that "the real genius of ballet is predominantly romantic," he cannot accept insipience of whatever form of art. Speaking of a ballet by Vestris III, called *Jucundus,* he exclaims somewhat irritatedly: "How wanting is this ballet . . . ! nothing but garlands, flowers, sashes with which beautiful ladies adorn their cavaliers, or which shepherdesses exchange with their lovers—and dance in honor of these sashes." He contrasts such feeble attempts at artistic creation with a ballet by Viganó which has a strong story line and deals with the problem of jealousy in which—we must assume today—Stendhal may have seen more psychologically justified motivations than Viganó may ever have thought of.

Stendhal thought Viganó's ballet *Othello* better motivated than Rossini's opera of the same title. No reference to the play of his God Shakespeare is made, although there may be some hidden implication when he says:

Viganó was clever enough to insert in the second act a great scene of noble and gentle conception: it was a nocturnal festival arranged by Othello in his gardens. In the midst of the feast his jealousy is awakened. It then happens that, at the beginning of the last act, we do not feel surfeited with terror and violence, and soon there are tears in everybody's eyes. Rarely have I seen anyone cry at Rossini's *Othello.*

Viganó's *Othello* and *The Vestal* may be singled out as the best of his works, or, at least, as the ones that made the strongest impression on Stendhal, who reported enthusiastically about them to Baron de Mareste. In reply to the Baron's question about the program notes, Stendhal answers on September 3, 1818:

I found the program notes to the Viganó ballet, but they are pointless when one wants to draw any conclusions as far as the ballet itself is concerned. For instance, you find the note in *Othello:* "The senators express their surprise," But in which way? Here comes in the talent of this great man. He must have keenly understood how to observe human gestures. Thus, for instance, in the third act of *La Vestale* she gives in to the demands of her lover: the pantomime which takes a quarter of an hour is so true to life and so graceful that—it can be said without immodesty—it sweeps the audience. . . . Viganó's program notes are put together by the next best writer at hand. The program notes from one of his most important ballets were written only after the creation of the ballet. . . . Viganó can only verbalize under great pains what he actually wants to express.

To what is Stendhal so attracted? It is less the dancing per se, it seems, than the development of an idea expressed through movement, gesture, and pantomime, expressed in a manner coming close to what is to him "ideal beauty," which his sensual aestheticism defines as something akin to "promise of happiness." In our day, Stendhal would have been a staunch defender of the modern dance of free rhythms and dramatic dimensions. Approaching the dance as a literary person, he might have accepted a ballet like Jerome Robbins's *The Age of Anxiety* or *Cage,* he would have been enthusiastic about Antony Tudor's ballets with their psychological insight in motivation and its translation into movement, but he might have labeled *Swan Lake* or *Giselle* as dusty museum pieces which were appropriate in another period. When Rossini once told Stendhal that in his opinion Viganó "has too much pantomime and not enough dancing," it was something that Stendhal could not agree with, for in the eternal fight between the pure and the expressive dancer he would naturally side with the latter.

Théophile Gautier, poet-journalist

Degas is famous for having given ballet the visual image of its romantic being. Théophile Gautier gave ballet the spiritual image of its romantic visualization. Gautier began his career as a painter, and he always saw the dance with the eyes of a painter. He went so far as to say: "If ever I had the honor of being director of the Opéra, I should have the ballets composed by painters."

In 1830 Gautier was still an art student in Rioull's studio in Paris. A meeting with Victor Hugo attracted him gradually towards writing. His attitude towards the dance can best be understood by his attitude towards himself as a writer. Gautier, the poet, felt that words should be used in the way that painters and sculptors use their tools in creating a visual image and plasticity. He was convinced that poems appear to the eye and ear rather than to the mind and that prose tales had to escape with you into the fantastic or macabre.

Whatever he did, basically he was a poet. When he wanted to do something really well, he always began in verse. He once said, he felt a certain hesitancy about prose, about his complete success with it. He was surer of himself writing poetry, and only the exigencies of life turned into prose many tales originally begun in verse. This explains why so many poetic images enrich his prose which has rhythm and fluidity as if meters measured its cadences. Because he also wrote poetry with the eye of a painter, his descriptions have the power of immediacy and plasticity. "Radiant words, words of light, full of rhythm and music, that's poetry," he said. "It proves nothing, it relates nothing."

The poetic precision of his expressiveness had an amazing

lightness about it. He wrote his many critiques and feuilletons with a flair and great literary style, and, even if he had not told us, one could sense that the flow of his words was put down with very few corrections. This had to do with his pronounced gift as a causeur. We find the following passage in The Goncourt Journals:

Gautier delivers himself inexhaustibly of paradoxes, lofty ideas, original notions, and marvellous phantasies. What a conversationalist! Far superior to his books, however great their value, and invariably better in the spoken than in the written word. What a feast for artists is this speech in two registers, the timbre of Rabelais sounding so often with that of Heine, the lusty enormities of the first mingling with the tender melancholy of the second.

Everyone interested in literature, painting, music, the theater, and dance must thank Providence for having treated him roughly and forced him to become a journalist. His reviews and critical studies fill dozens of volumes. The poet as journalist for thirty-six years! On August 2, 1836, he began with his daring article on Delacroix in *La Presse;* his last review was written on February 28, 1872, and the play was *Ruy Blas* by Victor Hugo, whom he adored and who had given him the passport to his literary career.

He wrote on all manifestations of the arts believing that all artists strive towards the same end which is the exaltation of beauty in life, the ultimate of ecstasy. He felt that there should be no barriers between the various artistic disciplines and wished for all artists to command the same tools with the same goal in mind. The musician, painter, sculptor, poet, novelist, dramatist, actor, and dancer should join forces in order to picture beauty in its most unified, integrated, complete form.

Gautier never thought much of virtue per se. If we can believe the Brothers Goncourt, he explained himself one day by saying:

I am very badly constituted. I am totally indifferent to mankind. In a play, when a father rubs his refound daughter against the buttons of his waistcoat, I remain absolutely cold: all I see is the folds of his daughter's dress. I am a *subjective* person. That is the truth: I am talking about what I feel.

On another occasion he referred to art alone as holding the key to everything positive in life:

We do not want the theatre to be a chair of ethics; the poet is under no obligation but beauty; but the beautiful is the path of the good, and men who trouble their heads over the perfection of a line of verse and who are transported with enthusiasm by a tirade are always decent people.

In paraphrasing Keats, Gautier could have said: Beauty is goodness, goodness is beauty.

He was a romantic knight on an eternal quest for beauty, and he spelled beauty with capital letters throughout his life. ("Beauty is found nowhere but in nature and the arts.") To him, "ugliness is always indecent" and "true voluptuousness is always chaste." There is something compulsive in his attitude towards everything that pleases the eye. He thought that "ugliness is only excusable in the theater when it is accompanied by great talent" and physical beauty was "the first condition required in a dancer . . . she has no excuse for not being beautiful, and she can be blamed for her plainness as an actress can be blamed for her bad pronunciation."

No one could ever claim that Gautier was impartial in his judgment nor that his weakness for female flesh did not determine his critical attitude. He never tried to conceal his predilection for the aesthetically enticing beauty of the ballerina. His critiques ostentatiously reveal the thinly disguised eroticism in his sensual enjoyment with phrases such as "The languorous seduction of the ballerina;" "Her bosom is full, a rarity among dancers . . . her breast does not exceed the fullness of an hermaphrodite of antiquity"; "Her swooning arms"; "intoxicated passion which sways in a frenzy of pleasure."

He is a master in describing impressionistically, almost fastidiously, the immediate response of his eyes. The enraptured feeling with which he can paint the ruffles and folds of a dress is as erotic as his exclamations about the body of a dancer. It is as if his hands would glide over the ballerina's dress, bosom, and legs, as if his hands would see and his eyes speak. When, for instance, writing about Fanny Elssler's dancing in *Cachucha*, his eyes finger her entire appearance and make us sense his lusty delight in seeing so much beauty:

She comes forward in her pink satin *basquine* trimmed with wide flounces of black lace; her skirt, weighted at the hem, fits tightly over the hips; her slender waist boldly arches and causes the diamond ornament on her bodice to glitter; her leg, smooth as marble, gleams through the frail mesh of her silk stockings; and her little foot at rest seems but to await the signal of the music. How charming she is with her big comb, the rose behind her ear, her lustrous eyes and her sparkling smile! At the tips of her rosy fingers quiver ebony castanets. Now she darts forward.

One is all prepared for his final ecstatic exclamations: "How she twists, how she bends! What fire! What voluptuousness!" And when Gautier leaves us with the question: "Would you not say that in that hand which seems to skim the dazzling barrier of the footlights, she gathers up all the desires and all the enthusiasm of the spectators?" one is convinced with Gautier that "Enjoyment seems to me the aim of life, and the only useful thing in the world."

His dictum that "The dance is essentially pagan, materialist and sensual" makes it understandable that he preferred Elssler to Marie Taglioni. Gautier agreed with Théodore de Banville who said about Taglioni that she was "the most perfect incarnation of correct, chaste and poetic dancing." Gautier saw in her a mystical and spiritual quality, transfiguring the physical into pure poetry. When she appeared in *La Sylphide* he echoed the general enthusiasm when he wrote: "She is just as much a genius as Lord Byron or M. de Lamartine. She has shown us ronds de jambe and ports de bras which are the equal of long poems." He recognized that Taglioni "has wonderfully understood the ideal side of her art."

With the appearance of Elssler on the scene, he made a telling distinction between the two great rivals of the romantic ballet:

Fanny Elssler's dancing is quite different from the academic idea, it has a particular character which sets her apart from all other dancers; it is not the aerial and virginal grace of Taglioni, it is something more human, more appealing to the senses. Mlle. Taglioni is a Christian dancer . . . she flies like a spirit in the midst of the transparent clouds of white muslin . . . she resembles a happy angel . . . Fanny is a rather pagan dancer; she reminds one of the muse Terpsichore, tambourine in hand, her tunic, exposing her thigh, caught up with a golden clasp; when she bends freely from her hips, throwing back her swooning, voluptuous arms, we seem to see one of those beautiful figures from Herculaneum or Pompeii which stand out in white relief against a black background, marking their steps with resounding cymbals.

Taglioni did not have a pretty face, but Gautier recognized and accepted her great artistry of poetry made visual, the spiritualized purity of her style. However, he said in a facetious manner: "Undoubtedly spiritualism is a most respectable thing, but where dancing is concerned, one can well make a few concessions to materialism." And he did not mean a few only.

Elssler was closest to his Grecian ideal. "We no longer love pure form and beauty enough to endure them unveiled," he once exclaimed and undoubtedly he would have been glad to sacrifice the entire nineteenth-century ballet if he could have witnessed the dances of the naked Grecian maidens. But Elssler fulfilled many other ideals and demands he made on the ballet. He considered pantomime an essential part of the ballet which is "mimed poetry," and Elssler had not her equal as a mime. She was dramatically strong, and Gautier stressed time and again that she acted much better than her rival. Moreover, true to the romantic spirit, Gautier was attracted by the exotic and Oriental as much as by the weird and fantastic. When he wrote the book for the ballet *La Périe* he remarked: "I am a Turk from Egypt. I seemed to have lived in the East." He also became a champion of the Spanish dance which had enough of the far-away or Oriental touch for him, and Elssler triumphed in her *Cachucha* as much as in her *Tarantella* or *Cracovienne*. Gautier's incessant stress on voluptuousness goes hand in glove with the romantic cliché images of Oriental languor and Spanish passion.

Exaltation is the usual trademark of the romanticist, and Gautier possessed it to a great measure. The Goncourts said of him that his "gaiety is like the gaiety of a child; it is one of the great graces of his intelligence." This observation invites comparison with Jean Cocteau: both blended beautifully childlike exuberance with a sophisticated mind; there was their utter belief in youth and the creative power of youthfulness; their predilection for the circus, for acrobats, clowns, and tightrope dancers, both applauding the mimic parodies of trained monkeys, loving bullfights and boxing; their gift for speech, for being causeurs par ex-

cellence; their identification with poetry; their love of beauty
(Cocteau: "Beauty in art is shrewdness which makes it eternal");
their flamboyant gesture of being different from the bourgeois in
a bourgeois world—and their intoxication with the dance, even
though the love affair of these two writers with ballet was caused
by different motivations and expressed in a different manner by
each.

Gautier sincerely believed in total escape through the arts
("An evening at the Opéra rests you from real life and consoles
you for the number of frightful bourgeois in overcoats you are
obliged to see during the day"). In order to free himself from the
snares of Philistinism, any unconventional idea was aggressively
formulated and accented with an exaggerated gesture. Freedom
from the limitations of ordinary existence provoked his denial of
all utilitarian aspects ("What is useful is ugly and base, the most
useful part of a house is the latrine"). The make-believe world of
the theater offered him the ultimate of illusion and therefore the
only truth:

The footlights are a frontier of fire dividing the auditorium from the
stage, the real world from the world of imagination; the audience
must not be allowed to cross it. Beyond its frontier reigns illusion;
perspective creates new depths, light creates new enchantments; tinsel
seems gold; rouge seems the freshness of youth; the characters, like the
decorations, are painted, and from this collection of harmonious lies
emerges relative truth, which is the truth of art.

The plays he was forced to review gave Gautier little gratification and rarely the same rewarding illusion as ballet. He was
dismayed by the decadence in the theater, by the slickness of the
well-made and little-meaning play. ("Manufacturing is taking
over everything, a play is cut together just as a suit. One of the
collaborators measures the actor, another cuts the goods, and the

third assembles the pieces; the study of the human heart, the style, the language to be used—all these qualities are disregarded.") He was very emphatic in his demands: "We should like the romantic, the fantastic, the ideal and the poetic to play a greater part in the theatre." All this he found in the dance which alone was able to give wings to his feelings and from which he never went away "with a broken heart." A ballerina like Elssler could convey the sensation of "a thousand joyful things." She was the incarnation of mystery-turned-flesh as much as Taglioni was flesh-turned-mystery.

Both ballerinas represented the two sides of the romanticism that Gautier thought he saw united in Carlotta Grisi. His enthusiasm and love for her inspired him to conceive a ballet for her which resulted in *Giselle.* In the early 1840s Gautier felt that there was too much ethereal flight, too much whiteness on stage, too many *ballets blancs,* as he termed the deluge of Taglioni imitations patterned on *La Sylphide.* He tried to create a composite of what Taglioni and Elssler symbolized. The sylphide was only a creature in the hero's mind, a dreamlike being with whom one can never identify. There should be a real creature which, through dramatic events, would become the unreal creature that was the romantic ideal. And, logically, *Giselle,* with its realistic first and sylphide-like second act, symbolizes the two sides of Gautier's romantic concepts: flesh and flight from reality, the sensuousness of passion and the poetic dream of love.

Gautier's love for Grisi, with whose name on his lips he was said to have died, has become historic evidence for romantic idealism and exaltation, for the woman as symbol of the unattainable, the ideal, the dream. It was no mere coincidence that, in 1832, when Marie Taglioni danced *La Sylphide* in Paris, Goethe should have written the last lines of *Faust:* "The Eternal Feminine leads us on!" But there was also the materialist and sensual side to Gautier which found consolation in his love for Mlle Forster, who danced the part of Princess Bathilde in the opening performance of *Giselle* and for whom he wrote a little-known poem.

As we see *Giselle* performed today, the ballet closes with Albrecht's despair. Gautier, however, described the final scene in his first draft differently: "The young man kneels by the mound, plucks a few flowers and clasps them to his breast, then withdraws, his head resting on his shoulder of the beautiful Bathilde, who forgives and consoles him." Gautier's intention to end *Giselle* with the notion of life triumphant seems to have appeared banal to Petipa, who changed the ending when he restaged the ballet in Russia years later. As for the poem that Gautier wrote to the lovely Mlle Forster, it was called *Ode à Bathilde:*

At last the early morning bell tolls the hour
When the pale Wilis, caressed by too much light,
Glide near the sleeping sylphs silently
Between the water lily and pretty-by-night.
And Giselle, departing with soft, sensuous poses
Slowly disappears under a pall of roses.
All one can see of this lovely phantom
Is a little hand reaching out for her lover.

Then you would appear, enchanting huntress,
A smile on your lips, a gleam in your eyes,
Dragging your velvet over velvet of grass,
Fresher than any dawn on the edge of the skies.
The very Graces on their white altar
Of pure Parian marble had adored
Your beauty with its blue look and golden tresses
And had admitted you in their midst as their sister.

The magic woods are flaring up with light
In a dazzling blaze—and wonders

Whether this daybreak, so glaringly bright,
Comes from your presence or from the sun.
Giselle dies, Albrecht, lost in despair,
Rises, and reality is sweeping away the dream.
But in divine beauty and chaste voluptuousness,
What dream could ever equal your existence?

Two years after the premiere of *Giselle,* Gautier created another ballet for Grisi, *La Péri.* He continued to mingle reality with fairyland notions out of a dream of Arabian days and nights. Achmet is in love with one of the Péris, the Oriental fairies, the counterparts to Heinrich Heine's Wilis from the Harz Mountains. La Péri enters the dead body of the slave Leila, who was shot as a fugitive from the harem. More so than in *Giselle* reality and unreality were blended with metaphysical subtlety, and everything ends with the triumph of spirit over matter. It was an exotic dream and effective on stage, proving one of Gautier's maxims:

For a ballet to have some probability everything in it must be impossible. The more fabulous the action . . . the less will probability be offended. Legends, fairy stories, hashish and opium-inspired dreams, all the fantasy beyond the realms of possibility are the true sphere of ballet.

Gautier stretched the plausibility of the flight of imagination in *Giselle* to a point of no return: a peasant girl going mad after discovering she is deceived by her lover, a metamorphosis within a moment's notice with ensuing death from a broken heart. He also defied all logic in La Péri. He was essentially concerned with creating a framework for the dancing only ("The true, the unique, the eternal subject of a ballet is dancing"), dancing which he never lets us forget is visual beauty and sensual excitement. When he entered the theater, Gautier seemed to have said with a polite gesture: Please, beauty before logic.

Beauty in ballet, as indicated, was of female gender to him. He helped establish the prominent position of the ballerina when, in shaping the romantic ideal of the dancer, Gautier at best tolerated men in ballet. "For us a male dancer is something monstrous and indecent which we cannot conceive. . . . Strength is the only grace permissible to men." This attitude was emphasized when he could not help praising Jules Perrot, admitting in his review: "This praise is all the less suspect from us because we do not in the least care for male dancing. Perrot has made us lose our prejudice."

Gautier never gave up his basically sensual approach, but he modified it with his growing experience of looking at dance. As a writer and painter he had hardly any technical knowledge of the dance. In the beginning of his career as a critic he did not understand the need for the turned-out feet to which he referred as "one of the most abominable positions ever invented by the pedantry of the past" and made fun of basic positions and figures. At first he undoubtedly approached the ballet from a literary viewpoint, but, later on, the eyes of the painter created his set of aesthetics. This becomes quite clear through some of his pronouncements:

Dancing is nothing but the art of revealing correct and elegant forms in various positions favorable to the development of line.

Dancing after all has no other object but the revelation of beautiful forms in graceful attitudes and the development of lines which are agreeable to the eye.

A ballet should be a kind of painted bas-relief or sculptured painting.

Gautier was very much aware of being dependent on his visual impressions and once complained, as noted in the Goncourt Journals on April 11, 1857: "Nobody has ever remarked that all my value lies in the fact that I am a man for whom the visible world exists." His influence on the development of the ballet was formidable. He not only held a key position as a critic, writing daily for *La Presse* and *Le Figaro*, he was also creatively shaping the ballet and decidedly pointing out the road nineteenth-century dance was to take. His almost sickish adoration of the ballerina made her all-powerful. The male dancer was not the only one to suffer in his degrading role as a *premier porteur,* the corps de ballet was also strongly neglected though it should have been recognized as the source of the future ballerinas. Gautier never found fault with the mediocre music that so often served as aural background only and was acceptable to him as long as it was danceable. He would describe the costumes of the ballerinas as meticulously as their flesh-in-movement, but he had no critical eye for the décors which meant little to him, even though he was a painter.

His contemporary Charles Baudelaire looked up to him with admiration: "Théophile Gautier is the writer par excellence because he is the slave of his duty, because he constantly obeys the necessities of his function, because a feeling for beauty is his destiny, because he has turned his duty into an obsession." On the other hand, our own contemporary, André Gide, said about him: "Yes, Gautier occupies an eminent position; it is a great pity that he fills it so poorly."

Since Gautier was essentially a poet ("For the superior writer, the inexpressible does not exist," he said) and believed in the multiple creative gifts of the artist, he was able to react to the dance as a writer and painter and sculptor. His ability to re-create the poetic image of the moving figures into verbal images of poetic power saved for us the likeness of the romantic ballet. It did not save the ballet itself, however. On the contrary, Gautier must bear much blame for the ballet having gone the way of all flesh towards the end of the last century. Without inner motivation and meaningfulness of which he deprived the dance, it lost itself in the stereotype and sterile communication of visual splendor, acrobatic bravura, sensual and voluptuous impressions. When Gautier died in 1872 he may have realized that there was much flesh to the ballet but too little meat.

Jean Cocteau's protean playfulness

"As far as I am concerned," Jean Cocteau said, "dancing is the language in which I would prefer to express myself, and my favorite theatrical formula."

He was always attracted by movement, and his entire personality gave the impression of being in movement. His gait and gestures were unusually meaningful and suggestive. He himself said his "feet and hands . . . are admired because they are long and very expressive." Some of his movements were dance arrested, unfulfilled. Misia Sert tells us in her autobiography *Misia and the Muses* "that Jean was irresistible at the age of twenty—for instance, when he started dancing on the tables at Larue's at the supper that always followed a first night." For all we know, Cocteau may have felt like a frustrated dancer. He certainly became a frustrated choreographer with the years and his more intimate knowledge of dance technique. There are pictures taken during the rehearsals of his ballet *Le Jeune Homme et la Mort,* which show Cocteau demonstrating positions and movements to the dancers. Through them we can appreciate that dancing was his favorite theatrical formula.

The secret of his intimate relationship with the dance may also lie in the very fact that he was attracted by the ballet because of its inherent poetic quality which addressed itself to the poet in him. Moreover, ballet's physical immediacy, symbolic of the life force itself, and its imperceptible fusion of the real and imaginary opened unforeseeable possibilities for Cocteau. He felt he could impose on the dances the most abstract ideas in a most poetically suggestive and sensitive form. He himself remarked that "poetry is a dance on a tight rope, but tight-rope dancing at the risk of one's life."

Cocteau was a keen observer of the dance scene, spoke about it like a seasoned dance reviewer, and learned the craft by being associated with the Ballets Russes. He always looked for and always recognized the poetic element in the dance. In *Cock and Harlequin* he said of Bronislava Nijinska's staging of Stravinsky's Cantata with Dances, *Les Noces,* that "I had better confess that I do not like the choreography of *Noces.* I admire it, however, without liking it, for although I may blame the form of a piece of furniture I can respect the skill of the cabinetmaker." In his comparison of Nijinska's ballet *Les Biches* with her staging of *Les Noces,* Cocteau made it quite clear that he saw ballet in terms of the poetic image. After having discussed *Les Biches,* he said:

The poetry of these dances was not expressly written down. The dances in *Noces* oblige us to recognize a Russian poem about sacrifice, maternity, birth, marriage, and death. Here nothing forces us. We are free. There is no poetry except the poetry that resides in figures and clear outlines.

In 1909, the year in which Diaghilev's Ballets Russes gave the ballet a new lease on life, Cocteau was twenty years old. The unusual brio with which he could write and converse catapulted him—perhaps too soon—into the foreground of the world of the intellectuals and artists who, at that time in Paris, had not yet altogether overcome the dandyism of the *fin de siècle.* The influence of pleasure-loving friends was noticeable in many of Coc-

teau's reactions in those days. Everything seemed to induce him
to embrace aesthetic values that were threadbare and had either
the recognizable stamp of the nineteenth century or of a decadent
atmosphere heightened by the *bel esprit* of the literary salons. It
was a world that did not recognize the daring experiments of
some artists, such as Picasso or Kokoschka, and did not grasp it
was on the way to burying itself.

In his formative years Cocteau, surrounded by actors, writers,
and critics, was understandably susceptible to praise which was to
always fan his vanity starting from the day the actor de Max arranged a reading of his poems at the Théâtre Fémina. The critic
Catulle Mendès was among those who constantly predicted a
great future for Cocteau and thus nourished his innately narcissis-
tic trend. This was the environment that forced upon Cocteau the
role of the dandy as much as the literatus. It was characteristic of
this period in his life—in which the initial success arrived at, too
easily blinded him—that Oscar Wilde's sophistication impressed
him most. Then and there the foundation was laid to an under-
current of frivolity and playfulness which accompanied him all
his life and found expression in many of his attitudes and in some
of his works. "I played an absurd figure at that time, I was not
myself," he wrote much later with an astounding objectivity towards himself. "Some celebrated me out of foolishness, others
credited my youth for many things. I became ridiculous, loqua-
cious, wasteful and took my loquacity and lavishness for articu-
lateness and generosity."

By then his first three volumes of poetry had been published
of which he was to say later that he wished they had never been
written. But at that time he plunged himself into the world of art
without knowing that it was more or less shallow water, the ecstasy of a lovable dilettantism which took itself seriously. He was
the witty, worldly poet, who roamed through life with wide-open

eyes, adoring and being adored. He believed himself to be *au courant*. Another three years, until 1912, he remained in this world of enthusiastic superficialities. His first escape from it took place on the Place de la Concorde one night in 1912.

We were coming home from supper after the performance. Nijinsky was sulking as usual. He was walking ahead of us. Diaghilev was amused at my behavior. When I questioned him on his reserve (I was used to praise), he stopped, adjusted his monocle, and said to me: "Surprise me!" The idea of surprise, so entrancing in Apollinaire, had never occurred to me.

In many ways, this moment was the beginning of Cocteau's flight from himself and of his search for his artistic identity. It was also the hour of conception of what has turned out to be a long experimentation in the theater arts which has grown from decade to decade, restlessly groping for the image of its time, with ever-changing surprise as its most expressive feature. Cocteau gave it life. He set it in motion. It has not yet stopped to move from extreme to extreme.

The three years that preceded this event on the Place de la Concorde were years of initiation and preparation for Cocteau. The great event in his life, in the artistic life of Paris and the Western World was the arrival of Serge Diaghilev with his Ballets Russes which started its first season at the Théâtre du Chatelet on May 18, 1909, one of the older theaters of Paris where Cocteau had seen many melodramas as a boy. Diaghilev entered the scene at a moment when a lull in the artistic life had to be broken. To many the appearance of this company was sensational, to a few who foresaw its consequences it was revolutionary. For Cocteau and some of the greatest creative minds, the emergence of Diaghilev had the effect of spiritual liberation.

Everything seemed to fall into place. Politically, it was an uneasy time before the storm, a time when the big powers formed alliances against each other, and both France and Russia encouraged any form of political or cultural exchange. Serge Diaghilev, who did not get along with the director of the Imperial Theatre at home, had been in Paris twice before presenting concerts, an opera, and an art exhibition.

The French impresario Gabriel Astruc suggested that Diaghilev return with a group of dancers. He returned with a group of dancers, destined to achieve legendary fame and to establish Russia as the leading country of ballet: Pavlova, Nijinsky, Karsavina, Fokine. Diaghilev brought with him Russia's famous scene designers, Benois, Bakst, and Roerich. The greatest names in French literature wrote and worked for the Ballets Russes in some way in certain periods: Paul Claudel, Marcel Proust, Jules Lemaître, Marcel Prévost, Henri Ghéon, and the critics Camille Mauclair, Anna de Noailles, Jean-Louis Vaudoyer. The literati were not deeply concerned about the development of the balletic art, but they realized that Diaghilev reawakened powers that had been dormant, that he gave the theater greatness again and that all the other arts would profit by it. To some Stéphane Mallarmé's dream of the aesthetic importance of the ballet became reality; in the eyes of others Richard Wagner's dream of the theater as a synthesis of all the arts found fulfillment, although in a somewhat different form. The great composers of that time were ready to serve the master magician Diaghilev, whose genius it was to recognize genius in others and to nurture it. Among his discoveries were Nijinsky as a choreographer, Leonide Massine, George Balanchine and, above all, Igor Stravinsky. Henri Matisse, Pablo Picasso, Georges Rouault, José-Maria Sert, and many other well-known painters were gradually added to the roster of his collaborators. The Ballets Russes could not fail to impress Jean Cocteau.

The young poet was invited to write and illustrate a booklet announcing the coming marvels. Later, Cocteau designed posters for the company and became its voluntary press agent. He wrote about its productions and talked ecstatically about Diaghilev and Nijinsky in the salons of Paris. He had met Diaghilev in the home of Madame Sert. "Instantly I joined the company," which he saw on opening night. He wrote about it:

The Ballets Russes of Serge Diaghilev played its part in one of my crises. He splashed Paris with colors. The first time I attended one of his ballets (*Pavillon d'Armide* was being presented), I had a seat reserved by my family. It all took place far off behind the footlights, in that burning bush where the theatre flames for those who do not see behind the stage.

Cocteau's development was strangely paralleled by the growth of the Ballets Russes which during its first three seasons did little more than climax the nineteenth-century achievements of ballet with its romantic, impressionistic, and exotic works. It was exciting balletic theater, no doubt, but still in a highly traditional form. Diaghilev knew how to present artistically unified works, impeccable in their craftsmanship, dazzling spectacles with sumptuous and picturesque dance images. It was convincing, because it was perfect in its way, a theater which, moreover, spoke the most international language: movement and color. But there was a great deal of sameness in style and content. The great change came in and after 1912. It also was at that time that Cocteau found himself.

Before the Ballets Russes came into being, Cocteau had seen some of the ballet productions at the Paris Opéra, whose ballet company had by then deteriorated into a cliché existence, best illustrated by Degas's paintings. Because of its slight artistic attraction he paid little attention to it. Only the Russian ballet made him see the poetic meaning in the art of ballet to which he became completely addicted. It seems it was the great revelation to him for which he had waited and to which he was fully attuned. The child in him—of which he could never rid himself and which gave him that inimitable touch of eternal youthfulness—enjoyed the fairy-tale world so germane to ballet. He hardly ever missed a rehearsal of the company, and Tamara Karsavina tells about it in her reminiscences, *Theatre Street:*

A permanent figure of the theater was Jean Cocteau, the *enfant terrible* of rehearsals. Like a mischievous fox terrier, he bounded about the stage and had often to be called away: "Cocteau, come away, don't make them laugh." Nothing could stop his exuberant wit; funny remarks spluttered from under his voluble tongue—Roman candles, vertiginous Catherine wheels of humor.

This is a very telling impression of the twenty-three-year-old Cocteau, sketched by someone who could observe him almost daily. Karsavina realized that there were two different Cocteaus when she told the story of how he visited the studio of a painter who did her portrait:

The sudden appearance of Cocteau in the studio would bring a boisterous note. As if he had vowed never to locate himself anywhere, his voice now spoke from behind canvasses, now called from the garden, unexpectedly addressed us from the top of the gallery. Standing there he forestalled our remarks and, pronouncing himself a preacher, a flow of extemporaneous speech immobilized him for a little while. Once only I saw him quiet: "Tell me the plot of the Fire Bird," he asked. While I was telling him the fairy tale he sat attentive as a child. He had just begun work on the book of *Dieu Bleu.*

Le Dieu Bleu was the first ballet scenario Cocteau wrote. He had become familiar with the terms, forms, and needs of the craft. He was surrounded by the atmosphere of *Schéhérezade.* It did not occur to him to turn against it. Strangely enough, Cocteau saw no reason for wanting to break out of the confinement of established rules and codes at an age when it is natural for young writers to rebel and seek new ways of expression. He bowed to the conventionalities of romantic exoticism when writing his first scenario. It has often been said that Reynaldo Hahn's music was so pedestrian that it destroyed all hopes for the ballet to succeed or last more than a few performances. Cocteau's story line, however, was cliché-ridden and pallid also. What is still worth remembering are the deep and clashing colors of Bakst's costumes and scenic design. The décor showed the court of a Hindu temple in a tropical forest with orange-colored rocks, complete with serpents and a sky in a bold blue. Lotus petals opened, and the audience discovered Nijinsky as Krishna, his body blue and silver, his garment beautifully embroidered. The story told of the efforts of a young girl—danced by Karsavina—who tries to stop her lover from becoming a priest. Choreographer Michel Fokine did his best to model Nijinsky's poses on temple sculptures, but the topic did not lend itself to more than poses.

If nothing else, the failure of *Le Dieu Bleu* convinced Diaghilev that it was no longer enough to continue on the path of the classical ballet with Oriental or exotic motifs, even though it corresponded with the *Zeitgeist* and delighted the masses.* As far as Ballets Russes was concerned, Fokine had served the purpose of getting the company started, and, with the uncanny instinct of

---

* During the first decade of the twentieth-century Western man became sated with a second-hand experience of everything Oriental. From 1904 on Giacomo Puccini's *Madame Butterfly* triumphed in the opera houses all over the world. People were still speaking of Paul Gauguin, who, in 1903, perished in the Marquesas Islands. Ruth St. Denis Americanized Oriental themes in her dances. Pierre Loti's and Lafcadio Hearn's exotic tales were favorites among readers. In these days people had a flair for the mingling of an Oriental background with occidental attitudes.

the explorer, Diaghilev was on the lookout for something new and startling.

During the winter of 1911, his company gave performances in Vienna and Dresden where at nearby Hellerau his dancers were introduced to the method of Dalcroze, the inventor of Eurhythmics. It was at that time that Nijinsky was feeling his way towards a new style of choreography, different from classical dancing. His rhythmical movements accentuated by rigid and angular poses and danced in bare feet—as applied in his first choreography, *The Afternoon of a Faun*—were a far cry from all established rules. But Diaghilev believed in the choreographic genius of Nijinsky.

It was not a ballet in the traditional sense at all, it was a choreographic tableau, rather two- than three-dimensional. It achieved dramatic images not yet seen in ballet and a new expressiveness for the dancer's body. It was a breakthrough. It was the first step in the process of liberating the theater arts from the nineteenth-century conventions. The ballet was received with a storm of disapproval, and applause. It turned into a battle between the faunists and antifaunists. After the catcalls subsided at opening night, Diaghilev ordered the ballet—it lasted twelve minutes—to be danced a second time in its entirety. The applause won the day, and Nijinsky won the battle for Diaghilev. This happened sixteen days after Cocteau's failure with *Le Dieu Bleu*.

Diaghilev was then quite certain what he wanted and what was needed. Out of this realization and mood came the challenge thrown at Cocteau: "Surprise me!"

It took Cocteau five years before he surprised Diaghilev and the world. First, he went through a period of apprenticeship on a high level. There was André Gide's influence while Cocteau worked on a collection of poems, prose dialogues, and drawings under the title of *Le Potomak*. The great inspiration and prompting came from the men who shaped the Ballets Russes and gave it a new direction.

The artistic revolution that had begun with the *Faun* had a second and more forceful installment exactly to the day a year later, on May 29, 1913. Stravinsky conceived a dramatically powerful ritual, *The Rite of Spring*. The first part celebrated the coming of spring, a fertile rite; in the second part the tribe meets on a hill top and watches the girls elect the "chosen virgin" who dances herself to death. Stravinsky's music was complex, with a quality of immediacy, rhythmically reaching far back into unashamed primitivism. It was stirring in its denuded purity, and it puzzled as well as antagonized the audience. Nijinsky's choreography anticipated a mood which became a characteristic feature of the decades to come. His was a sophisticated approach to archaic movements. His visualization of a circular dance in unbroken, endless motion was exciting and theatrically conceived. For the second time Nijinsky dared to contradict the classical positions by making all steps and gestures turn inward.

The premiere of *Rite of Spring* evolved into a tumultuous affair.* In theater's annals it takes a place of honor among the *scan-*

---

* Cocteau described the scene in his aphoristic book *Cock and Harlequin:* "*Le Sacre du Printemps* was performed in May 1913 in a new theatre, untouched by time, too comfortable and too cold for a public used to experience its emotions in the warmth of red velvet and gold. I do not for a moment believe that *Le Sacre* would have met with a more polite reception on a less pretentious stage; but the error of bringing together a work of youthful strength with a decadent public was at first glance symbolized by this luxurious auditorium. A tired public, reposing amidst Louis XVI garlands, Venetian gondolas, soft couches and Oriental cushions—for all this the Russian Ballet must be held responsible. It was under these conditions that one digested this complete novelty as if dozing in a hammock and drove it away

dales célèbres. Cocteau was deeply impressed and admitted that *"Le Sacre du Printemps* totally upset me." He noticed that Diaghilev was delighted about the public's resistance; it seemed to him to be the safest sign of progressing artistically. For Cocteau tells about Diaghilev's reaction to the great success he had some time later with the ballet *The Legend of Joseph,* by Hugo von Hofmannsthal: "After the tenth curtain call Hofmannsthal leaned over to Diaghilev: 'I should have preferred a scandal,' he said to him. And Diaghilev replied, as he had to me when he had said 'Surprise me,' 'the fact is—a scandal is not easy.'"

After the scandal of *Rite of Spring,* Cocteau joined Stravinsky in Leysin. He "was the first to teach me how to insult habits, without which art stagnates and remains a game." It was at that time that Cocteau began to work on a text for Stravinsky. He did not realize that he was not yet ready to turn against the past and start a new adventurous road. He visualized a theme that contained the major elements of the new and startling. He had the idea for a ballet on *David,* and, after an exchange of letters, he joined Stravinsky in Switzerland.

Cocteau thought of an acrobat doing the "parade" for King David,

a big spectacle which was supposed to be taking place inside; a clown, who subsequently became a box, a kind of theatrical "pastiche" of the travelling phonograph, a modern equivalent of the mask of the an-

like a fly; it was disturbing. . . . The audience lived up to its part; it rebelled immediately. People laughed, booed, hissed, imitated animal noises, and possibly would have tired themselves out before long, had not the crowd of aesthetes and a few musicians, carried away by excessive zeal, insulted and even roughly handled the people in the boxes. The uproar degenerated into a free-for-all. Standing up in her box, red in the face, her tiara all askew, the old Countess de Pourtalès brandished her fan and shouted: 'It's the first time for sixty years that anyone has dared to make a fool of me.' The worthy lady was sincere; she believed it was a hoax."

cients, was to sing through a megaphone the prowess of David and implore the public to enter to see the piece inside.

As Cocteau later admitted, this first sketch of *Parade* was unnecessarily complicated by the Bible and a text, and, though it contained some fresh ideas, it had not yet crystallized in any precise and presentable form. "I was moulting, I was in a state of growth. . . . But my idea was not ripe."

Our "Surprise Me" age started with the final stage version of *Parade* in 1917. Leonide Massine choreographed Cocteau's ideas and informs us in his autobiography, *My Life in Ballet,* that

Cocteau told Diaghilev that he wanted to incorporate into the ballet every possible form of popular entertainment. Diaghilev agreed until the moment came when Cocteau suggested that the managers should be given lines which they would deliver through megaphones. This was going too far, even for Diaghilev, who pointed out that the spoken word was entirely out of place in a ballet. Cocteau, however, insisted that in this case the use of megaphones was perfectly valid and in tune with the cubist conception of the production. Although he lost the argument, he eventually persuaded Satie to introduce into the score a number of realistic sound effects, such as the clicking of a typewriter, the wail of a ship's siren, and the droning of an aeroplane engine. All these, Cocteau explained, were in the spirit of cubism, and helped to portray the feverish inanity of contemporary life.

Erik Satie corroborated this statement: "I composed a background for certain noises which Cocteau considered indispensable in order to fix the atmosphere of his characters." Who were these characters? A Chinaman who "pulls out an egg from his pigtail, eats and digests it, finds it again in the toe of his shoe, spits fire, burns himself, stamps to put out the sparks, etc.," Cocteau recollects. A little girl who "mounts a race-horse, rides a bicycle, quivers like pictures on the screen, imitates Charlie Chaplin, chases a thief with a revolver, dances a rag-time, goes to sleep, is shipwrecked, rolls on the grass, buys a Kodak, etc." And then: "As for the acrobats . . . the poor, stupid, agile acrobats—we tried to invest them with the melancholy of a Sunday evening after the circus when the sounding of 'Lights out' obliges the children to put on their overcoats again, while casting a last glance at the 'ring.' "

Parade also introduced Pablo Picasso to the theater ("I am responsible for his becoming a stage designer," Cocteau exclaimed with pride). The poet Guillaume Apollinaire wrote in his explanatory note on *Parade et l'Esprit Nouveau* in the Ballets Russes program bill for the May 1917 season at the Théâtre du Chatelet:

From this new alliance—for until now costume and décor on the one hand, choreography on the other, have been linked only artificially—there has resulted in *Parade* a kind of *surrealisme* which I see as the point of departure for a series of manifestations of this New Spirit that today finds an opportunity to show itself. It will not fail to captivate the élite and promises to transform arts and manners into universal joy, for common sense wants them to be at least on a level with scientific and industrial progress.

This ballet had the atmosphere of the street, the music hall, the circus without re-creating their vulgarities. It was full of realistic suggestiveness, it had an ecstatic quality of the ordered chaos of life, an intense, nostalgic, lyric feeling as if of childhood memories, with a touch of the disintegrating society after World War I. Everything about it was contemporary. *Parade* was new, it was different, it was a scandal. (A later production in 1920, however, was applauded by the audience of which Cocteau said: "For centuries one generation has handed down a torch to another over the heads of the public, whose breath has never succeeded in extinguishing it.")

At that time Cocteau was convinced that "reality alone, even when well concealed, has power to arouse emotion." He wanted to strip things naked, to see with the imaginative eyes of a child.* He felt that in an age of subtlety and sophistication the return to simplicity was essential—and that it could be restored from the banal. It was "the rehabilitation of the commonplace" he sought, which would lose its ordinariness through the element of surprise.

We must not forget that Cocteau's development took place in the midst of a variety of dissonant *isms:* Orphism, Futurism, Purism, Expressionism, Cubism, Dadaism, and later Surrealism. But to understand really his dazzling daring and zest for anticipating tomorrow's artistic fashion, only to turn at once to new ideas, one must summarize the personal influences which shaped the man and artist.

Besides the visual example of Nijinsky and the prodding power of Diaghilev, four man, however different, were to give Cocteau the confidence he needed to find freedom for himself. Erik Satie taught him to liberate art from all adornment and to create in a simplicity which condenses richness in a refining process of economy. Pablo Picasso taught him "to run faster than beauty." ("If you keep step with her your product will be photographic 'kitsch.' If you run behind her, you accomplish only the mediocre.") Igor Stravinsky taught him to "insult habits"—for only in that way can art be kept from becoming sterile. Then there was his young poet friend Raymond Radiguet with whom he shared a passionate friendship. Cocteau learned from him to lean on no premise and to distrust what is new for the sake of newness. From each and all of these men Jean Cocteau gained perspective and stamina for his life with the arts. After a hesitant beginning Cocteau's genius understood how to become a virtual

* Paul Klee once said: "I want to be as though new-born . . . knowing no pictures, entirely without impulses, almost in an original state."

focus of everything that was new, how to play the rallying point for tomorrow's revolution. He played it by instinct which was uncanny.

Cocteau was in love with jazz, the music hall, the circus, "all that fertilizes an artist in the same way as life does . . . like machines, animals, landscapes, and danger." In 1920 Cocteau conceived and staged *Le Boeuf sur le Toit ou The Do Nothing Bar* as a mime show for the famous Fratellini clowns. His preoccupation with clowns and acrobats proves his desire to go to the roots of theatrical tradition and to carry the spirit of the *commedia dell'arte,* the heartbeat of Harlequin, into our mechanized world of whose gadgetry and din he tried to make full use. Clowns and acrobats—with their unsophisticated, popular appeal—gave Cocteau a heightened feeling of balance. "Balance on the brink of caricature without ever falling into it," or music whose "easy manner never lapses into mere facility" were the ideal he saw in Bronislava Nijinska's *Les Biches* (1924) in which he collaborated. It was one of the first "party" ballets which, as Cocteau said, combined classic steps with new gestures in an attempt to find the sophisticated expression of antisophistication.

About the same time Cocteau devised the idea for *Le Train Bleu,* a ballet based on beach games, swimming, tennis, and golf movements. He elaborated an idea created by Nijinsky in 1913. *Jeux* was the first ballet in a contemporary setting about emotional involvements with a game of tennis as a point of departure. *Le Train Bleu* emerged from Cocteau's predilection for acrobatics and clowning. He aimed at lightness and playfulness, at the rejuvenation of the theatrical dance, which he thought could be brought about by freeing it from the false and loud images of beauty and the insipid grace of the opera ballets. "What I aim at is to be sharp enough and quick enough to traverse laughter and tears in a single stride. I know that on this account I am taken for

an acrobat and a clown. No matter. I only wish my soul may be as perfect as the bodies of those acrobats." Cocteau felt akin to the man in the clown as much as to the clown in the man. He shared with the acrobat the awareness that life was a constant challenge because he dared it.

While the "realistic" *Parade* did not satisfy him completely since so many things he had visualized for it did not materialize —"theatre corrupts everything"—he derived greater satisfaction from the ballet which followed *Parade* and which he did for Rolf de Maré's Ballets Suédois, *Les Mariés de la Tour Eiffel.* He characterized it as "the first work to which I owe nothing to no one, which is unlike any other work and in which I found my code, I had forced the lock and bent the key in all directions."

He called *Les Mariés* a comedy-ballet and mixed ancient tragedy—(his actors wore masks) with music-hall numbers. He wanted to create a ballet-revue-play, an entity "in keeping with the modern mind . . . and still an unknown world rich in discoveries." He was aiming at a theatrical poetry that was contemporary—"Art is science made flesh"—classic in its formal expression of serenity.

In this comedy-ballet he achieved the triumph of the commonplace. He was fully aware of trying to revise "the rules of the game." He reduced the action to an almost embarrassing simplicity and clarity which created the impression of hiding more than revealing. Cocteau's ideal was the achievement of a refined simplicity in which the acquired riches are extracted and condensed; it was a certain soberness of expression, and the disguised commonplace. He realized that the greatest danger of our sophisticated age was our overcleverness, the very same quality which so often defeated him.

The danced and mimed action as it unfolded in *Les Mariés*

had surrealistic features and depicted the absurdity of life in a grotesque way. He dressed his two narrators as phonographs, an effect he wanted to create in *Parade* had Diaghilev not kept him from doing so. He also wanted to avoid a true-to-life appearance of his characters on stage. To give them visual power he had them wear masks and endowed them with the spirit of artificiality. He said in his preface,

These characters, instead of being too tiny, as so often happens in the theatre, too poorly real to justify the extent of the lighting and décor, are constructed, padded, corrected, repainted and enlarged by artificial means to a resemblance and scale which does not flare up like straw in the furnace of the footlights and projectors.

His concept in this respect was not too remote from Gordon Craig's idea of the super-marionette replacing the actor. "A theatrical piece," Cocteau said, "ought to be written, presented, costumed, furnished with musical accompaniment, played, and danced by a single individual. This universal athlete does not exist. It is therefore important to replace the individual by what resembles an individual most: a friendly group."

Cocteau was not so much interested in ballets as pure dance art at that time as he was in the new kind of total theater based on movement primarily. "This new genre, more consonant with the modern spirit, remains unexplored land, rich with possibility." And with prophetic emphasis he notes that "It is there, in this margin, that the future is being sketched." He was well aware of the artistic revolution which he helped to start and which would "fling doors wide open to explorers."

After Diaghilev's death Cocteau turned from the ballet for some time as if, with the passing of this man, his own interest in the ballet had passed. It coincided with illness and the work on novels, plays, and films which began to occupy him more and more. In one of his novels, *Les Enfants Terribles,* the elevated tone and the purity of the young people enveloped in tragic fate strongly influenced the generation of the Thirties. *The Infernal Machine,* a mature, nonrealistic retelling of the Oedipus myth with psychoanalytic overtones, is probably the most representative of his plays. But the greatest influence exerted by this iconoclast was through the medium of the film. Three of his films, and particularly the first, have revolutionized the art: *The Blood of the Poet, Beauty and the Beast, and Orpheus.* His contempt for rules was matched only by the daring of his fantasy, which pushed doors open with more keyholes into the unknown. His unrealistic and surrealistic film approach is a perfect counterpart to his balletic experiments. It has widened the range of all visual art forms. Theatrical dance has indirectly, but unmistakably, profited from it.

When, in 1946, Cocteau returned to the ballet, he had left behind the idea of any composite spectacle and tried to come close to poetic truth in a different way. Experimentation did not stop. *Le Jeune Homme et la Mort* was a great success when it was premiered by Ballets des Champs-Elyseés in Paris with Jean Babilée and Nathalie Philippart. Cocteau not only put on paper the story line but defined the choreographic patterns and images. The scene design, executed by Georges Wakhevitch, was outlined in detail by Cocteau, whose idea it was also to rehearse before the music was chosen. The ballet was whipped into shape to jazz rhythms of which Cocteau was so fond. Only after the dress rehearsal was the score decided on and Babilée and Philippart were then told they would dance this modern fable of tragic love to Bach's *Passacaglia* and *Fugue in C Minor.*

Cocteau's interest in the ballet was reawakened with this successful work. Two years later, he designed sets and costumes for another Babilée ballet, *L'Amour et son Amour* [Cupid and his

Love], which The American Ballet Theatre presented at the Metropolitan Opera House in New York in 1951. It carried the motto by Cocteau: "Love has no explanation—do not seek a meaning in love's gestures." He also designed sets and costumes for *Phèdre,* presented at the Paris Opéra. *La Dame à la Licorne,* his last ballet scenario, was choreographed by Heinz Rosen for the Munich Opera Ballet in 1953 and was later produced by the Paris Opéra and by Ballet Russe de Monte Carlo in New York in 1955. In that year, Jean Cocteau, the *enfant terrible,* was elected to the Académie Française and became an "immortal."

In an explanatory letter, addressed to Max Niehaus, Cocteau wrote in 1954: "With my ballets *Le Jeune Homme et la Mort* and *La Dame à la Licorne* I proved that one can deeply move the public without any verbal means as, some time ago, the ballet *Parade* could enrage the public as much as the word could have achieved." Cocteau has always felt interested in the ballet only if it was not content with being little more than *"guirlande ou grimace."* A century previously, Gautier saw in the ballet the sublime expression of the impossible, of a romantic unreality. Cocteau demanded that the ballet express unreality as much as truth. As a child of the twentieth century—a precocious child for that matter—he was only too much aware of the fact that through realism alone can we penetrate to, perceive, and embrace unrealness.

Cocteau's protean personality with its built-in fountain of exuberance bewildered and mystified many people. Brilliant and playful as he was, he struck many a quixotic note. While the world dashed from one cataclysmic event to the anxieties of the next, he could confess

the unpardonable and the scandalous, in an age which scorns happiness, I am a happy man. And I am going to tell you the secret of my happiness. It is quite simple. I love mankind. I love love. I hate hate. I try to understand and to accept. Every episode provides a dock from

which I can set sail and discover something now. . . . I am pessimistic
with optimism, with the conviction that all is better than it seems,
with a totally mad desire for harmony.

On other occasions he said that he was neither happy nor
sad, but that he could be excessively one or the other. He often
deluded everyone, including himself, about anything he really felt
and thought by the ease with which he could articulate. He expressed himself with equal facility as a poet, novelist, essayist,
draftsman, muralist, costume and scene designer, actor, mytholo-
gist, playwright, film director, and librettist. Sometimes one could
not help feeling that he enjoyed being thought of as an artistic
snob who made fun of his public, of wearing masks to entertain
by entertaining himself. There were times he appeared like a magician who let the public in on his tricks to fool them into believing that everything was easy.

Behind all the facility and exhibitionism, however, worked a
probing mind and behind the seeming constant inconstancy was
self-discipline and the desire for inner homogeneity. Now, looking back on the fulfilled life of Jean Cocteau, the paradox manifested in his work is no longer puzzling. It shows method in its
madness and little excess in its surprises. Cocteau's philosophy
brought him close to Nietzsche's ideal of being like "a dancer in
the battle," a dancer who could proudly say of himself, "I am a lie
that always says the truth."

Like his Orpheus, he insisted on having the right to be different. But the central theme of his work was in no way different
from any other important artist of any time: the probing and re-
creating of man. He felt that "every man is a night, and the artist's task is to bring this night into daylight."

In his sentence "To be reborn one must burn oneself alive"
lies the key to the understanding of his genius. This thought of
rising like a phoenix from one's own ashes was echoed in a later

statement: "My discipline consists in not letting myself be enslaved by obsolete formulae."

In retrospect, it becomes altogether clear that Jean Cocteau was a pioneer in transferring the reflection of everyday life onto the dance stage. Instead of the spectacular sequence of heightened unreality, the fairy-tale atmosphere on which ballet had fed for so long, he broke with the cliché and offered the gesture of heightened reality. What we have accepted as avant garde in dance in the Fifties and Sixties has been built, in more ways than one, on Jean Cocteau's graphic daring and tangible imagination, on his living and dying, and living again.

BIBLIOGRAPHY

Alighieri, Dante, *The Divine Comedy*. Translated by Carlyle-Wicksteed. New York: Random House, 1932, 1950.

Amberg, George, *Ballet. The Emergence of an American Art*. New York: Duell, Sloane & Pearce, Inc., 1949.

Andersen, Hans Christian, *The Complete Andersen*. Translated by Jean Hersholt. New York: Limited Editions Club, 1949.

Arbeau, Thoinot, *Orchesography*. New York: Dance Horizons, 1965.

Artaud, Antonin, Œuvres complètes. Paris: Gallimard, 1956.

Balanchine, George, *Complete Stories of the Great Ballets*. Edited by Francis Mason. New York: Doubleday & Company, 1954.

Barrie, James M., "The Truth About the Russian Dancers," *Dance Perspectives* 14 (Spring 1962).

Baudelaire, Charles Pierre, Œuvres. Paris: La Pleiade, 1931.

——*The Mirror of Art*. Critical Studies. Translated by Jonathan Mayne. New York: Phaidon Publishing Inc., 1955.

Beaumont, Cyril W., *The Complete Book of Ballets*. New York: G. P. Putnam's Sons, 1938.

——*A Miscellany for Dancers*. London: C. W. Beaumont, 1934.

Bergson, Henri Louis, *Henri Bergson, choix de texte* par René Gillouin. Paris: Louis-Michaud, 1910.

Boccaccio, Giovanni, *Decameron*. Florence: Per il Magheri, 1827–34.

Boswell, James, *Boswell on the Grand Tour*. New York: McGraw Hill, 1953.

——*The Life of Samuel Johnson*. London, New York: Oxford University Press, 1953.

Busch, Wilhelm, *Wilhelm Busch-Buch*. Berlin: Klemm, 1930.

Cage, John, *Silence. Lectures and Writings*. Middletown, Conn.: Wesleyan University Press, 1961.

Casanova de Seingalt, Giacomo Girolamo, *History of my Life*. Translated by Willard R. Trask. New York: Harcourt, Brace & World, 1966.

446

Chujoy, Anatole, "Russian Balleto-mania," *Dance Index*, Vol. VII, No. 3 (March 1948).

Cocteau, Jean, *Jean Cocteau*, nouvelle edition refondue et complète. Paris: Seghers, 1955.

———*The Journals of Jean Cocteau*. Translated by Wallace Fowlie. London: Museum Press Ltd., 1957.

Cunningham, Merce. *Changes: Notes on Choreography*. New York: Something Else Press, 1968.

Dante Alighieri (vide Alighiere).

Davies, Sir John, *Orchestra; or, A Poem of Dancing*. London: Chatto & Windus, 1947.

Degas, Hilaire Germain Edgar, *Huit sonnets*. New York: Wittenborn and Company, 1946.

Dinesen, Isak, *Seven Gothic Tales*. New York: The Modern Library, 1934.

Duncan, Isadora, *The Art of the Dance*. New York: Theatre Arts, 1928.

Durant, Will, *The Life of Greece*. New York: Simon and Schuster, 1939.

Ellis, Havelock, *The Dance of Life*. London: Constable, 1923; Boston: Houghton Mifflin, 1923.

Fletcher, Ifan Kyrle, Selma Jeanne Cohen, and Roger Lonsdale, *Famed for Dance; Essays on the Theory and Practice of Theatrical Dancing in England, 1660–1740*. New York: New York Public Library, 1960.

Fuller, Loie, *Fifteen Years of My Life*. Boston: Small, 1913.

Fuller, R. Buckminster, *Operating Manual for Spaceship Earth*. Carbondale, Ill.: Southern Illinois University Press, 1969.

Gautier, Théophile, *The Complete Works*. Translated by C. de Sumichrast. London: The Atheneum Press, 1900.

Goethe, Johann Wolfgang von, *Sämtliche Werke*. Berlin: Im Verlag Ullstein (no date).

Goncourt, Edmond and Jules De, *Journals*. Edited and translated by Lewis Galantière. New York: Doubleday Company, 1937; London: Cassell, 1937.

Grimm, Baron Friedrich Melchior, Correspondence littéraire. Paris: Garnier, 1871–82.

Guilbert, Yvette, *The Song of my Life*. Translated by Béatrice de Holthoir. London: G. G. Harrap & Co. Ltd, 1929.

Hawthorne, Nathaniel, *The Marble Faun*. Boston: Houghton Mifflin, 1879.

H'Doubler, Margaret, *Dance—A Creative Experience*. New York: Crofts, 1940.

Heine, Heinrich, *Sämtliche Werke*. Hamburg: Hoffmann und Campe, 1873.

Herder, Johann Gottfried von, *Outlines of a Philosophy of the History of Man*. Translated by T. Churchill. London: Luke Hansard, 1803.

Hofmannsthal, Hugo von, *Die prosaischen Schriften*. Berlin: S. Fischer, 1920.

——*Die ägyptische Helena*. Berlin: A. Fürstner, 1928.

——*Ariadne auf Naxos*. Berlin: A. Fürstner, 1912.

——"Her Extraordinary Immediacy." Translated by David Berger. In *Die Zeit* (1906).

——"The Conversation of the Dancers." Translated by James Stern. In *Partisan Review*, Vol. XVI, No, 5, (May 1949).

Hogarth, William, *The Analysis of Beauty*. Oxford: Clarendon Press, 1955.

Jonson, Ben, *The Works of Ben Jonson*. London: Printed by William Stansby, 1616.

Junyer, Joan, "On Painting," *Dance Index*, Vol. VI, No. 7 (1947).

Karsavina, Tamara, *Theatre Street*. London: Constable, 1950.

Kemp(e), William, *Kemps nine daies wonder*. London: J. B. Nichols & Son, 1840.

——*Knack to Know a Knave, 1594*. Amersham: Issued for subscribers by John S. Farmer, 1913.

Kirstein, Lincoln, *Dance*, New York: G. P. Putnam's Sons, 1935.

Kleist, Heinrich von, *Sämtliche Werke*. Stuttgart: Phaidon Verlag. (no date).

——*Kleists Aufsatz über das Marionettentheater*. Studien und Interpretationen. Berlin: Erich Schmidt Verlag, 1967.

Langer, Susanne, *Feeling and Form*. New York: Charles Scribner's, 1953.

Lawler, Lillian B., *The Dance in Ancient Greece*. Middletown, Conn.: Wesleyan University Press, 1965.

Lawrence, D. H., *Mornings in Mexico*, London: Heinemann, 1950.

Leonardo da Vinci, *The Literary Works of Leonardo da Vinci*. London, New York: Oxford University Press, 1939.

Levinson, André, *Meister des Ballets*. Potsdam: Müller & Co. Verlag, 1925.

——*La danse d'aujourd'hui*. Paris: Éditions Duchartre, 1929.

Lemaitre, Jules, *Impressions de Théâtre*. Paris: Societé française d'imprimerie et de librairie, 1920.

——*Les Contemporains*. Paris: Lecène, 1888.

Liebermann, William S., "Picasso and the Ballet," *Dance Index*, Vol. V., Nos. 11 and 12 (November-December 1946).

Lucianus, Samosatemis, *Lucian*. Translated by H. M. Harmon. London: Heinemann, 1967.

Mallarmé, Stéphane, *Œuvres complètes*. Paris: Gallimard, 1945.

Massine, Leonide, *My Life in Ballet*. Edited by Phyllis Hartnoll and Robert Rubens. London: Macmillan & Co. Ltd, 1968; New York: St. Martin's Press, 1968.

Medici, Lorenzo dé, *Poesie*. Milan: Louganesi, 1953.

Millay, Edna St. Vincent, *Collected Sonnets*. London, New York: Harper & Brothers, 1941.

Musset, Paul, *Œuvres complètes*. Paris: Gallimard, 1960.

Nietzsche, Friedrich Wilhelm, *Gesammelte Werke*. Munich: Musarion Verlag, 1929.

——*Thus Spake Zarathustra*. Edited by Manuel Komroff. New York: Tudor Publishing Co., 1936.

Noverre, Jean-Georges, *Letters on Dancing and Ballets*. New York: Dance Horizons, 1970.

Oesterley, William, *The Sacred Dance*. New York: Macmillan, 1947.

Peckham, Morse, *Man's Rage for Chaos*. Philadelphia: Chilton Books, 1965.

Pepys, Samuel, *Diary and Correspondence of Samuel Pepys*. New York: Dodd, 1884.

Petrarca, Francesco, *Rime, trionfi e poesie latine*. Milan: R. Ricciardi, 1951.

Priddin, Deirdre, *The Art of the Dance in French Literature*. London: Adam and Charles Black, 1952.

Read, Herbert, *Art and Alienation*. New York: Horizon Press, 1967.

——*Art and Society*. New York: Schocken Books, 1966.

Rilke, Rainer Maria, *Gesammelte Werke*. Leipzig: Insel Verlag, 1930.

Sachs, Curt, *World History of the Dance*. Translated by Bessie Schönberg. New York: W. W. Norton & Co., 1937.

Sartre, Jean Paul, *Baudelaire*. Paris: Gallimard, 1947.

Schechner, Richard, "Want to watch? Or act?" In The New York *Times,* January 12, 1969.

Sert, Misia, *Misia and the Muses*. Translated by Moura Budberg. New York: The John Day Company, 1953.

Shaw, George Bernard, *London Music 1888–89*. New York: Dodd, Mead, 1937.

Sontag, Susan, *Against Interpretation and Other Essays*. New York: Dell Publishing Co., Inc., 1966.

Sorell, Walter, *Hanya Holm. The Biography of an Artist*. Middletown, Conn.: Wesleyan University Press, 1969.

Stendhal, Marie Henri Beyle, *Œuvres complètes de Stendhal*. Paris: Champion, 1923.

Tabourot, Jehan (vide Arbeau).

Ter-Arutunian, Rouben, "In Search of Design," *Dance Perspectives* 28 (1966).

Toulouse-Lautrec Monfa, Henri de, *Toulouse-Lautrec* par Jacques Lassaigne. Translated by Mary Chamot. New York: Hyperion Press, 1939.

Valéry, Paul, *Œuvres*. Edition selected and edited by Jean Hytier. Paris: Gallimard, 1957–60.

——"The Exquisite Dancers." Translated by James Kirkup. "Dance and the Soul." Translated by Dorothy Bussy. In *Selected Writings*. New York: New Directions, 1950.

Wagner, Richard, *Nachgelassene Schriften und Dichtungen*. Leipzig: Breitkopf und Härtel, 1895.

Wieland, Christoph Martin, *Gesammelte Schriften*. Berlin: Weidmann, 1909.

Wigman, Mary, *The Language of Dance*. Translated by Walter Sorell. Middletown, Conn.: Wesleyan University Press, 1966.

Wilde, Oscar, *The Writings of Oscar Wilde*. London: Keller, 1907.

Winckelmann, Johann Joachim, *History of Ancient Art*. New York: F. Ungar, 1968.

SOURCES AND PERMISSIONS

SOME OF THE MATERIAL, in similar or different form, and some of the ideas presented in this book were dealt with in previously published essays. I wish to express my sincere gratitude to all editors and publishers—especially to those of *Dance Magazine, Dance Scope, Focus on Dance, Shakespeare Quarterly,* and *University of Kansas City Review*—for their kind permission to use material once written for them. Also, I wish to thank all publishers for allowing me to quote their authors.

Part one: Dance and dancers

THE AGE IS OURS

Focus on Dance II, 1962, and *V,* 1969. Washington, D.C.: American Association for Health, Physical Education, and Recreation.

Beckett, Samuel. *Waiting For Godot.* New York: Grove Press, 1954.

Dance Observer, Vol. XXVII, No. 8 (October, 1960); Vol. XXVIII, No. 4 (April, 1961).

TRENDS, TRAPS, AND TRAUMAS

cummings, e. e. "what if a much of a which of a wind," *Poems 1923–1954.* New York: Harcourt Brace Jovanovich, 1938.

Denby, Edwin. *Looking at the Dance.* New York: Pellegrini & Cudahy, 1949.

The Goncourt Journals (1851–1870) by Edmond and Jules de Gon-

court. Translated by Lewis Galantière. Copyright 1937 by Doubleday & Company.

Baudelaire, Charles. *The Mirror of Art.* Critical Studies. Translated by Jonathan Mayne. London and New York: Phaidon Press Ltd., 1955.

Shaw, George Bernard. *London Music 1888–89.* New York: Dodd, Mead, 1937. Permission by The Society of Authors, London.

Wilde, Oscar. *The Writings of Oscar Wilde.* London: Keller, 1907.

Dance Scope, Vol. I, No. 1 (Winter, 1965); Vol. II, No. 2 (Spring, 1966).

Dance Magazine, Vol. XXXVI, No. 6 (June, 1962); Vol. XXXVIII, No. 8 (August, 1964).

Dance Observer, Vol. XXVIII, No. 2 (February, 1961); Vol. XXIX, No. 9 (November/December, 1962).

Grohmann, Will. *Wassily Kandinsky: Life and Work.* Translated by Norbert Guterman. New York: H. N. Abrams, 1958.

PROFILES AND MEMORY PIECES

Duncan, Isadora. *The Art of the Dance.* New York: Theatre Arts, 1928; *My Life.* New York: Horace Liveright, Inc., 1927.

The University of Kansas City Review, Vol. XXI, No. 2 (Winter, 1954).

Dance Magazine, Vol. XXXX, No. 11 (November, 1966); Vol. XXXVIII, No. 3 (March, 1964).

Dance Observer, Vol. XXIX, No. 6

(June–July, 1962); Vol. XXVII, No. 5 (May, 1960).

Dandré, V. *Anna Pavlova.* London: Cassell and Company, 1932.

Pavlova, Anna. "Notes by Marianne Moore." In *Dance Index,* Vol. III, No. 3 (March, 1944).

Magriel, Paul David. *Pavlova,* an illustrated monograph. New York: Holt, 1947.

Thomas, Dylan. *The Collected Poems.* New York: New Directions, 1946, 1953; London: J. M. Dent & Sons, 1953; Copyright 1952 by Dylan Thomas. Reprinted by permission of New Directions Publishing Corporation and the Trustees for the Copyrights of the late Dylan Thomas.

Part two: Poets of palette and chisel

Degas, Hilaire Germain Edgar. *Hui Sonnets.* Translated by the author. New York: Wittenborn and Company, 1946.

Dance Magazine, Vol. XVII, No. 3 (March, 1953).

Guilbert, Yvette. *The Song of My Life.* Translated by Béatrice de Holthoir. London: G. G. Harrap & Co., Ltd., 1929.

Fuller, Loie. *Fifteen Years of My Life.* Boston: Small, 1913.

Morinni, Clare de. "Loie Fuller. The Fairy of Light." In *Dance Index,* Vol. I, No. 3 (March, 1942).

Magriel, Paul., ed. *Chronicles of the*

American Dance. New York: Henry Holt, 1948.

Goncourt, Edmond and Jules De. Journals. Edited and translated by Lewis Galantière. New York: Doubleday Company, 1937.

Rilke, Rainer Maria. Rodin. The Fine Editions Press, 1945; Gesammelte Werke. Leipzig: Insel Verlag, 1930.

Ter-Arutunian, Rouben. "In Search of Design." New York: Dance Perspectives No. 28, 1966.

Junyer, Joan. In Dance Index, Vol. VI, No. 7, 1947.

National Sculptural Review, Vol. XI, No. 1 (Spring, 1962).

Part three: Dance and actors

TRENDS OF THE TIME

Dance Observer, Vol. XXVIII, No. 10 (December, 1961).

Dance Magazine, Vol. XXXVII, No. 5 (May, 1963); Vol. XXXVII, No. 8 (August, 1963); Vol. XXXVIII, No. 1 (January, 1964).

Merce Cunningham. Changes: Notes on Choreography. New York: Something Else Press, 1968.

Tulane Drama Review, Vol. X, No. 2 (Winter, 1965).

Schechner, Richard. "Want to watch? Or act?" In the New York Times, January 12, 1969.

Part four: Dance and poets

THE LITERARY IMAGE

Lucianus, Samosatemis. The Dia-

logues of Lucian. Translated by H. M. Harmon. London: Heinemann, 1967.

Pushkin, Alexander. The Poems, Prose and Plays. Translated by Babette Deutsch. Random House, The Modern Library, 1936.

Dinesen, Isak. Seven Gothic Tales. New York: Random House, 1934.

Millay, Edna St. Vincent. "Sonnet XLIV." In Collected Poems. New York: Harper & Row. Copyright 1923, 1951 by Edna St. Vincent Millay and Norma Millay Ellis. By permission of Norma Millay Ellis.

Andersen, Hans Christian. The Complete Andersen. Translated by Jean Hersholt. New York: Limited Editions Club, 1949.

Boccaccio, Giovanni. Decameron. Florence: Per il Magheri, 1827–34.

Alighieri, Dante. The Divine Comedy. Translated by Carlyle-Wicksteed. New York: Random House, 1932, 1950.

Rilke, Rainer Maria. Gesammelte Werke. Leipzig: Insel Verlag, 1930. Excerpt translated by the author.

THE ENGLISH SCENE

Davies, Sir John. Orchestra; or, A Poem of Dancing. London: Chatto & Windus, 1947.

Jonson, Ben. The Works of Ben Jonson. London: Printed by William Stansby, 1616.

Shakespeare Quarterly, Vol. VIII, No. 3 (Summer, 1957).

Kemp(e), William. Kemps nine daies

wonder. London: J. B. Nichols & Son, 1840; *Knack to Know a Knave*, 1594. Amersham: Issued for subscribers by John S. Farmer, 1913.

Hogarth, William. *The Analysis of Beauty*. Oxford: Clarendon Press, 1955.

Shaw, George Bernard. *London Music 1888–89*. New York: Dodd, Mead, 1937. Permission by The Society of Authors, London.

Eliot, T. S. "Burnt Norton" from *Four Quartets* in *Complete Poems and Plays*. New York: Harcourt Brace Jovanovich, Inc., 1952.

Yeats, W. B. *The Collected Plays*. New York: The Macmillan Company, 1953. Reprinted by permission of M. B. Yeats and the Macmillan Company.

Joyce, James. *Finnegans Wake*. New York: The Viking Press, 1939.

GERMAN DREAM AND AMBIVALENCE

Goethe, Johann Wolfgang von. *Sämtliche Werke*. Berlin: Im Verlag Ullstein (no date).

Wieland, Christoph Martin. *Gesammelte Schriften*. Berlin: Weidmann, 1909.

Herder, Johann Gottfried von. *Outlines of a Philosophy of the History of Man*. Translated by T. Churchill. London: Luke Hansard, 1803.

Heine, Heinrich. *Sämtliche Werke*. Hamburg: Hoffmann und Campe, 1873. Translated by the author.

Dance Magazine, Vol. XXXV, No. 1 (January, 1961).

Kleist, Heinrich von. *Sämtliche Werke*. Stuttgart: Phaidon Verlag (no date).

Nietzsche, Friedrich Wilhelm, *Gesammelte Werke*. Munich: Musarion Verlag, 1929. By permission of Allen & Unwin, Ltd., London.

Hofmannsthal, Hugo. Excerpts from "Her Extraordinary Immediacy," Translated by David Berger. In *Die Zeit* (1906); Excerpts from "The Conversation of the Dancers." Translated by James Stern. In *Partisan Review*, Vol. XVI, No. 5 (May, 1949).

THE FRENCH ESPRIT

Beaumont, Cyril W. (compiled and translated) *A Miscellany*. London: C. W. Beaumont, 1934.

Musset, Paul. *Œuvres complète*. Paris: Gallimard, 1960.

Flaubert, Gustave. *Correspondance*. Paris: Charpentier, 1905; *The Selected Letters of Gustave Flaubert*. Translated and edited by Francis Steegmuller. New York: Farrar, Straus and Young, 1953.

Valéry, Paul. Excerpts from "Dance and the Soul." Translated by Dorothy Bussy; Excerpts from "The Exquisite Dancers." Translated by James Kirkup; both in *Selected Writings*. Copyright 1950 by New Directions Publishing Corporation. Reprinted by permission of New Directions Publishing Corporation.